Women Out of Place

The Gender of Agency and the Race of Nationality

Edited by Brackette F. Williams

ROUTLEDGE

New York ✦ London

Published in 1996 by
Routledge
29 West 35th Street
New York, NY 10001

Published in Great Britain by
Routledge
11 New Fetter Lane
London EC4P 4EE

Copyright © 1996 by Routledge

Printed in the United States of America on acid-free paper.

Library of Congress Cataloging-in-Publication Data

Women out of place : the gender of agency and the race of nationality
   / Brackette F. Williams, editor.
      p.   cm.
   Includes bibliographical references and index.
   ISBN 0-415-91496-5 (hbk). — ISBN 0-415-91497-3 (pbk)
   1. Feminist theory.   2. Gender identity.   3. Agent (Philosophy)
I. Williams, Brackette F.
HQ1190.W689   1996
305.42—dc20   96-28854
                                                              CIP

Women Out of Place

To my brothers, Lorance Williams,
the late Jodie V. Williams, Willie Austin, and Myron Murff,
and to my best friend, Drexel G. Woodson

Contents

Introduction: Mannish Women and Gender After the Act   1
Brackette F. Williams

Part I   Essentialism and Gendered Movements

1. Gandhi and Feminized Nationalism in India   37
   Richard G. Fox

2. Race/Class/Gender Ideology in Guatemala: 50
   Modern and Anti-Modern Forms
   Carol A. Smith

3. Multiple Alterities: The Contouring of Gender   79
   in Miao and Chinese Nationalisms
   Louisa Schein

4. "Fit Citizens for the British Empire?": Class-ifying Racial   103
   and Gendered Subjects in "Godzone" (New Zealand)
   Jacqui True

5. A Race of Men, A Class of Women: Nation, Ethnicity,   129
   Gender, and Domesticity Among Afro-Guyanese
   Brackette F. Williams

**Part II   "Wombs" of Nationalist Respectability and the
Problem of Patri-Racial Redemption**

6. "Feminism, the Murderer of Mothers": The Rise and Fall   161
   of Neo-nationalist Reconstruction of Gender in Hungary
   Éva V. Huseby-Darvas

7. "And Your Prayers Shall Be Answered   186
Through the Womb of a Woman":
Insurgent Masculine Redemption and the Nation of Islam
Paulette Pierce and Brackette F. Williams

8. Boudoir Politics and the Birthing of the Nation: 216
Sex, Marriage, and Structural Deflection
in the National Black Independent Political Party
Paulette Pierce

9. "Business Story is Better Than Love": Gender,   245
Economic Development, and Nationalist Ideology in Tanzania
Deborah S. Rubin

Notes on Contributors   271

Index   273

Introduction

Mannish Women and Gender After the Act

Brackette F. Williams

The genitals have always played a very important part in the lives of the Latin peoples, especially in the history of Italy. The true emblem of Italy is not the tricolour but the sexual organs, the male sexual organs. The patriotism of the Italian people is all there. Honour, morals, and the Catholic religion, the cult of family—all are there, in our sexual organs, which are worthy of our ancient and glorious traditions of civilization.

C. Malaparte ([1949] 1965: 72)

Human history becomes a part of natural history. But this rediscovered, reintegrated nature is not ordinary nature. It is historical nature: the *other* nature. *From nature back to nature.* . . . [T]he philosophical horizon of the ensuing naturalism (the union of man and nature) is the vanishing point where classless society appears.

J. J. Goux (1990: 214)

Definition:
Manhed: manhood; race.

> off women com duke and kyng
> I zow tell without lesyng
> of them com owre *manhed.*

M. S. Ashmole, 61, f. 60
in J. O. Halliwell ([1924] 1967: 540)

Mannish 2: relating to or characteristic of an adult male as distinguished from a child.

Webster's Third International Dictionary (1961: 1377)

To say that scholars are of two minds about the value and meaning of nationalism as concept and practice in the contemporary world is to put the case gently. Some, joining politicians, have proclaimed it one of the great ideas of Western thought. They hedge from time to time, remembering or living the ethnocidal horrors that have been committed in its name. Galloping past worst alternatives, so they claim, these scholars focus on nationalism's presumed associations with long-run stability and rationality in political, military, and economic processes. For them nationalism is a positive source of individual and group commitment, of loyalty, and of the principles in accordance with which allies can be identified and curried and enemies identified and subdued by force or by forcibly established conventions of persuasion. Thought of in these terms, nationalism, in short, is the *sine qua non* of modern earthly political order.

[margin handwritten: Scholars who adore nationalism]

Other scholars are less convinced that these positive potentials of nationalism actually override its built in sources of divisiveness and irrationality consistently enough to warrant such high praise and ideological centrality. They pause to wonder what alternative can be imagined. Interrogating national imaginings, these scholars reveal the history and contemporary manifestations of nationalist ideologies to be associated with the great tragedies of world wars, and smaller scale, but no less devastating to affected populations, racial and ethnic "purification" (or as reporters on Bosnia-Herzegovina have taught us to say, "cleansing") movements. Nationalism, interrogated from this stance, is demonstrably part and parcel of the environmental and economic irrationalities fostered by the manipulation of false commitments entailed in highly constrained conceptions of group and community loyalties, which nationally swayed conventional wisdom encourages. As Carlton Hayes (1960) noted long ago, nationalist ideologies transform patriotic commitment into nation-state loyalty overriding the very commitments to community welfare such ideologies are supposed to proclaim and promote. Above all, nationalist ideologies contain within their precepts the much too often realized potential to produce the biologically mongrelized, culturally diverse groupings of humans that become ideologically redefined new groups. "Nations" of the old school (i.e., biologically "pure" peoples), sharing "self-produced" cultural patrimony are intent on the realization of a "racial" destiny befitting their presumed biogenetic heritage. In the context of these precepts, no amount of actual "hybridity" within a racial "strain" or diversity within a state-defined population can stand as guarantors of hybridity and pluralism as ideologically valued end points.

[margin handwritten: Scholars who have problems with national ism.]

Nationalisms, like the ancient myths of origins with which they share a close, conceptual kinship and a related history, continually reinvent the classificatory moment of first dawn when people, places, and relations to divinely wrought destinies were all new. The material out of which the rope, dangling from the heavenly realm of the supernatural to the earthly realm of goods, services, and diverse pleasures below, is constructed varies from the ephemeral nature of divine substances to the scientifically ratified cascades of DNA and RNA. Yet in all these constructions of human substance we can still recognize the quests not simply to unlock the mysteries of appropriate linkages between the natural and the supernatural, but also to fathom the implications of such linkages for the pragmatics of being and becoming in a world of increasingly competitive physical and ideological juxtapositions. In these terms, nationalisms are supposed to help us recognize our "own kind" so that we might "stick by them." Its precepts are presumed to assist us in identifying our allegedly biologically given primordial urge to prefer "our own kind" to "other kinds." Nationalisms and their competing ideological configurations of classificatory systems intend to create, place, and justify the range of human matter and matters we encounter as we go about our earthly chores.

For citizens of nation-states, ostensibly the mythologics we construct need no longer explain how the valley people came to dwell in the valley or why the mountain people withdrew to the cold and frigid peaks than they need to tell us how and why the leopard got his spots. The myths of place, environmental relations, and rites of character are firmly supplanted by the mythologics of nationalist projects. Or are they? It would seem that the mythologics of nationalisms still tell us *who* we are as part of telling us *how* and *why* the rope to heaven was withdrawn and why we must substitute certain forms of behavior as the "modern" path of access if ever we expect again to have *any* access to the divine fates that are otherwise the destinies of strong, powerful, culturally superior peoples. We are encouraged to count on "tradition" to save us both from and for the future. Pride went before the "act"—the fall to earth (now read: modernism/progress)—and is reconstructed in the name of redeeming and maintaining national prowess through the protection of its cultural patrimony redrawn from an allegedly unsullied past.

Efforts to understand how nationalist ideologies are formulated and disseminated within and across institutional structures in class-stratified, racially varied populations thus require detailed attention to sites of ideological production in politically defined states. How are different concepts, categories, and practices, especially those pre-existing nationalist movements, assimilated to nationalist projects? How do these assimilations assist or hinder the consolidation of the constellations of ideas and practices referred to as nationalism? How are prior divisions, such as gender, age, caste, and class implicated in the generation of criteria for citizenship, loyalty, and the legitimacy of social actions statistically or stereotypically associated with status classification? In short, studies of nationalism now turn to questions such as: out of what are nationalist ideologies formulated and how or to what extent do they come to subsume or dominate prior conceptual and ideological forms into which pre-existing ideas had been configured? Within the constraints and possibilities posed by the shifting configurations that we call nationalist ideologies, how are practices formulated, by whom, and to what consequence for the range of categoric identities that constitute the systems of social classification sharing the terrains of politically defined states? Posing questions of historicity and practice in a broader analysis of the ideological content and structure of nationalist ideologies allows us to begin to understand how the same configuration of ideas and interpretations results in varied possibilities and realities of cultural and political citizenship for the myriad of subnational-nationals typically referred to as ethnics, minorities, or other forms of non-dominant "races" within the same putative nation-state.

Such a two-dimensional approach is especially critical to understanding how constructions of gender within nationalist ideologies produce varied forms of domesticity within and across such groupings despite continuities in the metaphysical inheritance that allow us to recognize particular configurations of ideas as nationalist ideologies. How have masculine and feminine, man and woman, come to "embody" the logics of the "national" in the shifting practices and ideas about norms of domesticity? How have the subordinated "subnationals" operating on the same terrains of various states confronted, contested, or assimilated these logics in diverse efforts to construct gendered selves and views of the morality and pragmatics of domesticity under continually changing economic regimes? Across these grids of difference and sameness, how does a member of such groups respect him or herself and at the same time show commitment to his or her "own kind," while demonstrating or contesting (or both) loyalty to the putative nation-state?

In conjunction with a particular conception of the metaphysical groundings of the national, each contributor to this volume confronts one or more of these questions. The contributors examine the historical and ethnographic specificity in which gender, race, and class become shifting dimensions of a nationalist problematic; sometimes at the point when independence is sought for a territory; at other times when a nation seeks a re-evaluation of its place among older nation-states in a changing international order; or at other times when a group called ethnic tries to find a place in the racialized, and class-stratified status rankings of either an old or a new state. One possible rendering of the intellectual formation of a metaphysics of nationalist gender constructions can be seen in how each essay in this volume addresses aspects of the problems refining and ethnographically qualifying issues posed by nationalism's metaphysical groundings.

Metaphysical Groundings of Nature, Respectability, and the Nationalist Fall to Grace as a Movement from Predatory Amoeba to Racial Scavenger

In his pathbreaking *Nationalism and Sexuality: Respectability and Abnormal Sexuality in Modern Europe* (1985), George Mosse focused attention on how public attitudes toward respectability and sexuality—as aspects of nationalist ideologies and the formulation of appropriate forms of sociality, especially those adopted and legitimated by the diverse groupings of the middle classes of European nations—functioned to shape social attitudes toward the human body and its sexuality. He sought to demonstrate that ideals concerning decent and correct manners and morals, as well as the proper attitudes toward sexuality, which by the twentieth century were taken-for-granted features of respectability, had a documentable history in which nationalism played a crucial role. It was "within the developing framework of nationalism and respectability," Mosse argued, that special attention was given to sexuality not only because it was basic to human behavior, but also because it was employed to inform aesthetic sensibilities, so that ideals of human beauty and ugliness, which were presumed to stand at the boundaries of erotic passion, preoccupied the moral concern of respectability (2).

His goal was to show how sexuality, which was "to be acknowledged yet curbed, deflected from the physical onto an ideal stereotype of male and female beauty," "haunted bourgeois society and nationalism" (2). Focusing primarily on Germany, England, and France, but with some attention to Italy, Mosse shows how respectability became entrenched in modern Europe during the first decades of the 19th century, within the life span of a single generation, as an accompaniment to the triumph of the bourgeoisie, and as the means to legitimize and define the middle classes (8–9). By the "nineteenth century [respectability] was to serve the needs of a class seeking stability amid changes it had itself initiated" as its economic practices brought forth industrialization and the "travails" that produced a "nervous age" (9).

In this "bewildering world," again and again men and women reached out "to grasp a 'slice of eternity,' whether embodied in nature, the nation, or religious belief, in order to counteract 'the vibrations of modernity'" (Mosse 1985: 9). In this process, as the bourgeoisie attempted to cope with the result of industrialization and political upheaval, Mosse characterizes nationalism as something akin to a parasitic, predatory amoeba which in

> its long career . . . attempted to co-opt most of the important movements of the age, to absorb all that men thought meaningful and held dear even while holding fast to certain unchanging myths and symbols. It reached out to liberalism, conservatism, and socialism; it advocated both tolerance and repression, peace and war—whatever served its purpose. Through its claim to immutability, it endowed all that it touched with a "slice of eternity." But however flexible, nationalism hardly wavered in its advocacy of respectability. (1985: 9)

Despite what we might rightly criticize as an overly anthropomorphic view of an almost agentless ideology capable of doing its own bidding for its own preservation, Mosse was careful to note that nationalism did not absorb all it came in contact with, nor over time did it retain all that it had earlier consumed. Instead, particular features of these diverse movements and the forms of respectability

they invoked came to characterize some of the basic premises of nationalist ideologies, especially with respect to the precepts of gender and its dimorphic
relationship to images of the nation, national stability, and the advancement of civilization. The general destiny of the nation's "race" was linked to conceptions of its
gendered respectability. Hence, Mosse concludes:

> The ideal of manliness was basic both to the self-definition of bourgeois
> society and to the nationalist ideology. Manliness was invoked to safeguard the
> existing order against the perils of modernity which threatened the clear dis-
> tinction between what was considered normal and abnormality. Moreover,
> manliness symbolized the nation's spiritual and material vitality. It called for
> strength of body and mind, but not brute force—the individual's energies had
> to be kept under control . . .
> Women also played a symbolic role in the national mystique; indeed, they
> furnished the national symbols like Germania and Marianne. But these female
> symbols were . . . sedate rather than dynamic. They stood for immutability
> rather than progress, providing the backdrop against which men determined
> the fate of nations. The stereotyped embodiment of manliness was modeled on
> an ideal of male beauty born in the eighteenth-century Greek revival, while the
> image of woman in German or English national iconography was frequently
> fashioned after traditional portrayals of the Virgin Mary. (1985: 23)

Mosse depicts in detail the features of respectability that ultimately came to
construct men as active agents of the nation, fashioning themselves through both
self-control and a redirecting of their lower passions to higher purposes. In contrast to this respectable manliness, he argues, women came increasingly to be
perceived as creatures of passion to be kept under control within carefully guarded domains, wherein they were allocated the role of protector and keeper of
traditions. Continuities within the changing precepts of nationalism thus reinforced views of manliness as the symbol of the nation when the nation was viewed
as an active agent capable of determining its own destiny against threatening
forces outside and within its state-defined boundaries. Womanliness came to be
symbolized as a container to house, physically and socially, the accomplishments
of masculine action. The traditions created through men's historical agency were
those of which the women of the nation were to be guardians. To some extent, in
the role given them as good women, they could also assure that men lived up to
the ideals of manliness and, thereby, in a superficial way, could be viewed as the
reproducers of these traditions (see Modghadam 1994: 18).

Men did not, however, simply make the history that became nation. Across
generations, as the opening quotes from Malaparte and Goux suggests, history
took a turn through nature, and in turn, this became the stuff out of which the
nation is made as generations of men of a race sought to embody the accomplishments of past generations' historic actions. Manliness without a distinctive history
of accomplishments, was thus judged effeminate (now read: lacking in originality

and self-imposed controls), accused of aping the prowess of "true men" as they assimilated to the "multiracial," but putatively homogenized, nation-state through established forms of respectability (see Newman 1987: 63–87 for an example of this process in the rise of English nationalism). Men's action in and on nature set the terms for manly character construction. Men of different politically defined states or classes and "races" within the same state could then be seen as having separable histories and, therefore, would make it possible for the mythologic of a nationalism, that absorbed the middle-class ideology of respectability, to reposition nature and culture in efforts to order (inter)national competition. Yet, with criteria of the masculine and feminine in the construction overlapping with criteria for other high- and low-status categories within a politically defined territory, most repositioning of the international had the potential to fracture and restructure masculinity and femininity within politically defined states. At the same time both genders were assimilated to the nation as features of race and a race's historicized process of biogenesis, making race an increasingly central and critical feature of conceptions of nation and nationalist ideologies.

In contrast to nationalism as predatory amoeba, Mosse dubs racism the "scavenger ideology, which harnessed to its banner the fears and hopes of bourgeois Europe" (134). First, he notes that: "Racism strengthened both the historical and the visual thrust of nationalism; it emphasized the stereotypes of superior and inferior races. While the distinctive history of each people was said to determine their superiority or inferiority for all time to come. Racism was a heightened nationalism: the differences between people were no longer perceived as chance variations, but as immutable, fixed in place" (1985: 133). Second, while recognizing that the uses made of *racisms* (for these constructions were by no means uniform and stable; see Todorov 1993: 90–170, 246–63) within European nationalist ideologies differed, and had varying results, he argues that each emphasized "the distinction between vice and virtue, the necessity of a clear line between the normal and abnormal according to the rules society laid down" (133). Through appropriate forms of culturally constituted interactions with external nature, men could transform their internal (i.e., divinely given) nature and thereby raise the character and quality of the races to which they belonged.

As numerous critiques of social evolutionism have amply demonstrated, the characteristics of those races deemed inferior at any given time by particular nationalist ideologies shared a common set of stereotyped masculinities. These stereotypes focused attention on the subordinated or "othered" males' lack of control over their lower passions. They attributed to them a lust for the "pure" woman of other races, especially those "belonging" to the dominating race sharing their political terrain. Such stereotypes also generally proclaimed that subordinated men (and to some extent their women) developed perverse forms of sexuality, a supersexuality, leading to physical and moral exhaustion. Within such races, to the extent that higher faculties were thought to exist at all, caught in the throes of such supersexuality, subordinated men were accused of neglecting higher faculties and thus failing in the respectability necessary to control and contain the sexuality of females of their race.

Viewed through the lenses provided by Mosse's work, one can readily see that the first groupings to be labeled "racial other" were as likely to be insiders to a biogenetically defined "own kind" and to a politically defined territory as they were to be in-migrating outsiders to one or both of these constructs. These early inside/outside divisions viewed as new or distinctive races resulted, in part, from lay and (pseudo) scientific efforts to develop and employ histories of difference to explain any lack of appropriate attention to particular forms of respectability within class-stratified populations (see Todorov 1993). Therefore, Mosse contends: "[nationalist ideologies] emphasize certain distinctions between the normal and the abnormal which . . . served to nail down still more firmly society's preconceptions and prejudices about looks and behavior" (1985: 134). As the socially different came be viewed as races which were products of histories of their abnormal relations to nature, nature was continually refigured in nationalist ideologies to account for what were deemed to be socially irretrievable forms of humanity. Normality came to be viewed as that which was made possible by "keeping in touch with the immutable and genuine forces of nature" (137). Yet, during the same period that nature returned as embodied manly historical agency, Mosse argued, "the quest for rootedness which formed the bourgeoisie set it against its place of origin—the cities and other man-made founts of culture" (137).

> Its members feared the impersonal monster they themselves had created: the monumental streets and buildings, the anonymous mass. Thus on one level the bourgeoisie sought to establish historical continuity—city halls were to imitate Gothic cathedrals, private villas, the palaces of the Renaissance. But above all the healing power of nature, symbolizing the genuine and the immutable, could serve to reinforce human control over a world on the brink of chaos. Such a use of nature was common in the nineteenth century, and became ever more popular with the speed of industrialization and urbanization—the need of men and women to annex a piece of eternity in order to keep their bearing.
>
> Nationalism, racism, and bourgeois society all sought to base themselves upon nature in order to partake of its immutability. (137)

In the relationship between nature and its curative power, however, the racialized insider became fundamentally different from a racial outsider at the same time that woman, as a categoric identity, became, by nature, the inside/outsider. Male insiders deemed racially aberrant due to a lack of respectability (i.e., the lower class, the homosexual, the insane, the social misfit considered diseased and probably insane by virtue of being a misfit) could all regain their manliness and, hence, their place in the race-as-nation by personal submission to patterns of respectability and through a direct manipulation of their physical relations to the challenges of nature. Especially important avenues to manliness were hard work, control over sexual passions, exhibiting the proper respect for women, and maintaining an engagement with the morality-reinforcing powers of physical games and other contests of prowess. With respect to the last of these avenues, unorganized play was deemed more valuable to the cause than were organized games and rule-regulated sports (Park 1987). Nonetheless, both organized and informal contests against nature were deemed adequate to restore distorted or inappropriate masculinity. The femininity of woman as inside/outsider could not be so redeemed. Instead, in this scheme, woman was, as Mosse argues, conceptualized such that her action in the world could only contain her abnormality. In the increasingly medicalized nineteenth-century views of biology and physiology, woman could not be "cured" by any reordering of her relation to nature because, if left to her own devices, her true (inherent) nature was defined by sexual passion wrought of her ever-present desire to reproduce.

Thus, by the end of the nineteenth century it was more often than not presumed that for the sake of the nation and its racial destiny, the more feminine the woman, the more masculine the man, the more intimate was family life, and, of course, the healthier was society for all this well-placed order. The obverse was no less frequently voiced: the less feminine the women, the more feminine the men as a race and a nation, the more disturbed the race's family life, and with it the more diseased the society produced of such malformations of the genuine relations of nature. If this naturalism was, as Goux argues, the vanishing point where classless society appears, it was also the vantage point from which the visibility of difference as race and gender was sharply focused.

Naturalized nature, when considered in the context of competing races as nations, was deemed both *genuine* and *spurious* and, no less critically, construed as *ancient* and *modern*. "Inferior" races were the historical products of an older nature, a decayed or degenerate "ancient" nature. This view remained even as other competing racist discourses proclaimed inferior races to be products of an immutable nature (see Todorov 1993). Consistent across competing racist discourses, inferior races were fundamentally and permanently different in true character as a result of their actions *in* and *on* nature. Consequently, within national orders, these types of racial outsiders, male or female, could never truly step outside of their natures defined as devoid of potential for historical rehabilitation. In opposition to the humanly embodied ancient or backward forms of race, modern nature could be seen as the particular histories of racial production and creativity (i.e., group genius) wherein the "trajectory" of superior human character was immutably formed. Hence, Mosse concludes: "Through its appeal to history and nature [nationalist ideology] attempted to make time stand still, to provide men and women not only with a usable racial past but also with a piece of eternity that would give them support. The outsider fulfilled a crucial function as the antitype—warning of what the future might hold if society relaxed it controls and abandoned its quest for respectability" (151). And he adds: "Always the outsider confronted a society dependent upon keeping the division between insider and outsider intact because it was thought as vital to the distinction between what was normal and what was abnormal as to the division of the sexes." (151–52)

Read in connection with the plights and pragmatics of subordinated genders, Mosse's historical analysis of nationalist precepts helps to flesh out insights contained in the passing comments and the metaphors and symbols that assessed the role of gender in the construction of nature, culture, nation, and race, long featured in works on nationalism (Julien Benda 1928, Carlton Hayes 1960, Hans Kohn 1965). Since Mosse's (1985) work, numerous historians, anthropologists, and literary critics, working through a variety of different types of data, have supplemented and refined the relevance of his conclusions for the construction of gender and the problematics of domesticity in nationalism (see Parker et al. (eds.) 1992, Moghadam 1994). Mosse's initial conclusions and his subsequent work on the relation between Jewish nationalism and the general precepts of Western European nationalism (1993) allow us to see that, when the analogy, man is to culture as woman is to nature, is revisited in the context of nationalism and its relation to respectability and race, subordinated forms of masculinity (whether identified as races or ethnic groups) become to culture what women are deemed to culture: its natural enemies. These subordinated races, as natural enemies to a culture now defined as progressive civilization, are construed as only partially redeemable, insofar as when properly behaved, they can, like woman-the-insider/outsider, become containers for, but not producers of, culture as a civilizing process. Moreover, like woman, if left to their own devices these races are deemed threats to the continuity of the social order created by the true manhood of the dominant/modern race, yet they are considered unable to produce a worthy successor manhood and associated civilization.

Against a background of nationalist mythologics, understanding subordinated forms of masculinity and their relation to constructions of varied forms of subordinated femininity requires first a clear specification of the nature of woman as an analogic conception of the inappropriate-unacceptable forms of masculinity. As such, these masculinities viewed as nondominant races qua nations are also taken to be ancient forms of nature and their spurious cultures. The precepts of nationalism out of which gender constructions are dialectically produced are therefore themselves cybernetic renderings of those aspects of the metaphysics according to which analogic constructions of substance (or essence) are transformed into culturally constituted homologies (races as "own kind" of humans) (see Williams 1994).

Nationalism's Construction of Nature:
Screwing (Up) the Past to Make a Virgin of the Future

What has been the relation between the amoeba and the scavenger functions of nationalist precepts in the production of gendered essences? How can we ferret out the implications of the identity processes and power struggles these relations imply for the multicultural, multiracial, class-stratified domesticities that make up the range of empirical realities we call nation-states? By treating nationalism as a dialectical interplay of amoeba and scavenger, Mosse makes clear that the ability of nationalist ideologies to convincingly portray the necessity and legitimacy of nation, as the social formation both dictated by nationalist precepts and implemented through codes of respectability, depended on appropriations of the complex and varied materials available in philosophical, religious, and scientific discourses. To address the aforementioned questions, we can look to the extensions of Mosse's insights available in recent works on gender in the science of culture and difference. Even if these works are not directly concerned with the nationalist construction of subordinated race as inappropriate gender, their findings and insights speak to the issue. In this regard I turn now to, among others, Tuana (1993), Poovey (1988), Huet (1993), Park (1987), and Hoberman (1995).

Efforts to understand the intertwining of philosophical, religious, and scientific discourses as background to and for the naturalism in nationalist mythologics are greatly served by Nancy Tuana's *The Less Noble Sex: Scientific, Religious, and Philosophical Conceptions of Woman's Nature* (1993). Therein Tuana demonstrates that pre-Christian creation myths, Euro-classical philosophies, and pre- and post-Reformation interpretations of the Genesis creation myth all rendered woman's nature inferior to that of man. Through an analysis of the basic premises of these myths, Tuana shows how certain now highly familiar beliefs about woman's nature became features of an inherited metaphysics that has served as a source of assumptions that directly and indirectly influenced the goals and methodology of scientific investigations among eighteenth- to nineteenth-century scientists, even as some of them proclaimed the equally of men and women.

She argues that throughout the eighteenth and into the nineteenth century, interpretations of creation myths influenced scientific discourses on woman's and man's natures and the consequent proper social relations between the genders. These, she notes, also influenced subsequent theological and philosophical writings. Consistent across these multiple sources, Tuana argues, woman's nature is viewed as less perfect than man's; sometimes as a result of divine purpose or at others by consequence of the process of creation (for example, man was created first and woman second, or man was created of original material whereas woman was created of material already shaped to masculine nature). Pre-Christian and Christian creation myths differed in the images they constructed of how the natural was created of or by the supernatural, but all converged in the view of woman's nature as inferior to that of men. In accordance with these myths and the metaphysical foundation they established for theological and scientific discourses of the eighteenth to nineteenth century, women possessed inferior rational capacities and were morally defective slaves to their passions and to their overriding desire to reproduce. Consequently, if society was to be protected from the dangers inherent in woman's nature, women must at all times be controlled by men; not just any men, but rather those deemed worthy by dint of their successful control of the negative aspects of their internal nature through the curative powers of their active manipulation of external nature (1993: x–xi, 155).

Tuana is not concerned with the rise of nationalist ideologies in particular or with general political and economic motivations for patterns in the selective appropriations of philosophical premises and mythical contents. Thus, her examination of these diverse discourses on woman's nature provides a relatively independent supplement to Mosse's general conclusions for nineteenth-century uses of gender and nature in nationalist ideologies. First in this regard is her treatment of gendered representations of the supernatural in the natural universe; second is her analysis of how natural beings created of supernatural forces are able to maintain connections to the supernatural properties of their creation through, that key feature of nineteenth-century masculinity, the control of passion; and third is her related interpretations of gendered views of creative versus passive forces in the generative process that turned male action into "social agency" and rendered female action as destructive "inference."

On the first point she concludes that, in both pre- and post-Christian creation myths, and the theological and philosophical interpretations rendered from them:

> Man contains within him the image of the universe; woman contains only the image of the image of the universe. Borrowing Calvin's words, woman is in the image of the universe only in the second degree. Paracelsus concluded that man's being is more perfect than woman's because it most directly mirrors the universe. Woman, unlike animals, is a microcosm, but in a manner less perfect than man. (1985: 17)

Across mythological and philosophical interpretations, man was said to have retained the godhead within him by exercising control over his human passions. In some of the more extreme renderings of the connection between control of passions and the ability to retain the true nature of the masculine, men who failed in this regard were thought to be reincarnated as females. In less extreme versions, he was dominated by the female aspect, effeminized, with a consequent distortion of his true inherent nature and the obstruction of his chances for perfection and salvation through curative reformations. Woman, by nature a slave to her passions, could, in some pre-Christian, Christian, and post-Reformation Christian views of creation and gendered natures, nonetheless achieve perfection or salvation. She did so, however, only by rejecting her own inherent nature to assume that of man (Tuana 1993: 12, 57). To accomplish even this rejection she required the assistance of and had to be at all times under the control of man or men.

Whereas woman's nature was partially defined by, and her otherwise out-of-control passions were directed by, her innate desire to reproduce, she was also deemed a passive vessel complementing or endangering male agency. Either because she was a "misbegotten male," a "mutilated man," or a mindless or soulless image of an image; woman's seed, in the extreme, was not simply inferior, but for some classical philosophers, it contributed nothing necessary to the process of generation. Paracelsus, for example, not only likened woman to a field that nourishes a seed but lends nothing of its character to the final product, but also imagined a generative process that could take place outside the womb, if only the right conditions were met. His recipe for the right conditions included, in the place of the female womb, the substitution of horse manure, kept at a constant temperature. This would produce a perfect child, only slightly smaller in size than that typically born of a female womb (Tuana 1993: 146).

An image of the generative process as a male domain was consistent with a pattern of belief Tuana details in creation myths that imaged fathers as the true progenitor of their "sperm children" or of offspring produced through acts of "birth reversal" whereby the fetus is taken from the female (as conceiver) to be carried to term and issued from (begot of) man. Thus Tuana concludes:

> The female creative force, it seems, functions properly only when passive and acting in harmony with the male creative force. On her own, the female force creates defective children—monsters and madness.
>
> . . . a set of themes common to classical, Christian, and Gnostic versions of the creation story . . . credit the male principle as the primary creative force. The male actively forms his offspring; the female merely receives what is placed in her by the male and nurtures it. The male seed provides form and purpose; the female provides only the material of creation. (1993: 128–29)

Implied by all the issues stemming from woman's nature was the need of "rational" men for codes of conduct adequate to assure containment of the physical woman (empirical woman), and the preservation (and reservation) of her body as a clean vessel available for the proper mode of conceiving racial patrimony. Woman's threat to the social order through her amoral or non-moral inherent drive to participate in reproduction anywhere, anytime could be handled by keeping her in the home. Her easy submission to passion, said to limit her rational capacities and to foreclose the sense of justice necessary to properly function in the public realm, would thereby be eliminated as well.

Such a rich and highly diversified metaphysical inheritance provided material highly conducive to the development of nationalist precepts and was, no doubt, also influenced and further shaped by those developing precepts. Hence, despite her lack of attention to changing economic structures and political motivations that influenced the selectivity and timing of appropriations of aspects of this inheritance, Tuana's analysis provides students of nationalism and its gender problematic with both a richer and clearer understanding of the philosophical, religious, and scientific supports for modesty as a code of conduct for women within the broader frame of respectability Mosse detailed. Against this background, we can have a better sense of the manner in which constructions of woman's nature and man's action on nature were consistent with developing precepts of nationalism as amoeba and its dependence on respectability as the means by which to transform male nature while maintaining female nature. The ideological directive was to bend both forms of nature to tasks presumed to be necessary to the "rational" ends of social progress and, with them, the advancement of civilization. A civilization manifested through an embodiment of the masculine defined as actively engaged nature was, however, a highly volatile and dangerous process of race making for nations because splits and fragmentations of any culturally constructed sameness was continually threatened by the reality of heterogeneity wrought in *intra*nationally produced class, religious, and other philosophical differences, as well as from equally diversifying forms produced of *inter*national movements of persons and cultural properties. In sum, the amoeba consumed metaphysical material adequate to nourish the production of a gendered view of nature that in turn set the coordinates within which the scavenger racisms would link these views to the genesis of a presumed hierarchy of races.

The production of "own kind" still was no easy task in which a single dominant ideology provided all forms and types of men interested in the subordination of women with the ready means to socially naturalize their interests on gendered fields and establish a proper, easily defined, male agency. Instead, maintaining the purity of woman-as-field of nourishment in a class-stratified, racialized world of nation-states posed a complex set of problems for nationalism as scavenger. First, woman's function was deemed to be tied to her biology, but the quality of the individual woman's biology, like that of men, was influenced by her actions in the world. Whereas men's action in and on nature as active conquerors could both strengthen and otherwise improve the overall quality of masculinity, energy spent by females in areas other than quiet modesty and biological reproduction sapped their potential as a field for the nourishment for the children who were to embody racial patrimony. The negative result of improper female agency, as Charles Meigs, a leading nineteenth-century obstetrician, argued, was an exhausted, innervated state wherein "the biliary organs give way, the kidneys fail to cast out the nitrogenous surplusage of the economy, and the whole mass of blood loses its fine and delicate crasis, and the endangium itself loses the power to keep up the constitution of the blood to its normal standard" (quoted in Tuana 1993: 75–76).

Meigs was by no means alone in his concern with the quality of female blood, for, as Tuana notes, such views were consistent with Spencer's application of Helmholtz's principle of conservation of energy to the human body. Spencer saw the body as a closed system of energy in which the battle for energy was between the brain and the reproductive organs (76). Neo-Darwinian views prevalent during the same period argued that women contributed more energy to the reproductive act than did men. These views also may be taken to have supplied potentially problematic material relevant to the racist element of nationalist ideologies focused on how to maintain the purity of woman-the-field of nourishment for racial reproduction (i.e., as the transmitter of the historically constructed blood of the nation, now defined as hierarchically positioned race). That these additional meanings were not lost on certain leading elements of the contemporary bourgeois population may be seen in the conclusions Tuana argues Edward Clarke (a member of the medical faculty at Harvard at the time the founding of Radcliffe was proposed) drew from the assumed debilitating consequences of female intellectual labor. "[Clarke] predicted that members of the poor, uneducated, and immigrant classes would soon outnumber the middle class, whose reproductive capacity he insisted would be unalterably diminished" (1993: 77). Although he spoke initially of the decline of the middle class without reference to the race of this class as the leading element of the nationality, Tuana adds, "Using warnings of race suicide and moral degeneration, Clarke . . . rejected educational opportunity for women as a 'crime before God and humanity'" (78). Tuana rightly notes that his concern was most directly applicable to the white, middle-class females as those most likely to be admitted to such institutions. Thus, the problem of "race suicide" and its relation to the use and conservation of energy was both a male and female problem, and it was a dominant and subordinate race issue. While women's energy was to be conserved as much as possible for reproductive purposes, the same principles of a closed system of energy also applied to men. The proper male character was to be created out of a balance between work (intellectual and physical) and athletic pursuits of a type that allowed men to integrate the moral and physical, the mind and body.

Speaking of this problem in the context of U.S. nationalism and the formation of the "man of character," Roberta J. Park (1987) links views of football, manliness, and the problem of "race suicide" during the Victorian era of U.S. nation-building. She argues, American nationalism borrowed from British, German, and Swedish views of the roles of contests in and on nature in the formation of manliness and consequences for racial health and longevity.

> Football, it was believed, not only fostered courage and obedience; it also provided a means by which men (i.e., white Anglo-Saxon or perhaps northern European men) might avoid "physical degeneration". Although football was the pre-eminent manly sport of the collegiate ranks, baseball, crew, and track were also held to be of value in "building manhood" of the nation. The ability to survive the struggle with other nations was seen to be important to a country now intent upon fulfilling its destiny as a world leader, so was the ability to match the reproductive capacity of the tens of thousands of immigrants from Central and southern Europe who began to arrive after 1870. Alarmed by falling birth-rates, middle-class Americans worried about "race suicide", a rising tide of mental disease, crime and pauperism. Theodore Roosevelt waned his contemporaries that a race was ". . . worthless and contemptible if its men cease to be willing and able to work hard and, when needed, to fight hard, and its . . . women ceased to breed freely." (1987: 23)

In general, athletics as peaceful wars became one of the means by which men, Park contends, could witness their struggle in and with nature to form new, more durable selves. Thus, of the role of athletics as part of a broader concern with exercise and other forms of physical culture in U.S. nation-builders' views of the relation between nature and manliness, Park concludes:

> The athlete personified new ideals of achievement and success. The athlete's body also united all that modern biology had separated into systems, tissues, cells and the like. His achievement—over himself and over an opponent— were demonstrable proof that man was not unduly fragile *and* the social order would not necessarily come apart. Through their own actions such men could make an impression on the world and perhaps, even control parts of it. Such were the men of character. (1987: 29–30)

In the formation of male character, organized athletics joined informal play in the recapitulation of racial ontogeny as some educators and physicians linked "motor education" to what in the work of psychologist G. Stanley Hall became recapitulation theory. According to Park, educators joining physicians saw "Spontaneous play and games as more valuable than gymnastics because the former called forth the acting out of the stages through which the race had passed" (Park 1987: 25). Park also provides examples of the opinions of some U.S. proponents of physical culture as the means to racial vigor, such as A. A. Livermore and Oliver Wendell Holmes, who, wanting to put a fine enough point on the matter that it left no space for their readers to doubt the connection between "pallid effeminacy" and the absence of manly pursuits, argue for analogies among physical work, war, and games.

> Livermore declared that whereas such hardy rural pursuits as hunting and woodcraft, and the French, Indian and Revolutionary Wars, had once been America's "Olympic games"—the ramparts against disease and ". . . the effemination of a whole race of men"—with the growth of cities, a mercantile class had arisen and indulgence had set in. The result was a deterioration of both the body and the *character* of the native-born American male. In 1858 Oliver Wendell Holmes similarly warned his contemporaries of the dire consequences of inattention to the development of physical vigour: ". . . such a set of black-coated, paste-complexioned youth as we can boast in our Atlantic cities never before sprang from the loins of Anglo-Saxon lineage." (Park 1987: 19)

In these terms we can see that Clarke's mid-eighteenth-century views on the engendering of the physical and intellectual in a closed energy system were consistent with other much earlier views wherein, as Tuana notes, such thinkers assumed that the more highly civilized the race, the greater disparity one should expect (barring constructive efforts to the contrary) between the physical and mental capabilities of the male and female of the race (1993: 66).

Mary Poovey's work (1988) further clarifies aspects of the amoeba and scavenger dialectic and its implications for the gendered nature of agency. Poovey notes that W. Tyler Smith, Clarke's contemporary, was much more straightforward in his views of female biology and its relation to race and the danger, for racial continuity, of contamination posed by woman's agency when he argued that "the uterus is to the Race what the heart is to the Individual: it is the organ of circulation to the species" (quoted in Poovey 1988: 35). Poovey goes on to indicate that it was as if Smith, and thinkers like him, dissolved women "into one enormous, universal uterus—a disembodied, faintly threatening womb, continuously generating offspring who seem dwarfed and short-lived in contrast to their great original" (1988: 35).

The womb, having been dismissed by Paracelsus as sufficient but not necessary to reproduction, was for M. L. Holbrooke, in the age of nationalist consolidation, so fundamental to the definition and purpose of woman that it was "as if the Almighty, in creating the female sex, had taken the uterus and built up a woman around it" (quoted in Poovey 1988: 35). Yet, if for Paracelsus and his contemporaries the womb in the age of nationalist race making was only faintly threatening, the woman around the womb was terrifying in the consequences her actions, observations, and thoughts could have on the genesis process and its ability to produce a strong and virile race. It is on this point that students of nationalism and gender can ill-afford not to consider the relation between those problems of agency thus far discussed and the powers of the imaginations detailed in Marie Hélène Huet's treatise on the maternal imagination as the monstrous imagination (Huet 1993). Whether eighteenth- to nineteenth-century medical men took positions as ovist or pre-formist, and whether they argue for what Huet dubbed "parental singularity" based in either a male or female principle, or whether they argue for some form of joint male and female principle in generation, Huet (1993) contends, they all, in numerous and diverse ways, fell prey to *vis imaginativa*. Few medical models and practices escaped the connection this pre-geneticist era drew between the role of imagination in the process of generation and the potential horrors they associated with the maternal imagination. In generation, the maternal imagination was a source and mechanism for the production of monstrous abnormalities. During this process, the female imagination was a potential usurper of the male's role and as such could disrupt the proper patriarchal transfer of historically constituted "blood" as metonym of racial genius and with it the intergenerational transfer of patri-racial culture (patrimony).

Whether behind women's backs or "up in their faces," men made the history of the race, but to embody that history in the reproduction of its next generation they had to get it safely through the womb. Here the woman around the womb and her experiences in the world were mediated by the power of imagination to distort resemblances and thus to provide mothers the opportunity to usurp the fathers's role as active agent in the process of generation. This was an era in which women were thought to be greatly affected by images, especially statues, paintings, and other such artistic renderings, as well as by the distortions they imagined in connections with the horrors of everyday life—crime, punishment, and other extraordinary events they might witness. This female weakness for images becomes a fatal flaw during conception and generation because women, deemed unable to distinguish between image and reality, were said to confuse nature and art at the same time as their imaginative productions usurp the active and normal role of the father as progenitor and the reproducer of proper resemblances. Although the mechanism for transmission of distortions from mother to child was never clearly and indisputably established in lay or scientific discourses, nonetheless ideas persisted that the mother's desires and yearnings could deeply mark and distort the products she carried in her womb. Hence, Huet summarizes the resulting view of woman-the-usurper and the consequences of her indirect agency.

> When the mother takes art, rather than nature, as the model for the child she is carrying, she not only subverts an important hierarchy, but also shows herself to be an undiscerning and misguided artist. The desiring imagination that leads her to usurp the father's formative role in procreation drives her to a series of fateful confusions; confusions between art and nature, between *physis* and *technè,* and between imitation and reproduction. Whereas the artist imitates with discernment, the mother's imagination artlessly reproduces a model that is already an imitation of nature.
>
> When the mother's imagination substitutes the lines of a portrait for the father's features, it inverts yet another hierarchy, that of the primacy of nature over art. The father's image is erased and the resulting disorder in fact reemphasizes the respective places of models and imitations. Every transgression of this hierarchy will result in monstrosity. . . . It is because the mother's imagination [as plastic art] has been led astray that it gives shape to a monstrous child; and it is because imagination shapes only the exterior part of the child's body that the monster is human. Moreover, since the progeny imitates a model that belongs to art rather than nature, it can be seen as the most illegitimate of offspring. (1993: 24)

Like the ideological configurations that anchored Tuana's and Poovey's works, those on which Huet's analysis depends were, as she is careful to point out, by no means stable throughout the Age of Reason, nor were the shifting configurations into which they formed and reformed during the period of nationalist consolidation at any time free of contested views, internal contradictions, and uneven popular distributions. Nonetheless, the agency of the woman around the womb and the implications of her experiences for the reproduction of racial patrimony and nation-building were *consistently problematic.* In a variety of ways, through feminine agency, it was argued, masculine agency could be erased and the consequence, while initially producing individual monstrosities, if numerous and sustained across generations could also become mechanisms for the production of monstrous races. Nationalism as amoeba-employed naturalism to define constructive agency as male, at the same time, nationalism as scavenger fractured race as manhood into varied, presumably, rankable nationalities. What were or could be the relation between the mythologically constructed male as agent of patrimonial continuity and the varied forms of empirical men and women who were citizens of the same political unit?

Dead on Arrival? Racial Subordination as Effeminized Man and Mannish Woman

Subordinated races were viewed as internally human but externally distorted and subject to racial death brought on by a suicidal venture in improper agency—effeminate men and mannish women. Whereas the male of the "master race" ultimately was viewed as a highly intelligent, aggressive dominator, paradoxically conceived by an air-headed femme fatale. "What," as a trite contemporary riddle asks, "is the newest form of artificial intelligence?" The answer: "a blonde who dyes her hair brunette," quickly sexes the historicity of this intraracial stupidity. Where monstrous distortions were averted, the master-race male, (prototype for "successful" masculinity) is begot by the history of his racial patrimony rather than mere biological reproduction. No more appropriate vessel or process of generation could be imagined for nationalism built on racialized respectability. In short, Mosse's historical treatment of nationalism and sexuality suggests that European nationalist ideologies found ways and means of selectively absorbing available mythic, philosophical, religious, and scientific renderings that defined and redefined nature in ways that emptied civilized woman of potentially contaminating essences, the better to bring forth future generations shaped by the history of masculine action in and on the world as the foundations for competing civilizations or contests between civilization and barbarism. That nationalist ideologies were convincing and durable may well be attributed in large measure to the absence of significant amounts of novel and unfamiliar material added during the period of its nineteenth-century consolidation as the reigning political philosophy for race making, formulations of unity, stipulations of codes for solidarity, and the specification of racial destinies within and across politically defined boundaries. Nationalisms were kept busy consuming the natures they had helped to produce. No claim is being made here for a perfectly coherent ideology, but rather the claim is that disparate ideological precepts cohere *well enough* to produce adequately flexible, and hence, enduring mythologics for nationalisms as amoeba and racial scavengers.

In sum, the position taken is that, between 1850 and 1950, nationalist ideologies worked and reworked an exceedingly rich metaphysics of nature, sexuality, and power. In the spread of nationalisms, both within and outside Europe, nationalism, in historical and dialectical tensions, differentially consumed the raw material of centuries of European thought, adjusting singular and complexly configured sets of ideas to competing, complementary or supplementary conceptions from non-European sources (i.e., "tribe," "clan," "caste," religion, and other classificatory distinctions). If this metaphysics and its diverse configurations confronted a difficult and entrenched gender problematic with respect to male versus female agency in production and reproduction, this problematic was itself part of a racial scaffolding on which nationalism as scavenger displayed fears about social and economic difference within genders and the nationalities they produced.

In many ways race constructed as a fear of difference was also a fear of the monstrous undead—those presumed dead on arrival to the modern age. The living dead, ancient forms of natures, were conceptualized as the "less civilized" men and women of the less noble races. Contrary to the social evolutionary expectation that they would die before the onslaught of stronger, superior races, instead found themselves on nationalism terrains again and again aiming to retrofit themselves to particular economic regimes in diverse geopolitical spaces. They would foster struggles to emancipate political territories, elevate subordinated cultural forms, and re-value racial histories through their own adoption and adaptation of the precepts of nationalism and its code of respectability. On this point Hoberman's (1995) extension of Mosse's discussion of Jewish identity and masculinity, as an oppositional set of stereotypes with which bourgeois Europeans conjured their own modern identity and sexuality, provides a worthy example of the issues we confront. To contextualize Otto Weininger's personal response to the problem of Jewish masculine identity,[1] Hoberman turns to the dialectical interplay between Jewishness as a subordinated form of masculinity and it exclusionary relations to transcendent "Indogermanic" bourgeois manliness (Hoberman 1995: 152).

> What is certain is that Weininger's ostensibly ungendered defamation of the Jews as a type is in fact an unerringly precise defamation of the Jewish male as he was commonly portrayed at this time by Jews and gentiles alike. In classic projective fashion, Weininger unloaded a set of anxieties about being Jewish and male onto an abstraction he calls "Jewry" or "the Jew." The anxieties cohere to form the syndrome I will call the "Jewish male predicament." The fact that Weininger's scathing portrait of the Jewish male did not even arouse controversy suggests that the predicament was a real factor in the lives of European Jews at this time. . . . The alleged deficiencies must be interpreted in the context of the social world in which many Jewish men struggled to achieve a viable male identity in the face of anti-Semitic folklore and discriminatory practices that limited Jewish access to privileged male venues such as the officers corps, university fraternities, and gymnastics clubs. (Hoberman 1995: 142)

Hoberman's analysis of Weininger's motivations reminds us that nationalisms' uses of respectability, race, and nature did not merely subordinate women, eliminating them from the domain of productive nature as culture, thereby setting them outside of the constructive means by which history played a role in making race. It also established a competition between racialized forms of masculinity within and across nation-states as political and cultural terrains. Could and would racialized forms of subordinated masculinity imitate their competitors, or could and would they provide and validate alternative criteria for manliness?

This competition was especially compelling for racialized forms of masculinity in search of nation-states in which to house their own masculinity or to find spaces for ethnically marked selves within nation-states already occupied by a predominant form of racialized masculinity. Unfortunately, the domestication and nationalization of gender in private lives and the intricate consequences of nationalism's absorption of racism by subordinated groups remained outside the scope of most scholars who studied the history of nationalism. Nonetheless, Mosse's text, supplemented by analysis of the philosophical and theological backgrounds to the metaphysics of respectability points in a fruitful direction. Following this lead through works such as that of Hoberman and others concerned with so-called self-hate critiques of racialized identity and gender, we not only learn to expect the death of those forms of race deemed inappropriate to the nationalist project, we can also foresee such an expectation for "inappropriate" forms of masculinity and other such "monsters." For example, Mosse indicates (in his discussion of death and funeral practices in the images of race and nation) that the Jews and homosexuals that Nazi Germany would attempt to exterminate, pre-Nazi German nationalism and its code of respectability had already been labeled as those who "knew neither how to live nor how to die." Speaking from the standpoint of gender, Huet echoes this warning when she comments that: "to give life to a monster is to give death as well by anticipating in the creation of a being doomed to live only a few hours, a progeny unfit to live in any sense of the term." *Traité du droite criminel français,* published in 1826, made this chilling statement: "Il ne peut être commis d'homicide ni sur un montre ni sur un mort' (there can be no homicide committed against a monster or a dead man)" (1993: 122).

In the same terms we can say that when males embodying other forms of masculinity entered as immigrants to racialized nations that were, by the twentieth century, guarding their masculinity from threat of external infection (other races) and internal decay (inappropriate femininity and effeminate masculinities), such males, as alternative forms of masculinity, were dead on arrival insofar as, in accordance with the general precepts of nationalist discourses, the less noble races were forms of either obsolete nature or inappropriate juxtaposing of nature and agency on nature.

As we have seen in the equation of war and sport contests, obsolete nature, the ancient natures of racial difference had a highly significant connection to the place of violence in constructions of the masculine. Whereas the right to violence and other forms of overt aggression were arrogated to male agency (Gay 1993: 292), such actions committed by inappropriate males did not contribute to a positive assessment of the role of violence in constructing masculinity. These assessments were sufficient to raise, but not to answer, questions about the relativity of "courage" as a feature of the prototypical male. Thus, on courage before death, and death before the invisibility of assimilation, Hoberman points out in the connection with his view of the "Jewish male predicament," that the issue of courage and its relativity was at times viewed as having a "degenerate as well as a genuine form" (1995: 149). The former lead to recklessness and the latter to controlled rational uses of violence. This dichotomy could be variously employed to produce contrasting stereotypes of masculine potential that misrecognized the empirical sources of their grains of truth. Excluded from most of the social, political, and symbolically favored economic domains, also meant, Hoberman argues, Jewish males were "exiled from an entire world of male drama—the stage upon which a man could demonstrate a spectrum of masculine qualities: loyalty, self-control, chivalric feeling, and that capacity for spontaneous exuberance that enabled a man be a courageous soldier, a boon companion, a passionate lover" (1995: 145).

Men representing alternative masculinities remained problematic for the coherence of masculine prototyping and its function in nationalist projects. The problem was to be temporary. In the parlance of the social evolutionary schemes of the era, the disappearance of such men and the races they produced was to be the proof of the superiority and rationality of nationalist ideology's definition of the proper means to civilization. As obsolete natures these races of man had made history improperly and proper history would erase them as embodied errors. Women, as members of the less noble sex in general and within "their own race," remained static containers for the preservation of the accomplishments of their males who actively engaged modern nature. Yet, the metaphysics that informed nationalism may have, as Malaparte intoned, created a history of tradition to be stored in male genitals and retrieved through wombs, but it still had to confront the problematic of how to keep the womb symbolically static in a world of moving, real women.

What is empirically preserved must also be symbolically inscripted in forms, acts, and practices, which can be read as "conquest" by all of those fluent in the language of power. In this order of symbols, acts of physical abuse join enactments of ritual humiliation. In his fictionalized witnessing of the U.S. occupation of Naples during World War II, in a chapter simply entitled "The Virgin," Malaparte (originally published in 1949) describes one such enactment and the grounds of its staging.

> "She is a virgin. You can touch. Don't be afraid. She doesn't bite. She is a virgin. A real virgin," said the man, thrusting his hand into the room [where a virgin is on display to be observed and touched for a fee of one dollar/viewer] through a gap in the curtain.
>
> Some laughed, and seemed to repent of it. The "virgin" did not move, but stared at us [Malaparte and Jimmy the U.S. soldier who took him to view the "virgin of Naples"] with eyes full of fear and loathing. I looked about me. Everyone was pale—pale with fear and loathing.

Suddenly the girl closed her legs bringing her knees together with a soft thud. She raised herself up with a jerk, pulled down her dress, and with a rapid movement of the hand snatched the cigarette from the mouth of the English sailor who was standing near the edge of the bed. . . .

"You people ought to be well satisfied to see Naples brought to this pass," I said to Jimmy when we were outside.

"It certainly isn't my fault," said Jimmy.

"Oh no," I said, "it certainly isn't your fault. But it must give you all great satisfaction to feel that you have conquered a country like this," I added. "Without such scenes how would you make yourselves feel that you were conquerors? Be frank Jimmy: You would not feel that you were conquerors without such scenes." (1964: 59)[2]

Castration by humiliation and the defilement of men's property in purified women are wrought by these scenes. Among subordinated races of men, the symbols of humiliation and the metaphors of conquest become a central feature of what liberation and revolution are intended redress. Movements for freedom from racial domination come to be equated with redemptions of racialized masculinity. Dominated men find it difficult to imagine alternative forms of femininity that do not reinscribe the effeminate position into which their masculinity has been placed relative to the dominant form of racialized masculinity with which they compete within a state-defined polity or in the international order of such polities.

Instead, turning to the formation of subnationalist identities as liberation projects allows these men to play the game. The game, however, takes place in nature, which as we have seen becomes historicized in a manner which fixes subordinated masculinities' relations to the win/lose column as long as these men play by rules that *legitimate* the preestablished *criteria* generated out of contests with nature redefined as social and political orders. The game permits, even requires, a division of labor between the sexes *within* a race, but it does not recognize legitimately distinct forms of masculinity *across* races within a putative nation-state. Not surprisingly, under these conditions, womanist scholars, writing from the latter spaces, tend to employ death metaphors when referring to the predicament such male-dominated efforts produce. In their death throes, these males become suicidal. More significantly they opt for homicidal suicide—the killing of self through the destruction of others.

This lack of *ideologically* preordained space for subordinated masculinities has profound implications for how we can formulate strategies that liberate the social order from oppressive forms of domination. For these reasons, women sharing the fate of such dominated groups find it difficult to struggle against sexist domination without appearing to undermine the quest for masculine redemption. From the standpoint of these ideological reckonings, to permit such an undermining is deemed tantamount to genocide.

For subordinated races, where does violence, symbolically arrogated to processes of male history/race making, enter and how are men and women to participate in projects of racial redemption within these turns to violence?

"Degenerate Courage" and the Gender of Violent Redemption

In war zones and times of crisis the relations between subordinated agency and death draw in grand relief which is fundamentally problematic to the everyday order of social classification that transforms death into a special form of agency—the agency of last resort. Even last resorts are racialized and gendered. An extension of Huet's thesis into the domain of the racialized subordination suggests, because no act of homicide can be committed against monsters or dead men, that when racially defined men and their women are declared dead as monstrous forms of humanity, it is also the case that their death dealing and defying acts—be these acts homicidal, suicidal, or homicidal suicides—cannot automatically undermine the order of that which defines them as monsters. Violence, like courage, can be treated as "degenerate" or "genuine." Within the construction of the degenerate and genuine, the urge to, and forms of, violence are gendered. Zombies, the living dead, male and female, can and do kill, and their violence is feared, but nationalist constructions of subordinate forms of masculine agency treat such violence as, at best, the devious, underhanded violence of congenital cowards, their barbarian tendencies unbound. Masculine subordinate views of women's acts of violence all too often absorb and project back onto women of their "own kind" the identity predicament they themselves are trying to escape. Racialized subordinate women that fight for their freedom at the sides of these men all too soon find themselves out of place when the moment of violence as last-resort agency has passed.

The issue for students of nationalism who would shed light on the problematic of gender reform and its links to liberation politics, is not one of violence versus non-violence, but rather is a matter of disclosing the ideological constraints within which decisions are made and judged as to who can and should die (literally and symbolically), in what manner, and to what consequence for the production of subordinated agency. When nationalist ideology, deeply rooted in the metaphysics of gender and genesis, fixes this place, women's metaphorical and actual deaths become forms of agency already overdetermined by their relation to historically constituted men of nature. For these men's women folk, there is thought to be no parallel agency. Instead the effort is more often seen as a masculine quest for means to eliminate "empirical woman," replacing her with the "metaphorical woman" as a field for patri-racial reproduction.

Although argued in racially neutral terms, in *Over Her Dead Body: Death, Femininity and the Aesthetic,* Bronfen (1992) sets forth a final critical consequence of the social order viewed as a patri-racial accomplishment. She argues that the death of women, constituted as the quintessential Other, authorizes cultural regeneration out of particular forms of death when, in literary representations, the death of a beautiful woman "emerges as the requirement for a preservation of existing cultural norms and values or regenerative modification" (181). Connecting the literary imaginary to the more general otherness of woman, she asserts: "The [construction] of Woman-as-Other serves rhetorically to dynamise a social order, while death marks the end of this period of change. Over her dead body, cultural norms are reconfirmed or secured, whether because the sacrifice of the virtuous, innocent woman serves a social critique and transformation or because a sacrifice of the dangerous woman reestablishes an order that was momentarily suspended due to her presence" (1992: 181).

In racial subordination, otherness, male and female, is continually doubly constructed, and the conventional norms they would regenerate forever unstable as subordinated features of cultural production in a putative nation-state. All too often, these men's sense of danger and their need for regeneration through retraditionalization of wayward norms/women are as much felt in relations to *inside forms of womanly virtue* as they are to *outside dangers* to those virtues. Under these conditions, the problem comes to be viewed as one of how the Other-as-racialized-male can select and properly kill the improper forms of the Other-as-his-female. Under these circumstances we must ask, when, where, and how can masculine redemption be taken as the best purchase from which to define and privilege the needs of an oppressed community, even a racially defined community, when the lauded form of masculinity by definition faces outward?

Women Out of Place, Races in Space: The Act Part Two?

Against the background of this metaphysic, the essays in this volume are explorations in the meaning and practical consequences of the gender of agency and of the races of nationalities.[3] They aim to advance our understanding of the interrelations of race, nation, gender, and domesticity as dimensions of subordination and commitment within nationalist projects for political change. They focus on the relations between constructs of gender, race, class, and the historical and economic conditions that selectively shape the range, type, and organization of nationalist precepts that configure any given nationalist ideology and its moments of struggle. As nationalist consolidation moves into a new era of nation-building and race making, phrasing our problem in terms of continuities and discontinuities in nationalist precepts and their underlying metaphysics, the essays in this volume examine the "act" part two as previous constructions of naturalized gender fall to postmodernity. The contributors explore the diverse and ever-shifting, complex linkages amongst various forms of gendering, domesticity, and the naturalization of power in nation-building projects as these are embedded in and produce a range of economic regimes. How, we ask, are the everyday pragmatics of gender related to reproduction, transformation, or both for nationalisms that have been highly flexible and enduring configurations that have absorbed the best and worst of numerous and complex "social logics"—each, perhaps, "poor" in its own right, but when taken together richly endow the politics of obfuscation and its pragmatic misrecognitions (Bourdieu 1977)? Our greatest attention is devoted to subordinates in each field of power and the processes by which genders are naturalized. In some instance, such as those in nations of the post-communist formation, the essays witness nationalism's amoeba expelling a previously consumed set of ideological precepts as its adherents aim to reposition gender and race in national rehabilitations, masculine redemptions, and feminine traditionalizations. In others, on the terrains of post-colonial nationalist awakenings or births, we examine its efforts to better digest a variety of competing social logics at the same time it contends for mythic space with nationalism as racial scavenger.

We have divided our task into two parts: "Essentialism and Gendered Movements," and "'Wombs' of Nationalist Respectability and the Problem of Patri-Racial Redemption." In the first part the contributors are primarily, though not exclusively, concerned with varied forms of essentialization and the manner in which the empirical conditions of their enactment influence both the ideological selectivity and pragmatic outcomes for political movements during which such precepts are either absorbed and recasted, or contested and rejected by either intranational leading political elements of racialized subordinated groups or a nation looking for an international place for its "civilization" in the order of nationalized cultures. In the second part the contributors focus on the relation between symbolic capital in women, as wombs of racial reproduction, and the economic and political constraints and options that variously shape masculine motivations to utilize such capital.

By paying careful attention to gender during moments of nationalist formation, the contributors disclose how twentieth-century nationalist and sub-nationalist ideologies differentially utilized nineteenth-century nationalist precepts. Among the uses to which these precepts are put is that of imagining woman as the site of cultural continuity which must be kept "pure and protected" from the manipulated and changing definitions of purity and danger. The purity concept and the construction of the dangers of impurity, they demonstrate, shift with the relativized (national and international) status of the elite males whose masculinity is constructed of varying and, often, tenuous, representations of history as the active interface between a biological inheritance (the godhead inherent) and manly accomplishments (both individual prowess and racial superiority).

Ethnographically, the essays of Part I explore geographically dispersed constructions of respectability as they move into the historical particulars of race, class, and gender concept formations as these are produced and reproduced in nationalists and subnationalist ideologies. Across the cases, we see how different circumstances encourage and discourage absorption and utilizations of various features of the metaphysical heritage. They also allow readers the opportunity to assess how such constructions are implicated in class stratification, the formation of ethnic patterns of domesticity, or both, at the same time they suggests ways in which aspects of racioethnic identities are simultaneously shaped by the constraints of particular economic regimes.

Fox opens the discussion by examining Gandhi's effort to overturn the patriarchal views of manliness, nation, community, woman's nature, and the place of women typical to western European nationalisms. While the content of Gandhi's rhetoric seems quite consistent with the pedestalisms and purified womb symbolism of woman fostered by gender naturalism, Fox focuses on what Gandhi's use of these precepts meant to Indian women, particularly those actively involved in the political actions made possible by Gandhian nationalism. He argues that Gandhian views serve as the model for both a "generative" reconstruction of the moral basis of masculinity as well as for a reimagining of an Indian nation. His essay brings us face to face with the question of the contextualization of naturalism in its consequence for empirical women as against its textual configurations for representations of metaphorical woman. We are encouraged to ask of whose essentialism we speak when we assess reproductions as continuities rather than discontinuities. Smith, building on Foucault's "symbolic of blood," and Martinez-Alier/Stolcke's political economy of blood, marriage, and the problem of class reproduction, continues the essentialist critique as she examines the implications of female purity and racial distinctions in the reproduction of Guatemalan Mayan ethnic and gender relations. Viewed through the dialectic of what she terms modern and anti-modern forms of blood, Smith finds that Maya men's and women's active reproduction of racially naturalized "blood" as cultural patrimony and marker of its community boundary provides the means by which they seek to mediate their community's relation to the economic order and its dependence on the forms of racial domination and subordination that structure the "marriage market." Treating the market as a total order of reproduction and viewed in terms of the interrelations of concept formation, Smith discloses further parallel between the reproductive capabilities of impure, sexually suspect White Guatemala women and those of Ladino and Maya women. She argues that like these fallen vessel of purity, neither Ladino, nor Maya women are among the forms of woman ideologically positioned to reproduce the ruling strata of the national order. Under such ideological constraints, Maya women, she argues, exchange an ideologically idealized individual autonomy for actual group-defined social relations of gender. While both Fox and Smith raise questions about the meaning of the essentials in essentialisms, Smith adds to the picture questions about the meaning of control. Maya men's relation to the economic order and to the order of biological reproduction are controlled by a ruling strata of White and Ladino male and female Guatemalans. Within these constraints Maya men in turn control the means and manner in which Maya women can reproduce within the Maya identity. The latter control, she notes, influences the "essentials" of dominant masculinity that are either pragmatically, ideologically, or both, acceptable to Maya men as they construct their own forms of masculinity. Louisa Schien, further problematizes the question of whose essentials, for what purposes. Exploring an example of subnational identity (the Miao), formed on the terrain of an ancient civilization, but now "underdeveloped" nation (The People's Republic of China), Schien directs our attention to what she terms the "multiple alterities" of an "internal orientalism." She argues that Chinese nationalists, struggling to position China as an ancient venerable civilization against the image of China as a culturally backward, economically undeveloped state, search their geographical terrain and "ethnic diversity" for the site and essential form best representative of China's unsullied imperial past. They find what they seek, she argues, in the romanticized, rural representations they construct of the "unspoiled" contemporary ethnic Miao and the presumed traditionalism of Miao women. Such representations of Miao identity and gender are not, however, the products of the contestation between a dominant ideology and a subordinate ideology. Instead, Schien argues, "three types of nationalism were actively molded in 1980s China, each with an ambivalence structured by gender difference." On this complex ideological field, she concludes: "The nationalism of the Miao (and other minorities) came to terms with the desired modernity of the dominant other by domesticating their women as the symbolic (and in many ways practical) conservators of valorized traditions, thereby consigning them . . . to a new subordination in the service of their people."

The problem of fit subjects for imperial representation takes a different turn when it resurfaces in True's analysis of the settler nationalism of New Zealand's "Pakeha." True explores European immigrants' efforts to imagine themselves as racially "fit" citizens of the British Empire. Dubbing New Zealand "Godzone," True argues, these "refugees from European industrialism" confronted the Maori as the "ignoble savage," managing, after a century and a half, to develop an appropriate discourse of racial and gender supremacy consistent with their image of national unity. In the mode of legitimation and everyday practices through which European immigrants asserted their dominance over the land and its indigenous inhabitants, True discloses how "nineteenth-century discourses of racial supremacy" operated "similarly to late twentieth-century discourses of national unity." In both discourses, racialized others posed problems for "homogenized" images of the nation, at the same time "woman" was seen as both a "worthless womb" and a danger to man; encouraging segregated spaces for men and women and manly displays of masculinity. Courage, bravery, and toughness take on larger-than-life portions as men confront these "dangers." The result, she contends, of their effort to make sense of being European in New Zealand was to come to see themselves as a superior form of the Anglo-Saxon. The struggle out of which this was achieved, over time, produced the "multiple forms of subordination based on identities of race, class, gender, and ethnicity," with which New Zealanders now contend as some of them try to image the fit citizens of the "Godzone," as a nation of "coffee-coloured" kiwis, while still others now see it as a nation of "white—not

British—natives." Williams closes this section with another look at contested fitness in a British post-colonial order. She focuses on constructions of race and class as dimensions of Afro-Guyanese ethnic identity in opposition to other ethnic identities, especially Indo-Guyanese, where these identities are thought to be producers of distinctive cultures which can be deemed more or less fit to serve as foundations for Guyana as a homogenizing nation-state. The consequence, Williams argues, of the particular conjunction of race and class in the construction of ethnicity is the creation of conditions among Afro-Guyanese in which a "race" of men interact with a "class" of women to produce forms of Afro-Guyanese domesticity that they then consider to be culturally distinctive from that of other ethnic groups. The essentials of their cultural distinctiveness, she argues, must be understood as part of historically constituted notions of the dialectical interplay of race and class in the differential construction of masculinity and femininity.

The essays of Part II begin with the symbolic and ideological constraints of the "womb" as the space of racio-national reproduction (Huseby-Darvas on antifeminism in post-communist Hungary, and Pierce and Williams on masculine redemptions and feminine re-traditionalism in the rhetorical practices of the Nation of Islam). Although focused on the symbolism of the womb and its relations to the mythologics of nationalism, both essays note how these aspects of identity and gender are simultaneously shaped by the constraints and possibilities of particular economic regimes as these change over time and in space. Yet, cases as seemingly far removed as Hungarian males rethinking their position in post-communist Hungary, and "insurgent" African-American Muslims seeking redemption in the racist, advanced capitalist United States, these essays demonstrate how the quest for masculine rehabilitation as racio-national redemption converge in their antifeminist quest for the purified womb. Bringing empirical women in line with metaphorical women is seen as the first step in a presumed economic reordering adequate to produce a more just class stratification. In both cases the health and longevity of the race is thought to depend on masculine control of women's wombs. One degree removed from this struggle to purify the womb as a field of patriarchal reproduction by regaining control over the women around it, is found in the "structural deflection" of the "woman problem." Pierce details in her sociohistorical analysis of "boudoir politics" in the National Independent Political Party. Her essay reopens, on a different venue, issues initially presented in the "movement" dimensions of the Part I essays. Despite a numerical predominance of women, and the centrality of their work for the Party's functioning, Pierce finds that the "naturalism" of womanness initially placed the woman problem at the bottom of the Party's political agenda and erased from the movement's organizational memory the roles women played in the historical development and functioning of the Party. Although an effort to confront this "erasure" in a subsequent reorganization of the Party resulted in doubling organizational positions such that each position had both a male and female counterpart, the view of active agency in these positions remained masculine. The females were seen as the passive occupants expected to leave decision-making, and public action to the male occupants.

The interconnected tales of power and intimacy began in Pierce's look at boudoir politics find a completion in the public spaces of Tanzania's reforming economy as Deborah Rubin's "Business Story is Better than Love" closes this section with an analysis of gender and development ideology in post-Ujamaa Tanzania. Rubin focuses on Tanzania's contemporary struggle to fashion an appropriate sense of gender distinction and gender roles under conditions where nationalism as amoeba tries to consume a "development ideology" that can facilitate the Tanzanian government's effort to transform Ujamaa socialism into sustainable capitalist development. In this new world, Rubin argues, Nyerere's nationalist vision, wherein "business" and "love" were unified in the "essence of *ujamaa* or 'familyhood'" for a nation imagined as "the African extended family writ large," has given way to programs fashioned in response to "structural adjustment policies which are partly responsible for redefining and newly appropriating women's work," to make business story better than love, but only from the vantage point of males with the resources necessary to enter the game. Even as the policies tout the "genderless economic actor" and calls for "gender equity persists," Rubin demonstrates that women's role as "support" for masculine agency is reinscribed and again underscored.

Overall the essays demonstrate that the business of love and hate—love of race, love of nation, hatred of others and of otherness within—are dialectics of power and intimacy that were never simply subsumed by either the gendered public/private dichotomy, or the numerous racial hierarchies that imagine nation and its relation to ethnic groups, or the relations between class privilege and state authority. These constructions, the essayists show, are intertwined at times, conflated at others, and at still others they confront the limitations of numerous contraries[4] wrought of centuries of metaphysical accretions and their relations to economic shifts and geopolitical discontinuities. Whether as effeminized forms of masculinity or manly forms of femininity, naturalisms seek to put agency in its properly gendered place.

Notes

Thanks are due to all the contributors of this volume who read and commented on drafts at various stages. I also thank Connie Sutton, Aihwa Ong, Helán Page, and Pamela Wright for their comments on earlier drafts and their involvement with the project over the years since we began in 1990. As we look forward to continuing our dialogue with them, we regret deeply that their work could not be part of the volume. I also offer thanks to Sara Berry, Charles Carnegie, Michel-Rolph Trouillot, Katherine Verdery, Drexel G. Woodson, and the two anonymous reviewers for their substantive comments, and to Ulrike Bode for special editorial assistance. You were all immensely helpful, though seldom did you agree on all points, and, hence, I hope I have taken constructive advantage of your diverse comments and suggestions. Where I have not, the fault and the outcome are, of course, my responsibility.

1. Otto Weininger, a Jew converted to Protestantism, authored the highly influential *Sex and Character,* first published in 1903, the 6th edition of which was translated into English in 1906. Weininger's goal was to prove the natural inferiority of "the woman" and "the Jew." His work, influence, and the sociohistorical context in which he developed and worked are the subjects of a recent collection, *Jews and Gender: Responses to Otto Weininger,* edited by Nancy A. Harrowitz and Barbara Hyames.

2. Thanks are due to Virginia Kay who brought Malaparte's work to my attention.

3. The term mannish as used in the title of this collection follows the Webster definition, which serves as one of the epigrams. Broadly speaking, it refers to agency of place; to one who does not have the authority to act in a certain way, time, or place, but who behaves as if he or she had such authority. In this broader sense it is used to label the behavior of very young male and female children who engage in actions that are deemed appropriate either for children of an older age or for adults. The term mannish should not be confused with any expression denoting homosexuality. Mannish males are not necessarily inappropriately manly but rather are politically "uppity" boys when their efforts to behave as adults is considered racially inappropriate. "Effeminized" by race they are considered to usurp the authority of an adult (racially dominant) male, whereas women as subordinates are mannish when they assume male agency regardless of their other patttterns of comportment, dress, and sexuality.

4. In relation to practical logic's divisions of the world into Pythagorean-like columns of contraries that define the sense of limits and legitimate transgression of limits, Bourdieu (1977) argues the necessities of practice demand both separation and reunion within the same concept and its limits. Consequently, ideological renderings of separations and their limits tend to emphasize the manner in which the illicit is made licit in relations to unavoidable transgressions of boundaries. Thus objects and concepts in an ideological field are perceived in terms of both their aspect of separation and of union. See Bourdieu 1977: 124–24, 132–39.

References

Benda, Julien. 1928. *The Treason of the Intellectuals.* New York: Norton.

Bronfen, Elisabeth. 1992. *Over Our Dead Body: Death, Femininity, and the Aesthetic.* New York: Routledge.

Epstein, Barbara Leslie. 1981. *The Politics of Domesticity: Women, Evangelism, and Temperance in Nineteenth Century America.* Middleton, CT: Wesleyan University Press.

Gay, Peter. 1993. *The Cultivation of Hatred: The Bourgeois Experience, Victoria to Freud, Volume III.* New York and London: W.W. Norton & Co.

Goux, Jean-Joseph. 1990. *Symbolic Economies: After Marx and Freud,* translated by Jennifer Curtiss Gage. Ithaca, NY: Cornell University Press.

Harrowitz, Nancy A. and Barbara Hyams (eds.). 1995. *Jews & Gender: Responses to Otto Weininger.* Philadelphia: Temple University Press.

Hayes, Carleton. 1960. *Nationalism: A Religion.* New York: Macmillan.

Hendricks, Margo and Patricia Parker. 1994. *Women, "Race" and Writing in the Early Modern Period.* New York and London: Routledge.

Hoberman, John M. 1995. "Otto Weininger and the Critique of Jewish Masculinity." In *Jews & Gender: Responses to Otto Weininger,* edited by Nancy A. Harrowitz and Barbara Hyams. Pp. 141–54. Philadelphia: Temple University Press.

hooks, bell. 1990. *Reflections on Race and Sex in Yearning: Race, Gender, and Cultural Politics.* Pp. 57–64. Boston: South End Press.

Huet, Marie Hélène. 1993. *Monstrous Imagination.* Cambridge, MA: Harvard University Press.

Kohn, Han. 1965. *Nationalism: Its Meaning and History.* Princeton, NJ: D. Van Nostrand.

Landry, Donna and Gerald MacLean. 1993. *Materialist Feminisms.* Cambridge, MA, and Oxford, U.K.: Blackwell Publishers.

Malaparte, Curzio. 1965. *The Skin.* New York: Vintage.

Mangan, J.A. and James Walvin (eds.). 1987. *Manliness and Morality: Middle-Class Masculinity in Britain and America, 1800–1940.* Manchester: Manchester University Press.

May, Larry and Robert Strikiwerda. 1993. *Gender on the Divide: The Dandy in Modernist Literature.* Ithaca, NY: Cornell University Press.

Melosh, Barbara (ed.). 1993. *Gender and American History Since 1890.* New York and London: Routledge.

Mitchell, W. J. T. (ed.). 1983. *The Politics of Interpretations.* Chicago and London: Cambridge University Press.

Moghadam, Valentine (ed.). 1994. *Identity Politics and Women: Cultural Reassertion and Feminism in International Perspective.* Boulder, CO: Westview Press.

Mosse, George L. 1985. *Nationalism and Sexuality: Respectability and Abnormal Sexuality in Modern Europe.* New York: Howard Fertig.

———. 1993. *Confronting the Nation: Jewish and Western Nationalism.* Hanover & London: University of New England for Brandeis University Press.

Newman, Gerald. 1987. *The Rise of English Nationalism: A Cultural History 1740–1830.* New York: St. Martins Press.

Park, Roberta J. 1987. "Biological Thought, Athletics and the Formation of a 'Man of Character,' 1830–1900." In *Manliness and Morality: Middle-Class Masculinity in Britain and America, 1800–1940,* edited by J. A. Mangan and James Walvin. Pp. 7–34. Manchester: Manchester University Press.

Parker, Andrew, Mary Russo, Doris Sommers, and Patricia Yaeger (eds.). 1992. *Nationalisms and Sexualities.* New York: Routledge.

Poovey, Mary. 1988. *Uneven Developments: The Ideological Work of Gender in Mid-Victorian England.* Women in Culture and Society Series, edited by Catharine R. Stimpson. Chicago: University of Chicago Press.

Roper, Michael and John Tosh (ed.). 1991. *Manful Assertions: Masculinities in Britain Since 1800.* New York and London: Routledge.

Therborn, Göran. 1980. *The Ideology of Power and the Power of Ideology.* London: Verso.

Todorov, Tzvetan. 1993. *On Human Diversity: Nationalism, Racism, and Exoticism in French Thought,* translated by Catherine Porter. Cambridge, MA and London, England: Harvard University Press.

Williams, Brackette F. 1993. "The Impact of the Precepts of Nationalism on the Concept of Culture: Making Grasshopper of Naked Apes." *Cultural Critique* (Spring) 24: 143–91.

———. 1994. "Classification Systems Revisited: Kinship, Caste, Race, and Nationality as the Flow of Blood and the Spread of Rights." In *Naturalizing Power: Essays in Feminist Cultural Analysis,* edited by Sylvia Yanagisako and Carol Delaney. Pp. 201–36. New York: Routledge.

Part I

Essentialism and
Gendered Movements

I

Gandhi and Feminized Nationalism in India

Richard G. Fox

Nationalist movements have often projected essentialist images of women as part of their attempt to create a sense of heritage, a peoplehood, by which to activate cultural resistance. Are such gender essentialisms all of a kind? Do they at their worst create a new bondage for women, more dire than their position under colonialism, or, at their best, admit women to the nationalist project only as an affirmation of the continuing power of (indigenous) men over women? Do they always deploy purified images of women in the hope of remasculinizing colonized men by contrasting the genders? Therefore, do they never lead to real changes in the balance of gender power?

In this paper, I shall show that Gandhian nationalism in India before 1947 kept women "in their place" and exhorted them "to follow their natures" in order to advance India's independence. These essentialist understandings of gender, however, proved liberatory rather than restrictive. Keeping women in their place required neither domesticity nor passivity from them; following their nature, as Gandhi defined it, led to a celebration of women's strength, not their purity. Curiously, Gandhian nationalism endeavored to remasculinize Indian men, effeminized under British colonialism, by feminizing them, that is, by urging them to behave "essentially" like women. Gandhi thought women more courageous than men; thus Indian men could only gain the self-discipline necessary for nonviolent resistance by becoming feminized. Gender essentialism at the behest of the nationalist movement therefore redefined gender roles, at least for middle-class women, and reworked their relationship to the public sphere.

Partha Chatterjee (1989) advances the opposite position, that Indian nationalism established a new patriarchy, which associated "female emancipation with the
historical goal of sovereign nationhood" (1989: 629). Therefore, what might
appear superficially as Indian nationalisms, liberation of women was nothing other
than a new "subordination." When Indian nationalism advocated educating women
and ending purdah, when it strove for women's right to travel by public transport
and attend popular entertainments, when it even promoted women's freedom to
work outside the home and participate in political demonstrations—in sum,
when Indian nationalism pursued any gender "liberation"—all it in fact enabled
was a new dichotomy of feminine/masculine, or so Chatterjee maintains. The
result: "the production of a nationalist discourse that is *different* from that of colonialism, nonetheless . . . trapped within its framework of gender essentialisms"
(1989: 633). Chatterjee's analysis portrays Indian nationalism as similar to the
European nationalisms that Williams (in the Introduction) shows advanced new
forms of patriarchy, that is, the power of men over women.

Chatterjee comprehensively characterizes Indian nationalism in this way, but
his empirical references actually refer to a very restricted period and place: the
late nineteenth century and Bengal. Furthermore, Chatterjee's piece, like much
of the anti-essentialist literature, perpetrates its own essentialism: women—
specifically nineteenth-century Bengali women (the only ones Chatterjee actually
deals with)—are portrayed as passive, propped up only by the new patriarchy that
forced "liberation" on them.

Ketu Katrak (1992: 395) also argues that Indian nationalism, and especially
Gandhism, victimized women at the very moment it promised to liberate them.
In her judgment, Gandhi failed to challenge the domestic patriarchy that
oppressed women (a mistaken view, as I shall show below). Gandhi's satyagraha
campaigns (which Katrak assimilates incorrectly to "passive resistance") "feminized the usually masculinist struggle against the colonizer," but Katrak believes
they never threatened Indian or British patriarchy (1992: 400).

Chatterjee and Katrak inspect Indian nationalism for the hidden messages on
gender it contained, rather than its overt statements, and they find that its
promise of liberation for women actually transmitted a new subordination.
Although they moved into new public spaces, they were still goaded to do so by
men, under whose yoke they remained.

Although Chatterjee and Katrak do not cite them, other scholars have written
extensively on the relationship between Indian nationalism and the women's
movement. This literature indicates that any judgment of Indian nationalism in
relation to gender issues cannot be as summary as Chatterjee's and Katrak's.
Before presenting my own understanding, I briefly review this literature for two
reasons: to indicate to non-South Asianists, who have often taken Chatterjee's
position as authoritative, the other scholarship that exists; and to present the
wide-ranging estimations of Gandhian nationalism's effects on gender, advanced
by this scholarship.

Geraldine Forbes (1981: 52–53) classifies the literature on Gandhian nationalism and the women's movement into two opposing viewpoints: One view holds
that Gandhi took over a developing women's movement in India and pushed it forward; the other view is that Gandhi coopted the movement and stymied it. Forbes
suggests that a good deal depends on the criteria used. If, as Gail Omvedt argues,
the measure of Indian nationalism is the extent to which it freed women from
domestic drudgery and exclusive child care, then clearly it did not truly liberate
women. If, however, the real indicator is access to public political space, as
Aparna Basu believes, then women did help liberate themselves by joining the
nationalist movement. Although Forbes (1981: 54) concludes that "feminism and
nationalism are compatible," she also indicates that those who advocated women's
rights before Independence gradually lost out to those who embraced nationalism. Led by Sarojini Naidu, who declared she was not a feminist in 1931, the
All-India Women's Congress disowned a "sex war" with men and a Western-
styled aggressive feminism that they felt might damage the nationalist movement
(Forbes 1981: 61; also see Caplan 1985: 112–15). Because many of the outright
feminist organizations weakly supported or even opposed the use of civil disobedience as a nationalist tactic, the apprehensions of nationalist women were
reasonable. In like manner, Aparna Basu and Bharati Ray (1990: 11) contrast the
repression endured by suffragettes in England with the encouragement Indian
nationalists gave to feminists. KumKum Sangari and Sudesh Vaid (1989: 19ff.) try
to adjudicate the real nature of Indian nationalism by distinguishing between modernizing nationalisms, which aim to change the material conditions and ideology
of patriarchy, and democratizing nationalisms, which reform social mores in the
interests of middle-class women. Their distinction breaks down, however, when
applied to Gandhism and Indian nationalism. There were attempts to reform
domestic relationships, in line with Sangari and Vaid's expectations for modernizing movements, but Indian nationalism was also shot through with middle-class
values, in accord with their so-called democratizing movements.

The relationship among Indian nationalism, gender essentialism, and changed
roles for Indian women is obviously more complex than Chatterjee's and Katrak's
that it perpetuated a new patriarchy by reformulating gender essentialism. Gail
Minault (1981: 11) nicely captures this complexity. She reviews Gandhi's use of
the goddess Sita as a model by which to mobilize women into nationalism.
Gandhi's evocation of Sita, according to Minault, emphasized the duty of a wife to
her husband but it also allowed women the power for independent public action.

Was Indian nationalism and Gandhism, which so informed this nationalism, a
repressive gender essentialism or a liberating representation of women? How do
we resolve this issue? Perhaps it cannot be done if we stay within the framework of
argument that I have just presented. We end up either with premature closures of
the analysis, as Chatterjee and Katrak make, or with unresolved complexity, such
as Minault provides. Perhaps we should start with this point: at a time when the
constructionist view of culture is commonplace, we seem strangely reticent to

allow that essentialism and Orientalism can construct anything other than the pejorative and the denigrated. It is as if we still require a residual notion of the authentic with which to celebrate progressive and liberatory social movements.

I think we need to sophisticate our understanding of cultural essentialisms, including gender ones, because it might help us deal better with issues of resistance. Anthropologists and historians busily engage in the hunt for cultural resistance. But we often appear to look in exactly the wrong places for it. On the one hand, we sympathize too readily with minor acts of foot-dragging and noncompliance—namely, where people squirm out of oppressive systems rather than break out of them—and we label them, following Michel de Certeau and James Scott, effective acts of social sabotage. On the other hand, we are very quick to write off as not really effective social protest that is ostensibly novel, as, for example, when Chatterjee dismisses the entry of Indian women into public politics. By the former, almost any social action constitutes resistance; by the latter, almost none does.

I want to pursue an intermediate position in this paper: Gendered resistance is a happening or process, not a suddenly attained state or a knee-jerk outcome of material conditions (to place E. P. Thompson's insight about class in another context). Chatterjee may be right that Indian nationalism only deployed a new gender essentialism, but he fails to recognize that it still enabled women to begin to take on new and effective social protest actions. They can do so for two reasons: the gender essentialism positively empowered and mobilized them; and eventually, it even led them to take over the essentialism and make the most of it. Gender essentialisms are neither historically static nor the testamentary property of only one group. The boundaries of power that an essentialism once demarcated can be redrawn by the purposeful actions of people as they work with these essentialisms in everyday life.

This more flexible approach to essentialisms originally came to me in research on the historical relationship between British Orientalism and Sikh identity in northern India (Fox 1985). The Orientalism the British visited upon the Sikhs exemplified a debilitating ethnic essentialism. The Sikhs became the very image of a martial race, loyal to their British "salt" and foolhardily courageous in defense of the Raj—an image cultivated by the colonial authorities through their control of Sikh temples and by their recruitment of Sikhs into the British Indian army. This Orientalism, although it shackled Sikhs to the British military and the imperial Raj for nearly 75 years, later (in the 1920s) came to empower a militant anti-colonial movement, which the British mightily feared.

If even this oppressive and pejorative essentialism could be reversed, then what of other essentialisms, such as gender essentialisms sponsored by nationalist movements, whose intent might be benign or even celebratory? I want to propose that not all gender essentialisms within nationalist movements are equally oppressive (or perhaps better put, equally patriarchal). These differences can have real consequences for the ultimate agency of women and their ability to resist patriarchy in nationalist movements.

I therefore distinguish "affirmative" essentialisms from "pejorative" or "negative" ones. This distinction came to me in working on Gandhi's utopian vision (Fox 1989). I found that the Gandhian resistance to British colonialism depended on the same sort of cultural stereotypes as British condemnation of India did; in many respects, Gandhian utopia was a reverse Orientalism. Gandhi based his hopes for a future perfected India on its traditions of spirituality, nonviolence, and long suffering. Gandhi's construction was precedented by European Orientalist scholars like Max Müller, by "Indian-lovers" like Annie Besant and Margaret Noble, and by other Indian nationalists. What distinguishes Gandhian essentialism from British pejorative stereotypes is its intent, which was affirmative rather than negative. The term "condescending veneration," which Raymond Schwab used to characterize Orientalist scholarship, captures this quality well. Hitherto, we have rightly paid most attention to the element of "condescension," which took form in European scholarship's control over the representation of India, even when the stereotypes used were positive ones. Here, I want to explore some of the consequences of "veneration," and especially, the positive valuation of what Gandhi took to be the traditional strengths of Indian women (he took them as the strengths of all women, but he thought them better preserved by Indian women, unaffected by the modern civilization that had corrupted most European women). I begin therefore with an analysis of Gandhi's ideas about women, to show that they were essentialist but also to indicate that they were affirmative and empowering.

Gandhian Gender Essentialism

Gandhi believed that women and men were essentially different, and his feminism was always of the "separate but equal" variety. In 1917, for example, he advocated education for men and women but not of the same kind. "True, [men and women] are equals in life, but their functions differ," he wrote. Man earns, woman "saves and spends." Women were the domestic managers and the guardians of children. As such, they upheld dharma or tradition, and they could give men courage by their loving support. For Gandhi, this was "the scheme of Nature," and he thought that a nation in which women had to earn their living was "no good": "such a people must be bankrupt." So women needed education, all right, but only of certain sort, namely, how to manage the home.

At the same time, Gandhi believed that "renunciation and nonviolence come naturally to women." Gandhi wrote in *Young India* (1930): "To call women the weaker sex is a libel; it is man's injustice to woman. If by strength is meant brute strength, then indeed is woman less brute than man. If by strength is meant moral power, then woman is immeasurably man's superior. Has she not greater intuition, is she not more selfsacrificing, has she not greater powers of endurance, has she not greater courage? Without her man could not be. If non-violence is the law of our being, the future is with woman." This essentialist belief promoted

Gandhi's incorporation of women in the nationalist campaign from a very early time, as we shall soon see.

In a peculiar way, Gandhi did combat gender essentialism—in respect to men, not women. When his spinning program was disparaged as unmanly, Gandhi replied that "it is contrary to experience to say that any vocation is exclusively reserved for one sex only" (Gandhi 1942: 173). Because he also recognized the power that husbands had over their wives, he advised college women not to marry, and instead, he suggested they devote themselves to national service—a pretty radical message in 1927.

Like European nationalisms, Gandhian nationalism hoped to foster an improved and more militant self-image among men. But this heightened self-esteem was not to come about through remasculinizing or through appeals to a new national domesticity, otherwise Gandhi would not have required men to spin or women to remain unwed. Gandhi set out to *feminize* men, using a model of the feminine that was essentialist. For himself, Gandhi had always wanted to feel like a woman, in keeping with the precedent of the Paramahansa Ramakrishna (the guru of Swami Vivekananda) in the late nineteenth century, who claimed he could become male or female at will. Feeling like a woman, Gandhi believed, would give him access to the strength and resolve that contemporary nationalist men so obviously lacked and so badly needed if they were to pursue nonviolent resistance.

Gandhi believed that women were essentially stronger than men because they could bear suffering better, especially better than cowardly men. The ability to suffer, as Gandhi's nonviolent methods required, came from an inner strength and spiritual discipline. It could be found in soldiers, who, in Gandhi's mind, also bore suffering well, but it was most prevalent in women (perhaps through the pain inflicted by childbearing and male sexuality). Empowering men in Gandhi's nationalism meant turning them into women—and he held up British suffragettes as models of courage and moral strength for Indian men.

Ashis Nandy (1988) makes a superficially similar argument when he claims that Gandhi relegitimated androgynous elements in the selfhoods of Indian men. Androgyny, according to Nandy, was deeply rooted in India, but the British colonization had devalued it as effeminate. The evaluation of androgyny in ancient India, whatever it was, does not seem to have determined Gandhi's position, however. Gandhi believed that men and women had separate qualities, as I have indicated, and, rather than some sort of androgynous composite, he hoped that by an act of self-discipline, cowardly nationalist men could come to act like courageous, long-suffering women. Androgyny implies a mixing of traits; instead, Gandhi called for a radical absorption of the female other by men—a condition I have labeled as "feminizing men."

Gandhi's essentialist emphasis on women as virtuous and respectable was not mainly to "domesticate" them at home (as I show below). Rather, it was to "domesticate" (that is, feminize) what he saw as the violent—and therefore, cowardly—emotions of male subalterns. By emphasizing woman's noble nature, he was actually trying to contrast his own middle-class sense of discipline with what he took as the wildness and uncontrolled behavior of the Indian masses.

Gandhi worried that under the influence of modern civilization, Indian women could lose these essential qualities. For example, in the late 1930s, he started a running battle with young college women over his conception of the "Modern Girl," Westernized and educated, who led men to "impure thoughts." Under attack, Gandhi insisted he did not include all educated women as "Modern Girls," but he refused to give up the notion altogether. The modern girl lacked (sexual) self-discipline, and as a result, she had lost courage as well as her Indian national virtues, or so Gandhi feared. I shall return to Gandhi's Modern Girl run-in with young feminists later on, when I discuss the resistance to Gandhian essentialism that emerged from within it.

Over the course of the nationalist movement, Gandhi's gender essentialism defined somewhat different political roles for women, and, although all of them kept women within his affirmative essentialism, they began to remove women from domesticity. Initially, he appealed to women's domestic power and especially charged them with supporting the swadeshi program against imported British cloth. By the early 1930s, however, he urged women to look beyond their "narrow domestic chores" and "by completely identifying herself with her husband, learn to identify herself with the whole world."

There was an inherent contradiction in Gandhi's essentialism, however, which develops out of the very essentialist affirmation of women. Because Gandhi urged women to develop their better, nonviolent nature; because he rallied them to recognize their "true selves," Gandhi thereby had to allow that self-realization was possible for them. Almost immediately after his return from South Africa (and until the end of his life), Gandhi insisted that women would have to raise themselves, and that it was not for men to lead them to liberation. He enunciated this theme in 1935: "women alone can emancipate themselves, not men." Eventually, trapped in this contradiction, Gandhi became the victim of his own essentialism, when women used it to take political action against his wishes.

Gandhian Essentialism in Practice

From the beginning of what was then called "passive resistance" in South Africa, Gandhi depended on women's labor and support, at first Europeans like Sonya Schlesin and Olive Steiner. Later, in 1912, when Gandhi's political fortunes were at a low point, and he took the major risk of mobilizing Indian laborers working in South Africa under indenture, Gandhi used women to initiate a mass protest. About a dozen women living in Tolstoy Farm harangued mine and sugar workers against a recent South African law that delegitimated non-Christian marriages. The result was a massive strike and march by indentured laborers, which gave Gandhi the reputation of a revolutionary after his return to India in 1915.

In the early years of his return, Gandhi concentrated on mobilizing women behind the swadeshi movement, which meant, in effect, getting them involved on the domestic front. It is worth remembering how physically and socially constrained Indian women were, even in 1920. Burgeoning reformist associations labored and lobbied hard for women's literacy, in favor of widow remarriage, and against purdah and prostitution. We remember only too well how elitist their efforts were, but all too often we forget how truly revolutionary their aims were. Feminists of the South Asian diaspora criticize Western feminists for only reinforcing Orientalist stereotypes of Indian women as passive and dominated (see Grewal 1993: 227). Women's public participation in nationalist meetings and reformist associations developed very quickly and almost entirely from Gandhi's legitimization after 1920. The Gandhian Constructive Programme became a training ground for their further participation. As they worked to spread homespun cloth and other so-called village industries, as they protested Untouchability and agitated for prohibition, women gained leadership experience and developed cadres—which is exactly what Gandhi said he had in mind. For him, the Constructive Programme was a way to educate and train women for civil disobedience. Yes, it was very much still with the permission of men and it still involved elite women overall, but it did happen, and it was a radical initiation.

Amrit Kaur, Gandhi's co-worker and one of the main leaders of nationalist women, testified to Gandhi's accomplishments in this manner: "I do not know if any other man has ever acknowledged in such terms the equality of status of man and woman" (Amrit Kaur n.d.: 26). Did Gandhi never protest domestic patriarchy (as Katrak intimates)? Amrit Kaur says otherwise: "He spoke against enforced widowhood, against purdah, against the dedication [as dancers and prostitutes] of girls to temples, against prostitution, against early marriage, against the dowry system, against the economic and marital bondage of women" (Amrit Kaur n.d.: 179).

She then goes on to note the most significant affirmative element in Gandhi's gender essentialism: "he was a severe critic of the weakness that had crept into the mind of woman whereby she had willingly subordinated herself to man" (Kaur n.d.: 180). According to Kaur, although Gandhi believed a woman's greatest service was in the home, he also allowed that women should be eligible "to work in all spheres" (n.d.: 180).

Gender Essentialism and Gendered Protest

How truly radical could Gandhian affirmative essentialism be? How well could it prepare Indian women for greater social mobilization and political/gender resistance? I think the best illustration comes from two incidents when women who had been mobilized and brought to consciousness disputed the gender essentialism within the nationalist movement.

The first incident took place in 1930 when Gandhi chose not to fulfill his promises to women, mainly because of his gender essentialism. In 1921, Gandhi could easily turn aside a protest by one of the most militant women nationalists, Sarladevi Chaudharani, when she protested that Indian women served mainly as sex objects for male nationalists. He also gave no credence to her statement that the lot of Indian women was just as bad as that of the Untouchables. This was a Gandhi who still saw women's role in the nationalist movement as primarily an extension of their domestic duties.

Soon after, however, women came to resist more directly and more effectively Gandhi's gender essentialism, at the same time that they demanded a greater voice in Indian nationalism. The war against the British and the war against Gandhian essentialism came together at one moment for these women, which, I hope I am right to say, is not typical of many nationalist movements.

The Salt March in 1930 was to prepare Gandhi's re-entry into Indian public politics, after the caesura caused by his imprisonment and by his self-imposed rustication. Not only an affirmation of nationalism, the Salt March was also to prove the vitality of nonviolent resistance against the increasingly violent and Leftist militancy that was then overtaking Indian nationalism.

At the outset, Gandhi expected to exclude women from the Salt satyagraha. His argument was that since there would be many more men than women, women's participation was not essential and would win them no special recognition. Later, in early April 1930, Gandhi justified his decision more essentially: women, he said, have greater moral power, endurance, courage, and nonviolence than men—therefore "when women of the Ashram insisted on being taken along with men, something within me told me that they were destined to do greater work in this struggle than merely breaking salt laws" (Gandhi 1942: 164). In place of the Salt March, Gandhi gave women exclusive rights to publicly demonstrate in front of foreign cloth and liquor shops—in such places, he thought, women could show what they had learned and how they had organized in the Constructive Programme. Gandhi wrote:

> Let the women of India take up these two activities, specialize in them: they would contribute more than men to national freedom. They would have an access of power and self-confidence to which they have hitherto been strangers. . . . The charm will lie in the agitation being initiated and controlled exclusively by women. They may take and should get as much assistance as they need from men, but the men should be in strict subordination to them. . . . Highly educated women have, in this appeal of mine, an opportunity of actively identifying themselves with the masses, and helping them both morally and materially. (164–65)

Less publicly, Gandhi feared that if women participated, British "chivalry" would make them hesitate to attack the satyagrahis, and thence Indian nationalism would be accused of hiding behind women. Of course, the issue was not only or mainly British chivalry but Gandhi's own essentialist chivalry.

In the event, women simply refused to let Gandhi get away with it. There were protests directly to Gandhi himself, as well as in the print media and in public meetings. When Gandhi made salt at Dandi, his closest companions were two women, who came along anyway. Because anyone making salt joined the protest and because it was a simple act, thousands of women joined marches and participated in salt making. A woman, Sarojini Naidu, later took control of the protest at the Dharsana salt works.

At the same time, women decided for themselves to initiate the boycotts of liquor and cloth shops that Gandhi had left to them. On April 13, 1930 a self-styled conference of women met at Dandi, where the Salt March ended, and formally adopted the boycott of liquor and cloth shops that Gandhi had assigned them (Gandhi 1942: 167). When they picketed liquor stores, women sometimes used protest techniques, like blocking the entrances with their bodies so as to prevent entry, very much like the Pro-Life movement does today—techniques that some now say are too coercive to be truly Gandhian. They often endured verbal abuse from male patrons, and in the Punjab and other locales, many boycotts had to be terminated because of the violence threatened by men.

At least from this period on (and perhaps earlier), women trained themselves for nonviolent direct action, such as forming a protective cordon between nationalist protesters and the British police. Although their protective role was to be nonviolent, the fact that they formed the front line put women in the immediate way of official brutality and tested their determination severely. In one incident at Bombay in late June 1930, women satyagrahis, who had trained under male drill masters and who were led by a woman municipal counselor, marched out to protect male nationalists after four baton charges by the police against them. The police chief urged the women, who all wore saffron saris they called "the cloth of sacrifice," to submit to arrest and thereby insure their safety, but they refused. "'We shall die with our menfolks because we, too, are volunteers,'" they said. Mounted native police attacked the demonstrators regardless of the women, and five hundred people were injured (*New York Times* June 22, 1930: 14/3,4).

The women who led the liquor and foreign-cloth boycott showed a similar resolve. After being sentenced to six-months of imprisonment for harassing cloth merchants, one woman was reported to say: "'Do what you like with me now but I shall continue picketing the minute I am free again'" (*New York Times* July 4, 1930: 4/7).

Women volunteers not only lived out opposition to a Gandhian essentialism, they also opposed it in print—and consciously. An example is the "modern girl" controversy that erupted in the pages of Gandhi's *Young India* in 1938. In response to several letters from young women asking him how ahimsa (nonviolence) could counteract the rudeness and foulness they encountered from men when they ventured out in public without a male escort, Gandhi strongly condemned this male behavior. He suggested that perpetrators have their names published and in other ways be exposed to public condemnation. Additionally, he wrote (Gandhi 1942: 68): "But I have a fear that the modern girl loves to be Juliet to half a dozen Romeos. She loves adventure. . . . She improves upon nature by painting herself and looking extraordinary. The non-violent way is not for such girls."

Gandhi shortly received a letter from eleven "girls" who charged him with blaming the victim. They admonished Gandhi for putting the burden on women not to provoke men, when "in these days when women are coming out of closed doors to help men and take an equal share, . . . it is indeed strange that they are maltreated by men" (69–70). Gandhi replied to their complaints in essentialist terms: "I hold myself incapable of writing anything derogatory to womanhood. My regard for the fair sex is too great to permit me to think ill of them. She is, what she has been described to be in English, the better half of mankind" (70–71). He later says that he meant a special kind of behavior as the "modern girl" whereas his correspondents took him to refer to anyone getting an English education.

By this point, it seems, Gandhi's essentialism had provoked and legitimated women's active involvement in nationalist protest to the extent that they could break with the restraints he would have placed on them, the so-called "fair sex" (although this is a translation of Gandhi's Gujarati original, which might carry a different connotation). His essentialism, although still affirmative, could not any longer contain the modern consciousness of Indian women, even though it had once been a major inspiration for that consciousness.

By the early 1940s the Indian National Congress had organized a Women's Department, following the lead of other nationalisms, especially the Communist Party, which aimed to organize women much more widely than ever before. In the aftermath of the 1942 Quit India movement, when most of the Congress leadership was interned, a few women organized an underground Congress radio station, and some of them went so far as to break with Gandhian nonviolence. Their acts of sabotage and terrorism told Gandhi that qualities other than renunciation and nonviolence could come naturally to women.

Conclusion

I do not make excessive claims for affirmative Gandhian essentialism, but I think I claim more than we often allow such utopian visions or ideologies encased in nationalist movements. Clearly, it elevated mainly elite women and primarily gave such women the possibility of resisting this elevation, when it began to trap rather than to liberate them. In most respects, it was not an ultimate emancipation, not only in the sense that it did not involve the Indian masses, but also because even the women it did involve had often adopted atypical gender roles: they were the celibate, the unmarried, or the separated. To be sure, much more remained and remains to be accomplished. Yet if Gramsci's idea of passive revolution applies to

India, as some scholars have argued, then surely we should not expect greater upheavals in matters of gender than we find in class relations. The passive revolution accomplished by Indian nationalism was to free the country from colonial domination, even though it perhaps did too little to alter the distribution of power and wealth among Indians, including the distribution of power between Indian males and females. In fact, I could argue that the revolution in civil society has not been deferred so completely on gender issues as in other political-economic relations, at least within the educated class. At the least, I would like to consider that Gandhian nationalism did not generally work against such a revolution and often worked for it by the very nature of its gender essentialism. In India, an affirmative essentialism produced action and consciousness that superseded the original gender stereotypes. Perhaps that can serve as a political and a critical lesson for us as we observe the politics of identity today.

The alternative is to write off everything that Indian nationalism accomplished as, nevertheless, still entrapped within gender essentialism, with the implication that nothing substantially altered between Indian men and women. In this view, which Chatterjee has championed, unprecedented action in public by Indian women becomes only a means by which men redefine their masculinity without altering basic gender inequality. Indian women, hitherto trapped in domesticity of the most restrictive sort, that is, purdah, now challenge men in front of liquor shops, but Chatterjee assures us that no matter what they may think, they are still trapped. And should we interpret Gandhi's suggestion to nationalist women that they not marry as an underhanded way of preventing these women—tainted by nationalism—from reproducing themselves in the national "blood stream"?

In fact, Chatterjee and others given to poststructuralist critiques never tell us how people can escape any of the hegemonic and epistemic traps in which they get tangled. We have a right to ask them: what would pass inspection as an effective redistribution of power, other than a complete revolution in gender categories and their abolition? If we take gender essentialism to refer to viewing men and women as having basic and homogeneous natures, sentiments, and personality traits, unmodified by variables like class, history, and the like (the definition I give it in this paper)—then has any nationalism or any society or even any social movement ever completely escaped entrapment by such notions? The struggle for universal suffrage could be written off, after all, as only giving women the right to vote for mostly male candidates. Gandhi—and, one imagines, the women nationalists he sensitized—knew better: they recognized that "experiments with truth" over time would accumulate the lived experience and the critical self-discipline necessary to begin to break humanity free of any trap.

References

Amrit Kaur, Rajkumari. n.d. [c. 1961]. *Selected Speeches and Writings,* edited by G. Borkar. New Delhi: Archer.

Basu, Aparna and Bharati Ray. 1990. *Women's Struggle*. New Delhi: Manohar.

Caplan, Patricia. 1985. *Class and Gender in India*. London: Tavistock.

Chatterjee, Partha. 1989. "Colonialism, Nationalism, and Colonized Women: The Contest in India." *American Ethnologist* 16: 622–33.

Forbes, Geraldine. 1981. "The Indian Women's Movement: A Struggle for Women's Rights or National Liberation?" In *The Extended Family,* edited by Gail Minault. Pp. 49–82. Delhi: Chanakya.

Fox, Richard G. 1985. *Lions of the Punjab: Culture in the Making*. Berkeley: University of California Press.

———. 1989. *Gandhian Utopia: Experiments With Culture*. Boston: Beacon.

Gandhi, Mohandas Karamchand. 1942. *Women and Social Injustice,* edited by Amrit Kaur. Ahmedabad: Navajivan Publishing House.

Grewal, Inderpal. 1993. "Reading and Writing the South Asia Diaspora." *Our Feet Walk the Sky,* edited by Women of the South Asia Descent Collective. Pp. 26–236. San Francisco: Aunt Lute.

Katrak, Ketu H. 1992. "Indian Nationalism, Gandhian 'Satyagraha,' and Representations of Female Sexuality." In *Nationalisms and Sexualities,* edited by Andrew Parker, Mary Russo, Doris Sommer, and Patricia Yaeger. Pp. 395–406 New York: Routledge.

Minault, Gail. 1981. "Introduction: The Extended Family as Metaphor and the Expansion of Women's Realm." In *The Extended Family,* edited by Gail Minault. Pp. 3–18. Delhi: Chanakya.

Nandy, Ashis. 1983. *The Intimate Enemy*. New York: Oxford University Press.

New York Times. 1930. 22 June; 4 July.

Sangari, Kumkum and Sudesh Vaid. 1989. "Recasting Women: An Introduction." In *Recasting Women,* edited by Kumkum Sangari and Sudesh Vaid. Pp. 1–26. New Delhi: Kali For Women.

2

Race/Class/Gender Ideology in Guatemala

Modern and Anti-Modern Forms

Carol A. Smith

More often than not, women bear the burden of displaying the identifying symbols of their ethnic identity to the outside world, whether these be items of dress, aspects of language, or distinctive behavior. Men of the same ethnic group, especially when filling lower-order positions in the local division of labor, usually appear indistinguishable from men of a different ethnicity but in similar class positions.[1] Thus in Guatemala, for example, one readily identifies a Maya Indian woman by her distinctive and colorful dress, her tendency to speak only the local dialect of a Maya language, and her modest demeanor when in public settings, especially those involving non-Maya. Most Maya men, in contrast, are not so easily distinguished from non-Maya (that is, Ladino[2]) men of equivalent class in Guatemala.[3]

In this essay I attempt to explain why women, rather than men, carry the emblems of the stigmatized position of a lower-order ethnic group in places that the West has colonized by examining the gender politics of this behavior in Guatemala, where the pattern is especially pronounced. I also attempt to show how ideologies of descent and rules of marriage operate in such systems, in ways that both parochialize women and conflate beliefs about race,[4] class, and culture. For this purpose I contrast the subordinate Maya belief system about identity with the dominant non-Maya or Ladino belief system—which differs on some propositions about race, class, and gender, but shares others. Finally, I consider how these two different belief systems, as they were first articulated into a race/class/gender ideology[5] and then reformulated within a revolutionary context, affect the construction of ethnic and national identity. In addressing this latter question, I offer some suggestions for why ethnic nationalists are more resistant than others to liberating or modernist ideologies, whether revolutionary or feminist.

I beg more questions than I can fully address by raising so many questions simultaneously, but there is a certain logic to this method. Ultimately I want to argue that race, class, and gender are conjoined systems of belief about identity and inequality in much of the contemporary world and that they are linked by certain assumptions about descent and inheritance and by certain social practices that enact these beliefs. If this is so, it will be useful to trace out the ways in which various beliefs and practices concerning social identity (that is, race, class, gender, ethnicity, nation, and individual subject) interact with and constrain one another in two interactive cultural systems, one part of the dominant national ideology, the other, not. As this wording implies, I do not want to separate out and juxtapose one form of social identity, such as race, to another, such as gender. Instead, I want to consider several different ways in which social categories are linked to social practices in the general realm of identity construction.

The particular cultural matrix from which I work is that of modernity, which I assume to be linked to European colonial expansion and capitalism. In my view the hierarchies of race, class, and gender associated with capitalism are not necessary or even logical outcomes of capitalism, but are based on the cultural baggage that came along with the way the material world of capitalism was historically constructed: with particular kinds of racialized, gendered, free and unfree labor, as they were constituted by Western categories and institutions. With the expansion of Western culture through capitalism, the systems of race, class, and gender were no longer separate, competitive forms of oppression, but came to be linked and mutually reinforcing in practice and through Western cultural precepts about race/class/gender hierarchies.

I begin by trying to make the case for the general social and ideological links between race, class, and gender, first in Western culture generally and then in modern nation-states of the West, as others have constructed the case. I conclude by attempting to reformulate the meaning of modernity for race/class/gender systems in social relations that involve colonialism, nationalism, and ethnicity, as well as ideologies of modern liberation. I illustrate my argument with the case of contemporary Guatemala, an interesting historical mix of modern and anti-modern[6] elements, some of them congruent with each other, most of them deeply contradictory. Guatemala makes an interesting and complex case because it was colonized by the West in the sixteenth century (during which a pre-modern symbolics of blood became dominant among the colonists); it separated in the late nineteenth century into two competing national potentials (hispanicized Ladinos and culturally resistant Maya); and it has been pulled since then in three different directions: the creation of a modern authoritarian state, ruled by elite white men; the creation of a modern revolutionary state, representing the mixed blood of the proletariat; and an anti-modern multicultural state, representing the diverse Maya communities.

Ideological Links Among Race, Class, and Gender in the West

Throughout Western history, people who assumed powerful positions in class society defended their class privileges in terms of their blood—a descent ideology that was implicitly racist. Michel Foucault (1980) describes the pre-modern system as a "symbolics of blood" upon which an emerging bourgeoisie erected the more directly biologist, racist system of modernity. As he sees it, the "blood relation" remained a significant ideological precept[7] in "modern mechanisms of power, its manifestations, and its rituals" (1980: 148). In "blood regimes" the value of descent lines are predominant, and blood constitutes one of the fundamental signifiers of position in a society. Systems of marital and political alliance are linked and based on blood status ("blue blood"); the political legitimacy of the sovereign is based on blood lines; and society is differentiated into orders and castes on the basis of blood descent (Foucault 1980: 147–48). Later (that is, under capitalism) "the symbolic function" of blood comes to predominate:

> Beginning in the second half of the nineteenth century, the thematics of blood was sometimes called on to lend its entire historical weight toward revitalizing the type of political power that was exercised [in a new disciplinary form]. Racism took shape at this point (racism in its modern, "biologizing," statist form) . . . Nazism was doubtless the most cunning and the most naive . . . combination of the fantasies of blood and the paroxysms of a disciplinary power. (Foucault 1980: 149)

Other scholars have described the significance of Western "blood regimes" for women's reproductive and sexual roles. Jack Goody (1976: 41–65), for example, described how monogamous European marriage systems, organized as heir-producing devices, institutionalized class distinctions in the West. Only the certified wife (whose blood lines were equivalent to those of her husband) produced a legitimate heir; the offspring of (lower-class) concubines would remain distinct and propertyless. Goody developed a contrast between Eurasia and Africa, noting that in Africa, where polygyny prevailed (and all wives were of equivalent marital status), the blood lines of the upper classes were not so clearly distinguished. Goody only implicitly notes the difference in sexual standards between men and women of the upper classes in regimes of blood. But from his descriptions it is clear that social expectations concerning the sexual behavior of an upper-class woman were very different from those concerning the upper-class man.

Gerda Lerner (1986) theorizes the linkage between sexual standards and race/class/gender hierarchies. She argues that the Western caste-like system of stratification that arose with the Western patriarchal state required that women's bodies and social freedoms be controlled because women had been construed as the biological "repositories" of descent systems (blood regimes) that ideologically and materially bolstered Western class systems. Thus, differences in blood explained differences between genders as well as between races and classes because blood differences could only be maintained through control of women's sexuality and ultimately their social freedoms. In this way class and race oppression based itself upon the control over women's sexuality and socially constructed differences put in biological terms to such an extent that race, class, and gender were seen to be linked. Lerner then goes on to explain how Western regimes of blood required the sexual purity and ideological complicity of upper-class women. Elite women could retain their status and reproduce themselves (in both class and biological terms) only through their sexual conduct. They had to remain virgin until marriage, monogamous after marriage, and socially protected throughout their lives from even the suspicion of improper sexual behavior. Only by controlling elite women's sexuality could the upper classes (both men and women) proclaim that their progeny were of pure or legitimate blood. Those elite women who violated the rules of sexual conduct could lose their class status to become, like lower-class women, the concubines, prostitutes, and sexual playthings of elites; they could even become mates for the lower classes. Elite men faced no such restrictions on their sexual behavior—they had access to many women of many ranks throughout their lives, some of whom became their legal wives, others of whom became their irregular concubines. In this way, Lerner argues, the ideological foundations for class reproduction in the West were as much rooted in the control and oppression of women as in biologism (or racism).[8]

Verena Stolcke (1981) suggests how the Western "symbolics of blood" shifted under capitalism to create an even more virulent form of racism (see also Hobsbawm 1975), together with a greater concern with the sexual conduct of upper-class women. Stolcke argues that the ideology of capitalism attacked at one level the aristocratic ideas in Europe that pure blood lines should define and limit political and economic rights. Bourgeois society espoused the ideology that all men are created equal and that the best of them will win out in fair market competition; yet, the rising bourgeoisie wanted to maintain their holdings or family property over time. In order to rationalize existing and continuing class inequalities, and to reproduce a class system over time, bourgeois society explained the maintenance of classes over generations with a notion of the survival of the fittest.[9] Fitness, of course, was assumed to be based on inherited qualities; and fitness required even greater concern with eliminating the non-fit (that is, those thought to have inferior blood) from competition in the market.[10] Stolcke, who terms this new ideology "scientific naturalism," explains its paradoxical development in the following way:

> The age of the French and American revolutions not only proclaimed the ideas
> of freedom, equality, and tolerance, but also saw the birth of racial classifica-

tions and hierarchies. The crucial issue was how to reconcile freedom and equality of all men with perceived inequalities. Racial classifications from the start collapsed phenotypical, cultural, and social traits and were applied not only to the "savages" abroad but also to differences at home. . . . If the self-determining individual seemed to prove incapable of making the most of the opportunities society appeared to offer him, it must be due to some essential inherent natural defect which was hereditary. The result was a sociopolitical and cultural elitism grounded in theories of biological class superiority. (Stolcke n.d.: 2)

Stolcke goes on to argue that scientific naturalism found its fullest expression in Nazi Germany as well as in the white-ruled colonies of the West. It resulted in systematic forms of racism (often apartheid, sometimes genocide) and increased concern for women's purity as reproducers of the biologically fit. She makes clear, however, that the ideology of scientific naturalism was not an imperialist mutant but, rather, was basic to social life under Western capitalism, remaining a "diffuse social sentiment" today (1981: 38).

The Impact of Nationalism and Colonialsm on Race/Class/Gender Ideology

The European assumptions that conflate race, class, and culture were diffused throughout the world not simply as a cultural accompaniment to capitalism but also as elements in the widespread ideological construction of modern nations—a political as well as cultural effect of capitalism's European origins.[11] Thus, in the third world and in Europe, national sovereignty was proclaimed everywhere and came to be justified by certain identical ideological claims, which logically integrated notions of territoriality, biological purity, cultural homogeneity, and status stratification, indicating how earlier notions of nation as blood group remain tied to the formation of the state as a political unit (see B. Williams 1990, 1993). Partha Chatterjee (1986) suggests how this might have happened in non-Western cultural contexts in his study of Indian nationalism. Indian nationalists such as Bankinchandra, Gandhi, and Nehru were all anti-colonialists united mainly in an attempt to create an autonomous national state and culture. They were doomed to fail in this enterprise because they were forced to derive the cultural meaning of what they were attempting to construct (a single and homogeneous state, nation, and culture) from Western discourse about them. He summarizes this argument in a later article:

> [Indian] nationalism located its own subjectivity in the spiritual domain of culture, where it considered itself superior to the West and hence undominated and sovereign. . . . [The] formation of a hegemonic "national culture" was *necessarily* built upon the privileging of an "essential tradition" [in which "women"

and "home" were not to be "modernized" or Westernized], which in turn was defined by a system of exclusions [of women, ethnic minorities, lower classes]. . . . [This] went hand in hand with a set of dichotomies that systematically excluded from the new life of the nation the vast masses of people [e.g., women, minorities, lower classes] whom the dominant elite would represent and lead. . . . In the confrontation between colonialist and nationalist discourses, the dichotomies of spiritual/material, home/world, feminine/masculine, while enabling the production of a nationalist discourse *different* from that of colonialism, nonetheless remain trapped within its framework of false essentialisms. (Chatterjee 1989: 631–32)

As Chatterjee sees it, then, the adoption of Western nationalist discourse by Indian nationalists led to a homogenized and essentialized cultural self-representation—a "derivative discourse" on the Indian state, nation, and culture—necessarily couched in Western terms. Thus, Indian nationalists, even as they struggled against a colonial discourse on gender, began to see the relation of gender to the nation in a Western way. They also began to exclude their ethnic minorities and lower classes from their conception of the nation in a Western way. In this fashion anti-colonial precepts came to embody Western precepts about the nation—and about the links between the nation, race, class, and culture. In this way, too, gender played a pivotal role in essentializing the spirit of the nation.

Chatterjee's argument suggests that in modern nationalist ideologies, whether European or non-European, the female will always come to stand for the spirit of the nation and the site of its reproduction because the female is (always?) the "essentialized" home-bodied other. In my view, however, Western beliefs about inheritance (in its material, biological, and cultural senses)[12] provide the key ideological element linking race, class, culture, and nation to gender. In Western ideology, a person's race, class, and culture are thought to be more clearly inherited from women than from men because it is assumed that women's uncontrolled sexual lusts will muddy or make uncertain paternity. Europeans institutionalized these concerns about patrilineal inheritance with particular kinds of sexual controls and marital arrangements. As Goody (1976) points out, they created separate roles for wives and concubines, controlling the sexuality of each (and the progeny of each) in different ways. As colonialists, moreover, Europeans linked different marriage and mating patterns to women of different classes, races, and national origins in such a way as to maintain separate hierarchies for different races, classes, and cultures (see also Martinez-Alier 1974; Stoler 1991). Women thus became the key icons around which a modern nation or culture would be built in cultural, biological, and material terms. And reproductive control over women—control of their sexuality—became the instrumental means by which economic, political, and cultural dominance of the elite in a new nation was assured. While obtaining such reproductive control over women is not a necessary or universal pattern to instituting a modern nation state, it is certainly predominant in those nation-states that were former European colonies. In this way the formation of different and unequal forms of marriage and concubinage became a pervasive feature of modernity.

The Colonial Construction of a Guatemalan "Symbolics of Blood"

Different colonial powers of the West created the political and cultural conditions by which new nations would interpret race, class, and gender in distinctive ways.[13] Verena Stolcke is the best source on the intersection of marriage and kinship with race and class in historical Latin America.[14] A recent article (Stolcke 1991) summarizing her work suggests how the Spanish conquest of indigenous and African slave women and the institutionalization of different and unequal kinds of marriage patterns between people of different social origins (African, American, European) affected race/class/gender ideology in the hispanic parts of the New World:

> When social position is attributed to inherent, natural, racial, and therefore hereditary qualities, the elite's control of the procreative capacity of their women is essential for them to preserve their social preeminence. As a nineteenth-century Spanish jurist argued, only women can bring bastards into the family. By institutionalizing the metaphysical notion of blood as the carrier of family prestige and as the ideological instrument to guarantee the social hierarchy, the state, in alliance with families that were pure of blood, subjected their women to renewed control of their sexuality while their sons took their pleasure with those women who lacked social status without having to assume any responsibility for it (Stolcke 1991: 28).

> The mestizo and mulatto population multiplied as a result of the ubiquitous concubinage between white men and Indian or black women . . . and inspired deep distrust because they . . . placed in doubt or actively threatened the emerging racial hierarchy. . . . For the elites and for those who sought to get close to them, legitimate birth from a legitimate married couple thus acquired new importance as the only proof of purity of blood. Illegitimate birth, on the other hand, was a sign of "infamy, stain and defect" stemming from the mixture of races. The only guarantee of racial purity, hence social prestige, was marriage between racial [and class] equals. (Stolcke 1991: 26–27)

In this way, a "dual marital strategy"[15] was produced throughout colonial Latin America, wherein men of European descent established legal monogamous marriages with women of their own race and class, whose offspring became their legitimate heirs, while engaging in irregular liaisons, frequently by force, with non-European women, and rarely recognizing those offspring. At the same time elite men felt the need to vigorously safeguard the purity of women they considered theirs from men other than their legitimate spouses, especially from men of lower-ranking social origins.

Severo Martínez Pelaez (1973), the foremost Guatemalan historian of the colonial period, recapitulates the importance of these assumptions in understanding the positions of the white (Spanish) elite in Guatemala (whom he terms *creoles*) and Ladinos (who are people of non-legitimate lineage in the eyes of creoles). His understanding about the linkage between race, lineage, and class is exceptionally keen; his understanding of gender only implicit. I quote him at length here because of the clarity and specificity of his exposition of Guatemalan ideology concerning race, class, and gender:

> The (male) Spaniard—as well as the hispanic creole—carried out very different acts when he copulated with a Spanish woman and when he copulated with an Indian one. . . . [H]e took the Spanish woman, or had to take her, to the Church and there, in a ceremony to which the assembled attributed transcendental meaning, he committed himself to live with her in everlasting union, to protect and educate his children, and to make them, and eventually her too, heirs to his goods. These children received certain material goods as well as a certain capacity to conserve and expand them. They entered a group their parents and other families belonged to which also had something to conserve, inherit, and expand. They became part of the dominant class.
>
> . . . The Indian woman was not simply fertilized by the Spaniard or the creole. Whether she was raped, deceived, bribed, seduced, or persuaded . . . the fundamental condition of the relationship that occurred between Spanish men and Indian women was, after all, the superiority of the colonizer over the native—not only the pretention of superiority but effective superiority in terms of economic and social advantage. . . . [The important point is that] the Indian woman was not the wife of the Spaniard or the creole who occasionally or regularly possessed her. She was rather his Indian concubine (his *barragana* in the judicial lexicon of the era), which in this context meant his extramarital servant supplying the commodity of sex.
>
> No law, no moral code obligated the colonial gentleman to his Indian concubine, nor to the children he procreated with her. Inheritance of blood equalled inheritance of power. The protection of wealth within a small European nucleus of heirs of the conquest demanded that the nucleus remain closed and its racial "character" protected—a racial character to which was attributed from the beginning a false significance as a source of distinction in every sense. . . . [S]ocial opinion was not bothered by concubine relations and spurious children—common happenings in colonial life—as long as the man's conduct left it clearly understood that these were escapades that did not threaten the structure nor the patrimony of the legitimate [creole] family. The colonial aristocracy, the creole class, . . . remained closed to the people of mixed blood and to the Indians during the respectable lapse of three centuries.
>
> Let us understand, then, that the initial *mestizaje* (the creation of mixed-blood offspring) was an act realized in the context of and as a consequence of

the social inferiority and disadvantage of a woman from the dominated class facing a man from the dominant class. It was the result of a biological union based on profound human disunion and inequality—of fornication as an act of veiled domination or, in many cases, simple and open rape. The children of these unions, the original *mestizos,* were what they were—workers without patrimony . . . as a consequence of their parents belonging to two antagonistic classes. Neither could give them a place without bringing harm to their class or themselves.

The secondary mestizaje, the multiplication of mestizos combining among themselves and with various other groups—including of course the Spaniards and creoles themselves—could not be anything other than the prolongation and compilation of what resulted from the initial mestizaje. From the multiplication of beings who were born outside the wealthy dominant class and outside the servile Indian group, was a proliferation of individuals in search of middle-level and inferior vacant positions and occupations. Individuals without inherited property, or authority, or Indian servants, had to make themselves useful in order to survive. The need for free workers acted as a mold into which the human stream of mestizos was poured [thus was born the Guatemalan Ladino]. (Martínez 1973: 355–60, my translation)

In the post-colonial, nationalist context of Latin America in the nineteenth and twentieth centuries, according to Stolcke, "scientific racism came to replace the metaphysics of purity of blood" (1991: 28), but the kinship, marital, and sexual patterns institutionalized in the colonial period remained essentially the same (for documentation of this, see Arrom 1985; Stepan 1991). The major shift that occurred in the post-colonial period throughout Latin America is that the ruling class tended to become more mestizo and less white. Color distinctions among mestizos remained important, however, and extremely gendered (see C. A. Smith, n.d.)

In post-colonial Guatemala, for example, some Ladinos rose to positions of wealth and prominence, while others remained the disenfranchised workers to whom Martínez alludes. Upwardly mobile Ladinos, however, took on the beliefs and kinship practices of the white creoles, who remained Guatemala's true ruling class—and the producers of the hegemonic national and race/class/gender ideology (Martínez 1973, Casaus Arzú 1992). After Independence, lower-class Ladino women were more likely to be preyed upon by upper-class males than Indian women, leading to what Martínez terms secondary *mestizaje.* Ortmayr (1991) documents that the marital practices of upwardly mobile Ladinos began to resemble those of the creole elite in the nineteenth century.[16] And McCreery (1986) observes that virtually no prostitutes in late-nineteenth-century Guatemala were Indian; most were lower-class Ladino women. In this little-studied period, Maya beliefs concerning race, class, and gender also reformulated themselves, and sexual (reproductive) contact between self-identified Maya and Ladinos seems to have diminished considerably.

Few anthropologists have followed up on Stolcke's pioneering work on historical Latin American race/class/gender relations and their impact on contemporary marriage and kinship systems, though she has been extremely influential in the Caribbean literature (see, for example, R. T. Smith 1984, 1992). I find her arguments for contemporary Guatemala generally persuasive, though incomplete. As formulated, her arguments do not treat the contemporary or nationalist periods, nor do they consider the impact of colonizing ideologies on colonized peoples, such as the Maya. In addition, she pays relatively little attention to the strategies of oppressed women and their complicity or resistance to a masculinist elite ideology. Despite the advantage of those in power to impose on others their new institutions, beliefs, and sentiments through persuasion or force, we would be perpetuating elite delusions of omnipotence to confuse their race/class/gender metaphors and evaluations with those of society as a whole. The problem, then, is to discover or suggest if and how colonial elite race/class/gender ideology has been accepted, resisted, or reformulated by the oppressed races, classes, and genders. I explore this notion further by examining Guatemalan race/class/gender ideologies in the contemporary period, concentrating on the beliefs and behaviors of Maya women, who are the triply oppressed in terms of race, class, and gender. I begin, however, with the dominant ideology—that held by the elites and Ladinos of modern Guatemala.

Race/Class Ideology Among Modern Guatemalan Elites

Class in Guatemala is inextricably bound up with constructions of race and blood in ways that we might suspect from the above.[17] Guatemalan elites still consider themselves white in race (though few are without some non-white admixture) and European in culture (Casaus Arzú 1992). They attempt to maintain both their racial purity and their legitimacy as the main power-holders in Guatemala by maintaining their cultural and marriage ties to the whiter and more dominant parts of the world—namely, Europe and the United States. This makes it virtually impossible for them to create a unified Guatemalan nation. On what basis—other than a racist ideology—can a white, basically non-Guatemalan elite claim to have the right to rule all of Guatemala, which is more than half Mayan? And if persuasive, does not this racist ideology impugn even the rights of white Guatemalans—who are assumed to be less racially pure than the white foreigners they emulate? This problem has forced Guatemala's white anti-colonial nationalists to do a lot of soul searching and hand wringing, even though it has caused surprisingly few of them to challenge the underlying assumptions about their own rights to rule over Guatemala. The assumption that creoles (those of European descent) should rule in Guatemala has rarely been challenged, even to the present day.[18] Although those of more clearly mixed descent have been "invited into history" by changes in ethnic and racial labels, which no longer distinguish between Ladinos and creoles (both groups now being labeled Ladinos), Guatemalans of predominantly European ancestry clearly remain Guatemala's ruling class and continue to make distinctions between themselves and those of mixed ancestry (Casaus Arzú 1992; Gould 1994).

There is little question that Guatemala's middle- and lower-class Ladinos, whose class and race position is considered intermediate between that of Guatemala's elites and Maya Indians, support the elite ideology, even though they are exploited by it. The class position of most Ladinos is that of salaried workers and petty bureaucrats, which in the context of an economy that is not fully capitalist puts them in the middle, rather than lower, class rungs of the system. Lower positions are reserved for Indian peasants and artisans who bear the burden of absolute, rather than relative, class exploitation. Because Ladino race and class position is thought to be intermediate between that of Indians and creoles, the two systems, race and class, bolster each other in the actual material organization of Guatemala's economy. The Ladino proletariat is happy to accept a system that basically exploits them, not only because salaried work is better paid and more secure than non-proletarian forms of labor, but because it allows them to identify with creoles vis-a-vis Guatemala's Maya Indians and, thus, to more easily exploit Guatemala's Maya majority, who are less fully proletarianized (C. A. Smith 1990).

As in much of Latin America, race is largely defined through culture rather than through descent (for an especially good depiction of this complexity, see Stutzman 1981). A person who is publically recognized as Ladino can be virtually any biological mixture—from all Mayan to all European—but must acquiesce to the dominant "national" culture, sever kinship ties with indigenous community members, and speak Spanish. In fact, state policy in Guatemala since independence from Spain has promoted the cultural assimilation of Maya, accepting assimilated individuals as Ladino citizens with the full political rights that unassimilated Maya do not have. At the same time, however, lighter and more Europeanized Ladinos are more highly valued by other Ladinos, especially as marriage partners, than darker, more Mayan, individuals. Color, education, and connections to Europe and or North America are as important as class in positioning different Ladinos vis-à-vis the creole power elite.

Sex and Marriage Among Guatemala's Ladinos

Ladino sexual and marital patterns in Guatemala, which I consider modern, if somewhat more traditional than most, are similar to those found throughout Latin America. Class position has a much more dramatic impact on the sexual and marital options available to Ladino women than to Ladino men. There are three statuses for women descended from the white elite, based on their sexual activity: virgins, legitimate wives, and prostitutes. (Women whose sexual activities violate the elite sexual standard are labeled prostitutes, which effectively declasses them). These statuses reinforce the race/class/gender system as follows. Legitimate wives in Guatemala mostly come from the same race and class background as the men they marry. Legitimacy in marital status, following upon virginity, is especially important to upper-class white women. Laurel Bossen describes the sexual status of elite women in the mid-1970s in the following terms:

> The . . . woman who produces children without a contract of paternal recognition (legal marriage) from a man of her class jeopardizes her membership in the class. She must be able socially to "prove" the paternity of children in order to maintain class privilege. Social proof generally consists of the absence of any evidence or insinuation of independent interaction with males other than a woman's kin or husband. She must be above suspicion. Hence, virginity for unmarried women and the appearance of absolute sexual monogamy for married women are means by which legally married parents of middle or upper socioeconomic status ensure the right of their children to inherit their class status and privileges. (Bossen 1984: 294–95)

Even though birth control and abortion are now widely available to these women, most have internalized what we would consider a Victorian notion of their sexuality. A twenty-one-year-old unmarried woman, member of the creole elite, described sexual differences between men and women to Bossen as follows:

> I think sex is more important for a man. Men want to demonstrate their *hombría* (manliness). A woman can reserve herself. She must deny sexuality. If she did not do so, she would be like the prostitutes. In my environment, there are some girls who are freer for love, but later, it is thrown in their face. (Bossen 1984: 292)

This woman, like most members of the elite, thus reduces women of her class into the three groups described above: unmarried virgins (like herself), legitimate wives (whose sexual-reproductive activity is reserved for their husbands), and prostitutes (who can no longer reproduce elite status).

The reduction of elite women to race and class reproducers is reflected in their high birth rates within legal marriage, together with their low employment and divorce rates (Bossen 1984: 288–95). Elite women with children rarely work outside of the home. Indeed, until recently Guatemala's Civil Code allowed men to restrict their wife's employment:

> The husband can oppose the wife's dedication to activities outside the home, as long as he supplies what is necessary for the support of the same. . . . Once procreation starts with the birth of the first child, the woman must understand that her mission is in the home, and except for very special circumstances she must not neglect her children under the pretext of personal necessities or the desire to aid her husband. (Código Civil Dto. Ley 106, Articulo 114, cited in Bossen 1984: 274)

Some women interviewed by Bossen resisted this restriction in various ways, but few questioned male authority in this domain. Most reasoned that men forbade women to work outside the home out of (appropriate) sexual jealousy or to protect the reputation of the family—both the man as breadwinner and the woman as sexually circumspect.

Upper-class women's views about work and marriage help explain the contradictory position of lower-class Ladino women vis-à-vis work and marriage. Lower-class Ladino women would also prefer legal (civil) marriage, but they rarely attain it. Roughly two-thirds of the lower-class Ladino women interviewed by Bossen (half in an urban squatter settlement, half in a rural plantation area) were not legally married, and most had had more than one sexual partner. Because these women worked, most outside of the home, they were sexually suspect. Those few women who were legally married were mostly married to men who had stable employment; these men could (and did) "demand a high degree of control over their wives' activities, typically seen in a curtailment of sexual freedoms and social relationships outside the family" (Bossen 1984: 167). Even so, married women were not immune to abandonment by their husbands. As Bossen saw it, lower-class Ladino women faced strong competition from other women for men who had stable jobs or good incomes:

> While alcoholism and male peer groups may be contributing factors, wives generally perceive their real competition to be other women: prostitutes in town who are interested in a worker's paycheck and local women . . . who may hope to establish a permanent support relationship. An insecure wife is reluctant to jeopardize her position by directly attacking her husband when he wrongs her [which] would challenge his authority or drive him even more surely to the comforts of a new partner. Instead, women who feel severely threatened are prone to attack the competition. While such attacks may begin with verbal abuse, they may well culminate in physical violence. (Bossen 1984: 154)

Where possible, lower-class Ladino women would exchange a poor provider for a better one—for example, the role of wife to a poor man for the role of concubine to a richer man. This was not a major sacrifice, for in severely reduced economic circumstances, there is not a great deal of separation between legitimate wives (who can legally make certain property claims for themselves and their children) and concubines (who can make no such claims). It seems fairly clear, in fact, that people in the upper classes saw most lower-class Ladino women as precisely that: sexual objects who could be either prostitutes or concubines—that is, women who could not press property claims for themselves or their children.

Lower-class Ladino women who possess some form of social capital (lighter skin, education, personal connections) can sometimes marry up—mostly to darker, richer men.[19] But more frequently lower-class women form non-legitimate liaisons with higher-class men—the *casa chica,* or kept woman, phenome-non. Women who make such liaisons cannot expect much in the way of day-to-day assistance or companionship from their higher-status mates—some-thing not easily obtainable from same-status mates either. But they can expect greater social and sexual freedom than is possible in a relationship with a same-status Ladino man.[20] Because of this option for lower-status Ladino women (who in this respect have options that upper-class Ladino women lack), there is a scarci-ty of women at the bottom rungs of society. Richer and more powerful Ladino men have more than one woman, leaving poorer, less powerful men with less than one. Little else distinguishes upper- and lower-class Ladino men with respect to marital and sexual options.

Traditional Maya Beliefs About Race and Gender

How do Ladino sexual/marital patterns affect Maya women in Guatemala? Do Maya women marry up by making liaisons with the darker, poorer Ladinos? My evidence suggests that they do not—or that they do so only rarely. The reasons they do not, moreover, enhance and solidify Maya ethnic identity. Let me try to explain this phenomenon beginning with a discussion of the main symbols of Maya ethnic identity to traditional Maya: These symbols include local community descent, language, women's dress, gender roles, and rules of sexual conduct with-in the community.[21]

In the 1970s the Maya, like all other Guatemalans, accepted an essentialist con-struct of the bases of ethnic identity. They believed that the Maya formed distinct peoples descended from local community-specific ancestors, and that they obtained both their identities and social positions in their communities through descent or biology (see Warren 1989, Watanabe 1992). Identity was community specific, based upon an extremely high rate of community endogamy.[22] All Maya were expected to marry within the community, and virtually all of them did so. Particular Maya communities were thought to have existed as separate social enti-ties since time began. They were marked as particular in two main ways: community-specific forms of language and of dress. These differences distinguished Maya communities from each other as well as from non-Maya communities. Most Maya women, unlike most Maya men, could be immediately classified as to com-munity by both language and dress: that is, Maya women spoke mainly the local Maya dialect and dressed in a community distinctive form. Women, then, bore the burden of maintaining the main markers of Maya ethnic identity. While there were significant pre-conquest elements in the Maya local identity pattern, traditional Maya culture in the twentieth century (which included Maya gender relations, marriage, and kinship patterns) was clearly a product of Maya interaction with Spanish colonial precepts, like most other cultural elements identified as traditional Maya today (see Wolf 1959; Warren 1989; C. A. Smith 1990).

The maintenance of Maya women's parochialism (through dress and language) helped to maintain Maya women as marital partners for Maya men, in community-specific ways. Most Maya women married local men at a fairly young age and then were expected to bear and nurture as many children as possible, imbuing those children (especially daughters) with community-specific Maya values. Thus, Maya women were seen to be (and were) the reproducers of the Maya community, both culturally and biologically. On these grounds, one could argue that ethnic identity and Maya community solidarity was based on the reproductive control of traditional Maya women. But before reaching this conclusion too hastily, let us look more closely at gender roles and rules of conduct within various Maya communities.

Until very recently, the rate of male migration from Maya communities far outstripped that of female migration (Demarest and Paul 1981). This provided a strong contrast to the Ladino migration pattern, where women found it easier than men to position themselves in urban areas—as servants, as traders, and as sexual partners for Ladino men. It also suggests that Maya women, who could easily have been accepted as Ladinos in urban areas, did not feel confined within their communities.[23] Previous sexual experience or marital failure did not jeopardize the chances of remarriage for either women or men. There were no prostitutes or concubines within Maya communities, and virginity was not highly prized.[24] Maya men would occasionally have more than one wife but made no distinctions among their wives—all wives (whose status of wife was achieved simply by taking up domestic relations with a Maya man) could make equal economic claims for themselves and their children. "[Maya] women also form[ed] sexual and exchange relationships with more than one man simultaneously, although with greater discretion" (Bossen 1984: 122). Bossen provides an example:

> [A Mam woman] Maria Lazaro, roughly 60 years old, is married to Efrain [of the same community] who is about the same age. Both have been married twice previously. Efrain's first wife ran away with another man after she had had two children with Efrain. [Such a woman would be socially recognized as the "legitimate wife" of her second mate, once the relationship was securely established, as long as he was a member of the same community.] His second wife bore more children and died, leaving him with young dependents. Maria Lazaro had also been widowed, first, and then separated from her second husband. She was in her mid-50s and living with her father when Efrain came to ask for her. She had never had any children and at any rate was beyond childbearing age when Efrain came to ask for her. He officially petitioned her father, although it is understood that the father cannot command a grown daughter, only a young one. (Bossen 1984: 117)

Maria Lazaro was married to her third husband by Maya custom (a small brideprice was paid for her), despite the fact that she had earlier been widowed, had married a second time, was abandoned by her second husband, and was now well past the age of childbearing.

Maya women, unlike other Guatemalan women, were relatively autonomous subjects (socially and economically) within their communities. They inherited their own land; they usually had their own sources of income; and they were relatively free to move about (within the community). Maya women, moreover, could seek divorce, mediation, or redress from the community if mistreated by their husbands and were more or less guaranteed a relatively secure place in the community, with or without their original husbands, if they followed the local rules of cultural and sexual conduct. The rules of sexual conduct did not require them to abstain from social contact with men other than kin in the community, to be virgins at marriage, or to risk abandonment by kin and community if discovered in sexual relations with men in the community other than their husbands—the demands made of legitimate wives in the rest of Guatemalan society. Instead, Maya women were mainly required to wear the emblems of their community identity, marry local men, and bear and nurture children of the community.

There was one other requirement, a product of colonialism: Maya women were expected to avoid contact with men outside the community, especially Ladinos, and were expected to conduct themselves modestly, which is not the perceived behavior of Ladino women.[25] While a Maya woman raped by a Ladino would not be repudiated by her community (nor would the child of such a union), a woman who voluntarily left her community for a mating arrangement with a Ladino (usually in the process adopting Ladino identity) would not be welcomed back into her community. In Totonicapán, the Maya community where I lived in the 1970s, women who changed to Ladino dress (which was interpreted as a public announcement that they were seeking a relationship with a Ladino man) were called whores and rarely married within the community.[26] Those women who took up employment as domestics in Ladino households—where they were often sexually abused—were able to contract marriages with Maya men from their community but appeared to contract less advantageous marriages than women who did not take up such employment. In this sense, Maya women appeared to be stamped as community property, if not individual male property, in a sexual sense.

As I see it, then, Maya women exchanged the freedom to abandon their communities (socially, culturally, sexually, and reproductively) for a certain personal security within their communities—a security that no other Guatemalan women had. By following the rules of cultural and sexual conduct, the Maya woman, at least traditionally, could expect full community support against abandonment or mistreatment by her husband. Because of her economic autonomy and value, a Maya woman who was abandoned or who wished to repudiate her marriage could return home, remarry, or live independently with her children. It should be noted that Maya women were no more likely to be abandoned than Maya men, for most Maya men also eschewed Ladino norms of sexual and social conduct (that is, machismo and promiscuity), if not other patriarchal rights. In order to find legitimate spouses within their communities, Maya men were expected to be as hard working, responsible, and non-promiscuous as Maya women.[27] Maya men still were given wider sexual latitude than Maya women, however.

Given that male sexual and cultural behavior outside of their community was not as closely circumscribed as female sexual and cultural behavior, were not Maya women still oppressed vis-à-vis Maya men? And did not their conduct reproduce, though in a different form, the dominant race/class/gender ideology of Guatemala—making both Maya and Ladino women icons of race and class identity? As a feminist I would have to say yes to both questions, but I would also have to say, as those few other students of Maya women have also said, that Maya women were freer than any other Guatemalan women in this regard. Their actions, moreover, challenged certain elements in the dominant ideology. By exchanging what was assumed to be their essential position in reproducing Maya culture at a community level for basic protections by the community, protections that no other Guatemalan women had, Maya women put certain conditions on the sexual and marital conduct of Maya men. We should not be surprised, then, that Maya women basically supported the limits placed on them which produced the community solidarity that confined but protected them. Maya women were, in fact, mostly proud to produce and wear the symbolic emblems of their stigmatized status as Maya and as women.

Gender, Race, and Ethnic Nationalism in Revolutionary Politics

Let us now look at the implications of traditional Maya beliefs about race, class, and gender for reproducing ethnic nationalism in Guatemala and for creating certain contradictions within it. The dominant race/class/gender ideology is based on the expectation that everyone plays by the same rules, that is, that everyone competitively strives for individual position in society by accepting the same norms, by assimilating to national culture and belief systems, and by making the most advantageous marriages possible. Thus, since independence in 1821, the dominant classes in Guatemala have attempted to draw Maya into the Guatemalan (Ladino) nation by getting them to take on Ladino norms of language, dress, and sexual conduct—not in order to accept them as equals but to deal with them as part of the overall race/class/gender hierarchy rather than as a separate cultural system.

The existence of distinct beliefs about race, class, and gender within Maya communities clearly conflicted with this expectation. Traditional Maya neither accepted nor rejected their position in the national race and class hierarchy: They operated by a different set of principles. Rather than competing in the national hierarchical system, they attempted to remain separate from it in economic as well as ideological terms. By retaining a relatively autonomous economic existence (refusing proletarianization), Maya communities managed to remain separate from the national class system. And by keeping their women out of the national marriage pool, Maya communities maintained their separatist (anti-assimilationist) cultural and political stance against the Ladino nation.

The particular form that Maya resistance took to the national race/class/gender hierarchies required the Maya to remain divided as separate communities rather than united as a (potentially) revolutionary or ethnic-nationalist force. Most Maya, both consciously and unconsciously, refused to stand as a separate nation within Guatemala: They stood as separate nations or communities, united only by the same basic principles that divided them as a political force. Gender politics in Maya communities played a key role in defining separatist Maya ethnic-national politics. To substantiate this claim, let me briefly describe two distinct moments—one in 1979 and one in 1989—in Maya resistance to incorporation in a revolutionary national race/class/gender system. These moments depict changing Maya stances toward the revolutionary ideology, which shared many cultural precepts with the nationally dominant (Ladino) ideology on matters concerning race and gender. The main point on which the revolutionary ideology differed on gender, was its belief that all Guatemalan women, Ladino and Maya alike, should be free to deploy their sexuality as they wished.[28]

Between 1978 and 1979, for a variety of reasons that cannot be fully explored here, significant numbers of Maya men and women joined a Marxist-Leninist revolutionary movement intended to topple Guatemala's corrupt, repressive military-state regime that Ladinos had always exclusively controlled.[29] By that time, the revolutionary movement was perceived to be of and for the Maya, even though it was clearly led by Ladino commanders. Those Maya who became active participants in the revolutionary movement were subjected by the Ladino leadership to an intense barrage of revolutionary rhetoric designed to break down the parochial bases for their grievances against the state and unite them (with lower-class Ladino cadre) into a national-liberation movement against the state in which they would be unified by the grievances of all oppressed—that is, all workers, whether Indian or Ladino, presumably also whether women or men. The revolutionary language was Spanish, the revolutionary dress was military (for both men and women), and a primary revolutionary goal was to end the divided, exploited, and assumed marginal existence of Maya communities. The presence of large numbers of Maya in this revolutionary movement forced the revolutionary leadership to at least consider certain separate Maya issues and thus a number of revolutionary position papers on what was termed "the Indian question" were produced. Symptomatic of deeper problems in the Ladino-led revolutionary project, none of these papers was able to address adequately the issue of Maya autonomy in the revolutionary project (C. A. Smith 1990, 1992). By 1984, many Maya had left the revolutionary fold (see C. A. Smith 1990; Jonas 1991; Wilson 1991), having become quite disillusioned about the revolutionary agenda.

In discussions with these dissidents in 1988 and 1989, I found to my considerable surprise that race and sexuality had become key issues to them, leading many Maya to renounce the vanguardist politics of Ladino revolutionaries and to support more traditional forms of Maya resistance.[30] Most of the Maya I interviewed complained about Ladino dominance of revolutionary rhetoric and goals and were disturbed by Ladino insistence on a unified, as opposed to a particularized (community-based), political agenda for the Maya. Almost all of them pointed out that Ladino revolutionaries had no understanding of or respect for Maya traditions and women's dress codes. Many hinted at their dismay about revolutionary sexual beliefs and conduct that required Maya women to deal with unacceptable sexual practices. The people who complained were women as often as men.

Had I heard these stories of revolutionary disillusionment among Maya cadre in 1979, I probably would have concluded that the Maya were simply unable to accept the universalizing modernist message basic to a revolutionary movement. I would have agreed with Ladino revolutionaries that the Maya, for both economic and cultural reasons, remained too parochial for revolution. By 1989, however (partly because of discussions I was having with Maya cultural nationalists), I saw Maya complaints about revolutionary unity in a somewhat different light. The demands of revolutionary unity would, in a sense, destroy the structural props of Maya ethnic identity—the main revolutionary goal of most Maya and one for which which they had been willing to fight and die.

The experience of Guatemalan (marxist-leninist) revolutionaries among the Maya suggests some of the limits to revolutionary recruitment among community-based peasants. Revolution requires the destruction of local (parochial) communities for the purpose of meeting some higher goal—to create a larger "imagined community" (cf. Anderson 1983) or some other utopian set of social relationships. In the practice of revolutionary struggle, most Maya found that they were unwilling to substitute a utopian community for their real community bases, which were rooted in a particular pattern of sexual and gender conduct. It may be worth noting that few women in traditional agrarian societies have been attracted to the revolutionary promise of sexual autonomy. This suggests that they recognize, as traditional Maya women did, that sexual autonomy without family or community support is more of a burden than a liberation (see M. Wolf 1985; Molyneux 1985).

The evidence also seems clear about the relation between ethnic identity and traditional Maya beliefs about race, class, and gender. The strongest material prop to community-specific forms of ethnic identity among Guatemala's Maya Indians was community endogamy or in-marriage and the kind of sexual conduct that supported and reproduced it. It now seems clear to me that the complex set of beliefs and social relations that underwrote Maya practices concerning race and gender was that which preserved community-specific ethnic identity in Guatemala. The retention of non-capitalist social relations within these communities was also important, to be sure—as most of my other writings have emphasized. But I now doubt that the economic autonomy of Maya communities could have been preserved without the support of the Maya marital and sexual practices described here—especially insofar as the particular economic system of

Maya communities (artisanal production) required a willing household labor force that was not lured away by the promise of better jobs or higher status outside the community. The only people who did leave Maya communities in significant numbers before the 1980s were unmarried youths (Demerest and Paul 1981). Being properly married within a Maya community meant that one's Maya identity was relatively fixed. Many traditional Maya beliefs and practices concerning community, class, and gender appear to be transforming rapidly in the post-revolutionary period, but they are not going in the directions desired or expected by conservative Ladino elites or Ladino revolutionaries.[31]

I cannot claim that a complex of beliefs and practices similar to that described for the Maya operates in most other cases of ethnic resistance to homogenizing nationalist appeals. Not all ethnic groups are as anxious as the Maya to retain multiple, locally based, ethnic communities. Yet, there appear to be some aspects of ethnic resistance important in this case that are more generally significant. Most obvious is that ethnic groups typically construct themselves around ideologies of common descent, which politically motivates and mobilizes people in terms of rules of marriage and sexual conduct. Without defining a line across which marriage or sexual (reproductive) relations are forbidden, it is very difficult to make an imagined ethnic community appear real to people. Feminists have often observed that feminist mobilization is very difficult in cases where ethnic mobilization is already a strong social force. The intertwined sets of relationships described above may help explain why.

Modern and Anti-Modern Race/Class/Gender Ideologies

To deal with some of the more difficult issues of nationalism, as well as with the difference between modern and non-modern ideologies, let me refer to an apparently very different case that Claudia Koonz (1987) examined. Koonz depicts the race/class/gender ideology of Nazi Germany as "anti-modern" because it rested upon the total rejection of modernizing freedoms—of sexuality, of the individual, of social mobility, of strong elements in civil society such as organizations for workers and for feminists—that characterized the Weimar republic and erected in their place folk notions of family, traditional gender roles, security, and commitment to ideals of community. It was an "imagined community," to be sure, that was completely subservient to the demands of a militarist state; but its founding premise was reconstructing Germany as a "natural" (racially pure) community. Control over women was key to constructing what the Nazis deemed a racially pure German community. Concentrating on middle-class women in Nazi Germany, Koonz documents their complicity in their own and other women's subjugation as well as in the horrors perpetrated by the Nazi state.

Yet modernity was not erected anywhere in the world on Weimar-like freedoms for women. As I argued above, most modern class systems and most forms of modern nationalism, whether anti-colonial or not, rest upon a Western folk-ideology of descent or biological inheritance. That is, they rest upon biological explanations for the social relations created by humans, bolstering the kinds of racist ideologies and racism that found expression among the Nazis. All of us who want to immortalize and perpetuate ourselves through descendants of our own blood buy into this ideology to some extent. It is, as Verena Stolcke observes, a "naturalized" belief and thus natural in Western society. In this way, kinship cemented in blood relations—which can include ever-larger communities up to the nation—appears to us to be a natural part of the human condition. Although the modernist impulse of capitalism works against it, human beings have resisted the creation of alienated individuals who are totally without ties to and claims on blood kin.

Marxist-Leninist revolutionaries, such as those who led Guatemala's recent revolutionary movement, are more likely than regular modernists to support Weimar-style freedoms—of sexuality, of the individual, of status mobility, and of strong elements in civil society such as organizations for workers and for feminists. But as Stacey (1983) and M. Wolf (1985) have argued for revolutionary China, and as Molyneux (1985) and Randall (1992) have shown for revolutionary Nicaragua, the sexual and marital freedoms of revolutionary society are largely illusory. Just like the conservative modern (Ladino) race/class/gender ideology, revolutionary ideology appears to offer women the possibility of using their sexuality and reproductive potential as they will, even though the free woman is likely to reap dire consequences for her actions, should she actually break the rules of appropriate sexual and reproductive conduct. Truly anti-modern belief systems (which the Maya had, but the Nazis did not), on the other hand, reject that illusion. That is, they more clearly deny to individual women the possibility of sexual (reproductive) freedom. More importantly, however, they substitute for that freedom the security provided by some kind of protective and real, rather than totally imagined, community. Both systems are socially supported by the reproductive woman's extreme social vulnerability.

Almost all kinds of nationalism build upon our attachment to the supports and claims that we can make of blood ties, kinship, and family. (In the words of many nationalist ideologues, "the family is the microcosm of the nation.") This is as true of Ladino-Guatemalan nationalism, with its modern race/class/gender system as it is of Nazi nationalism. The various attempts that Guatemalans have made to create a nation, contradictory as they have been, required the incorporation of Maya into the Guatemalan family—which to the Maya has meant the death of their own cultures, nations, and kinship systems. When it appeared to Ladino Guatemalans—erroneously as it turned out—that all Maya were united in an attempt to claim the nation, they did not hesitate to consider a "final solution" that required for Guatemala, as for Nazi Germany, the eradication of those unfit or unwilling to become part of the Ladino-Guatemalan nation. In the early 1980s, the Guatemalan military chased over half of the Maya from their homes in a campaign of terror specifically directed against Indians—a campaign that involved the death and torture of more than 100,000 Maya—with the implicit consent of most ordinary Ladino Guatemalans.

How could ordinary Guatemalans, most of them at least partially descended from the Maya, support this campaign? I believe they could do so because they accepted the idea that Maya (revolutionary) nationalism would destroy the foundations of their own nation, together with the blood and kinship supports they had constructed within that nation. The Ladino Guatemalan is inscribed in a modern race/class/gender system that promises individual freedom and mobility, but the complex of beliefs that undergird it is still rooted in non-modern blood sentiments which mainly circumscribe women and minorities. These non-modern sentiments, which are part of all modern nationalist ideologies, were readily mobilized by the Guatemalan military state. It remains a major question how readily they can be mobilized in any modern nationalist conflict.

The differences between these ideological systems—modern, anti-modern, and revolutionary—I conclude, are only ones in degree not in kind. A truly different kind of system would have to base itself outside of blood ties, which would require an end to kinship and marriage as we know it. Until we construct a different kind of system—a system that disempowers the sentiments of blood and descent—we will have to live with the consequences of racism and sexism and to guard against the very real possibilities of the sort of racial holocaust recently enacted in Guatemala.

Notes

I am especially grateful to Charles R. Hale, Suad Joseph, and G. William Skinner who discussed with me many of the issues involved as I worked out these arguments. Since I did not always take their good advice, they cannot be blamed for my views. Different versions of this essay have been delivered to several different audiences (anthropological, feminist, and Latin Americanist) at the University of California, Davis; Stanford University; the University of Texas, Austin; and the University of Wisconsin, Madison. I would like to thank members of the audiences for useful comments, questions, and challenges. I would also like to thank Diane Nelson, Nora England, and Abigail Adams for suggesting that I historicize my discussion of contemporary Maya Guatemalans.

1. It appears, however, that when an ethnic minority is not at or near the bottom of the local status hierarchy—as in the case of the Hasidic Jews of New York—men are as likely as women to be labeled with a special ethnic marker. Why this should be so will be apparent as the argument unfolds.

2. The meaning of Ladino in Guatemala is very specific to the nation of Guatemala. People who are currently classified Ladinos are any people who are non-European or non-Maya; but the identity of people categorized as Ladinos has changed over time (see Gould 1994). I more fully explain the meaning of the term Ladino as I describe the historical particulars of Guatemala.

3. In several dozen Maya communities where women still weave the bulk of the clothing, some men continue to wear ethnically distinctive clothing; even in these communities, however, younger men wear general rustic clothing indistinguishable from that of rural non-Mayans, especially when away from their community. Virtually all Maya women, in contrast, maintain community-distinctive dress as a moral commitment, even when they do not weave it themselves (see Otzoy 1988, 1992). For a sophisticated discussion of class-, ethnic-, and gender-specific cultural patterns in another indigenous area of Latin America see Gill (1993) and de la Cadena (1991).

4. Throughout this essay I use race to mean the conflation of social origin (Europe, Africa, native America) and color (or general phenotype) that is embedded in North American and Latin American racial and racist discourse. Naturally, I repudiate the idea that race is a scientific biological category.

5. When I create words joined by slashes (as in race/class/gender) throughout this essay, I am highlighting the fact that the elements in the series are discursively joined. For example, race, class, and gender (in either ideology or social practice) are conjoined systems of oppression in which the social construction of each element powerfully affects the nature of the other elements: The social construction of race (often derived from phenotype, which is taken to be the marker of a biological or descent category) is affected by the class and gender of the person; the social construction of class is also affected by race (or phenotype) and gender; and the social construction of gender is affected by race (or phenotype) and class. These linked forms of social construction are especially prominent in modernity when the individual is not as fully enmeshed in relatively permanent communities which carry the weight of social position.

6. I take the idea of "anti-modern" from a recent article by Joel Kahn (1990), who depicts peasants as anti-capitalist rather than non-capitalist or precapitalist. I use the term anti-modern rather than anti-capitalist in order to extend the idea that peasants are resisting assumptions of the modern nation-state as well as capitalism.

7. By the term ideological precept, I mean essentially what Brackette Williams means, that is, "rules and standards, often expressed in principles, maxims, or proverbs, which declare the world to be of a certain composition and to work in a certain way. Precepts become ideological when they are linked to politically privileged interpretations of human experiences which ignore or consider irrelevant information that contradicts the logic of these rules and standards" (1993: 184).

8. Irene Silverblatt (1988) assures us that the reproductive (gender) kernel of class and race domination in the West, which required control over women's sexuality and reproduction, is not a functional prerequisite of class society everywhere. Her own work on the Inca (1987) describes an alternative sexual/reproductive system associated with class stratification and the state. Jack Goody, in a large number of publications (see especially 1976), must be credited with showing that this linkage is not universal in all social systems with class stratification. Developing a contrast between African and Eurasian systems of stratification, Goody shows that African class systems are based on entirely different rules and beliefs concerning proper marriages, inheritance, sexual conduct, and the like.

9. Hobsbawm, in noting the difficulty the bourgeoisie had in justifying its own success by the rules of "freedom, opportunity, the cash nexus and the pursuit of individual profit," makes a similar observation:

   > Hence the growing importance of the alternative theories of biological class superiority, which pervade so much of the nineteenth-century Weltanschauung. Superiority was the result of natural selection, genetically transmitted. The bourgeoisie was, if not a different species, then at least the member of a superior race, a higher state of human evolution, distinct from the lower orders which remained in the historical or cultural equivalent of childhood or at most adolescence." (1975: 247–48)

10. Given the link between capitalism and imperialism, the notion of fit races made a lot of sense to both lower and upper classes in the centers of the very unequal capitalist world economy, which came into being upon the production of basic commodities with the labor of African slaves, New World Indians, and other non-white serfs all over the world.

11. The belief that all classes within a nation shared the same basic culture, if not blood, is now widely acknowledged to be a modern or nineteenth-century invention; such a belief was not at all typical of early archaic states made up of a mosaic of different peoples (see for example, Anderson 1983, Gellner 1983).

12. It is noteworthy that the Western term inheritance means not only "(1a) the act of inheriting property," but also "(1b) the reception of genetic qualities by transmission from parent to offspring," and "(1c) the acquisition of a possession, condition, or trait from past generations" (*Webster's New Collegiate Dictionary*).

13. Ann Stoler has described the patterns institutionalized during the nineteenth and twentieth centuries in colonial Southeast Asia (1992), which bear a general resemblance to those institutionalized much earlier in Latin America.

14. Stolcke's first major work was written on Cuba under Martinez-Alier (1974). Since then her ideas on the relationship between race, class, and gender in the Americas have been taken up by others, most prominently Arrom (1985) and Seed (1988), who treat colonial and post-colonial Mexico. See also Lavrin (1989) on colonial Latin America and C. A. Smith (n.d.) on the pattern throughout the Americas in the post-colonial period.

15. R. T. Smith (1984, 1992) defines and describes a dual-marriage strategy as one where upper-class men typically maintain both legitimate and "outside" wives or concubines. Smith has worked mainly on the pattern in the Caribbean but notes that the strategy is also common to Latin America.

16. According to Ortmayr (1991), who treats marriage and society in nineteenth-century Guatemala, the rate of marriage for Ladino women rose between 1850 and 1950 substantially. Ortmayr, however, makes no distinctions by class, so he is really documenting the upward mobility of some Ladinos in cultural and class terms. As Ladino economic and political fortunes rose with independence from Spain, they become more closely identified with Spanish creoles and eventually assume most creole cultural patterns. This is not true of lower-class Ladinos, however, whose marital and other cultural patterns remained different from that of creoles. Silvia Arrom (1985) makes this argument much more clearly for nineteenth-century Mexico city.

17. See, for example, Brintnall 1979; Smith 1990; Knight 1990. There has been a long and misleading debate on the matter (described in Brintnall 1979) among anthropologists, which is only now being rectified.

18. In this regard, Guatemala is more conservative than Mexico (though see Knight 1990); on Guatemala, see Martínez Pelaez 1973, C. A. Smith 1990.

19. Alan Knight (1990) observes that no Mexican president has ever married a woman "darker" than himself. He notes the racism, but not the sexism, involved in such practices.

20. Martínez-Alier (1974) argues that this factor more than any other was responsible for the high rate of concubinage among mulattos in nineteenth-century Cuba. It may also be a major factor in mestizo Latin America, about which less is known.

21. The Maya of whom I speak here are traditional community-centered Maya—still the vast majority of Maya in Guatemala—rather than those Maya who emerged in the 1980s and 1990s identified with a broader pan-Mayan community, a community with some classic nationalist characteristics (see C. A. Smith 1991).

22. The Maya rate of in-marriage is about 90 to 95 percent in communities now averaging about 10,000 individuals, one of the highest rates of community in-marriage in the world (Adams and Kasakoff 1975).

23. See Chaney and Garcia Castro (1989) for a discussion of female migration patterns in Latin America. In most areas the number of women migrants far outstrips that of men because they are more easily employed in urban areas then men.

24. Evidence from more remote and traditional Maya communities (such as Chiapas, Mexico) make this clear (see, for example, Collier 1973, 1974; and Rosenbaum 1993). But in certain Maya areas of Guatemala, where contact with the Catholic Church and with Ladino sexual and marital mores has been relatively strong, there is greater concern for female virginity (see Ehlers 1990, 1991).

25. For discussions of the code of conduct for both Maya and Ladino women that support this argument, see Rigoberta Menchú's autobiography (Burgos-Debray, 1984), Laurel Bossen (1984), Rosenbaum (1993). I am not so sure any sanctions are applied to Maya women who marry Maya men of other communities. In precolonial times elite Maya did marry across communities.

26. I cannot claim that this is common to all Maya communities. Women in some communities have changed their dress as a group without major repercussions or without losing community identity (Ehlers 1990). The highly politicized nature of this labeling of non-traditional women in Totonicapán, where I worked, may reflect particular sexual or ethnic tensions in that community.

27. This pattern may be changing somewhat for the Maya who are part of the pan-Maya nationalist movement. At the same time Maya nationalists are attempting to challenge Ladino nationalist discourse, they may be appropriating certain assumptions about the world (see C. A. Smith 1991), as much as about appropriate masculine and feminine behavior. If this becomes a clear pattern in succeeding years, Partha Chatterjee's argument about "derived" modernist discourses (1986) gains further support.

28. On the parallels between dominant and revolutionary ideology concerning ethnicity, or the necessity of assimilating Maya into the Ladino nation, see C.A. Smith (1990, 1991, 1992). On the revolutionary position concerning "the women's question," see *Women's International Resource Exchange* (1983) on Guatemala.

29. The most useful discussions of Maya participation in the revolutionary struggle, from my perspective, can be found in Burgos-Debray (Rigoberta Menchú) 1984, Carmack 1988, Manz 1988, C. A. Smith 1990, and Wilson 1991.

30. These traditional forms of resistance have now been described by a small group of Maya intellectuals—who call for recognition that "Guatemala is a multicultural nation" (see C. A. Smith 1991). These intellectuals appear to be unaware of the gender politics that grounds their multicultural nationalism.

31. The significant changes that are occurring in the post-revolutionary period have much to do with the development of a pan-Maya movement in Guatemala, led by intellectuals whose sense of identity is no longer community-based. One indication of this change relevant to the thesis presented here is that Maya women who are part of this movement typically wear Maya clothing from many different communities (thus proclaiming their pan-Mayanism). While Maya women who are part of the movement can associate with Ladinos (though usually only in a group context), they are still much more strongly sanctioned than Maya men for marrying Ladinos. As could be expected, both men and women who are part of the pan-Maya movement are much more likely to marry outside of their community of birth than traditional Maya.

References

Adams, John W. and Alice B. Kasakoff. 1975. "Factors Underlying Endogamous Group Size." In *Regional Analysis* Vol. II, Social Systems, edited by C. A. Smith. New York: Academic Press.

Anderson, Benedict. 1983. *Imagined Communities: Reflections on the Origin and Spread of Nationalism.* London: Verso.

Arrom, Silvia Marina. 1985. *The Women of Mexico City, 1790–1857.* Stanford: Stanford University Press.

Bossen, Laurel. 1984. *The Redivision of Labor: Women and Economic Choice in Four Guatemalan Communities.* Albany: State University of New York Press.

Burgos-Debray, Elizabeth, ed. 1984. *I, Rigoberta Menchú: An Indian Woman in Guatemala.* London: Verso.

Brintnall, Douglas. 1979. "Race Relations in the Southeastern Highlands of Mesoamerica." *American Ethnologist* 6: 638–52.

de la Cadena, Marisol. 1991. "'Las Mujeres son Más Indias': Etnicidad y Género en una Comunidad del Cusco." *Revista Andino* 9: 7–47.

Carmack, Robert, ed. 1988. *Harvest of Violence: The Mayan Indians and the Guatemalan Crisis.* Norman: University of Oklahoma Press.

Casaus Arzú, Marta. 1992. *Guatemala: Linaje y Racismo*. Guatemala City: FLACSO.

Chaney, Elsa and Mary Garcia Castro, eds. 1989. *Muchachas No More: Household Workers in Latin America and the Caribbean*. Philadelphia: Temple University Press.

Chatterjee, Partha. 1986. *Nationalist Thought and the Colonial World: A Derivative Discourse?* London: Zed Books.

————. 1989. "Colonialism, Nationalism and Colonialized Women: The Contest in India." *American Ethnologist* 16: 622–33.

Collier, Jane. 1973. *Law and Social Change in Zinacantan*. Stanford: Stanford University Press.

————. 1974. "Women in Politics." In *Woman, Culture, and Society,* edited by Michelle Rosaldo and Louise Lamphere. Stanford: Stanford University Press.

Demarest, W. J. and B. D. Paul. 1981. "Mayan Migrants in Guatemala City." *Anthropology UCLA* 11: 43–73.

Ehlers, Tracy. 1990. *Silent Looms: Women and Production in a Guatemalan Town*. Boulder, CO: Westview Press.

————. 1991. "Debunking Marianismo: Economic Vulnerability and Survival Strategies among Guatemalan Wives." *Ethnology* 30: 1–16.

Foucault, Michel. 1980. *The History of Sexuality, Vol. I*. New York: Vintage Books.

Gellner, Ernest. 1983. *Nations and Nationalism*. Oxford: Basil Blackwell.

Gill, Lesley. 1993. "Proper Women" and City Pleasures: Gender, Class, and Contested Meanings in La Paz." *American Ethnologist* 20: 72–88.

Goody, Jack. 1976. *Production and Reproduction: A Comparative Study of the Domestic Domain*. New York: Cambridge University Press.

Gould, Jeffrey L. 1994. "What's in a Name? From Ladino to Mestizo in Central America." Paper presented at the 18th International Congress of the Latin American Studies Association, Atlanta, Georgia.

Hobsbawm, Eric. 1975. *The Age of Capital*. London: Weidenfeld & Nicolson.

Jonas, Suzanne. 1991. *The Battle for Guatemala: Rebels, Death Squads, and US Power*. Boulder, CO: Westview Press.

Kahn, Joel. 1990. "Towards a History of the Critique of Economism: the Nineteenth-Century German Origins of the Ethnographer's Dilemma." *Man* (N.S.) 25: 230–49.

Knight, Alan. 1990. "Racism, Revolution, and Indigenismo: Mexico, 1910–1940." In *The Idea of Race in Latin America, 1870–1940,* edited by Richard Graham. Austin: University of Texas Press.

Koonz, Claudia. 1987. *Mothers in the Fatherland*. Rutgers, NJ: Rutgers University Press.

Lavrin, Asunción, ed. 1989. *Sexuality and Marriage in Colonial Latin America*. Lincoln: University of Nebraska Press.

Lerner, Gerda. 1986. *The Creation of Patriarchy*. New York: Oxford University Press.

Manz, Beatriz. 1988. *Refugees of a Hidden War: The Aftermath of Counterinsurgency in Guatemala*. Albany: State University of New York Press.

Martínez-Alier, Verena. 1974. *Marriage, Class and Colour in Nineteenth-Century Cuba.* London: Cambridge University Press.

Martínez Pelaez, Severo. 1973. *La Patria del Criollo.* Guatemala: Editorial Universitaria.

McCreery, David. 1986. "Female Prostitution in Guatemala City, 1880–1920." *Journal of Latin American Studies* 18: 333–53.

Molyneux, Maxine. 1985. "Mobilization Without Emancipation? Women's Interests, the State, and Revolution in Nicaragua." *Feminist Studies* 11: 227–54.

Ortmayr, Norbert. 1991. *Matrimonio, Estado y Sociedad en Guatemala (Siglo XIX y XX).* Guatemala: Ediciones CEUR, Universidad de San Carlos.

Otzoy, Irma. 1988. *Identity and Higher Education Among Mayan Women.* M.A. Thesis, Anthropology, University of Iowa.

———. 1992. "Identidad y Trajes Mayas." *Mesoamérica* 23: 95–112.

Randall, Margaret. 1992. *Gathering Rage: The Failure of Twentieth Century Revolutions to Develop a Feminist Agenda.* New York: Monthly Review Press.

Rosenbaum, Brenda. 1993. *With Our Heads Bowed: The Dynamics of Gender in a Maya Community.* Austin: University of Texas Press.

Stanford Central America Action Network, eds. 1983. *Revolution in Central America.* Boulder, CO: Westview Press.

Seed, Patricia. 1988. *To Love, Honor, and Obey in Colonial Mexico: Conflict over Marriage Choice, 1574–1821.* Stanford: Stanford University Press.

Silverblatt, Irene. 1987. *Moon Sun, and Witches: Gender Ideologies and Class in Inca and Colonial Peru.* Princeton: Princeton University Press.

———. 1988. "Women in States." *Annual Review in Anthropology* 17: 427–60.

Smith, Carol A. 1990. *Guatemalan Indians and the State, 1540–1988.* Austin: University of Texas Press.

———. 1991. "Maya Nationalism." *Report on the Americas* 25: 29–33.

———. 1992 "Marxists on Class and Culture in Guatemala." In *1492–1992: Five Centuries of Imperialism and Resistance,* edited by Ron Bourgeault et al. Halifax, Nova Scotia: Fernwood Press.

———. n.d. "The Symbolics of Blood: Mestizaje in the Americas." forthcoming in *Identities.*

Smith, R. T. 1984. "Introduction." In *Kinship Ideology and Practice in Latin America,* edited by R. T. Smith. Chapel Hill, NC: University of North Carolina Press.

———. 1992. "Race, Class, and Gender in the Transition to Freedom." In *The Meaning of Freedom,* edited by F. McGlynn and S. Drescher. Pittsburgh: University of Pittsburgh Press.

Stacey, Judith. 1983. *Patriarchy and Socialist Revolution in China.* Berkeley: University of California Press.

Stepan, Nancy Leys. 1991. *"The Hour of Eugenics": Race, Gender, and Nation in Latin America.* Ithaca, NY: Cornell University Press.

Stolcke, Verena. 1981. "The Naturalizations of Social Inequality and Women's Subordination." In *Of Marriage and the Market,* edited by Kate Young et al. London: CSE Books.

———. 1991. "Conquered Women." *Report on the Americas* 24: 23–49.

———. n.d. *The Individual Between Culture and Nature.* Unpublished ms.

Stoler, Ann. 1991. "Carnal Knowledge and Imperial Power." In *Gender at the Crossroads of Knowledge,* edited by M. di Leonardo. Berkeley: University of California Press.

———. 1992. "Sexual Affronts and Racial Frontiers: European Identities and the Cultural Politics of Exclusion in Colonial Southeast Asia." *Comparative Studies in Society and History* 34: 514–51.

Stutzman, Ronald. 1981. "El *Mestizaje:* An All-inclusive Ideology of Exclusion." In *Cultural Transformations and Ethnicity in Modern Ecuador, N.E.,* edited by Whitten. Pp. 45–93. Urbana: University of Illinois Press.

Warren, Kay. 1989. *The Symbolism of Surbordination: Indian Identity in a Guatemalan Town.* 2nd ed. Austin: University of Texas Press.

Watanabe, John. 1992. *Maya Saints and Souls in a Changing World.* Austin: University of Texas Press.

Williams, Brackette F. 1991. *Stains on My Name, War in My Veins: Guyana and the Politics of Cultural Struggle.* Durham, NC: Duke University Press.

———. 1993. "The Impact of the Precepts of Nationalism on the Concept of Culture: Making Grasshoppers Out of Naked Apes. *Cultural Critique* 24: 143–91.

Wilson, Richard. 1991. "Machine Guns and Mountain Spirits: The Cultural Effects of State Repression Among the Q'eqchi' of Guatemala." *Critique of Anthropology* 11: 33–61.

Wolf, Eric. 1959. *Sons of the Shaking Earth.* Chicago: University of Chicago Press.

Wolf, Margery. 1985. *Revolution Postponed: Women in Modern China.* Stanford: Stanford University Press.

Women's International Resource Exchange. 1983. *We Continue Forever: Sorrow and Strength of Guatemalan Women.* New York: Ragged Edge Press.

3

Multiple Alterities

The Contouring of Gender in Miao and Chinese Nationalisms

Louisa Schein

Women have seldom escaped becoming sites onto which nationalist agendas are projected. Gender relations are thrown into flux by this process, and everyday local practices may be contradicted by those mandated by nationalist representation. This was the case in China where, in the 1980s and for the century preceding, an attempt was made to elaborate a national identity in part through the manipulation of images of minority women. Minority norms of gender and sexuality, explicitly marked as "other," became grist for the mill of a nationalist cultural production project seeking to reconcile itself with modernity. At the same time, minorities (in the case of this paper, the Miao people) were experiencing profound change and the opportunity to craft anew their own subnational identities. The resulting intersection of discourses inspired much contestation over the content of such categories as tradition, domesticity, femininity, and masculinity.

Tradition Recast: Gender and Sexuality in Two Nationalisms

Two nationalisms antedate and inform contemporary Chinese concerns over identity: Han nationalism and Chinese nationalism. The former was concerned with

79

boundaries between peoples *within* the territory of the Chinese polity; the latter rose in response to incidences of foreign imperialist aggression.

Han nationalism had its roots at least as early as the fall of the Han-ruled Ming dynasty to Manchu conquest in 1644 (at which time it is perhaps more appropriately referred to as Han "ethnicism"). It crystallized over the course of the Qing dynasty (1644–1911) as a reaction against control of the center of the Chinese state by "barbarian usurpers," the non-Han Jurchen people from the north. Organized around a myth of primordial purity, it advocated an inviolable "racial" separation as the basis for preservation of the Han culture held to be legitimately ascendant. Such sentiments of separation or hostility vis-à-vis the non-Han within China continued to constitute an important focal point for resistance and/or activism before and into the twentieth century.

Meanwhile, the figures of Western and Japanese power at China's shores, classed also as "barbarians," tended to diminish the salience of inter-ethnic issues at the domestic level in favor of protection of what was constructed as the Chinese nation from the territorial, political and ultimately cultural incursions with which it was confronted. In the wake of defeat in the Opium and subsequent wars in the 1840s and 1850s, certain Chinese elites became committed to a sweeping political and cultural overhaul. While the valorization of tradition was not absent from the ideology of these nationalists, they were more willing to dispense with cultural continuity if doing so was seen to be of benefit to China in the larger world context of sovereign states.

The revolution of 1911, the overthrow of the Manchu regime, and the ending of the dynastic order in China did little to temper the preoccupation on the part of the mainstream Chinese intelligentsia with what they perceived as China's relative weakness and cultural bankruptcy. In the years surrounding the May Fourth and New Culture movements in 1919, intellectuals sought a new identity for China that took inspiration from the differences persisting among the Chinese people. At this point burgeoning nationalism, sharpened by Chinese intellectuals' outrage at unfavorable treaty agreements at the Versailles Peace Conference, began to penetrate more deeply into the cultural domain, giving rise to an intense search for alternative sources of strength and vitality to be found among the Chinese folk, Han and non-Han alike (see, for example, Hung 1985, Schneider 1971). This iconoclastic climate of cultural transformation laid the groundwork for the appropriation of minority cultural forms for national purposes, a practice which was to recur at moments of cultural crisis throughout the century.

Meanwhile, women and sexuality also came to be favored ground for the working out of issues of national identity. Certain cultural conservatives of the May Fourth period, for instance, held fast to otherwise widely rejected gender practices precisely because they were seen as emblematic of Chinese tradition. The Western-educated scholar Gu Hongming, who published a short-lived journal entitled *The National Heritage (Guogu),* was an unyielding apologist for footbinding as an important element of the Chinese spirit (Levenson 1967: 276) and asserted that concubinage was "as natural as a teapot with several teacups making a tea set" (Chow 1960: 62).

In contrast, from the 1920s on, a newly constituted group of (predominantly male) intellectuals (*zhishifenzi*) stridently advanced the imported trope of individuated, universalized woman (*nuxing*) cut loose from her former kin-inflected positionality who would stand as a sign of New China's modernity (Barlow 1991). But at the same time, the Guomindang under Chiang Kaishek was moving toward a conservative stance on women that, according to Diamond (1975), was to persist for decades after the flight to Taiwan. Scandalized by unbound feet, bobbed hair, so-called "free love," and resistance to parental marriage arrangement, Guomindang ideology sought to restore women to their place in the service of the patriarchal family and, by extension, the nation.

In the folklore field, directives for collection betrayed both a repression of and a fascination with sex/gender practices. In 1918 students were urged to collect: "folksongs concerning the customs and habits, the history and society of the respective places . . . songs of far-off soldiers, rustics, *longing girls and sorrowful women, in so far as they have natural beauty and are not obscene*" (in Eminov 1975: 259, emphasis mine). A Custom Survey Society in 1923 collected data on such "reactionary" old customs as "concubines and slave-girls," "brothel-frequenting," and "abandoned children" (in Eminov 1975: 261).

As for non-Han cultural material, two apparently contradictory approaches can be identified as emerging from this historical moment. Coinciding with the two forms of nationalism described above, they differ in their perspective on gender and sexuality. From the perspective of Chinese nationalism, minority cultural production was a source of lost vigor and renewed identity in an atmosphere of repeated humiliations by foreign powers. Accounts of strong women and less constrictive gender attributions promised ideological liberation from the Confucian straitjacket. Much celebrated and recounted practices of courtship, romance, and free love suggested a passionate vitality that could revivify a stilted and suffocating Han urban culture. But a subtext associated with these representations reveals the workings of a Han nationalism, soon to be recast as Han "chauvinism." Here the same material was employed as evidence of Han "positional superiority" (see, for example, Nader 1989) on a scale of "civilization": fluidity of gender roles became transgressive of the prescribed social order; openly expressed "love" became sexual promiscuity, a breach of morality. That these contradictory approaches co-existed is not surprising: they mirror, I would argue, the ambivalences generated by the tensions between competing constructs of tradition and modernity that were to prevail throughout the twentieth century. In the face of imperialist foreign powers, "tradition" was at once a source of independent identity and a crippling obstacle to development. "Modernity," on the other hand, was desired as a vehicle to wealth and power at the same time that it was rejected as alien and corrupting.

Internal Orientalism: Distilling the Feminine Other

As a peasant village, the community of Xijiang, where I did fieldwork in 1988,[1] was anomalous for several reasons. Nicknamed the "Thousand Household Miao Village" (*Qian Jia Miao Zhai*),[2] it was hardly a village, but instead a sprawling settlement with a population of over 5000. It was the administrative seat of a district (*qu*) governing about seventy outlying villages, and consequently had a significant state presence in the form of over three hundred state employees, a government office building, a middle school, a post office, a bank, a courtroom, a grain depository, and other offices. It was spatially oriented around a town-like main street that was the terminus of a long-distance bus route and the site of a periodic market thus qualifying it as what Skinner (1964–65) defined as a "central place." Despite its location in the remote mountainous region of southeast Guizhou, an otherwise abhorred province in China's southwest, Xijiang had an air of relative worldliness about it, of which its locals were proud.

At the same time, Xijiang's reputation as a locus of "typical" (*dianxing*) Miao culture has been growing, and it has become one of the most popular destinations in Guizhou province for Chinese urbanites looking for a taste of the exotic and/or authentic. In recent years, Xijiang has seen a constant stream of artists, photographers, journalists, ethnographers, officials, and tourists coming through in search of something—whether images or information—to take away from the Miao people that live there. These were domestic travellers—this particular county has remained closed to foreign tourism—and they were primarily male. Where images were being made, the subjects were primarily female.

Travelers usually stayed in the government guest house and went out from there into the village in search of interesting angles. They often came back disappointed from these initial forays and sought me out as the "expert" ethnographer. The local Miao people, they complained, were Sinicized (*Hanhua*): the women wore pants, and many of the people even wore Western-style clothing. Could I recommend a village in the region where they might see the "real" Miao? What they were referring to was the elaborately embroidered festival costume and silver headdress that they had seen for decades on magazine covers and television documentaries as "typical" Miao women's attire. When they discovered that what they sought was precious festival regalia reserved only for wear on special occasions, they frequently paid to have the young man at the local "culture station" (*wenhua zhan*) organize a photo shoot. Carefully selected Miao girls would don their best costumes, marks of their beauty and emblems of their difference, and pose as directed for the replication of the images expected and craved by urban consumers.

In this process, Xijiang's undesirably "modern" look was elided (camera angles were chosen to conceal the concrete buildings that lined the paved main street), and its fictive typicality was reproduced in the distilled image of the colorfully dressed, smiling, young woman—a young woman who was decidedly and visibly other. The Miao, as a consequence, were feminized and rendered as symbols of the tradition-bound past, untouched by decades, even centuries, of change. China, in the eyes of urbanites who consumed these images, could take its place in a world of nation-states that could both invoke a particular, identity-bestowing history and also distance it.[3]

These practices of othering occurring within the so-called Orient are what I have elsewhere described as "internal orientalist" (Schein 1993). The creation of representations by a dominant group that portray a subordinate group as deserving of their structurally inferior position were not unique to the colonizing West, but persist in the post-colonial era and within multi-ethnic states. I borrow from Edward Said the notion that orientalist practices are productive in nature and that what is produced are ideas and statements that constitute a hegemonic description of the object. The culture of the producers of such ideas "gains in strength and identity" by contrasting with the Other as a "sort of surrogate and underground self" (1978: 3). For China, this underground self was internal, yielding an indigenous identity that allowed distinction from the West, and simultaneously marking the modernity of Han urbanites by offering a "traditional" alter-ego, as signified by the subordinate sex.

A Seductive Simulacrum of Time Travel

A closer look at the specific sites of the reproduction of difference in 1980s China reveals the ways that gender dichotomies framed both the interactions and the images that emerged out of them. As I've said, visitors to the village of Xijiang were primarily male, and came under various auspices. These travellers brought with them, along with their easels, their tape recorders, and their preferred seasonings with which to doctor local food, a relatively unified metropolitan discourse by which they described their hinterland destinations. These places were "backward" (*luohou*), the ways of life "primitive" (*yuanshi*), and the people "simple, honest, unsophisticated" (*chunpu*). It was like going back in time: by visiting these places one could see the stages through which society had developed.[4] Most sought after were locales that had "distinctive ethnic flavor" (*minzu tese*). Consequently, Xijiang with its jarring emblems of modernity was frequently characterized as having "not much worth looking at" (*meiyou shenme haokande*).

In the quest for the unfamiliar, images of non-Han women came to represent antipodes to urban elite culture, signifying both a trajectory toward modernity and the nostalgia that kind of "progress" so often inspires.[5] Not surprisingly, then, the oppositions of modern-backward, civilized-wild were revealed through the association of minority women with nature and with youth. In mass media images she appeared communing with animals or nestled among trees and flowers. Youth was stressed not only by the physical appearance of the women represented, but also by their identity with the innocence of the natural. Child-like women were pictured accompanied by such companions as birds, lambs, or butterflies with whom they seemed to be in direct communication.[6]

The effect was of infantilizing and trivializing. Yet these representations were also imbued with a kind of warmth—albeit patronizing—and an intense fascination. One team that visited Xijiang was making a video documentary on atmospheric conditions and other natural phenomena for a meteorology institute in another province. Not content, however, with nature per se, this team decided that a bevy of local maidens would be the perfect companionship for their work and the perfect ornamentation for their meteorology video. They hired four local girls at nominal pay to accompany them on an arduous climb to a mountain pass 1200 meters above the village and to be filmed along the way. The girls were coached to wear their best clothing and hair adornments. As they climbed, they were stopped at strategically chosen scenic spots to perform such activities as washing in a stream or singing a Miao song on camera. The effect was to be of naturalness, the local women skillfully embedded in their wilderness environment.[7]

Joking and giggling characterized the mood of the climb as the filmmakers took pleasure in their ingenue escorts. When they reached the top of the pass, the girls rested with their employers in the thick mist on an expansive level area before beginning their long descent home. The filmmakers were to continue on to a more distant cluster of villages nestled in the next valley. One of them held out a handful of candy—a seldom-eaten luxury for peasants in this region—in what looked to be a gesture of gratitude and parting. The girls reached out to accept it, but he snatched his hand back and demanded that they sing him one more Miao song before he would compensate them.

In this episode, minority women experienced a double objectification. On the one hand they were arrayed among the massive trees and trickling brooks as part of the intriguing wildness which drew urban visitors. On the other, they were treated as ethnic automatons, expected to produce folk culture at a moment's notice for the reward of a mouthful of candy. This latter dynamic is of course ubiquitous in ethnic tourism worldwide. What I am examining here is in effect a pre-tourism moment in which peasants were being socialized to commodify their culture, to regard it as a discrete medium of exchange.

While Chinese internal orientalism commonly classed minority women as natural, non-human, or child-like, or as cultural conservators, this did not preclude their also being very human objects of erotic fascination. In many contemporary art and media images, their proportions appeared voluptuous and their expressions were unabashedly inviting. Sometimes their bodies would be more extensively revealed than would be appropriate for a Han woman; at other times, reminiscent of the French colonial postcards of Algerian women that Alloula (1986) described, the elaborateness of their costume would operate like the veil, suggestive by virtue of its concealment and its excess. Accounts that bespoke minority women's imagined availability were common. In whispered lore as well as in bluntly scientistic ethnographic reports, tales would circulate about non-Han courtship practices, freedom of choice in marriage partners, and especially sexual promiscuity.

The imaginings that surrounded minority women, thus, constituted a powerful attractive force. Yet they were also attended by a kind of repressive fear and repulsion toward the implied baseness and breaches of morality that made these women so other. It was not uncommon, upon mentioning to a Chinese urbanite one's interest in minorities, to be told in tones of confidentiality and admonition that, for example, the women "there" wear no tops, or that the unmarried young people are said to have orgies during courtship festivals. Tones of disapproval mixed with titillation characterized these furtively conveyed anecdotes. They recalled an earlier ambivalence now revived by 1980s ruptures in the familiar social order: unrepressed sexuality signified a relativizing of mores that was both threatening but liberating; and strong, unrestrained women meant the hopeful but unnerving potential for transgression of constrictive gender roles.[8]

Crafting a Marketable Native for the Nation

Over the course of the 1980s, as Chinese urbanites increasingly engaged with the West in the domains of cultural/economic exchange, the problematic nature of minority sexuality was intensified. As suggested above, non-Han cultures were appropriated in images that presented to the outside a picture of a vibrant and diverse China, politically harmonious and culturally intriguing. Influenced by Western modernist primitivism, artists creating representations for international consumption crafted eroticized images of the exotic other within. This gave the (hitherto) "forbidden" China an alluring authenticity and was to pique foreigners' interest by using visual codes suited to Western tastes. At the same time, it demonstrated that China was no longer isolated from a world system of culture in which artistic styles had become internationalized.

The 1980s, with its ostensible emphasis on diversity and tolerance, was a period filled with the excitement of breaking the taboos that had distanced the mysterious minority woman. She was brought in from the country to the city, domesticated, made into an object of consumption. A sharp increase in geographic mobility within China coincided with the advent of large-scale international tourism, setting in motion a wave of commodification of "things ethnic." The result was a proliferation of not unfamiliar hybrids that put folk material in "modern" forms.

Also re-imported was the quickly-naturalized identification of the female body with sale, an advertising ploy that had been repressed since liberation. The older minority-as-woman image merged with a commodity-as-woman marketing strategy, giving rise to an array of products that reworked raw, putatively traditional elements into portable, collectible, and *desirable* forms. Elaborately headdressed women appeared on greeting cards, on shoulder bags, on bookmarks. A wall calendar promoting avant-garde fashions made from batiked fabric adapted from

Miao designs used models in vogue-like postures, sporting leggings, pumps, and Western haircuts to complement their exotic outfits.

Many foreign tourists (and Chinese urbanites), daunted by the prospect of hardship travelling, still hungered for the experience of untouched territory, uncorrupted culture, ingenuous natives. This led to a demand for the "staging of authenticity" (MacCannell 1973) in the metropolis. One Han man, a Hunan native working as a musical director for the Guizhou Culture Bureau, conceived a "new" form of exhibition: a travelling display of words, photos, and artifacts portraying Guizhou folkways accompanied by re-enacted festivals in the form of a living museum. He travelled around the Guizhou countryside to recruit young people with particular talent and instructed them to bring with them not only their best festival attire, but also a song or dance that was typical of their locality. These "raw" materials were processed into a finely honed performance, carefully choreographed to be "realistic," which represented the songs, dances, and musical instruments of Guizhou folklife. The exhibition travelled to such major cities as Beijing, Xian, Tianjin, and Shenzhen.

While minority performing troupes have been commonplace in China for decades, what was seen as "novel" in this one was that the performers were minimally trained peasants from the countryside, holding out the promise of a kind of intimacy of (first) contact whose resonances with the lure of virginity were less than subtle. The director was the constructor and mediator of these desires. In the crafting of the festival show, passionate abandon could be rechanneled as enthusiastic appreciation. The effect was of sanitizing, deftly repressing the dangerous sexual subtext and creating a safe domain for the controlled consumption of festival practices which in their original context might have been frighteningly disorderly and spontaneous. The process evokes an ancient distinction applied to the Miao and other peoples at China's periphery in which groups were considered "raw" (*sheng*) until they were brought under Chinese rule at which point they were referred to as "cooked" (shu). For the culinary feat discussed here, however, a particularly skilled chef was required, because only by retaining the flavor of rawness would the fare be palatable to the discerning foreigner.

Like Father, Like State

In the foregoing sections I have described a plethora of agents that contributed to the production of orientalist representations of China's internal others. I turn now to the issue of how state discourses interfaced with the complex meanings generated in the public cultural domain. A number of themes informed state representations of China's cultural diversity (see, for example, Yau 1989), but the subtext was frequently that of the civilizing mission and a kind of paternalistic authority (Harrell 1995: 3–36). Ultimately, the dissemination of images of valorized/derogated difference may have more to do with the state's representation of itself—both to the people it aims to govern, and to the outside with whom it hopes to dialogue—than it does with the "others" it ostensibly portrays.

Official policy stresses a horizontal relationship among the nationalities, each of which is formally recognized as having equal status in the Chinese polity. This parity is made visual through the ubiquitous tableau—whether living or artistically reproduced—which arrays China's fifty-six nationalities, each in emblematic dress, in a dense, hand-holding throng in which—significantly—all stand on a level plane. Public events regularly feature this pageant as part of the opening ceremonies, and it is also common to encounter it on billboards, posters, and the like. Such images proclaim to the international community as well as to citizens at home that it is harmoniously and on an equal footing that the Chinese people are joined together.

Many publicly circulated images, however, betrayed a more vertical vision of China's social order. A 1985 billboard promoting development in southeast Guizhou showed two minority women in full festival regalia standing on either side of a Han male, taller and apparently older, in urban worker's clothing. The conflation of minority with such categories as female, rural, and "backward" stressed the vanguard role of the Han on the road to "progress." A further reading is suggested by Ann Anagnost's work in which the state, constituting itself as center, manipulates such contrasts in order to represent itself as a "modern, activist state opposed to all that is irrational, traditional and local" (1994: 229).

A 1984 poster betrayed the enduring paternalistic role of the Party through a generational disparity. Literally infantilized minority children—again in full festival regalia, some holding toys and some holding musical instruments, along with one or two Han—are shown playing gleefully with, holding the hands of, or even embracing a fatherly Mao Zedong, Zhou Enlai, Liu Shaoqi, and Zhu De. Both this image and the development billboard above invoked a Confucian vision of authority—the first employing the elder sibling-younger sibling relationship, the second conflating the father-child relation with that of the emperor-subject—to emphasize the ascendancy of the Han state.[9]

In 1980, new images began to be printed on the face of Chinese paper currency. Industrial and agricultural scenes were replaced with two elaborately adorned heads of minority women (or occasionally men) on each of the small denominations. These diversely headdressed, cheery tokens serve to remind all Chinese of the multi-ethnic make-up of the Chinese polity. The new 100 yuan bill, however, tells a superseding story. It pictures the solemn profiles—again—of Mao Zedong, Zhou Enlai, Liu Shaoqi, and Zhu De. As above, a flurry of bills barrages the cash-user with a "cross-section" of China's peoples, but the progression from small to large denominations leaves no doubt as to the ultimate relations of authority.

Miao Women's Reply to the Trope of Backwardness

I move now to the issue of how women came to terms with the confinements of the dominant gaze. Miao women, when transposed to urban centers dominated by ethnic Han and characterized by a kind of monocultural metropolitan homogeneity, experienced a strong ambivalence around the marking of their difference. Some told me of travelling to visit relatives now working in cities, and of the conflicts they underwent in deciding whether to put their hair up in characteristically Miao style. Young women working in a tourist hotel in southeast Guizhou told me that they would prefer to wear their hair down, living as they were among urbanites, but that they were required by the hotel to comb it up in ethnic style. By contrast, when they were seen on the street after hours, they often made themselves indistinguishable from the Han urban residents in more Western clothing and hair styles. I interpret this less as a desire for cultural assimilation than as an evasive tactic by which they hoped to avoid the public associations with backwardness that their appearance as ethnic provoked.

Depending on their situations, these dilemmas created two different types of internal conflict for Miao women torn between the felt imperatives of tradition and modernity (see, for example, Ong 1988: 86–90). For rural women travelling to cities for short periods of time, ambivalence derived from the fact that dressing like the Han felt like putting on a costume, a kind of denial of self. For women working in cities, such as those in hotels, or travelling ethnic performers, the source of ambivalence was that while their work brought them to the cities and accustomed them to its ways, it also required of them a maintenance of their otherness as the basis for them having this work in the first place.

These tensions were poignantly dramatized in a performance during the 1988 occasion of the "April 8th Festival" that Beijing Miao held annually on the campus of the Central Nationalities Institute. The Nationalities Institutes, colleges for the education of and research on minorities, function as sites for the forging of permissible alterities. Students and cadres-in-training learn to "be ethnic" within the parameters of state cultural policy. More subtly inculcated is the nostalgia for the romanticized past which accompanies participation in "modern," urban life.

The April 8th Festival, orchestrated by the Beijing Miao intelligentsia, condensed many of these themes. Among the numbers in an afternoon revue of performances of Miao song and dance—inter-cut with demonstrations of martial arts and of Han and Western music styles—was a solo dance by a young Miao woman. She entered the stage dressed conservatively in an urban-style pale pink shirt and black pants, her hair braided simply down her back. Her movements were graceful, controlled, dignified. After a few moments, she discovered in a heap some Miao silver jewelry and a flame-red diaphanous skirt in a pattern evocative of the stereotypical Miao pleats. She approached tentatively and began to try on the jewelry. As she adorned herself, her enthusiasm grew, and she quickly donned the rest of the ornaments and pinned her hair up in characteristic Miao style. She danced with the skirt as prop and then put it on, too. Her movements now became bold, flamboyant, confident. The music picked up tempo. She smiled with an expression of child-like mischievousness. She twirled to make the skirt flare out triumphantly. Then, as if pulled by some inexorable force,[10] her movements gradually slowed and she reluctantly began to shed her ethnic attire. When it was returned to a heap on the floor, and her hair again hung braided down her back, she brought her dance to a close by *fleetingly covering her face with her hands as if ashamed of her momentary transgression.* The dance embodied the problematic articulation of the Miao self, a self even more fractionated by urbanity and its pained relation to the rough vitality of the countryside. What the performance enacted was a structure of feeling—a la Raymond Williams (1977: 132–35)—in which standards of beauty and contours of identity were unsettlingly shifting and indeterminate.

In what ways, then, did Miao women who remained in the countryside come to terms with their imaging as quintessentially ethnic? The vast majority of these young women were peasant daughters living in rural settings perhaps more remote than those of most of the Han peasantry. Their interactions with Han Chinese were rare: Xijiang's population was 99.5 percent Miao and the population of the entire county was 82 percent Miao with the Han and other minorities clustered mostly in the county seat and in a handful of spatially distinct villages. Many of the outlying villages were without electricity and consequently without television; mail was delivered over the mountains on foot and the rare newspaper or magazine that arrived was scarcely glanced at by young women because of their widespread lack of literacy. Their choices to adorn their hair or wear ethnic clothing were governed by very local normative standards that as a rule called for everyday dress of simple Miao style but did not necessarily disdain more Western-style clothing. Decisions about other practices were also made on the basis of local pressures toward conformity and were unconcerned with image-management vis-à-vis the larger society. Thus in the countryside, Miao peasant women did not experience their actions as "minority" practices which defined them in relation to the Han per se.

It was only in the larger, more central villages, the sites of periodic markets or of important bus routes, that the heavier volume of traffic by Han and more cosmopolitan Miao brought a kind of self-consciousness to Miao young women. Xijiang, as a popular destination for domestic tourism, had a particularly intense degree of this kind of awareness. In Xijiang, young women knew that a handful among them would be chosen to pose for journalists' cameras or to sing for folklorists' tape recorders. Gossip circulated as to who was picked and for what reasons. There were a range of responses to this display element of their existence. Many young women, professing shyness, eschewed cameras and other forms of scrutiny under all circumstances. Others reluctantly complied, and were occasionally even persuaded to change into "better" clothes for photographs. A handful, however, were those discussed above, who routinely accepted remuneration in exchange for much more formal labors in the creation of "authentic" images. Some had become so accustomed to this commodification that they had altercations with a group of visiting journalists. When they demanded pay towards the end of a trying photo shoot, the photographers protested, claiming that what they were producing was good publicity (*xuanchuan*) for Xijiang that would result in social and material benefits for the community. The models, impervious to arguments about the wider advantages of their cooperation, insisted, through their advocate in the culture station, that they be compensated, and eventually they prevailed.

The young women's demands for payment revealed their resistance to the utilization of their bodies, their smiles, and their time in the interests of an amorphous community principle. In this way they refused to submit themselves unilaterally to the service of their community or their people just as they withheld themselves from the urban gaze until they were sure of remuneration. Although the end result was still the reproduction of orientalist representations, their insistence on payment may be seen as counter-orientalist practice in that it attempted to supplant a kind of colonialist cultural plundering with a more clear-cut market transaction.

Miao village women, however complicit in reproducing their image as "traditional," also had an acute desire for "modernity" and attached considerable value to its trappings. This was most clearly seen in their marriage strategies. Although subject to certain strictures of exogamy and to parental interventions, Miao young people had a considerable degree of latitude in choosing their partners. Since village exogamy was the norm, market days and annual festivals—when rural folk traveled out from their home villages—were the most common times for getting acquainted with potential partners. Miao young women participated actively in such courtship practices as improvised antiphonal singing between groups of boys and groups of girls at festival, and in the more routine promenading on Xijiang's main road with flashlights after nightfall.

Marriageable young people from all over the region shared a finely honed understanding of a system that ranked villages and their inhabitants according to desirability. Prized features included size, proximity to the road, and to long-distance bus routes, presence of a periodic market, availability of goods, electricity, television, and so on. Long-standing practices of patrilocality determined that young women would be acutely concerned with these distinctions. Courtship and its accompanying cultural production, then, provided for the active construction of otherness even among rural Miao youth. Not only the passive targets of elites and urbanites seeking to exoticize them, Miao young people also strove to mark themselves off through deployment of valorized criteria of "modernity." Thus, for Xijiang locals, distinctions crystallized less around gender and ethnicity than around a fluid status system based on derogation of the agrarian life. Those in more central locations identified their own periphery by contrasting their access to electricity, transportation, goods, and mass media with their sorry "backward" cousins over the mountains. The agency of Miao rural women reveals itself in their aggressive pursuit of the modern through a local form of hypergamy.

The Contouring of Gender in Miao Cultural Production

My digression into the nuances of marriage strategizing is intended to show that local Miao women were at least as concerned with striving toward the social and economic modernity so idealized in contemporary China as they were with manufacturing their cultural distinctiveness. Indeed, Miao peasants in general were rarely concerned with issues of national identity. Their belonging to the denigrated class of laboring agriculturalists was far more salient both in their everyday lives and in their dealings with higher echelons of Chinese society. Where Miao nationalism did come into play it was largely the product of elites. Their self-representation was largely concerned with securing a place of prestige within China's multi-ethnic social order rather than with carving out an oppositional space in contradistinction to the mainstream.

As mentioned before, the local culture station in Xijiang was staffed by a local Miao man, as was its parent organization in the county seat. These "culture brokers" were pivotal actors in the construction and presentation of "local color" for outsiders. When visitors to Xijiang wanted to organize a photo shoot or other event, it was to the local culture station that they made their requests. In the course of these transactions the young culture worker in Xijiang, who had little education, but a relative degree of worldliness from having served in the People's Liberation Army for four years, had been gradually socialized into the expectations of the dominant culture in terms of what to deliver from his own. He knew, he told me, how to find the girls with looks (*maoxiang*) and figures (*shencai*). It was he who explained to visitors that if they wanted to photograph subjects that looked more ethnic they would have to pay them to get dressed up. And it was he who collected the money and distributed it to the models when they were hired.

In this instance, the Miao male role involved a straightforward packaging of ethnicity for dominant consumption. But, minority men figured not only as key producers but also as consumers of difference. Their practices reflected the exigencies of cultural struggles that required of them the contouring of gender in service to both their own as well as the Chinese nationalist projects. Their complicity in commodifying and objectifying "their" women as "ethnic" had multiple significances, as they were called upon to highlight their otherness even as they sought to legitimate it in relation to China's status system.

Miao cultural producers encountered the tension, particularly acute in the 1980s, between two prevailing ideologies. The first, issuing both from the international socialist agenda and from the emulation of the "modern" in the form of Western feminism, valorized the progressive dissolution of gender differences. The second, spawned by the recuperative moves of the post-Mao era, sought to entrench gender dichotomies as emblematic of a Chinese identity. The modes in which Miao elaborated women's roles both echoed and reworked the contest between these two impulses.

For the Miao, a sharpening of distinctions in gender roles has often been experienced as "sinification." Historically, their ethnic identity was in part expressed,
as alluded to above, through the image of their women as strong, with unbound
feet, laboring in the fields and drinking copiously at festive occasions alongside
Miao men. A kind of parity symbolized by the engagement of both sexes in dialogue songs for courtship was also enacted in the voluntary entry of women into
romantic/sexual liaisons and in their active choice of marriage partners. There is
a certain irony to the fact that dominant Chinese society has turned to non-Han
groups for a model of intact femininity when these groups have so long been contrasted with the Han on the basis of their relatively lax gender differentiation. Yet
this turn has had the effect of an injunction, compelling the Miao and other
groups to package their women for dominant consumption in terms of widely circulated tropes of non-Han femininity. Simultaneously, their desire to mark
themselves as "modern" by participating in practices of nostalgia and cultural
objectification has led them to recast their women as keepers of tradition thus
accentuating gender separation. I will illustrate this process through the examination of three tropes that have been and remain complexly identified with Miao
womanhood: ethnic costume, hospitality, and the drinking of alcohol.

Costume. It has long been the case for the Miao, as with other non-metropoli-
tan groups around the globe, that women have been seen as the conservators of
customary dress. Consequently, it is women who are more commonly sought out
as the objects of an exoticizing gaze that favors color, ornamentation, and *difference.* In Xijiang, the directionality of this gaze was only rarely diverted to men,
and then it was for their wrinkled faces, their pipes, or their engagement in
activities such as silversmithing or the playing of the *lusheng* (bamboo reed pipe)
instrument.

For Xijiang villagers, the emphasis on "dressing Miao" has become virtually the
exclusive province of women. Wielding the Han saying, "*Nan geng, nu zhi*" (Men
plough, women weave), both sexes participated in reifying this de facto bifurcation as an element of Miao culture. That men's dress was not a site for the marking
of ethnic identity was evidenced by the indifference with which Xijiang villagers
regarded men's adoption of uniform Chinese peasant dress as their everyday wear.
Indeed, this process of "sinification" was linked to a centuries-old practice in
which men were the ones to "go out," to intercourse with dominant culture in
Han towns and cities, and to be subject to their influence or, in some periods,
their regulation in the form of strict bans on ethnic language and clothing. This left
women "at home" and conflated the use of Miao dress with the construction of
domesticity. The presumption of continuity in women's dress constituted a support for the image of Miao women tending the home fires segregated from the
potent changes that swept about their isolated mountain fastnesses. By the 1980s
this vision of gender difference had taken firm hold within Miao villages.[11]

But there was a counter-representation that was not entirely occluded by this
convention and that challenged women's consignment to the role of "traditional"

dresser. This issued from the claim that, historically, "authentic" Miao practice entailed both sexes adorning themselves elaborately. I encountered this rival vision in 1988 at the Shidong Dragon Boat Race (*Longchuan Jie*) in the neighboring county of Taijiang.[12] The annual event, which combined an age-old set of ritual practices with a highly staged media extravaganza, featured a young boy perched on the bow of each boat beating a gong to help orchestrate the rowing and decked out in the type of full festival regalia usually (in the 1980s) worn only by women. Journalists, photographers, and tour promoters, eager for cultural curiosities to make their material more marketable, have sensationalized this practice as a mysterious form of ritual cross-dressing. Local Miao elders, however, maintained that the boys' ornamentation with silver and embroidery was merely a preservation of the ways of old in which men and women both dressed elaborately at festival time. Everyday wear may also have been less differentiated in the past, as seen in the Miao albums of the eighteenth and nineteenth centuries in which men, distinguished only by their use of pants instead of skirts, are pictured wearing leggings, with their hair tied on top of their head in a variety of styles that the contemporary period tends to associate only with women (Ruey 1973a, 1973b). As late as 1923, it was reported that excessive ornamentation was a mark of a Miao "king" or "overlord" (Jamieson 1923: 380).[13] This high valorization of characteristic Miao dress for men, particularly its identification with rule, represents a counter-discourse that may have hardened during historical Chinese campaigns to suppress Miao dress, which took men as the chief target. It subverted a dominant logic of conformity not simply by the retention of Miao dress, but more specifically by the decidedly more gender-neutral character of that dress and the less differentiated roles that reflected. It is not surprising, then, that the flip-side of this Miao nationalist impulse would be the contemporary reproduction of mainstream masculinity through the casting off, by men, of the clothing that feminized them and marked them as other.

Hospitality. The generous hospitality of the Miao (and many other groups) has been a recurrent subject of praise by Chinese and Western commentators alike. At times, it has been framed as so excessive as to be a target of state regulation because of the economic consequences for Miao families too selfless in the receiving of guests at weddings, funerals, and New Year festivals (see, for example, deBeauclair 1970: 114). In the 1980s, with the groundswell of cultural revival came a renewal of issues around the expenses incurred by hosts as they attempted to restore vitality to rituals suppressed during the Cultural Revolution. Miao households, largely excluded from the explosion of wealth that characterized the coastal peasantry, ambivalently undertook the added material burdens entailed by the welcome return of their customary rituals.

Meanwhile, the state sent dual messages, still discouraging wanton expenditure for local hospitality obligations at the same time that it played up the trope of Miao hospitality as it was purportedly displayed toward travelers and particularly toward foreign tourists. A receptive demeanor toward the stranger became reified as a hallmark of Miao ethnicity, one of which many of the Miao I encountered were proud. The bestower of warmth and generosity was, of course, imaged as the Miao female. As the one who purportedly stayed put while those from afar came to partake of her offerings, she was once again linked to the home village from which her only venture was imagined to be vicarious, through the thrill of receiving travelers.

At home, engagement in the obligations of hospitality were shared by both sexes. Men often cooked, and both men and women sang the improvised songs of welcome and parting that constituted the etiquette toward guests. At larger rituals, men's and women's eating spaces were segregated, with the men's banquet table accorded higher prestige, but even then the welcoming practices were often parallel. The absoluteness of gender separation was also defused through the custom of placing elderly matriarchs at the head of the male table.

For outsiders, as described in previous sections, status asymmetry was mirrored in gender differentiation. Thus, in receiving male urbanites or foreign tourists, it was women who were tasked with the duty of proffering wine and singing welcome songs. The guests, unlike their Miao peasant counterparts, did not sing back; the inferior status of the women permitted this rupture of norms of reciprocity. The ritual, severed from its original context as an interchange between equivalent parties, became a vehicle for the expression of the deference of the subordinate. The nationalist Miao elite in turn re-integrated this latter form into their own rituals in a way that mirrored growing stratification within the ethnic group.

In 1988, members of the Miao intelligentsia in Guizhou province convened the first annual meeting of the newly-founded Miao Studies Association. The conference was characterized by a kind of hybridity in which intellectual production was combined with cultural consumption. In many ways, its content epitomized the exercise of selective traditionalism that Brackette Williams (1990, 1991) has described. Election of officers, formal speeches, and presentation of academic papers took place alongside such events as a visit to a Miao festival in a nearby village, attendance at an ethnic performance in the evening and banquets in which feasting, toasting, and Miao drinking songs were standard fare. Of relevance here, however, was the first event of the conference. When participants piled off busses at conference headquarters they were greeted by elaborately garbed Miao girls presenting them welcome wine out of the horns of bulls. The (again, primarily male) conferees were unconcerned that the hospitality ritual was transplanted to an urban compound in a county seat and took place between strangers. On the contrary, this dislocation effected for them a kind of re-location, a return to the bosom of rural Miao tradition (or a simulacrum thereof) for which they had longed in their absences.

Miao elites, then, were engaged in a kind of ritualized self-objectification in which they themselves partook of reified representations of their own "traditions." This, I would suggest, was especially common among those who had left the countryside for urban vocations and, living among the majority, separated in space from their home villages, had begun to cultivate a kind of nostalgic yearning for essentialized versions of their forgotten culture. The chief symbol of this still-recoverable past was the richly adorned Miao girl, usually in song. Their celebration of her as symbol had special significance because in so doing they were claiming her as their own, as contrastive with the dominant culture rather than simply constitutive of it. The hospitality of women was a fitting means by which to achieve this self-valorization without foregoing their status position as participants in the modern. The trope left Miao women guarding the hearth, preserving the past, welcoming the returned and simultaneously supporting the latter's (masculinized) absence. Through the bifurcation of roles it mediated the contradictions between "tradition" and "change" that have been especially problematic for the Miao and other groups in this era of flux.

Drinking. As noted above, Miao women as hearty drinkers have for centuries been sharply contrasted with their temperate Han female counterparts.[14] It has been a point of fascination for Han onlookers that Miao women do not seem to value sobriety as a virtue that distinguishes them from men. Among Miao peasants, alcohol consumption was perhaps one of the conventions of sociality most rigidly regulated by codes of etiquette. Politeness required that men and women participate evenly in administering liquor to their guests and in imbibing it themselves. A gracious wife was to be prepared to take over singlehandedly initiating and responding to toasts should her husband drink himself into unconsciousness before the guests did. Sex-segregated get-togethers, whether of males or of females, were likewise regulated by the equation of heavy drinking with proper and harmonious relations. A refusal to partake, referred to as being "unhappy," was tantamount to refusal of the social bond that brought relatives and friends together.

In official portrayals, however, the drinking Miao woman has been transmuted into one who merely offers libation to others. The opening ceremonies of the 1990 Asian games in Beijing[15] featured an array of colorfully dressed minorities, among whom was a Miao woman once again proferring liquor with both hands in a servile gesture, underscored by her sex, which constructed herself as giver and the audience as receiver. This image has become ubiquitous in characterizations designed for foreign tourist consumption that catalogue the pleasures of Miao country. A ritual in which visitors are met at the entrance to a village and required to take a drink before entering has been canonized in magazines and brochures promoting the region.[16] Once again, a practice structured by reciprocity in which men and women travelled periodically between villages for markets, festivals, and other ritual occasions, alternately hosting and guesting, and offering and drinking toasts in a manner strictly governed by norms of equivalent consumption was transformed into a more hierarchized interchange structured by gender and status asymmetry. In a socialist modernizing context which stigmatized ritual excess and the chaos and waste signified by drunkenness, Miao elites tended to reproduce this new order, recasting their women as wholesome and selflessly hospitable as seen in the Miao Studies Conference above. The association of Miao women with liquor, an important marker of ethnic identity, was retained, but in a manner that stressed their generous purveying rather than their unrestrained imbibing of it.

Miao women, socialized to the offering dimension of their role, were complicit in reproducing this sanitized version of their relation to alcohol. In countless contexts, they smilingly raised their two hands to put liquor to the lips of officials, tourists, and their own high-status men. More often than not, however, I observed a subtext to these gestures, one that strove to invert the power differential. It consisted of the apparent pleasure that Miao women derived from imposing a custom with which they were intimately familiar on those less schooled in the protocols of drinking. This dynamic allowed them to fix the form of the interchange, to establish a way of interacting structured by "Miao tradition." In true Maussian fashion, by assuming the role of unilateral givers, they established their control, relishing the opportunity to shame those who attempted to avoid their alcoholic prestations. Their favored targets were foreigners and Han women, those most likely to be put out by having to take even a mouthful of the fiery liquor. They pursued these superordinates-turned-victims relentlessly, aggressively forcing the cup or horn to their lips and swiftly tipping it to empty its contents down their recipients' chins and onto their shirts should they resist swallowing. Any attempts at polite refusal were dismissed as impolite on Miao terms. Thus, through a deft redefinition of the significance of the ritual, they recast their gender subordination as a kind of cultural superiority in which they set the parameters of appropriate behavior, taunting those who failed to comply with accusations of disrespect for "Miao custom" ("*Miaozu xiguan*"). In the process, they momentarily restored their status position as strong women unruffled by the physical exigencies of proper social interaction. Ironically, the fact that the new format did not require them to partake made it more feasible for them to pursue this reversal of power positions even though it was premised on the image of their seasoned familiarity with drink.

Conclusion

The contouring of gender, then, was a highly contested project involving a cacophony of voices and comprised of a combination of complicitous and counterhegemonic representational practices. This disorderly process confounds the uncritical application of Said's orientalism paradigm in the Chinese-minority context, because it shows that (at least some) Miao, as suggested at the outset, were not mute objects of representation, but rather active subjects engaged in the crafting of their public selves. The turbulence of reforms and the appeal of modernity touched all domains of cultural production in the 1980s, provoking myriad anxieties over the negotiation of identity. The consequence for minority women was that they became what Lata Mani has called the "site on which tradition was debated and re-formulated" (1987: 153).

In summary, three types of nationalism were being actively molded in 1980s China, each with an ambivalence structured by gender difference. Chinese nationalism, turning its face to the world, appropriated minority cultures in its imagining of a vibrant and historically-rooted nation, but betrayed its reluctance to fully incorporate these "survivals" by maintaining their distinction through the alterity of woman. Han nationalism, threatened at the core by decades of self-questioning and radical change, preserved its sense of integrity and superiority by contrasting with the impropriety and moral depravity of non-Han sex/gender norms even as it was irresistibly attracted by their purported vitality. The nationalism of the Miao (and other minorities) came to terms with the desired modernity of the dominant other by domesticating their women as the symbolic (and in many ways practical) conservators of valorized traditions, thereby consigning them, a la Chatterjee (1989), to a new subordination in the service of their people. At the same time, however, through a multiplicity of practices, they advanced a critique of their gendered subordination by presenting a rival and subversively gender-neutral self-representation.

Notes

1. Research was conducted in Xijiang *zhen,* Leishan county, Guizhou province from January through December, 1988, under the auspices of the Committee on Scholarly Communication with the People's Republic of China, the Fulbright-Hays Doctoral Dissertation Research Abroad program, the Chinese State Education Commission and the Guizhou Nationalities Institute. Shorter research trips in 1982, 1985, and 1986, under the joint sponsorship of the Central Nationalities Institute as well as the Yunnan, Guizhou, and Southwest Nationalities Institutes, were supported by a Samuel T. Arnold Fellowship, Brown University, a Humanities Institute Graduate Research Grant, a Department of Anthropology Robert H. Lowie Grant, and an Institute of East Asian Studies Travel Grant, University of California, Berkeley. I am grateful to all these organizations as well as to many local people, scholars, and levels of government within China for their support of my research.

2. "Miao" designates one of the fifty-five minority nationalities (*shaoshu minzu*) officially recognized by the People's Republic of China. My use of the term "Miao" in the following discussion is not intended to reproduce the reification of the official category used by the state nor the stigma associated with the term when it was used by the Han in previous periods. It should be noted that the people who comprise the current officially defined Miao are extremely complex in their internal diversity and are scattered across seven provinces within China as well as several southeast Asian countries. A strong case for the consideration of such regional and "sub-group" heterogeneity has recently been made by Stevan Harrell (1990) in his study of three Yi communities in Sichuan and by Gladney (1991) in his work on Hui communities across China.

3. In an extremely sophisticated reading of the 1987 cinematic event, *Red Sorghum,* Yuejin Wang suggests that the film "and many other culturally specific texts do *not* reflect the *appearances* of a culture; they mirror what the actual cultural landscape *lacks*. They reflect fantasies and imagined memories—that which society expels" (1989: 53). Wang's conclusions are highly resonant with those I propose here for Chinese cultural production on minority women. In the context of a collective consciousness of this "critical moment of historical transformation . . . issues of masculinity and femininity acquire more social and symbolic resonances than they may in the West. The problem of sexual difference is politically more displaced, more often figured as a signifier of social and ideological entities than of the immediate reality it denotes" (1989: 52–53).

4. The long-standing backbones of Chinese nationality theory, Lewis Henry Morgan's *Ancient Society* (1877) and Friedrich Engels' *Origin of the Family, Private Property and the State* (1883), have molded popular perceptions of minorities in terms of the fixity of evolutionist stages. For more detailed discussion of the importing of these approaches and their contemporary applications in China, see Gladney (1991: 66–96), Guldin (1987, 1992), Harrell (1991), McKhann (1995). For a critical discussion of these types of temporalizing moves, see Fabian (1983).

5. Rey Chow (1991) argues that reconstructed "tradition" is highly marketable in periods in which modernizing change is embraced with trepidation precisely because taking a nostalgic stance toward the past is a practice marked as "modern."

6. Historically, so strong was the association of the non-Han with the non-human, that the radical component of the characters used to designate groups was in many cases that of a dog or an insect. Only in the twentieth century were the characters revised to omit these indignities.

7. The filmmakers were very eager to have me join them on the hike. And, despite the apparent strangeness of the scenario, they often encouraged me to enter their camera frames. This was consonant with the tremendous desire that I encountered throughout my fieldwork for the production of representations of the white Western woman. As I have discussed elsewhere (Schein 1992), the anomalies created, by juxtaposition of the emblem of Western modernity with the signifiers of minority backwardness, were not without their specific and multiple meanings.

8. Norma Diamond (1988) has addressed the problem of the danger surrounding minority sexuality and marriage practices through an examination of allegations by the Han of Miao women's use of magic poisoning. Diamond suggests that the power attributed to Miao women to cause illness and even death through "*gu*" sorcery, was a kind of projection of the fear held by Han Chinese of the perceived strength and relative freedom in Miao women's gender roles. This was profoundly threatening to the Confucian moral order and was compounded by the fact that during the Ming and Qing dynasties large numbers of male migrants and demobilized soldiers who had been sent to suppress Miao rebellions settled in the southwest provinces. In the absence of Han women, they were dependent upon the Miao for marriage partners, making the maintenance of a "safe" distance impossible. The stories of poison potency constructed by the Han in this context continue into the present. They epitomize the kind of myth-making that may be generated by attempts to resolve a highly con-

tradictory relationship in which the "other" woman's attractiveness and sexual availability also constitutes her danger.

9. Heng and Devan (1992), in a powerful reading of Singapore's state discourses, found that the recent selective appropriation of Confucianism as antidote to the (now) contaminating West, also advanced the homology between family and state in ways that legitimated governmental authority. They proposed the term "internalized orientalism" to describe the careful and rationalistic crafting, by a largely Western-educated political elite, of an idealized "Chineseness" consonant with a modern market economy and a patriarchal order that the authors call "state fatherhood." While "internalized orientalism" is suggestive in identifying a practice of systematic knowledge production concerning a non-Western cultural form, it is conceptually weak in that it lacks the fundamental quality of othering that is central to notions of orientalism.

10. Growing up, conformity, modernity?

11. As temporary work in road-building, lumbering, or in factories in nearby towns and cities became available through economic reforms in the 1980s, the common strategy for Miao peasant families was to send one or two of the young males of the family (to the extent that their labor could be spared at home), out to earn cash income. However, as seen above, girls also went out for work, and not exclusively in "ethnic" occupations. During my fieldwork in 1988, some families were beginning to send daughters to work in factories in the Shenzhen special economic zone. In 1992, a Miao scholar stated that 25 percent or 10,000 of the Miao going out of the province for work were women (personal communication).

12. See Schein (1989) for a detailed discussion of the Dragon Boat Festival and its media aspect in 1988.

13. Inez de Beauclair, who conducted ethnographic surveys of the Miao in the 1940s also mentions in passing that in "some Miao groups special costumes also survive for the men" (1970: 49).

14. Symptomatic of the elaboration of typicality, it was actually only the Miao women in the region of eastern Guizhou and to some extent western Hunan, who were culturally expected to keep pace with men in drinking; the image however has been generalized to stand for all Miao despite wide variations between sub-groups on the ground.

15. Gladney (1994) provides further analysis of the minority presence in the ceremonies.

16. For instance, one issue of *Guizhou Huabao* (*Guizhou Pictorial*, 3: 1990), a colorful, bilingual pictorial which features Guizhou minorities as part of every issue, carried two articles: "Songs in Front of Stockaded Village" introduced the custom of offering liquor at the entrance to the village by picturing two foreign women (myself included) being urged to drink; and "Guangzhou Fascinated with Guizhou National Song and Dance Troupe," which foregrounded a grinning Miao woman presenting liquor to a high government official. Significantly, Guizhou province is the producer of the fiery "Maotai" perhaps the best known Chinese liquor. As an important index of status all over China, Maotai, which is exported abroad and in high demand all

over China, has been a great source of revenue for the province. Thus, it has been economically advantageous for Guizhou to perpetuate rather than suppress its identification with liquor, but in a way that can be seen as respectable by a broader consuming public.

References

Alloula, Malek. 1986. *The Colonial Harem.* Minneapolis: University of Minnesota Press.

Anagnost, Ann. 1994. "The Politics of Ritual Displacement." In *Asian Visions of Authority: Religion and the Modern States of East and Southeast Asia,* edited by Laurel Kendall, Charles Keyes, and Helen Hardacre. Pp. 221–54. Honolulu: University of Hawaii Press.

Barlow, Tani. 1991. "Theorizing Woman: *Funu, Guojia, Jiating* [Chinese Women, Chinese State, Chinese Family]." *Genders* 10: 132–60, Spring.

Chatterjee, Partha. 1989. "Colonialism, Nationalism, and Colonialized Women: The Contest in India." *American Ethnologist* 16(4): 622–33.

Chow, Rey. 1991. *Woman and Chinese Modernity: The Politics of Reading Between West and East.* Minneapolis: University of Minnesota Press.

Chow Tse-tsung. 1960. *The May Fourth Movement: Intellectual Revolution in Modern China.* Stanford: Stanford University Press.

deBeauclair, Inez. 1970. *Tribal Cultures of Southwest China.* Taibei: Orient Cultural Service.

Diamond, Norma. 1988. "The Miao and Poison: Interactions on China's Southwest Frontier." *Ethnology* 27(1): 1–25.

———. 1975. "Women under Kuomintang Rule: Variations on the Feminine Mystique." *Modern China* January 1(1): 3–45.

Eminov, Sandra. 1975. "Folklore and Nationalism in Modern China." *Journal of the Folklore Institute* 12(2/3): 257–77.

Fabian, Johannes. 1983. *Time and the Other: How Anthropology Makes Its Object.* New York: Columbia University Press.

Gladney, Dru. 1991. *Muslim Chinese: Ethnic Nationalism in the People's Republic.* Cambridge, MA: Harvard University, Council on East Asian Studies.

———. 1994. "Representing Nationality in China: Refiguring Majority/Minority Identities." *Journal of Asian Studies* 53(1): 92–123.

Guldin, Greg. 1992. "Anthropology by Other Names: The Impact of Sino-Soviet Friendship on the Anthropological Sciences." *Australian Journal of Chinese Affairs* January 27: 133–49.

———. 1987. "Anthropology in the People's Republic of China: The Winds of Change." *Social Research* 54(4): 757–78, Winter.

Harrell, Stevan. 1990. "Ethnicity, Local Interests, and the State: Yi Communities in Southwest China." *Comparative Studies in Society and History* July 32(3): 515–48.

———. 1991. "Anthropology and Ethnology in the PRC: The Intersection of Discourses." *China Exchange News* Summer 19(2): 3–6.

———. 1995. *Cultural Encounters on China's Ethnic Frontiers.* Seattle: University of Washington Press.

Heng, Geraldine and Janadas Devan. 1992. "State Fatherhood: The Politics of Nationalism, Sexuality, and Race in Singapore. In *Nationalisms and Sexualities,* edited by Andrew Parker, Mary Ruso, Doris Summer, and Patricia Yaeger. Pp. 343–64. New York: Routledge, Chapman and Hall, Inc.

Hung, Chang-tai. 1985. *Going to the People: Chinese Intellectuals and Folk Literature, 1918–1937.* Cambridge, MA: Harvard University, Council on East Asian Studies.

Jamieson, C. E. 1923. "The Aborigines of West China." *China Journal of Science and Arts* 1(4): 376–83.

Levenson, Joseph R. 1967. "The Province, the Nation, and the World: The Problem of Chinese Identity." In *Approaches to Modern Chinese History,* edited by Albert Feuerwerker, Rhoades Murphy, and Mary C. Wright. Pp. 268–88. Berkeley: University of California Press.

MacCannell, Dean. 1973. "Staged Authenticity: Arrangements of Social Space in Tourist Settings." *American Journal of Sociology* 79(3): 589–603.

Mani, Lata. 1987. "Contentious Traditions: The Debate on Sati in Colonial India." *Cultural Critique* 7: 119–56.

McKhann, Charles. 1995. "The Naxi and the Nationalities Question." In *Cultural Encounters on China's Ethnic Frontiers,* edited by Stevan Harrell. Pp. 39–62. Seattle: University of Washington Press.

Nader, Laura. 1989. "Orientalism, Occidentalism and the Control of Women." *Cultural Dynamics* 2(3): 323–55.

Ong, Aihwa. 1988. "Colonialism and Modernity: Feminist Re-Presentations of Women in Non-Western Societies." *Inscriptions* 3/4: 79–93.

Ruey Yih-fu (ed.). 1973a. *Eighty-Two Aboriginal Peoples of Kweichow Province in Pictures.* Taibei: Academia Sinica.

———. 1973b. *Sixteen Aboriginal Peoples of Kweichow Province in Pictures.* Taibei: Academia Sinica.

Said, Edward. 1978. *Orientalism.* New York: Vintage Books.

Schein, Louisa. 1993. Popular Culture and the Production of Difference: The Miao and China. Ph.D. dissertation: University of California, Berkeley.

———. 1992. "An Ethnography of Distinction: Fieldwork and the Chinese Social Order." Paper presented at the Association for Asian Studies Meetings, Washington, D.C., April 3.

———. 1989. "The Dynamics of Cultural Revival among the Miao in Guizhou." In *Ethnicity and Ethnic Groups in China,* edited by Chien Chiao and Nicholas, Tapp. Pp. 199–212. Hong Kong: New Asia College Academic Bulletin VIII, Chinese University of Hong Kong.

Schneider, Laurence A. 1971. *Ku Chieh-kang and China's New History: Nationalism and the Quest for Alternative Traditions.* Berkeley: University of California Press.

Skinner, G. William. 1964–65. "Marketing and Social Structure in Rural China." 3 Parts. *Journal of Asian Studies* 24(1): 3–44, 24(2): 195–228, 24(3): 363–99.

Wang, Yuejin. 1989. "Mixing Memory and Desire: *Red Sorghum,* A Chinese Version of Masculinity and Femininity." *Public Culture* 2(1): 31–53.

Williams, Brackette F. 1990. "Nationalism, Traditionalism and the Problem of Cultural Inauthenticity." In *Nationalist Ideologies and the Production of National Cultures,* edited by Richard G. Fox. Pp. 112–29. American Ethnological Society Monographs Series, No. 2.

———. 1991. *Stains on My Name, War in My Veins: Guyana and the Politics of Cultural Struggle.* Durham, NC: Duke University Press.

Williams, Raymond. 1977. *Marxism and Literature.* Oxford: Oxford University Press.

Yau, Esther. 1989. "Is China the End of Hermeneutics? Or, Political and Cultural Usage of Non-Han Women in Mainland Chinese Films." *Discourse* 11(2): 115–36.

4

"Fit Citizens for the British Empire?"

Class-ifying Racial and Gendered Subjects in "Godzone" (New Zealand)

Jacqui True

A land without a past; a race/set in the rut of commonplace. (William Pember Reeves 1899)[1]

I found myself asking an(other) unsuspected question. What was the European doing in this far away Pacific Ocean country anyway? Had he [sic] the right to be there? What were the ideas and ways of life which he had brought with him and how had they developed? Was a community being built which could continue to flourish, or was the European occupation a kind of tenancy which would eventually be terminated? Did I personally agree with the prevailing sentiments about these matters? (Frank Sargeson 1975)

Aotearoa/New Zealand,[2] according to the *Oxford Illustrated History* (and eminent nationalist historian Keith Sinclair) was "settled by two sea-faring peoples, Polynesian and British, after crossing immense oceans in small vessels" (Sinclair 1990: vii). On this official account, two *races* appear to be destined, from the outset, to become one *nation,* in spite of the fact that (approximately) 1000 years separate the respective settlement of peoples now known as *Maori* and *Pakeha* New Zealanders.[3] Indeed, most histories of New Zealand effectively begin with the signing in 1840 of the *Treaty of Waitangi,* by representatives of the British Crown (Queen Victoria) and several Maori chiefs (rangatira).[4] On the face of it, the treaty signifies an agreement guaranteeing mutual accommodation and autonomy of Maori people and Pakeha settlers. To the British in 1840, it was the means by which they gained sovereignty over New Zealand. To Maori people since, the treaty has had a very different significance. It marks more than one hundred and fifty years of adverse conditions under European rule and the loss of Maori "rangitiratanga," roughly translated as Maori governorship, authority, even "sovereignty" in the European-derived sense.[5] Today, more than ever, the *Treaty of Waitangi—Te Teriti O Waitangi* is a symbol of national unity (in diversity) and contestation, signifying the imperialist point of departure: the beginning of European colonization and settlement.

This essay explores the cultural (re)production of race, class, and gender privilege in the context of nation-building and nationalist hegemonic formation in Aotearoa/New Zealand. It considers the transmission and transformation of European (specifically, Victorian English) ideas about race, class, and gender in the making of *New Zealand* and *New Zealanders.* Not surprisingly, there are few really insightful studies on the adaptation of Victorian cultural ideologies as expatriate Katherine Mansfield (in O'Sullivan 1987) wrote, from "the other side of the world" to this "little land with no history." National(ist) myths and Victorian attitudes of race/class superiority and progress, have precluded serious reflection on the politics of meaning and materialization of culture as a struggle over power in the interstices of the Old World-New World. Thus, it is with a sense of ambiguity that I embark upon this project, as I both *belong* to Reeves' "race set in the rut of commonplace," and yet *do not belong* in so far as I question core *New Zealand* national(ist) precepts. These mutable, albeit taken for granted, precepts about race, class, and gender have motivated and delimited historical action—the historicity of (post) colonial New Zealand. Increasingly the site of cultural struggle, they legitimate the "tenancy" of *Pakeha New Zealanders* and "ground" their everyday practice. Before outlining the principles and origins of New Zealand nationalism, however, it is necessary to understand their historical constitution through the conception of historicity.

Historicity

> To have a history may be an old land's glory and safeguard: to make a history is a new land's perilous employment.[6]

Historicity helps us to think about society, a nation in an inter-national order for instance, as a dialectical process. "Rather than placing society in history," within a chronological and progressive narrative, Touraine places "historicity at the heart of society" (1977: 24). This conception emphasizes the symbolic capacity of a society to continually impose meanings on material practices, thus allowing it, "to turn back on itself" (1977: 15): "through historicity activity becomes meaning and meaning once again becomes practice" (1977: 17). The past and future of a society are always present and serve to both constrain and enable historical action. Past cultural models act as structuring meanings on the present, and the concreteness of accumulation—past economic activity—makes this abstract orientation materially possible. In this way, nineteenth-century British industrialism provided the economic model of accumulation for breaking-in the new land and the cultural model of creativity for socializing a new "people" according to Victorian puritanism (i.e., thrift, hard labor, and repressive social manners).

In 1904, Andre Siegfried wrote, "New Zealand may with justice be regarded as the English colony which is most faithful to the mother country" (quoted in Gibbons 1988: 308). Cohen comments on this cultural transmission:

> This is not to say that "Little England" was a homogenous collectivity and culture even within England. Regional and class differences have been crucial. . . . What is true, however, is that there was an hegemonic Victorian English middle class culture which was also exported to the Empire, where many "Little Englands" have been created, culturally and even in terms of landscapes.[7]

European settlers thought of themselves as creating a "little England" better than the "ole England." They wanted "great alteration but nothing new" (Newman 1987: 175). In their view, they were purifying the old society by creating a more equal country, with respect to free-for-all opportunities to property ownership and thus class mobility. And yet in its nineteenth- and early twentieth-century beginnings New Zealand's nation-building was never separate from imperial progress, the protection of the British empire, with "ole England" at the center. The compatibility and parallel development of imperialism and nationalism in New Zealand's history is encapsulated in Joseph Grimmond's speech opposing federation with Australia, to the New Zealand Parliament in 1889: "New Zealand should be a country for New Zealanders. With the wings of Great Britain over us we need not look to no other country or colony for protection. . . . We are here pioneers of a great nation, and shall, no doubt, have a glorious history . . . with a nationality of our own" (in Macintyre 1992: 342).

However, the tensions and contradictions of the old and the new, the past and the present, preclude any society from simply being re-produced. "The distancing of society from its own functioning," Touraine argues, leads a society to produce its own historical environment (1977: 16). Thus, the same society miraculously engenders a different one, although people continue to recognize themselves as part of essentially the same evolving society. The self-production of society is, to different extents, taken for granted. For Pakeha settlers, the past is not in a "foreign country," (cf. Lowenthal 1985) but rather in the "mother country," otherwise called "home." In this way, the legendary pioneer spirit of early settlers is recast in present tense as an expression of *Kiwi* ingenuity, toughness, and practicality.[8] The cultural model a society adopts limits its field of historicity: it creates the limits for the forms of domination and opposition that historicity makes possible (Touraine 1977: 30). Victorian middle-class England has arguably been the standard of civilization, the cultural and accumulation model that together have limited the historicity of New Zealand. As I will argue below, the dominance of Pakeha over Maori, men over women and nature is constitutive of the cultural model. However, as Touraine states "society is not merely a system of norms or a system of domination, it is a system of social relations, of debates and conflicts, of political initiatives and claims, of ideologies and alienations" (1977: 30). Historicity is further a "state of collective activity: its content is determined by the form of that activity" (Touraine 1977: 25). Thus, past meanings embedded in the cultural model are never fixed but always changing in relation to collective resistance and challenges to dominion over social practice.

New Zealand's *national character* is a site of cultural contestation and resistance. As a cultural model it is a motivating force for the construction of national identity *in* difference. The collective conduct of New Zealand's historicity gives rise to nationalist challenges to British class domination *outside*. Consider this assertion of difference in the face of *losing face:* "We NZers have far less in common with the English middle classes than we may think and at best they will patronize us and emasculate us. We could no more lose our national habits if we were to try, than we could, if we wanted to, disguise our kiwi twang" (Pearson 1974: 32).

"Every popular class," Touraine holds, "carries on an action that is defensive at the same time that it is contestatory" (1977: 302). Society, he adds, can only produce a new society in struggles "for and against domination, by war, the struggle for national independence, military organization against the invader or colonizer" or by the struggle of social forces inside for dominion over historical action (1977: 108). These inside-outside dynamics of change and continuity are thoroughly intertwined. In New Zealand, the colonization of territory was fought over by British forces and Maori tribal groupings, and national independence was imposed by the British Crown. Thus, Pakeha settlers have spent the majority of their history under the illusion that they are British, if not living in Great Britain itself. To the extent that there have been struggles in New Zealand history, their outcome—European victory—is seen as inevitable. Social and racial ideologies of colonialism persist in the Pakeha preoccupation with the formation of a national identity. This identity, which must increasingly express its difference from Britain (the external force of domination) and its unity to the world, produces and reproduces race and gender domination *inside*. Social movements of Maori and women, environmentalists, peace activists, and citizens organize against this (inter)national domination, and in doing so push back the limits of the field of historicity.

Historicity is the process in which structured inequality, dominant and subordinate power blocs, confront each other. Social change—the renegotiation of power relationships—emerges from both this confrontation and from the tensions and contradictions in New Zealand society (Weatherall and Potter 1992: 160). Cultural debates over national identity and nationalist representations open ideological spaces for domination and resistance. In this way, society rethinks the dialectical relationships between ideas and power, past meanings, and future utopias. New Zealand society invents itself and its history everyday in relation to inside-outside social forces of inclusion-exclusion which constitute its field of historicity. The politics of race, class, and gender identity arise out of the dominance of the nation-state as the primary unit of representation on this field. It is these *particular* identities which contest the national homogenizing process, the hegemonic configuration of universal and particular, dominant and dominated in an international order.

Nationalist Precepts

Austin Mitchell (New Zealand ex-patriate and British House of Commons Member) once said that "most New Zealanders would not recognize an ideology if it accosted them in the TAB" (the Horse-Racing Totaliser Agency Board, where you "$\underline{T}$ake $\underline{A}$ $\underline{B}$et!") (in Renwick 1987: 216). An apt statement, albeit not one particular to New Zealanders. Like most people, Mitchell and the *New Zealanders* he interpellates, misrecognize the way assorted commonsense ideas, discourses, and scientific logics become ideological practices embedded in our everyday social relations. Nationalist precepts constitute the ideological field on which this bricolage is integrated and made commonplace.

Typically, state-led and state-seeking nationalisms share similar precepts. They assume that the conjoining of territorial and cultural *unities,* by which the centralized state is wed to the homogenous nation, is both natural (primal) and normative (the most politically effective) (Williams 1993: 147). One nation, one culture, one people (deified by one Godhead) is the privileged representation of unity in the face of significant diversity and heterogeneity. "King Dick" Seddon's (New Zealand Prime Minister in the 1890s) reference to New Zealand as "God's Own Country," later to become affectionately known as "Godzone," symbolizes this dominant sense of national destiny through the appropriation of the glorious will of one deity—the Judeo-Christian Godhead. Whether nationalisms assert a universal myth of origin (in the case of the Old World) or a myth of destiny (in the New World), they commonly invent communities—giving meaning to the past in the process of constructing the future (Touraine 1977: 387; also Andersen 1983, 1991). On this view, our relations to each other and to the environment are presented as being always, already given: things could not and indeed should not be otherwise. In the nationalist construct, "the past is a foreign country" (Lowenthal 1985) that must be redeemed and re-invented. Domination practices that took place in the past must be rationalized from the point of view of the present and the most privileged (i.e., Pakeha men as the dominant group in relation to the existing politicoeconomic order). Nationalist representations of unity (in time and space) deny these historical ruptures and oppressive power relations in emphasizing progressivist futures.

Partha Chatterjee argues that post-colonial nationalism is a "'different discourse', but, one that, is dominated by another" (1986: 42). Nationalism emerges in ambiguous relation to the "large cultural systems that preceded it, out of which—as well as against which—it came into being" (Andersen 1983: 19). New Zealand nationalism is no exception. While belonging to, and separation from the mother country has not been an identity issue for Maori people, it has been an obsessive imperialist and nationalist theme in the history of European settlement. Differences and inequalities of race, class, gender, and ethnicity have been rendered largely invisible by the discourses of nation and empire. These differences, however, are constitutive of the *nation*. They position us in hierarchies relative to, rather than in egalitarian community with one another. In order to deconstruct the nationalist romance of unity, therefore, we must analyze the distinct but related ideological components of race, class, and gender on which it is based.

Race Precepts

> New Zealand . . . is a white man's country, if there ever was one (Henry Demarest Lloyd 1990: 5)

At the uttermost ends of the earth myths of New Zealand national origin, destiny, character, and sentiment, albeit mutations of British imperial culture and ideology, establish their dominion over historical action. As argued above, the historical experience of New Zealand is defined by colonialism and the power relations of colonized-colonizer. Prior to colonization, however, *New Zealand* was Aotearoa, a land inhabited by various Maori *iwi* (tribes). Thus at the moment of "landfall" (European discovery by Tasman and Captain James Cook), *New Zealanders* were the "tangata whenua," guardians of "Maori-land," who were later known to Europeans as "the Maoris." Following the signing of the Treaty of Waitangi, Queen Victoria's representative William Hobson declared: "He iwi tahi tatou—we are one people." With rapid European settlement after 1840, white settlers appropriated the name and identity of *New Zealander*. Maori, who formerly inhabited this universal category became hyphenated *New Zealand-Maoris* or simply "the Maoris." For European purposes they were now minorities in a majoritarian culture.

According to early twentieth-century nationalist myth "the stock from which *New Zealanders* are sprung is not only British, but the best British."[9] The myth is perpetuated by the distinguished economic historian J. B. Condliffe, who wrote in his 1930 edition of *New Zealand in the Making* and again in 1959:

New Zealand's social health depends primarily upon the quality of the stock from which the present generation has been recruited. Physically, mentally, and morally, the original stock was rigidly selected. (Sinclair 1988: 332–33)

As the later twentieth-century nationalist historian Keith Sinclair argues, this view of New Zealand's "selected stock" (as opposed to the *Australian convict breed*) is likely derived from the commonplace assumption that "New Zealand was annexed solely because of the insistence of (Edward Gibbon) Wakefield, who wished to found a second England and forced the British Government to forestall the French" (1988: 333). It was the *intent* rather than the *achievement* of Wakefield and his New Zealand Company in London to settle New Zealand as "Little England in the South" by selling (Maori) land to landed gentry in Britain and using the profits to secure laborers who would develop a civilized New World. Regardless of its scientific error, the myth of racial purity and good breeding has contributed to the moral superiority of many *Pakeha* New Zealanders in their gender, race, class, and international *relations* (Sinclair 1988: 334). Myths of superior origin, moreover, have practical utility in the Pakeha struggle to secure national hegemony and a place for New Zealand in the international political economic order.

To explain the particular form that nationalist precepts take in New Zealand, we need to review the Victorian racial ideologies revisioned there. Nineteenth-century nation-building was at the same time a process of "race-making." Civilized British stock were defined against a savage (albeit noble) race of natives. Confronting each other as colonizer and colonized erased the class and regional differences among Pakeha and the tribal differences among Maori. Leon Poliakov (quoted in Newman 1987: 162–63; also Williams 1993: 163) argues that this colonizing process of national homogenization, masked a previous conflation of race and class. In Britain, for instance, different socioeconomic classes were considered different races of qualitatively different bloods, embodying different cultures. In the New World, however, race privilege was not seen as related to class privilege. To this day, New Zealand social analysts comment on the double oppressions Maori suffer as members of an indigenous people and as the most deprived socioeconomic group, *as if the two are not related.*

Nationalist romances of the Maori people, while varied in their historical constitution, generally fall into the broader European categories of noble and ignoble savage. Pottier L'Horme, an officer on the St. Jean Baptiste in its journey to the *Antipodes* in 1769,[10] describes the "ignoble savage" people of Tokerau (on the east coast of the North Island of New Zealand) in his journal:

They have very limited intelligence. Their arms and fortifications are still in their infancy and doubtless their tactics are on the same level of perfection. As for fishing if they are familiar with the implements for it, they could be said to have been forced into this knowledge by the prodigious abundance of fish along their coasts. They have shy natures, but they are lazy to the last degree, treacherous, thieving, defiant and on the lookout to surprise you without thinking twice, which goes to show their limited intelligence, because from what I could see they paid not the slightest attention to the consequences. (quoted in Salmond 1991: 352)

On the other hand, Captain James Cook's record, generally promoted a "noble savage" interpretation of the Maori: "All their actions and behaviour towards us tended to prove that they are a brave open warlike people and voide of treachery" (Salmond 1991: 352). Similarly, Samuel Marsden, the first and leading Church of England missionary in New Zealand from 1814–1837 (although stationed in New South Wales, Australia) wrote: "From my first knowledge of these people [the Maoris], I have always considered them the finest and noblest race of heathens known to the civilized world" (in Elder 1932: 79). At the same time, he believed that without Christianity "they were cannibals . . . a savage race, full of superstition and wholly under the power and influence of the Prince of Darkness" (Ibid: 60).

However, European scientific worldviews, such as social Darwinism, overlaid romantic views of the "noble savage." The Victorian novelist, Anthony Trollope, on visiting New Zealand in the late nineteenth century expressed the prevalent European view that the Maori were destined to "die out" as a race, once they came into contact with a superior (Darwinian) race: "One can understand the hope and ambition of the first great old missionaries who have had dealings with them [the Maoris] . . . but contact with Europeans does not improve them. At the touch of the higher race they are poisoned and melt away" (quoted in Reed 1969: 133). Dr. Issac Featherstone, Superintendent of Wellington, argued in 1856, that the best Europeans could do, as good compassionate colonists, was to "smooth down their [the Maori's] dying pillow, then history will have nothing to reproach us with" (Macdonald 1989: 104). Callous Von Tempsky, the Prussian adventurer who fought for various militia in the 1860s–1880s New Zealand wars, including the British army, wrote of his experiences: "Of all the aboriginal races, the Maori character appears to me the most complex and peculiar. I don't pretend to read it clearly, but can see far enough into it, to understand how much bungling must have taken place with those who had had to deal with and confront that character (Macdonald 1989: 157). The "fatal impact" theory or law of nature applied as well to the Maori as it did to all "native" races who came face-to-face with the Anglo-Saxon. Reflecting on this cultural contest of (superior and inferior) racial character, von Tempsky wrote further: "With all the success that has attracted England's efforts to colonise the world, it has done so generally by crushing either the spirit or the very existence of native races; yet the Anglo-Saxon is not cruel, he is even kindly and his intentions are not destructive—[w]hat breaks then the fortunes of the races that go down the stream with him together? It [is] his character, his hard cold individuality . . . With all his just intentions, he continually shocks his partner to the very core . . . he will go the journey together with him but he is as cold at the end of it as at the beginning" (quoted in Macdonald 1989:

157). The prototype of this Anglo-Saxon racial character as rational, calculating, and benevolent is not particular to New Zealand. It closely resembles American ideologies of Anglo-Saxonism as cultural model, class disposition, and national character in the period prior to the American Civil War (see Horsman 1985). In both contexts, the violent methods of European conquest are rationalized with reference to a superior racial character embodied in English-derived culture and institutions.

While various Maori tribes suffered defeats and subsequent confiscation of land in the Anglo-Maori wars—now the *New Zealand wars,* in revisionist history—their racial stereotype as the most advanced "heathen or indigenous race," the bravest and most (Greek) warrior-like was emphasized in late nineteenth-century nationalist representations. What was once inscribed on war memorials of this era as Maori "fanaticism and barbarism" (Bollinger 1973: 355) has in recent years, been politely changed to "courage and loyalty." Maori heroism in wars *for* (in special battalions in the European World Wars) and *against* the British (in the *New Zealand wars*) is reclaimed as a narrative of national unity.

The race prototypes produced from these various stereotypes of both Pakeha and Maori compare very favorably in relation to other racial types in the "Great Chain of Being." Pakeha settlers claimed to be the "best of the British," superior to British Australians of convict stock, and to non-British—especially Americans and ex-colonials of mixed breed (Sinclair 1988: 334). The depiction of the valiant Maori—a European reflection of self—only adds to this Pakeha superiority. The "selected settler breed" and "the most advanced savages" make, in this view, a great team for the country renowned in the twentieth century for the best race relations in the Empire, if not the world! They prepare the "ground"—of *purity* out of impurity, national *homogeneity* out of racial heterogeneity—for the making of all-white, (all-male) New Zealanders (ironically symbolized by New Zealand's representative rugby football team known to the sports world as the "All Blacks," which has included Maori players). The nationalist task remains, however, to homogenize these all-whiters, distinguished by class and regional differences, the equivalence of racial differences in the mother country.

Class Precepts

> Consider the curious fate/of the English immigrant/his wages taken from him/and exported to the colonies;/sated with abstinence, gorged on deprivation,/he followed them; to be confronted on arrival/with the ghost of his back wages, a load of debt;/the bond of kinship, the heritage of Empire. (A. R. D. Fairburn 1966: 23)

In the twentieth century it was common for the people of New Zealand to be told by successive governments that they were a "classless society." Inequality, writes

Sinclair (1988: 331), was the dynamic of the old world, equality was that of the new. If this was not the lucky country (like Australia), it was surely, "God's Own Country," and therefore "Godzone." Renowned in the late nineteenth-century as a working man's paradise (coined at the time by Prime Minister Vogel) because of its high wages and easy property acquisition, and as the social laboratory of the democratic world, because of the Liberals' radical state reform (in land, welfare, and suffrage), there is *some* material basis to this egalitarian myth of classless origins (Dalziel 1988). At the same time, "egalitarianism establishes the ideological terms for the existence of inegalitarian distinction" (Kapferer 1989: 175).

In the New Zealand context, it seems that the classless society assertion reflects the need to reassert the naturalness of inequality (James and Saville-Smith 1989: 23). The nation is "classless," not only by ignoring significant class inequalities, but at the expense of Maori people, whose land has been plundered for white-settler gain, and at the expense of women whose status as "colonial helpmeets" renders them "offstage hands to an all male drama" (Enloe 1989). The idea of the classless society is a "different discourse" from the pomp and circumstance of the British monarchy and its inherited class privilege. An interviewee (Sargeant) in Weatherall and Potter's discourse analysis of racism in New Zealand comments:

> We like to think the best of, the aspects of the best New Zealander are, as I talked before, tolerance, a person who gets on easily with all sorts of races, a person who, in whom there is no class consciousness, we are very very different, far apart from the British class system and we want none of that system. (Weatherall and Potter 1992: 53)

From this stance, classless New Zealand is rather, a "discourse of difference," led by the dominant middle classes incorporating the working classes in their transformist national hegemony. At the turn of the twentieth century the American socialist Henry Demarest Lloyd (1900) observed that the dominant political force in New Zealand, the "Newest England," was the task of absorbing all classes into the middle class. Certainly, the values of the classless society are assumed to be middle class: respectability, Protestant work ethic, thrift, property ownership, traditional families, and good sportsmanship—all adapted from middle-class, nineteenth-century Victorian England. The Old World's moral regulation, if not its *rigid* class structure, persists in the hegemonic formation of this New-World society. "The dark places of industrial England, its poverty and disease were left behind/Only the best had been taken, it seemed, of the English tradition" (Curnow 1987).

To expose the class consciousness of New Zealand society is not, however, to argue that egalitarianism is merely a myth. To the contrary, egalitarianism is best understood as an idea arising out of material conflict and competition (the land grab of the nineteenth century) and embedded in social practice. For instance, rituals such as amateur *rugby* football, *race*-betting, and *beer* "shouts" at the local "pub," are "mateship" institutions of national pride.[11] This in-group behavior gives an illusion of equality, well grounded in certain embodied dispositions that qualify one as a "good joker" and naturalize one's socioeconomic distinction and/or privilege. For in this mateship culture, being different is equivalent to being superior and (thus) to be avoided at all costs. Setting yourself above the crowd is a threat to security in equality and conformity. In his celebrated 1952 essay "Fretful Sleepers," Bill Pearson scrutinizes this New Zealand *dream made reality*:

> The special quality of the New Zealander's version is that the evil is to disagree or be different. The chaos of existence is to be legislated into shape; the varieties of human quality and personality are to be levelled into conformity with the legislation. It is the development of individual talent that destroys the conformity: some men are left resenting their lack of another man's talent, so he must not use it, it is an unfair advantage. If life is (as the New Zealander assumes) a race, it is to be run by handicap. If nature can't be controlled then man must be: social boycott must keep the talented man in his place. (1974: 19)

The "Great New Zealand Clobbering Machine" as it is infamously known, lops off those *tall poppies* who succeed in the outside, artificial world: those who do not know their place and upset others sense of (limited) place as their sense of reality. At the same time, those whose exceptional status is natural(ized)—such as landed gentry, national sports heroes, and some professionals—are accepted; as long as they participate in ritual-levelling acts on the ideological fields of battle, sports and booze, each earns or is accorded the status and honor of "good mate." These cultural spaces/meeting places hide well the material inequalities among *Pakeha* men. "The mask of money" (of materialism), however, "hides too well the wound we cannot touch" (Baxter 1987: 284).[12] The relations between Maori and Pakeha, men and women are the "untouchables" in narratives of the classless nation. Contrary to Kapferer's (1989: 136) view, egalitarianism is *not* a perfect form of ideological nationalism. It recognizes both race and gender as legitimate hierarchies or specializations. To believe otherwise, is to be similarly deluded by the all-inclusive practices that consistently exclude others and legitimate the Pakeha male as the national norm. In a white-dominated "man's country," class privilege is also a race and a gender privilege. Hence, one cannot understand New Zealand's particular brand of nationalism without understanding its gendered construction and masculinist formation.

Gender Precepts

As I have argued, national identities in New Zealand have been forged against old-world oppressions and the cultural and economic dominance of the mother country. Separation from Britain triggered a nationalist dialectic where hostility to the "outside" originary civilization and its attendant class system produced a virulent assertion of nationalist egalitarianism and resentment towards domesticity and respectability embodied in feminine civilization now "inside." An inside-outside, public-private gendered division is institutionalized within the space of the national such that the birth of new national culture and set of practices becomes exclusively masculine/male.

Revisionist historians have pondered whether New Zealand is "a man's country," the title of Jock Phillips' 1987 history of the image of the Pakeha male, or a "mother-dominated country" (Macdonald 1989: 104; Pearson 1974: 27). Regardless, the outside projection of "real man," masculine values of war, sports, heroism, and mateship has been constitutive of New Zealand's nationalism and national identity. This gendered culture emerged from the interests of race and class, as discussed above, in nineteenth-century, early-colonial development and settler struggles over land and production. Stories of the "rugged individualism" of settler-pioneers serve as narrative evidence that New Zealand colonials were not emasculated by their detachment from Britain. Indeed, the unmediated relationship (without in(ter)ventions of women) between man and nature on the frontier, in common myth, constructs the "real" manhood of colonial settlers. Given that emigration was perceived in Britain as "only for Godhoppers and country bumpkins and not for civilized beings" (John Logan Campbell quoted in Graham 1988: 137), these nationalist myths have sparked pride in otherwise suspect origins and the perilous toil of breaking in the land. Ironically, English nationalism, on Gerald Newman's (1987: 81) account, was also concerned with throwing off the shackles of effeminacy and pretentious manners—in their case associated with the Frenchified aristocracy: "If only the nation would awaken from its hybrid effeminacy," bourgeois nationalists cried (Newman 1987: 73). Victorian nationalist ideology (1740–1830) also provoked the fear of moral "castration" (or worse "hermaphroditization") from foreign cultural influence. Real (bourgeois) Englishmen, like New Zealanders, boasted of the "native" manliness of their disposition (Newman 1987: 127).

The nationalist myth that the frontier creates new supermasculine men rather than emasculated men on a new frontier serves to naturalize the social construction of gender—native/natural masculinity and cultured/artificial femininity. New Zealand pioneer men were advised that investment in a colonial wife would be "more valuable than a patent plough or thoroughbred horse" (James and Saville-Smith 1989: 23) and that they should spend an extra day in London seeking the employ of a suitable helpmeet. The gendered division of labor between household and agricultural land production seemed clear-cut in colonial New Zealand (see Dalziel 1977). Nationalist narratives of this period, however, are more likely to recount the experience of male "mateship" or the "man alone" experience on goldfields, farming blocks, and new settlements. Anti-domesticity and awkwardness in civilized, inside places are the familiar sentiments echoed in these nationalist representations. The popular antithesis of (homosocial) mateship and (heterosexual) mating is strengthened by its association with the related oppositions of freedom-necessity, culture-nature, masculinity-effeminacy, and outside-inside. New Zealand masculinity defines itself against the image of the civilized English (gentle)man and their female/feminine agents of civilization within. Aware of the mutual exclusiveness of these cultural spaces, William Morgan, a visiting gentleman in 1860 commented: "I certainly pity the unfortunate individual who lives in the bush all alone. What indeed is the bush without female society!" (quoted in Graham 1988: 120).

Bev James and Kay Saville-Smith in their book *Gender, Culture and Power* (1989), argue that New Zealand is distinguished from Britain and South Africa by being thoroughly suffused with gendered—masculine and feminine—meanings, symbols, and practices. Although this claim is not uncontested, it suggests that in New Zealand the attempt to erase class and race differences has produced extreme social distance between genders—female-feminine and male-masculine: this distance takes the patriarchal form of mateship/fraternal egalitarianism—an expression of homogeneous "maleness" achieved through the exclusion of women and femininity, which are constructed as the unruly natures and artificial culture ("mannish women") out of place in (post)colonial New Zealand. Consider Austin Mitchell's matter of fact description of female exclusion in New Zealand from his (oft-quoted) book, *The Half-gallon, Quarter-acre, Pavlova Paradise*:

> Most countries have oppressed minorities. New Zealand has an oppressed near majority, sometimes called . . . *Sheila*. She's constructed locally from internationally approved patterns. Basic design is good and sturdy, though finish is unimaginative and trimmings limited . . . She needs little attention or maintenance: mumble at her occasionally, slap her on the back (never the bottom) and you can ignore her for hours. America is female dominated; France is male dominated. New Zealand you have to accept as a world divided into "his" and "hers." The "his" compartment included all the positions of power and interesting jobs, all the folk heroes and all the dominant myths: sport, war, virility. Woman's role is to run the home, raise the children and make the scones. (quoted in Gordon and Deverson 1985: 68, emphasis added)

This "sexual apartheid" institutes a patriarchal bargain/economic bond between respectable women and men, *other*-wise known as *sheilas* and *jokers*: "Sheila(s)" the New Zealand/Australian colloquial name for (othering) women as a group is a collectively trivializing and degrading term, which, while not individually offensive, serves to put all "women" in their place. Tellingly, the *Dictionary of Australian Colloquialisms* (Wilkes 1990: 291) notes that the meaning of *sheila* is "not derogatory, although no woman would refer to herself as a *sheila*." Similarly, the male bias of the *Oxford English Dictionary* (1989: 227) states that the name *sheila* is "playfully affectionate and predominantly in male use." When analyzed critically, *sheila* is unmasked as the linguistic device used by men to define themselves as the agents of history and culture at the expense of "women:" Such naming is a constitutive practice which (re)produces the subordination of women and the supermasculinity of men. The fact that comparable male referents "joker," "bloke," and "mate" are endearing terms mostly used homosocially, by and between men, only reinforces this point. In contrast, consider some of the following public, literary uses of *sheila* in the context of social discourse:

> "The Sheila wot I owns (C. Vaude, 1916 in Ramson 1988, p. 582)"; "Sheilas don't interest me. They're not worth a bumper" (Lawson Glassop, 1949, Wilkes 1990, p. 291); "Leave the sheilas alone they're sure to pool a man sooner or later" (Arthur Wright, 1928, ibid.); "We used to lie and talk about what we were goin' ter eat. An' the sheilas we was goin' ter do" (Patrick White 1965 in Wilkes op.cit); "Beats me how any bloke can enjoy himself talking with women. Sheila talk has always driven me up the wall" (H. Williams 1973 in Wilkes); "Fat, lazy and going to seed. . . . Thats yer spoilt [Ocker] sheila" (Australian 1975 in Wilkes op.cit.); "I've got a job in a grocer's shop and I'm trotting a sheila" (Sargeson in Simpson and Weiner 1989, p. 227); "Ned said he wasn't married yet. . . . 'Still looking for the right sheila?'" (M. Shadbolt in Brown 1993: 2820)

Here, women-called-sheilas are variously represented by (New Zealand/ Australian) men, as sexual objects of desire, the ruin of men and mateship, the controlling influence of the social order encapsulated in the compulsory marriage contract, and as "good for nothing" reproductive wombs. Moreover, the suspected origins of the generic *sheila* in Ireland, the female equivalent of "Paddy," suggests an attempt in the settler colonies of New Zealand and Australia to devalue the class pretensions/civilization of English settler women by associating them with the Irish, who were marginalized and considered racially inferior in the mother country. In P. W. Joyce's, *English as We Speak it in Ireland* (in Wilkes 1990: 291), the female Christian name *Sheela* is said to have been used "in the South as a reproachful name for a boy or man inclined to do work or interest himself in affairs properly belonging to women." Thus, the name *sheila* seems to be central to the creation of respectable men and women and nationalized gendered boundaries (male-female, inside-outside), emanating from the subnationalist fear of emasculation/effeminacy in colonial Ireland as well as in the settler state, New Zealand.

Respectable boundaries between sheilas and jokers are maintained through daily practice and cultural rituals, such as parties, *dos* after rugby matches, and other special occasions where hosts and hostesses ask that "men bring half a crown (or one dollar in the post-1960s generation) and ladies a plate" (of baked goods). My own early childhood memories are of social gatherings where men fraternized in the kitchen, or were outside talking business and politics while the women enjoyed the comfort of the lounge inside, chatting about families, kids, people they knew. In this bargain, women appear to have a great deal of control over the (inside) domestic sphere of household and family life: unlike their male counterparts they enjoy the taste for necessity and the necessity of taste (Bourdieu 1984). But, as James and Saville Smith (1989) contend, any move away from this domesticity potentially undermines the sheila's feminine identity and power in national space. With middle-class values predominating, there have been few respectable spaces for Pakeha women outside the private or moral realm, at least until very recently. In the national(ist) frame women take on distinctively negative characteristics and their influence is mostly derided.

The national hero "man alone" who appears frequently in Frank Sargeson's (1940s) New Zealand short stories is often a vehicle for the expression of masculine hostility towards women and domesticity (in so far as they are conflated). One fictional character bemoans, "you might as well be dead as work at a regular job and have to keep a nagging wife" (Wevers 1993: 132). Work and family, breadwinner and wife, financial responsibility and moral respectability go together; they are the oppositional sides of the national patriarchal bargain. While one can feel sympathy for the national "man alone" whose embodiment is the very antithesis of pious civility and class pretense, rarely have women been nationally celebrated for similar expressions of individuality and self-determination. The public spaces of escape from work and domesticity have been mostly male: the pub, the shouts of beer, and the infamous "six o'clock closing" where men once (until the late 1960s) swilled away their one hour of freedom between work and home and the rugby field where sexual and aggressive tensions could be released.[13] These are masculine spaces of resistance to civilization and the influence of women, against whom much of the anger is directed. Gendered culture, the subordination of women to man alone, or mateship traditions and masculine representations is constitutive of national identity. The Janus—inside-outside—faced nation is distinctly male, and rarely are women's activities and achievements representative of New Zealand.

The reduction of all conflict to gender conflict within "domestic(ated)" space, however, renders Pakeha oppression of Maori invisible and denies the role that Pakeha women especially have played in upholding the exclusionary standard of civilization. In Pakeha male culture the idea of male "comradeship in sport and leisure conceals Maori confinement to an inferior social and economic position and their isolation from Pakeha and each other" (James and Saville-Smith 1989: 76). In sum, gender, race, and class ideologies are mutually reinforcing components of a homogenizing process that produces the white, Western-bourgeois-male subject as the insecure national norm. This dominant subject is insecure because to be hegemonic the nationalist ideal requires the ongoing, active consent of heterogeneous subjects: the nation is therefore the terrain for constant cultural and ideological struggle.

National Hegemony in an International Context

> In reality the internal relations of any nation are the result of a combination which is "original" and (in a certain sense) unique: these relations must be understood and conceived in their originality and uniqueness if one wishes to dominate them and direct them. To be sure, the line of development is towards internationalism, but the point of departure is "national"—and it is from this point of departure that one must begin (Gramsci 1971: 240).

Gramsci theorized the concept of hegemony—the rule of a dominant group by political and ideological leadership of different, often contradictory social forces in relations of active consent and struggle—as a tool for understanding the formation of the "national" in order to move beyond it. National hegemony articulates and is made possible by dominant international forces: by the very construction of a world system based on the right joining of centralized bureaucratic states with homogenous cultural unities. Thus, to move beyond "the national" cannot mean to simply transcend it in the international space "outside." Such a space does not exist. Rather, the international dimension which is not merely a reunification of the national(ist) is to be found, Homi Bhabba suggests, "within the margins of the nation-space and in the boundaries in between nations and peoples" (Bhabba 1990: 4). Echoing Gramsci's point of departure, he reiterates Frantz Fanon's revolutionary creed that, "national consciousness, which is not nationalism, is the only thing that will give us an international dimension" (Fanon 1967: 199, quoted in Bhabba 1990: 4).

So far I have discussed the formation of race, class, and gender ideologies in relation to the construction of national unity and the hegemony of a particular dominant group. Gramsci argued that "the development and expansion of the particular group are conceived, and presented as being the motor force of a universal expansion, of the development of all the 'national' energies" (1971: 182). A particular social group, Gramsci held "becomes dominant when it exercises power, but even if it holds it firmly in its grasp it must continue to 'lead' as well" (1971: 57–58). We are all, therefore, included in the universalism of nation, but differentially so. The struggle is to deconstruct the homogenizing *we* and unmask the power behind the force of unity-in-hierarchy. Social movements based on race, class, and gender political identities challenge the unequal power relations that consolidate national formations in New Zealand.

Like most nations, New Zealand produces itself by constructing inside-outside boundaries of identity and authority. We know ourselves only in relation to what we are *not*. Foreign policy is constitutive of national identity, inside-out, but so is imperial moral regulation outside-in. In-groups and out-groups are constantly being renegotiated in relation to international forces—the situation of New Zealand in world political and economic alliances. I referred earlier to the ideological transformation of New Zealand nationalism in terms of New Zealand's loyalty and belonging to the mother country. In the first phase of state formation, New Zealand constituted itself as a selected peoplehood drawn from "the best of British" stock. An assertion of settler unity on the basis of a common and superior race, class, and cultural heritage, this ideology served to naturalize racial differences between Maori and Pakeha and legitimate Pakeha super-exploitation and subordination of Maori land, resources, labor, and culture as historical progress and destiny. The reproduction of Victorian racial interpretations, social ideologies, and cultural practices were necessary to this initial formation of Pakeha hegemony. It was a dialectical process of cultural transmission in the making of New Zealand into "Little England," and material transformation and exploitation in the production of agricultural goods for the British home market: each was necessary to the naturalization and legitimation of the other. Gender and class conflicts—in the form of male violence, rioting, intoxication, desertion, women and children's sweatshop labor, and poverty in the context of economic depressions (1880–90s and 1930s)—threatened to rupture the hegemony of the dominant bourgeois class.[14]

The second phase of hegemonic formation in New Zealand was less imperialist than *nationalist*-imperialist. In the late-nineteenth and first half of the twentieth century, New Zealand was reconstituted as a radical democratic paradise, *better than Britain,* if not the entire western world. The moral-political high-ground was the space for a New Zealand no longer a colony but a dominion of Britain. The need to constantly prove its imperial fitness and bourgeois credentials was reflected in New Zealand's eagerness to fight in every imperial war. The war sacrifice of a significant proportion of the male population on foreign territory is said to have ushered in the birth of the nation,[15] while the almost godly playing of the brutish contact sport rugby-football further established the distinction of New Zealand manhood abroad. Exporting farm products to Britain maintained the economic viability and "land of milk and honey" reputation of New Zealand as an outpost of the dominant metropole. In this hegemonic formation, by the turn of the nineteenth century, women had the vote (1893) and Maori four seats (1867) in the representative parliament. Their constant moral and political struggles were important to the development of the social democratic welfare state under the first Labour government in the 1930s depression years. Maori people and women, however, were still largely excluded from national representations and leadership.

After World War Two, the break up of empires and the decolonization process finally motivated New Zealand to ratify (in 1947) the Westminster statute of official independence passed in the British House of Commons in 1931. The hegemonic dream of assimilating all classes into the middle class was reasserted in this post-war period: what else could independence mean? In 1952, Bill Pearson criticised this conformist utopia as,

> [l]iving off the threats of communism, the coloured races and the bland terror
> of infinite space; trying to give their customs a universal validity flouted by life,

time and the multiplicity of planets. They [New Zealanders] huddle to reassure themselves that their habits are beyond question, and difference and unconformity questions them. It is a dream too, of the middle class wanting to compensate for the daily routine of competition: life is cruel, business forces you to shoddy tricks, but on our dream let us relax and be jolly good fellows. (Pearson 1974: 19)

Against the background of post-colonial and national liberation movements, Maori's blatant exclusion from this dream, their colonization "inside" New Zealand, was heightened and prompted a radical rethinking of "race relations." Long touted as having the best race relations in the world, by the 1960s Maori urbanization exposed the serious racial gap in living, health, and education standards and an increase in Maori poverty and related social oppressions. The infamous Hunn Report of 1961 outlined a new approach to race relations, choosing integration as a model for New Zealand over separatism, apartheid, and assimilation as the (limited) alternatives tried overseas. There was a renaissance of Maori culture in this era and the rise of Maori, feminist, peace, and environmentalist protest movements based on growing democratic consciousness and contestatory politics. In many ways a whole system—the nation and its unifying race, gender, capitalist, and imperial ideologies—was under threat. This was the beginning of a process which heightened the conditions of crisis and prepared the ground for an alternative hegemony—a new historical bloc of political-economic and ideological-moral leadership. Gramsci argues that on multiple levels (i.e., interpersonal, intergroup, international), criticism of the hegemonic

makes possible a process of differentiation and change in the relative weight that the elements of the old ideologies used to possess. What was previously secondary and subordinate, or even incidental, is now taken to be primary— becomes the nucleus of a new ideological and theoretical complex. The old collective will dissolves into its contradictory elements since the subordinate ones develop socially, etc. (Gramsci 1971: 105)

New Zealand nationalism today, as a consequence of competing identity groups and social movements, is avidly *not* British. The official transition from one nation, one people, one culture *to* one nation, two people, and biculturalism reflects the attempt to cement a hegemonic partnership against a sociopolitical background of gross inequality and severe racial tensions. This domestic shift is inseparable from the (re)construction of New Zealand's international identity. In foreign policy New Zealand is conscientiously pursuing a South Pacific regional role and responsibility.[16] In Weatherall and Potter's analysis "New Zealand could be said to be resuming its actual geographic position in the Southern hemisphere, as opposed to its imagined position in the English channel" (1992: 145). Still, these interrelated domestic and international hegemonic shifts have at least two faces: as regards New Zealand's situation in the South Pacific, the limits of gratuity are exposed by racist immigration policies which restrict the residency of Pacific Islanders and have a history of deporting them as "overstayers" (see Loomis 1990). As the official trustee of several Pacific islands since World War Two,[17] New Zealand has at least some pretensions of playing "big-man" in a South Pacific *empire,* which Shameem (1993) suggests has actually encouraged Pacific migration to New Zealand.[18]

Inside New Zealand, the nationalist impulse to unite two peoples, Maori and Pakeha, in one nation has led to what some have called the "nativist" representation of national identity (Oliver 1990). Again, negating all that is British-derived, this "nativism" appropriates Maori cultural resources, not just out of culturally or politically correct sensibilities but in the name of national *identity in difference.* Mark Williams critically comments:

> The present kind of nationalism stresses our utter uniqueness in the world. The need to break with European values and European origins is stressed. European culture generally is depreciated as materialistic, alienating, scientistic, commercial (European here means not so much Europe itself as Anglo-Saxon culture derived from England and most visibly expressed today by America). In opposition to this, the Maori qualities of New Zealand are emphasized. The values of spirituality, community and love are seen as peculiarly Maori. Here is nationalism which aims to chuck all the exotics out of the local garden and make the Pakeha into genuine New Zealanders by nativising them. Once they have remade themselves in the romantically interpreted image of the Maori, they will be able to feel truly at home. (1988: 35)

Appropriation being the latest strategy in a long line of hegemonic techniques, this new brand of nationalism seems remarkably like the old imperialist ideology that included military conquest, economic exploitation, cultural ignorance, assimilation, and integration. It is the same Pakeha obsession with searching for a national identity that "will show us these islands and ourselves" (Renwick 1987: 199) A kind of transformist hegemony, nativist ideology maintains the dominance of Pakeha society, its economic structures and cultural priorities, while projecting a distinctive and unified identity to the world. For the most part, differences and inequalities of race, class, ethnicity, and gender are still elided. Such elisions, however, do not go unchallenged. They provoke, in Homi Bhabba's words, "unmanned [sic] sites of political antagonism and unpredictable forces for political representation" (1990: 4). After over one hundred and fifty years of Pakeha disregard, Maoris especially see the *Treaty of Waitangi* as a major site of political bargaining and cultural struggle over New Zealand's national resources, culture, and identity. The treaty (te teriti) could be said to be an important instrument in the creation of an alternative hegemony that would reconfigure the power hierarchies of race, class, and gender.

Conclusion

In the course of a one sesqui-century various representations of identity have inhabited the island nation of New Zealand. At first contact, New Zealanders were "noble savages" in "Maoriland," but with European settlement they became a brown homogeneous race of "Maori," no longer fit to stand for the nation. Now, in the 1990s, Maori are recognized as diverse *iwi* (tribal) ethnicities, who are bicultural citizens of New Zealand/Aotearoa as well. What of those economic refugees of British industrialism? On antipodean soil, they became a selected breed of Anglo-Saxons, "fit citizens of the British Empire" for the best part of this century, a nation of classless New Zealanders in the booming 1950s, reluctantly *Pakeha* (white) New Zealanders, and lately the new bicultural natives of the South Pacific. Some analysts predict that in fifty years Pakeha and Maori might be joined in one *coffee-colored* (that is, mixed race) nation of Pacific kiwis! In spite of the national commitment to biculturalism, the globalized trend is towards multiculturalism and a population which is not easily differentiated by the political categories of *Maori* and *Pakeha*.[19]

Race-making—the cultural (re)production of homogeneity and difference—is a mode and means of nation-state making (Stanfield 1985). In the nation-space of Aotearoa/New Zealand the national identity formation process has created multiple forms of subordination based on identities of race, class, gender, and ethnicity. The construction of an overarching group identity in the nation privileges one identity as universal and normative and renders all other ties of loyalty and belonging as particular and deviant. In international political-economic competition this one identity has superior access and claims to the exercise of power and use of resources as national priorities and "national interests."

Europeans have asserted their dominance over Aotearoa and Maoridom in their struggle for material progress and prosperity and superior cultural identity. Nineteenth-century discourses of racial supremacy operate similarly to late twentieth-century discourses of national unity. In their unquestioned legitimacy and everyday practice both discourses maintain the universal-particular, self-other, rational-passionate, abstract-concrete, mind-body hierarchical relationships of Pakeha and Maori, but also of men over women, and the middle class over other classes. The question, "What is the European doing in this faraway Pacific Ocean country anyway?" has been variously answered, over the past century and a half: in the fraternal languages of racism, of masculinism, of imperialism, and of nationalism. However, it is the nationalism, of one people, of white—*not* British—natives, that is most disturbing in this historical period. It attempts to prove that New Zealanders are *not* imperialistic, *not* racist and in the last instance *not* responsible for the economic exploitation and cultural degradation of the Maori people. This "denial" is at the core of many Pakehas' ambiguous sense of guilt and identity. However, in the past two decades, the politics of cultural struggle have been heightened. As a result of Maori protest the *Treaty of Waitangi* has become a central discourse/discursive site in the political life of New Zealand society.[20] In Claudia Orange's (1987: 5) words, recent politics "have challenged the long standing assumption that the treaty forged "one people" and that New Zealand was a special experiment in relationships between a European and an indigenous people." An historical document, dishonored in the past, considered faulty or flawed by many, has (short of being rewritten) been reinvented as a means in the process of creating a more just and less oppressive future, where Maori are not merely party to a European legal contract and the man alone/mateship experience is not metaphor and metonym for the nation.

Notes

I would like to thank Brackette F. Williams for introducing me to many of the ideas in this chapter and encouraging me to contribute to this volume, and for her editorial support throughout. I would also like to thank my family in New Zealand for their encouragement and support of my Ph.D. studies abroad: I share the antipodean spirit of our settler forbears in striving for new worlds, if not, the "New World."

1. Taken from a longer poem by Reeves (the author of *The Long White Cloud* and reformist Labor Cabinet Minister in the 1890s Liberal Government), this excerpt is part of a heated conversation between a British gentleman and a New Zealand colonial settler on the topic of 'imperial fitness' (quoted in Pearson 1974, p. 30).

2. Aotearoa—which translates as *the land of the long white cloud* is the indigenous Maori name predating *New Zealand*—the name coined by the Dutchman, Abel Tasman in his 1642 voyage to the South Seas. Aotearoa/New Zealand is the official name of the state registered at the United Nations. In this chapter I refer to *New Zealand* more often as the specific name for the colonizing settler state.

3. *Pakeha* is the Maori name for foreigner or white man. It is a controversial and politicized term for white New Zealanders, distinguishing them from European and for the most part "British" origins. Increasingly, however, it is the self-ascribed ethnic identification of some "white" New Zealanders conveying their acknowledgment of the historical domination of *Pakeha* in the politico-economic (colonial) space of Aotearoa/New Zealand. (See King 1985, King 1991).

4. In the following months more than 500 signatures of various tribal chiefs were collected. For the best historical analysis, to date, of the treaty agreement see Claudia Orange, *The Treaty of Waitangi,* 1987.

5. For an analysis of the conflicting oral and written versions of the *Treaty of Waitangi* and the debate over discrepant English and Maori translations of "what was being given up by Maori to the [British] crown" and "what was the Crown's guarantee to the Maori in respect of their land etc." See David V. Williams, "Te Teriti o Waitangi—Unique Relationship Between Crown and Tangata Whenua?" (1989: 65).

6. The New Zealand Herald's report on announcing the election of Gordon Coates as the new Prime Minister (Sinclair 1986: 338).

7. Cohen cited in N. Yuval-Davis (1991: 15).

8. *Kiwi* has come to stand as the affectionate term for "New Zealanders" in recent years. It connotes toughness, practicality, and individual ingenuity in so far as it is associated with these same qualities symbolized by the flightless, nocturnal, and mostly solitary Kiwi bird, native to New Zealand, and mascot to the nation.

9. Here Sinclair (1988: 332) is quoting two eminent historians in 1902. He does not give an original source for their comments.

10. Anne Salmond describes Pottier L'Horme in her book, *Two Worlds: First Meetings Between Maori and Europeans 1642–1772,* as a "conscientious and thoughtful Companie Officer who quoted from Voltaire and had probably read Buffon" (1991: 314).

11. "Rugby, racing, and beer," is the cliche for the national preoccupations of Pakeha males in New Zealand, dating back to, at least, the heyday 1950s.

12. James K. Baxter "Jerusalem Sonnets, 18" (O'Sullivan 1987). Baxter comments elsewhere that, given the egalitarian ideology of a classless society, it is remarkable that "the only language which our country [New Zealand] speaks with understanding is the language of money and status" (quoted in Stead 1981: 247).

13. Jock Phillips's book, *A Man's Country?: The Image of the Pakeha Male,* is notorious for its passing interpretation of the rugby scrum as a licensed male hug and the game as generally imbued with homosexual desire.

14. For an insightful history of this era, see Miles Fairburn *The Ideal Society and its Enemies,* 1989.

15. New Zealand is said to have fought in every war that the British Empire has been involved since the 1890s Boer War in Southern Africa. As a result, the ANZACs (Australian New Zealand Army Corps) who fought for Britain on the Eastern Front (on the Gallipoli peninsula) in World War One, and suffered massive fatalities and military failure (e.g., New Zealand had the greatest per capita combatant loss of any country in this war), were lauded as a new "Greek race" of warriors. In spite of their tragedy, *the Anzacs* were mythologized as the colonials "fit" to lead the British Empire to victory once again. The loss and bloodshed at Gallipoli, in part due to the incompetencies of British officers, however, is a key event in the birth of the nations and nationalisms of New Zealand and Australia. For a revisionist historical record see C. Pugsley, *Gallipoli, the New Zealand Story,* 1984.

16. Examples of NZ's foreign policy commitments in the South Pacific include: support of the South Pacific Nuclear-Free Zone and the national nuclear-free stance, protests against French colonialism and nuclear testing, bilateral and multilateral development assistance to the region and political identification with the South Pacific Forum countries.

17. For example, Western Samoa 1945–1962, the Tokelau Islands, Niue, Nauru, and the Cook Islands.

18. Shameem (1993) notes that Pacific Islanders made up nearly nine percent of New Zealand's population by 1990.

19. Wendy Larner (1993: 88) argues that labor and capital mobility characteristic of a globalizing economy, has lead to the emergence of new collectivities and increased

complexity within and between conventional categories of race, ethnicity, colonial status, gender, and class in 1990s New Zealand.

20. See Sharp (1990) for an important analysis of the Maori-Pakeha cultural struggle surrounding "the Treaty," from the perspective of Western political theory.

References

Anderson, Benedict. 1983. (Second edition 1991). *Imagined Communities. Reflections on the Origin and Spread of Nationalism.* London: Verso.

Belich, James. 1986. *The New Zealand Wars and the Victorian Interpretation of Racial Conflict.* Auckland: Auckland University Press.

Bhabba, Homi. 1990. "Introduction: Narrating the Nation." In *Nation and Narration,* edited by Homi Bhabba. New York: Routledge.

Bollinger, Conrad. 1973. Protest and Conformity: Learning to Stand Upright." In *New Zealand Today,* edited by R. Knox. Wellington: Hamlyn.

Bourdieu, Pierre. 1977. *Outline of a Theory of Practice,* translated by Richard Nice. Cambridge: Cambridge University Press.

————. 1984. *Distinctions: A Social Critique of the Judgement of Taste.* Cambridge, MA: Harvard University Press

Brown, Lesley, ed. 1993. *The New Shorter Oxford English Dictionary, Vol. 2.* Oxford: Clarendon Press.

Chatterjee, Partha. 1986. *Nationalist Thought and the Colonial World: A Derivative Discourse?* New Delhi: Zed.

Dalziel, Raewyn. 1977. "The Colonial Helpmeet: Women's Role and the Vote in Nineteenth Century New Zealand." *New Zealand Journal of History* 11:2: 112–23.

————. 1988. "The Politics of Settlement." In *The Oxford History of New Zealand,* revised edition, edited by W. H. Oliver with B. R. Williams. Pp. 87–112. Oxford: The Clarendon Press and Auckland: Oxford University Press.

Easton, Brian. 1973. "Social Class: Jack and His Master. In *New Zealand Today,* edited by R. Knox. Wellington: Hamlyn.

Elder, J. R., ed. 1932. *The Letters and Journals of Samuel Marsden,* 1765–1830: senior chaplain in the colony of New South Wales and superintendent of the Mission of the Church Missionary Society in New Zealand. Dunedin: Coulls, Somerville Wilkie Ltd. and A.H. Reed for the Otago University Council.

Enloe, C. 1989. *Bananas, Beaches, and Bases: Making Feminist Sense of International Politics.* London: Pandora.

Fairburn, A. R. D. 1966. *Collected Poems.* Christchurch: Pegasus.

Fairburn, M. 1989. *The Ideal Society and its Enemies: The Foundations of New Zealand Society 1850–1900.* Auckland: Auckland University Press.

Gibbons, P. J. 1988. "The Climate of Opinion." In *The Oxford History of New Zealand,* revised edition, edited by W. H. Oliver with B. R. Williams. Pp. 302–333. Oxford: The Clarendon Press and Auckland: Oxford University Press.

Graham, Jeanine. 1988. "Settler Society." In *The Oxford History of New Zealand,* revised edition, edited by W. H. Oliver with B. R. Williams. Pp. 112–140. Oxford: The Clarendon Press and Auckland: Oxford University Press.

Gramsci, Antonio. 1971. *Selections from the Prison Notebooks,* translated and edited by Quintin Hoare and Geoffrey Nowell Smith. London: Lawrence and Wishart.

Gordon, Elizabeth and Tony Deverson. 1985. *New Zealand English: An introduction to New Zealand Speech and Usage.* Auckland: Heinemann.

Hindley, G., ed. 1993. *Trollope the Traveller: Selections from Anthony Trollope's Travel Writings.* London: W. Pickering

Horsman, Reginald. 1981. *Race and Manifest Destiny: The Origins of American Racial Anglo-Saxonism.* Cambridge, MA: Harvard University Press.

Hunn, J. K. 1961. *Report on Department of Maori Affairs.* Wellington: Government Printer.

James, Bev and Kay Saville-Smith. 1989. *Gender, Culture and Power: Challenging New Zealand's Gendered Culture.* Auckland: Oxford University Press.

Kapferer, Bruce. 1988. *Legends of People, Myths of State: Violence, Intolerance and Political Culture in Sri Lanka and Australia.* Washington: Smithsonian Institution Press.

Kawharu, I. H., ed. 1989. *Waitangi: Maori and Pakeha Perspectives of the Treaty of Waitangi.* Auckland: Oxford University Press.

King, Michael. 1985. *Being Pakeha.* Auckland: Hodder and Stoughton.

King, Michael, ed. 1991. *Pakeha: The Quest for Identity in New Zealand.* Auckland: Penguin Books.

Lloyd, Henry Demarest. 1900. *Newest England: Notes of a Democratic Traveller in New Zealand with some Australian Comparisons.* New York: Doubleday, Page and Co.

Loomis, Terence. 1990. *Pacific Migrant Labour, Class and Racism in New Zealand.* Aldershot, England: Avebury.

Larner, Wendy. 1993. "Changing Contexts: Globalization, Migration, Feminism in New Zealand." In *Feminism and the Politics of Difference,* edited by Anna Yeatman and Sneja Gunew. Pp. 85–102. New York: Routledge.

Lieberson, Stanley. 1985. "Unhyphenated Whites in the United States." *Racial and Ethnic Studies* 8(1): 159–80.

Lowenthal, David. 1985. *The Past is a Foreign Country.* Cambridge: Cambridge University Press.

Macdonald, Robert. 1989. *The Fifth Wind: New Zealand and the Legacy of a Turbulent Past.* London: Bloomsbury.

Macintyre, W. David. 1992. "Imperialism and Nationalism." *The Oxford History of New Zealand,* second edition, edited by Geoffrey W. Rice. Auckland: Oxford University Press.

Mitchell, Austin V. 1972. *The Half-gallon, Quarter-acre, Pavlova Paradise,* illustrated by Les Gibbard. Christchurch: Whitcomb and Tombs.

Newman, Gerald. 1987. *The Rise of English Nationalism: A Cultural History 1740–1830.* New York: St. Martin's Press.

Orange, Claudia. 1987. *The Treaty of Waitangi*. Wellington: Allen & Unwin.

O'Sullivan, Vincent, ed. 1987. *An Anthology of Twentieth-Century New Zealand Poetry*, third edition. Auckland: Oxford University Press.

Oliver, W. H. 1987. "A Destiny at Home." *New Zealand Journal of History* 21(1): 9–15.

Pearson, Bill. 1974. *Fretful Sleepers and Other Essays*. Auckland: Heinemann Educational Books.

Phillips, Jock. 1987. *A Man's Country?: The Image of the Pakeha Male—A History*. Auckland: Penguin Books.

———. 1990. "Of Verandahs and Fish and Chips and Footie on Saturday Afternoon: Reflections on 100 years of New Zealand Historiography." *New Zealand Journal of History* 24:2: 118–34.

Pugsley, C. 1984. *Gallipoli, the New Zealand Story*. Auckland: Hodder & Stoughton.

Ramson, W. S., ed. 1988. *The Australian National Dictionary*. Melbourne: Oxford University Press.

Reed, A. H., ed. 1969. *With Anthony Trollope in New Zealand*. Wellington: A. H. & A. W. Reed Ltd.

Reeves, William Pember. 1899. *The Long White Cloud: Ao tea roa*. Second edition. London: Horace Marshall.

Renwick, W. L. 1987. "'Show Us These Islands and Ourselves . . . Give Us a Home in Thought': Beaglehole Memorial Lecture, 1987." *New Zealand Journal of History* 21(2): 197–214.

Sargeson, Frank. 1975. *More than Enough: a Memoir*. Wellington: A. H. & A. W. Reed.

Shameem, Shaista. 1993. "Post-Coup Exodus: Indo-Fijian Women Migrants in New Zealand." In *Feminist Voices: Women's Studies Texts for Aotearoa/New Zealand*, edited by Rosemary Du Plessis with Phillida Bunkle, Kathie Irwin, Alison Laurie, and Sue Middleton. Pp. 91–111. Auckland: Oxford University Press.

Sharp, Andrew. 1990. *Justice and the Maori: Maori Claims in New Zealand Political Argument in the 1980s*. Auckland and New York: Oxford University Press.

Sinclair, Keith. 1986. *A Destiny Apart: New Zealand's Search for a National Identity*. Wellington: Allen & Unwin in association with Port Nicholson Press.

———. 1988. *A History of New Zealand*, second edition. Auckland: Penguin Books.

Sinclair, Keith, ed. 1990. *The Oxford Illustrated History of New Zealand*. Auckland: Oxford University Press.

Simpson, J. A. and E. S. C. Weiner, eds. 1989. *The Oxford English Dictionary*, second edition, Vol. XV. Oxford: Clarendon Press.

Stanfield, John. 1985. "Theoretical and Ideological Barriers to the Study of Race-Making." In *Research in Race and Ethnic Relations: A Research Annual, Vol. 4*, edited by C. Marrett and C. Leggon. Pp. 161–81. Greenwich, CT: JAI.

Stead, C. K. 1981. *In the Glass Case: Essays on New Zealand Literature*. Auckland: Auckland University Press/Oxford University Press.

Touraine, Alan. 1977. *The Self-Production of Society*. Chicago: University of Chicago Press.

Vowles, Jack. 1987. "Liberal Democracy: Pakeha Political Thought." *New Zealand Journal of History* (October) 21(2): 215–27.

Weatherall, Margaret and Jonathan Potter. 1992. *Mapping the Language of Racism: Discourse and the Legitimation of Exploitation.* New York: Columbia University Press.

Wevers, Lydia. 1993. "The Short New Zealand Story." *Southerly* (September) 53(3): 118–36.

Wilkes, G. A., ed. 1990. *A Dictionary of Australian Colloquialisms,* new edition. Sydney: Sydney University Press with Oxford University Press.

———. 1993. "The Impact of the Precepts of Nationalism on the Concept of Culture: Making Grasshoppers of Naked Apes." *Cultural Critique* (Spring) 3(24): 143–91.

Williams, David V. 1989. "Te Teriti o Waitangi—Unique Relationship Between Crown and Tangata Whenua?" In *Waitange: Maori and Pakeha Perspectives of the Treaty of Waitangi,* edited by I.W. Kawharu. Pp. 64–92. Auckland: Oxford University Press.

Williams, Mark. 1988. "Race and Nationalism: the Novel in New Zealand." *Island* 36: 31–37.

Yuval-Davis, Nira. 1991. "Anglomorphism and the Construction of Ethnic and Racial Divisions in Britain and Australia." In *Immigration and the Politics of Ethnicity and Race in Australia and Britain,* edited by Richard Nile. Pp. 14–26. London: Bureau of Immigration Research (Australia) and Sir Robert Menzies Centre for Australian Studies, University of London.

5

A Race of Men, A Class of Women

Nation, Ethnicity, Gender, and Domesticity Among Afro-Guyanese

Brackette F. Williams

In contemporary nation-states, where race is class stratified, and the symbolics of class status are racially hierarchicalized, we must explore gender developments in relation to racioethnic-based constructions on the ideological field whence is generated the criteria for masculine and feminine assessments. To demonstrate the implications of race, class, and gender conflations formed in the nexi of ethnic genderings, shaped themselves by the ongoing processes of nation-building and a history of group rights and obligations in changing economic regimes, I will examine conflations of race and culture in constructions of class, ethnicity, and gender identity for the implications they have for domesticity among Afro-Guyanese male and female residents of a community I have elsewhere named Cockalorum (1983, 1991). The community is located in the East Coast Demerara region of The People's Co-operative Republic of Guyana, formerly British Guiana. To situate, ideologically and practically, contemporary constructions of gender, requires a brief sketch of the society's historical background.

The Construction of Afro-Guyanese Gender and Domesticity in the Aftermath of Slavery

Guyana was settled as a sugar producing plantation society. Initially its development was based on unsuccessful efforts to enslave the native population.

Subsequently planters successfully imported enslaved Africans. The emancipation of slaves in 1834 resulted in an unsuccessful effort to import bound labor from European, Chinese, and Portuguese sources. The latter failure led, by 1839, to the successful mass importation of indentured labor from India—primarily from North India (with a much smaller representation from Madras)—which are today all known as East Indians. The current population of Guyana reflects this conquest and labor history. Its culture is constituted of the religious diversity of its constructed population—Christian, Muslim, Hindu, and forms of African, Indian, and Native American spiritualism.

The majority of scholars who analyze the transition from slavery to freedom in British Guiana speak of freedmen. Those who add women rarely go into sufficient detail about the practical, legal, and ideological differences men and women confronted during this critical transition. Studies of male/female relations in post-emancipation and contemporary Guyanese society that draw on such historical accounts confront tremendous gaps in the information available to them on issues relevant to how these men and women responded practically and ideologically to the new rights and obligations acquired through emancipation.

As eye-witnesses to this transition, from the standpoints of their different positions in the overall structure of racial domination, categorically dominant male planters, missionaries, and magistrates commented on the transitional experiences of African men and women in ways that are suggestive of the ideological underpinnings of these men and women's post-emancipation constructions of gender and domesticity.[1] From such accounts we can glean a sense of the interconnected construction of race, class, and gender. Planters commented on the inability of African freedmen to get African freedwomen to behave like proper wives (by moving into their husbands' houses and accepting their authority). These planters claimed that African men came to them and/or to their overseers seeking assistance, requesting that a woman to whom they were legally married be forced to assume the dutiful role of wife and mother. Magistrate accounts echoed these complaints as they reported on men who brought their legal wives before their court with similar complaints. They also indicated that even when women moved into their husbands' houses, they, as one magistrate put it, had an "indifferent attitude," suggested by their refusal to prepare meals, carry out decisions made by men, and even refusing their sexual advances while seeking their sexual pleasures elsewhere. Missionaries voiced similar complaints while lamenting that neither men nor women understood the real meaning of marriage. For whereas both men and women were interested in holding church ceremonies, in the opinion of missionaries they did so for all the wrong reasons. Missionaries complained that men and women often married every Communion Day not as a renewal of vows but to persons other than the ones married the previous year. According to such accounts, they married strictly for the symbolic status; status that women acquired through the title "mistress" (Mrs.) and which men and women attained as a perquisite of the big parties that accompanied wedding ceremonies.

Scattered throughout other journals and accounts one finds items which might also be viewed as symbolic of female resistance to some of the patriarchal implications of marriage, neolocality, and a nuclear domestic organization when they noted that during the ceremony many brides refused to allow the groom to push the wedding ring beyond the first joint of their finger because to do so would mean that they would be "ruled" by their husbands. Along these same lines, brides reportedly refused to kneel next to the groom before the altar, as is customary in some forms of English Christian wedding ceremony, for fear that this would also symbolize their subordination. Likewise, a practice developed, which continues today, whereby on the wedding night the marriage partners tried to trick one another into being the first to enter the marriage bed, believing that the first one in bed will be ruled by the other.[2]

In addition to this, admittedly anecdotal, material we also find in early and recent histories of the working class during this period accounts of active female involvement in the struggles for higher wages and to eradicate other forms of injustice that affected them not only as mothers and wives but also as human beings. For example, as Walter Rodney (1981: 205–10) and other economic historians report, women were among the unemployed "centipede" gangs that rioted against Portuguese merchants and Chinese and Portuguese pawnbrokers. Among the best-known of these women were Tigress of Tiger Bay, Georgetown, and the Centipede Queen, leading women who lived "bachee" (bachelor) lives, running in small gangs and refusing all forms of domesticity, or failing to become involved in a stable union or cohabitation with a male.

Material of this sort can only suggest the need to develop detailed historical knowledge of the ways emancipated men and women made the *ideological* transition from having many of their domestic social and reproductive relations defined and controlled by overseers and planters to defining and controlling those relations themselves. Although works on other issues have provided scattered information about West Indian women's responses to the transition from subordination to an owner to subordination to a husband/father, and West Indian men's response to taking on the subordination of women, these do not provide us with a systematic picture of the overall status of patriarchal ideology in Anglophone West Indian society, or of the institutional forms it implies.

Writing about the presumption of neolocality and monogamy as the prevalent social model of the era, R. T. Smith (1988) convincingly argues that what he refers to as the "dual marriage system" (i.e., a pattern of legal and non-legal unions within and across racial categories), now considered characteristic of the African lower classes, was prevalent and consistent throughout colonial society from its inception. Smith argues that this pattern only came to be associated exclusively with the lower classes as socially mobile mulattoes and others used these elements of patriarchal ideology to construct the norms and values of respectability, even as their own conduct continued to contradict the norms which were generated by this maneuver. In essence a form of domestication, deemed "illegitimate," became an element of the structures of racial signification made possible, and perhaps necessary, by the efforts to "place" class stratification in a system previously defined primarily in terms of racial criteria.

On the other side of the issue, under slavery, stereotyped conceptions of male and female roles and capabilities were implicated in the allocation of agricultural tasks and child rearing responsibilities. Despite the practical contradictions of these stereotypes when women carried out "male tasks" as adjustments required by the labor regime, the developing ideological conceptions of the naturalness of male dominance in non-household labor remained in tact. Yet, whatever the continuity of an ideology of male supremacy, ideologically slave women and their children were never fully the economic and social responsibility of the slave men who sired their children. Slave men, like slave women and their children were, first and foremost, all deemed subordinate to plantation owners, their overseers, and the administrators of the jural and other institutional structures of colonial society that buttressed these men's (and some plantation owning women's) personal domination as members of a race.

Whatever the nature of ideological and practical transitions might have been, for contemporary Guyana neither men nor women are exempt from the contradictory interactional demands of egalitarian and hierarchical ideological precepts that have historically constituted views of class appropriate conduct. These precepts give shape and substance to the ideological field on which local conceptions of social order and interaction are formulated. They structure the conceptions of class and with it race and gender. Femininity and masculinity, no less than race and class, are constructed within a social framework fashioned out of the integration of these competing, sometimes contradictory precepts.[3] Notions of class identity—expressed through the term *mati*[4] and "we iz awl wan famili"—are elements of the code for conduct fashioned around these precepts, and they demand of women and men the accomplishment of a *balanced* regard for egalitarian and hierarchical modes of behavior. However, the logico-meaningful and causal-functional integration[5] of ideological precepts associated with egalitarianism and hierarchy provide for different constructions of femininity and masculinity. Such differences require that we consider how these sets of ideological precepts intersect, compete, and contradict one another in the simultaneous construction of race, class, and gender as *masculinity* and *femininity* among Afro-Guyanese residents.

To accomplish this task, such an examination must include analyses of dilemmas posed by the local expectation that the individual will, for the sake of his or her ethnic group's position in the sociopolitical order, balance the demands of egalitarian and hierarchical precepts in a manner that is also consistent with his or her ethnic identification. Thus, to better understand their views of one another and of appropriate male-female relations, the focus will also be on how the integration of these same ideological precepts are implicated in formulation of ethnic identities and the competitive positioning of races. Although masculinity, femininity, and the associated gender role responsibilities are all shaped by the general logico-meaningful and causal-functional integration of these contrastive sets of ideological precepts, all are not equally influenced or constrained by the same aspect of this integration. Hence, I will also attend to how these differences create, shape, or close spaces for various forms of interactions considered to be "domestic."

In this regard, I will ask how Afro-Guyanese Cockalorums' efforts to meet the demands posed by different aspects of these sets of ideological precepts serve to shape their gender role expectations. I will suggest, for example, that the construction of femininity among Afro-Guyanese women is constrained most by the same contradictions and dilemmas which confront all humans aiming to live well with *mati* while climbing the class ladder. They must be *human and feminine* on an ideological field that constructs humanity as class-identity conduct (*mati*) and evaluates related behavior according to criteria defining cooperation, reciprocity, and sociability, and where femininity as a mode of subordination is diametrically opposed to a proper manifestation of such behavior. In contrast, I will suggest that constructions of Afro-Guyanese masculinity are most constrained by those contradictions and dilemmas confronted by all ethnically identified persons aiming to maintain their ethnic identity while climbing the class ladder. They must be *African and masculine* on an ideological field where ethnic cultures are perceived as competing biogenetic foundations of the nation-state, and the quality of the nation-state is believed to be dependent on the quality of the racially given male quantums from which such foundation are said to "grow" (Williams 1991).

During the formation of culturally valued domesticity, the result of this differential positioning on the same ideological field is to produce a race of men in interaction with a class of women because these forms of domesticity are not simply ways for men and women to interact properly to reproduce and rear children, they are also among the means by which the Guyanese participate in the state's business of making one nation of several competing ethnic groups. In practice and ideology, they draw from this nation-building business interpretations of its implications for their construction of gender and gender roles as racioethnically marked modes of domestication.

A Woman's Dilemma: Face and Contradictions in the Construction of Femininity as Humanity

Afro-Guyanese baby girls, as the often given nickname "princess" might imply, are the pride and joy of their parents.[6] With few exceptions both parents have high hopes that their little girl will, as one father put the matter, "grow-up to be more than a proud housewife mistress." Parents argue that, unlike in the "old days" when marriage was a woman's only source of security and children were expected to be her major source of old-age assistance, today formal education and various forms of technical training provide women other options. Although these options are not viewed as permanent alternatives to the goals of marriage and having a family, when possible they should be fully pursued before marriage, starting a family, or both. That is to say, a girl should remain a "school girl" as long as her intellectual capabilities and her parents' financial and social resources permit. She should, as another fifty-eight-year-old father of four daughters and two sons put it, "prepare she self as best she can fo' care she churen [children] who ah care fo' she in she ol' age" (1980, field journal). To remain a "school girl," however, implies more than simply remaining enrolled in school. The appellation implies a girl who is "growing well"—a girl who has not "fallen [from Grace]" and whose conduct does not suggest that she is stumbling towards a "fall." She is healthy, tidy in appearance, well-mannered, industrious, and diligent in applying her talents. She does not show undue, precocious interest in courtship and marriage.

Becoming a young woman, "taking the fall," requires leaving behind the often carefully cultivated school-girl reputation. It may entail marrying at an early age, or getting pregnant within or outside of wedlock. Such actions, however, in themselves only indicate how a girl is responding to her sexual maturity and what she is considering as she responds. They describe how far, fast, and hard a girl falls and, hence, from where she must pick herself up. Thus, generally speaking, the girl who becomes sexually active and/or marries at an early age falls faster, farther, and harder than a girl who waits until her early to middle twenties to marry, become involved in sexual relations or both, because in actuality judgments of the type of fall taken depends on the particular girl's circumstances. Such a judgment of too rapid and ungracious a fall is likely to be the public conclusion only if she is also of a certain background. A girl considered to be a poor student, from a poor family with few "lines" (social connections) to middle- or upper-class assistance who marries early and begins to raise a family, or who begins to have children who will grow up to assist her and/or her natal family, may be considered to be making the best of her options. In short, she has fallen as all women will, but she has not fallen far and she has already begun the climb back to responsible sociability.

The inevitability of the fall is "biologically" determined to the extent that as a girl matures into a woman she develops sexual needs, the meeting of which requires that she become involved with men and hence with the problems entailed in such involvements. These problems are numerous and shifting as the girl moves through the life cycle. At each point she confronts additional threats to her "good face" (personal reputation) and name (kin-group reputation and respectability). In the transition from school girl to young woman females confront the potential conflicts stemming from their efforts to gain the affective attention of males and to acquire from a particular male the constancy of involvement necessary in their lives to produce and to facilitate rearing children. Even when the timing of their interest in young men, courtship activities, marriage, and establishing their own households coincides with what their parents consider appropriate, the transition involves a division of their loyalty and of any financial resources they may acquire from salaried employment or other forms of income-producing activities. Such changes, at the same time, challenge the strategies and patterns of interaction a girl's parents, especially her mother, have established and of which she is an integral part. Although these potential conflicts do not inevitably lead to "stains" on (irreparable damage to) a young woman's good face, they are likely to do so if she does not, as egalitarianism demands, resolve them in a manner that allows others to conclude that she remains a good daughter who, at the same time, as hierarchical ideological precepts demand, exhibits the promise and ambition to advance herself and her family of procreation to the moral status and material rank of middle-to-upper class.

As she begins to renegotiate relations with her parents she must also start to negotiate relations with her boyfriend and his parents, especially his mother. Although she has a right to expect her boyfriend to demonstrate that he is serious about the relationship by expressing his loyalty and generously sharing his time and resources, she must also take care not to appear too demanding in the early period of the courtship. Sons are expected to remain in and contribute to their natal household long enough to "repay" some of the sacrifices their parents, especially their mothers, made while rearing them. Consequently, if the courtship begins while the couple is in its early teens, the girl must not appear too eager to marry and establish her own household. Even when the courtship begins in the late teens to mid-twenties, if she rushes matters along too quickly she may be considered to have a greedy and selfish attitude towards her future in-laws.

From an egalitarian standpoint, such an attitude is said to suggest, in general terms, that in the long run she might not "live well" with people. In specific terms it suggests that once married she may not allow the young man to continue to assist his natal household as his mother has a right to expect because such an expectation is consistent with the community (i.e., *mati* and *wan famili*) presumption that a young man should continue to support his natal household. Yet, from a hierarchical standpoint, she should quickly establish herself at the center of her boyfriend's loyalty, claiming his time and the disbursement of his financial resources in order to suggest that she has good "sense" and adequate ambition. If she is from a middle-class family she must have sufficient sense and ambition to maintain that status in her generation or, if she is not from that stratum, to propel herself and her family of procreation into that class rank. These contradictions establish the interethnic coordinates within which, as she seeks independence from, but gender identity with, her mother, she and her mate/husband will construct domesticity.

If a girl manages to balance the contradictory egalitarian and hierarchical demands entailed in these negotiations without unduly staining her good face and/or (family) name, the transition to womanhood also brings her into direct competition with other women and she must protect her face and her name from potential stains stemming from these competitive interactions. Her interest in a particular male as potential mate can bring her into conflict with one or more women interested in the same male. Egalitarianism demands that she manage to compete for his favors without encouraging gossip about her moral conduct or instigating public quarrels with other women interested the same man. Of course, the more men in which she shows an interest before settling on a particular male as her choice of a potential mate, the larger the number of women with whom she competes directly and the greater the chances she will become embroiled in a public quarrel with one of them. Further, because casual dating or playing the field is not an established practice in Cockalorum, showing an interest in several men at the same time is likely to result in negative gossip about the girl's sexual morality. Here egalitarian and hierarchical precepts intersect in the demands placed on her to control and appropriately direct her sexual desire.

Moreover, from an egalitarian standpoint, a "playgirl" may be judged greedy— trying to have all the men for herself. From the same standpoint, if she is especially pretty and does not, within a "reasonable" period of time, discourage the multiple suitors attracted to her beauty by making known her interest in and loyalty to a particular male, she may also be accused of flaunting her good fortune (i.e., beauty) in the face of the less fortunate (i.e., homely).

The intersection of the demands of egalitarian and hierarchical ideological precepts in matters relevant to the moral evaluation of feminine sexual conduct also underlie a fourth source of potentially face- and name-damaging conflicts—managing childrearing and the interhousehold mediations it frequently entails. Viewed in egalitarian terms, "sexual promiscuity" translates into charges of greed, flaunting one's good fortune and, in situations where the male already has children by another woman, covetousness (i.e., wanting material assistance, time, affection, and sexual favors that rightfully belong, respectively, to his children and their mother). In practical terms, egalitarianism therefore demands that a woman control and direct her sexual desire through commitment (legal or non-legal) to one man and that she, as the expression goes, "git all she picni wan place" (have all her children by the same man).

These practical egalitarian demands coincide with the ideological and practical demands stemming from the hierarchical precepts. From an hierarchical standpoint, criticism can be equally damning: a girl too taken with the game of courtship for its own sake, or too taken with her own beauty, exposes herself to suspicions of sexual promiscuity and to a public conclusion that she is lacking in the ambition and the good sense necessary to advance herself and her family of procreation into the middle-to-upper class ranks. Again, albeit for different reasons, the demands and, for the most part, the consequent judgments stemming from the egalitarian and hierarchical precepts do, nonetheless, interact to fashion a double link between morality and ambition. Also from this same standpoint premarital sexual chastity and post-marital monogamy are symbols either of accomplished "middle-classness" or of the ambition thereto. Hence, whether a woman's motivation is to avoid egalitarian-inspired charges of greed, flaunting good fortune, covetousness, or to manifest a hierarchically inspired representation of middle-class status, the protection of her face and name requires that she commit herself to a particular male who will become the father of her children. Although women who marry legally and have all their children by their legal mate are, other factors being equal, considered of higher moral status than those who establish non-legal unions, if the latter relationships are stable and the women have all their children by this common-law mate they too are considered to be morally worthwhile.

However, the potential damage to a woman's face/name is not limited to the morality of legal and non-legal unions: whether the woman has children within or outside wedlock the egalitarian demand that her children be fathered by the same man may pose both the greatest practical difficulty and the greatest general threat to her ability to maintain a good face and name. Just as the young girl who is interested in a number of young men at the same time increases the number of potentially competitive relations or interactions she has with other women, and thereby increases her chances of becoming involved in face-damaging gossip and/or public confrontations with one or more of them, so too does the woman who has children with more than one man or who establishes a relationship (legal or non-legal) with a man who already has children with another woman. In hierarchical and egalitarian terms, a man is morally obligated to continue to provide economic assistance to his children regardless of the state of his relationship with their mother. Women have both the right and the responsibility to demand that men meet this obligation to their children regardless of their obligations to other women and any children they might have with these women.

Love, as one of the "trigger mechanisms" that informants believe set into motion a woman's innate ability to control and direct her sexual desire, comes with no guarantee that she will not fall in love with a man who has not already become a father. It also provides no protection against one who is incompetent as a father/provider or impotent as a husband/lover. The other trigger mechanism, pragmatism (i.e., controlling and directing sexual desire on the basis of what appears to be the best choice for an economically viable, socially mobile, stable, monogamous union)[7] does not guarantee that the best available choice at any given time will not be a man who already has children with another woman or one who will not produce "outside" children once the union is established.

Whereas some informants argued that a woman who makes a wrong choice and creates a hard life for herself should simply bear the burden, they were out-numbered by those who argued that anyone can make a mistake but it is a very foolish person who does not try to rectify that error. Moreover, remaining with one's first choice in order to have all of one's children by the same man is not, from either an egalitarian or an hierarchical ideological stance, a solution without face- and name-damaging potential. From a hierarchical standpoint, to continue in the situation would demonstrate an absence of ambition, the lack of a desire to become "somebody" or to provide one's children with the opportunity to move up the class ladder. From an egalitarian standpoint, to the extent that such a woman manages to get by with assistance from her kin, continuing in the situation would mean running the risk of charges of selfishness and uncooperativeness—all take and no give. Generally, female kin are available to assist, however, one consequence of reliance on such assistance is that the elevation of sisterhood becomes the denigration of humanness, to the extent that humanness is defined in terms of egalitarian precepts.

In such a situation, a woman could rectify her mistake by attempting to make it on her own with whatever intermittent assistance she might be able to acquire from the man, either through direct requests or by "actioning" him (i.e., taking him to court to demand child support). She could also combine these efforts with a search for, and the eventual establishment of, a relationship with another man. Whatever her choice, the ultimate outcome is likely to increase the chances of gossip about her conduct and of public confrontations either with the man or with other women to whom he is financially obligated. Thus, despite the fortuitous intersection of these aspects of egalitarian and hierarchical ideological demands which are relevant to the evaluation of feminine sexual conduct, overall the conjunction does little to make easier a woman's effort to protect her face and name. Instead, the congruence poses tremendous obstacles as she aims to accomplish a viable humanity as a precondition for maintaining dignity in the crucible of domesticity. Stains do not merely lay on the surface of her name, they actively eat into the fiber of her socially constituted humanity.

Should she manage to develop a face- and name-sustaining relationship with a man, once she has children, childrearing adds yet another dimension to her personal conduct which is subject to competing egalitarian and hierarchically inspired evaluations of these dimensions of her self. For example, an important measure of a woman's interest in and ability to live well with people, and of her desire to become somebody is assumed to be expressed in the way she rears her children. Well-mannered children are a credit to their parents in general and their mothers in particular because their behavior indicates that the parents have respect for *mati* and have trained the children to conduct themselves appropriately. It also shows hierarchically important ambition because it is assumed that the well-mannered child is a sign of a household oriented to middle-class values. Children from such households are assumed to have the best chance of "growing well," completing school and thus being prepared to take advantage of economic opportunities to assist their natal family, and eventually to form and advance families of procreation.

Well-mannered children may in their early years become involved in fewer interhousehold conflicts than ill-mannered children, nonetheless childrearing inevitably draws women into interhousehold-conflict mediation in ways that differ from male involvement. From an egalitarian standpoint, the way a mother responds to conflicts between her children and members of other households is taken as a significant measure of her ability to properly integrate the role responsibilities of motherhood and those of good neighbor defined as a decent human being. She gains a reputation as one who takes her "eye past *mati*"[8] when she is quick to take her child's side in any conflict and to insist that when accused of some misdeed the accuser is either wrong or intentionally malicious.

As with other kinds of behaviors, where such conduct is considered to be consistent with a pattern developed by other members of her kin group, it deepens the stain already on the family name—"Iz 'ow dem people ah stay." The kinds of interhousehold conflicts in which children become involved will vary as they grow older and with the variations increase the possibility of others, godparents for example, intervening to mediate. Even so, for most of their lives it is their mother who will be the first adult drawn into conflicts they instigate or into which others draw them. Thus, she soon develops a reputation for being either a fair or foul mediator, which influences how others expect she will behave in all kinds of interactions. Increasingly, in relation to other gender-role responsibilities, her childrearing practices come to define her competence as a morally worthwhile human.

Woman Can Sit on Her Thumbs and Clap With One Hand?

Necessary sacrifices and compromises to a just construction of humanity should and must be made for women to have and successfully rear children, but these necessities do not exempt women from the potential damage to their faces that results from others' impressions that they have accepted a permanently subordinate position to a man, or men, thereby giving up an equality of dignity and respect to which they have rights as *human beings*. Therefore, whereas men and women must cooperate to raise a family, only the woman who lacks self-respect and who does not know how to "make life" without loss of humanity is believed to be satisfied with a domestic arrangement in which she is truly subordinate to her husband/lover. Hence, as already noted, for women this means that as wives and mothers they must be concerned with the moral and material well-being of their children, the social mobility of their nuclear families, and with maintaining the moral reputations of their extended kin groups. A person who manages to become a "real" woman and to carry out successfully the role responsibilities of a woman must also balance her concerns with producing and rearing children in a respectable middle-class oriented household against her concerns with developing and maintaining what I will here refer to as *autonomy* from male domination—an aspect of her overall quest for independence.

To the extent that women are successful in the construction of the ideologically defined human dimension of their personhood, they protect and/or improve the quality of their personal reputations (face) as they seek the sexual gratification, motherhood, and the material advancement that signal that they are also true women. Moreover, whether the true woman carries out her gender roles of wife and mother simply as a "housewife mistress" or as a working woman depends on her circumstances. In the construction of domesticity, to be discussed below, cooperation neither automatically demands that she work to contribute an equal share to the household income nor stipulates that, because she is a woman, she not work and make a financial contribution. Instead, taking into consideration her personal circumstances, male and female informants argued consistently that the woman who knows how to "make life" demonstrates to the satisfaction of others that she makes choices that establish a pattern that in the long run will allow her to decrease the degree of control men, as lovers/husbands/fathers, have over her and her children. Whatever she does, with increasing age becoming a "big" woman must entail an increase in personal autonomy if she is to avoid a decrease in peer and self-respect. Neither female dependence nor male independence, viewed in either interior or exterior psychological terms, can be understood without placing those terms in an economy of social identities that are themselves already situated in a politic of group identity formation and competition (see Craib 1987 and Pierce and Williams in this volume).

An extreme consequence of the autonomy versus subordination issue may be found in the comments and motivations of a numerically small, but not analytical-ly insignificant, category of Cockalorum's men and women who view themselves, and are coming to be viewed by the larger community, as permanent bachelors and bachelorettes. Some young men, ranging in age from the late twenties to mid-thirties, claim they will never marry or even settle into a non-legal cohabit-ing arrangement with any woman. They say women just use men up and leave them "to punish" (i.e., suffer gravely and unjustly) in their old age, so why not just love them and leave them; let them worry about supporting the children pro-duced from such unions because in the end these children will only be concerned with the welfare of their mothers. Even if such conduct means, as it does for the moment at least, that the community considers them doan-kay-damn men (i.e., faceless social dropouts who are an embarrassment to their name) at least they will have the satisfaction of saying they used but were not used by women.

Their counterparts are the equally few but far more vocal, and, in the eyes of "respectable" women of all class statuses, obnoxious and morally dangerous young women of roughly the same age category who not only vow that they will never marry or cohabit but add that they will get involved only with married men. They say it is true that married men do not have much to offer financially but, they add, whatever one gets from them one does not have to "hear their mouths everyday," and when sexually you do not want to be bothered with them they can be sent home to their wives. If one of them is not enough (sexually or economically), or cannot be available when needed, one has only to keep several on the string. Thus, involvements with married men are preferable to involvements with unmarried men, they say, because such involvements allow a woman to produce children, who in the end will be her true support, with the least sacrifice of autonomy and, hence, in their view, humanity and human dignity.

On this point I give the final words to a young woman, age 21, and mother of three, whom I dubbed Lady Day, after a not unambiguous but hopefully clear enough reversal of the spirit of Billie Holiday's "Ain't Nobody's Business If I Do."

Telling me about a quarrel she had with the wife of one of her lovers she conclud-ed: "So, me til she, iz you gaa the M.R.S., but iz me gaa de M.A.N., bu' naa worry when me done, me ga send 'e home."

A Man's Dilemma: Race and the Contradictions of Masculinity as Encultured Nature

Men say women start life ahead of men and remain ahead because they are born with an acre of land between their legs (i.e., their ability to have children) where-as men must buy land (i.e., work) in order to have the resources that give them access to this feminine acre. They invest in the cultivation of female sexuality— this sacred acre—but they charge that they can never be certain of a share in the products (i.e., the affection of children and their future assistance). Nonetheless, men who seek these resources, and the ties to women and children they necessi-tate, face many of the same dilemmas as women struggling to balance the demands of egalitarian and hierarchical ideological precepts. Although the dis-courses about gender and domesticity that are generated in the diverse intersections of egalitarian and hierarchical precepts allow that "boys will be boys" (i.e., rambunctious from time to time), from the standpoints of both sets of pre-cepts, in their youth, males are to be dutiful, obedient sons who grow up and settle down to raise a family. They should use their talents, parents' financial assis-tance, and any opportunities available to them to move themselves and an eventual family of procreation up the class hierarchy. While working to improve or to maintain their socioeconomic position, they too are expected to live well with people, avoid public quarrels, and the exhibition of behavior suggesting greed, jealousy, covetousness, the flaunting of good fortune, or the "doan-kay-damn" attitudes of the unambitious "limer" (i.e., one who idles away time).

Whereas men are not believed to have an innate ability to control and direct their sexual desire, they are thought to be capable of such behavior if assisted by a "good woman" and constrained by shouldering the responsibility of providing for children. They are, therefore, expected to seek out these control mechanisms. The school boy makes the transition from boyhood to manhood through the behavior he exhibits in seeking out a woman, asking for her hand, preparing for, and subsequently meeting the responsibilities of marriage and parenthood. The character of this conduct decides whether the male will either remain on and move up the social ladder or fall from it and have to start over. Men, unlike women, are not considered to be innately endowed with the potential to gain con-trol over their sexuality. Nonetheless, on issues relevant to the evaluation of masculine sexual conduct, hierarchical and egalitarian ideological precepts make intersecting demands on men. Like his female counterpart, he is expected to gain control over his sexuality, as a sign of adherence to the demands of egalitarianism, summed up in the expression "live well with people," and in adherence to the demands of hierarchy, summed up in the expression "become somebody," in order to become the morally worthwhile male.

In making the transition to manhood, however rambunctious in other respects, from the standpoint of both sets of ideological precepts the morally worthwhile school boy should not begin his first courtship as a "bush affair."⁹ Nor should he ask for one girl and then continue to play about, "spoiling other people's girl children." Instead, guided by physical attraction and, more importantly, a conscious decision and effort to gain and maintain control over his sexuality, he, like the morally worthwhile female, should begin to negotiate relations with his girlfriend and her family as he renegotiates relations with his natal family, especially his mother, in order that his loyalty and his use of time and resources may increasingly favor meeting his obligations as husband and father. If he does not begin this process, he exposes himself to the face- and name-damaging charge of not being serious about the relationship; or worse, that he is incompetent in these matters.

The transition from school boy to man also brings men into direct competition with one another for the attention and favors of the females to whom they are attracted. Informants, male and female, argue that such competition poses less of a threat to the face and name of males than it does to that of females. Men, they say, are less likely than women to become involved in public confrontations with their competitors because they can attempt to outdo such competitors through generosity, attentiveness, and, sometimes, by reinforcing their position in a woman's life by "giving her babies." The assumption underlying the latter contention is that once a woman has a child or children by a particular male, others recognize that he is "dar wid she" and (even when, at the time, there are no clear indications that the couple will marry) competitors will or should back off.

Somewhat ironically, however, the possibility of face- and name-damaging public confrontation increases among men once a man is legally married or has established a stable common-law cohabitation. Here the subtleties of differences in beliefs about the innate nature of males and females come into play. Women have an innate ability to control and direct sexual desire. This ability is *materialized* through the mechanisms of love and pragmatism, but in the process such mechanisms do not, and cannot, alleviate either the innateness of desire or the possibility that desire will be inadequately addressed in the particulars of any given materialization. Hence, the woman who does not receive adequate affective and physical satisfaction from her husband/lover will "naturally" seek it elsewhere. She will not be praised for such conduct but, informants say, she cannot be truly condemned for it either. In addition to these biologically based problems, women are also "sensible." That is to say, they know that for their own and their children's sakes they must seek material support. Where a husband/lover fails to adequately meet these needs women will be tempted to look elsewhere for assistance. In light of these contentions, unless there are compelling reasons to conclude otherwise, the sexual indiscretions of a married woman are taken to be the result of her husband's/lover's incompetencies—incompetencies from which other men may benefit, and which opens the husband/lover to face and name damage should he have to commit public acts to prevent other males taking advantage.

Here egalitarian and hierarchical ideological precepts again intersect to produce the demand that men "give one another a chance." That is to say, from an egalitarian standpoint, as *mati* living well with *mati,* real men should not take advantage of one another by tempting wives/lovers to follow their biological and/or material needs. From a hierarchical standpoint, as social beings ambitiously trying to become somebodies, real men should not waste their time, energy, and resources undermining another man's authority as head of household. Instead, such men should expend their energy and resources on true women who are available and who will assist them in their effort to move up the class ladder. They should, from this standpoint, demonstrate that they are firmly in control of both a woman and the economic advancement of a household.

Males who fail to meet these egalitarian and hierarchical demands create the conditions under which their faces and names are exposed to damage as they fail to improve their material condition; they publicly confront male competitors, or they otherwise become the focus of negative gossip. And, whereas public confrontations and gossip may be less damaging to the faces and names of men than they are to those of women, damages are not insignificant. From a hierarchical standpoint cuckolded men who confront their competitors admit that they cannot control their wives and/or, more importantly, that they do not give them sufficient reason to control themselves. From an egalitarian standpoint such men demonstrate their inability to live well with people. Cuckolded men who beat their wives or expose their indiscretions publicly are open to the aforementioned charges as well as to the hierarchically inspired accusation that they foolishly damage the very "property" that they are supposed to be protecting, and to the egalitarian inspired charges of "'vantage"—unfairly attacking a weaker party.

Childrearing also poses threats to a "real" man's good face and name. That men's faces and names may be less damaged than women's by interhousehold conflicts associated with childrearing results not from the fact of variations in closeness to reproductive functions, but rather from the fact that as "representer" (of family and household) in order to avoid charges of 'vantage men are expected to become directly involved in only the most serious conflicts. To do otherwise would be 'vantage by reason of bringing the full power of the household to bear on the conflict before trying a less powerful agent. In contrast, women should be involved in all but the most trivial matters—these being handled among children, arbitrated by an older sibling or relative in the same peer group. Nonetheless, men as representers are expected to encourage their wives and children to live well with *mati* by representing one another in a manner respectful of *mati.* Men who support their wives and children in unfair conduct, who, as premier representatives of their households, do not "give satisfaction" when others come to "complain" about their wives and children, "take their eyes past *mati*" thereby damaging their faces and, if their response is considered typical of their kinsmen, intensifying the stains on their names.

Note that, at this point in the construction of these *intraethnic* features of masculinity and femininity, Afro-Guyanese men and women confront many of the same dilemmas. Similarly, the dilemmas—of dependence and independence—faced by Afro-Guyanese men and women are structurally and ideologically consistent with those that men and women of Guyana's other ethnoracial groupings face as *mati* and countrymen of particular locals. Yet, between men and women and across ethnic boundaries the similarities of dilemmas do not always result from the demands of the same ideological precepts. Moreover, when the demands are generated from the same ideological source, they may not result from interpretations of the same aspects of that set of ideological precepts. For example, as we have seen, women try, for both egalitarian and hierarchical reasons, to have all their children by the same man. Men must, for egalitarian reasons, also try to produce children with only one woman. They are not, however, compelled by fear of being accused of promiscuity (after all, as the saying goes, men are "dogs") but primarily because they will be accused of living badly with neighbors—spoiling others' "girl children" and, thereby, creating grounds for disputes and hostile confrontations.[10]

Across the range of class strata such differences in the logico-meaningful integration of ideological precepts pose a range of problems for men and women as they construct gender, delineate gender-role responsibilities, and institutionalize these in patterns of domesticity. Moreover, when we consider how these sets of ideological precepts and their different aspects serve to inform and constrain the construction of *interethnic* features of masculinity, and how they are encapsulated in the stereotypes of ethnic distinctiveness and hierarchical competition to which these are oriented, we cannot but note that Afro-Guyanese men confront dilemmas that women of this category do not.

In the end, what most constrains masculine gender formation for these Afro-Guyanese men is the construction of race and its relation to the production of ethnic cultures of relative merit, and the ideology-made links between these cultures and the publicly assessed differential potentials of their members for socioeconomic mobility. In short, through analyses of the racialized positioning of forms of masculinity in the stereotypes of labor and laboring we can disclose how for men the boundary between class and race is blurred by the symbolic importance of work in the construction of their masculine identity and the acceptable range of gender role.

Blackness as "Unmanned" Manpower

According to Cockalorum's ethnoracial stereotyping, African men, when compared to men of other racio-religious cultural segments in Guyana, work only as long and as hard as they must to survive. They prefer to spend their time in the company of other men in rumshops, "gaffing" (i.e., idle or competitive "talk"), liming about the village paths, or chasing women to make babies for whom they will then be too irresponsible to provide care. African women, though hardworking themselves, are unable to control or significantly alter these aspects of African male behavior because these aspects derive from innate tendencies. That is to say, in these summary stereotypes African man is to nature what African culture is to its ethno-religious group competitors: an inferior variant. Consequently, Afro-Guyanese culture, although assumed to result from the interaction between men and women, because the character of all male/female interaction is shaped by the struggle to control innate tendencies in males, is deemed a male product and, as such, an inferior product, and, therefore, inadequate to serve as the foundation for a national Guyanese culture. Or so goes the basic assumptions of non-African-descent Cockalorums in their expression of a complex of historically developed cultural stereotypes[11] depicting the relations between Africanness as gender stereotype and Africanness as ethnic culture. These gender/culture stereotypes are frequently employed to define the masculinity of African men and to link it to the production, character, and relative merit of Afro-Guyanese culture.

Moreover, according to these stereotypical constructions, the presence of African men and the Afro-Guyanese culture for which, ideologically, they are largely held responsible, threatens the integrity and survival of all other racio-religious cultural segments in Guyana. As this part of the stereotyping argument goes, because African men are innately better endowed physically than are men of other races, and because they spend more time than men of other races practicing the art of seduction, women of other races, who are stereotypically assumed to be inexperienced and unaccustomed to this form of masculinity, are easy prey. Consequent to such stereotyping, even if they rejected the justice of such laws, sterotypes conclude that, without social, legal, and personal protection from African men, these women produce half-breeds instead of adding to the number of their own racio-religious cultural groups. In such interracial unions, even when they manage to establish a domestic arrangement with the fathers of their children, such women are deemed far less capable than the African woman of forcing or assisting these men to suppress their innate tendencies long enough and deep enough to construct a stable pattern of domesticity. Hence, domesticity is to maleness as maleness is to competitive constructions of culture: the best forms of masculinity necessitate the best forms of true womanhood in order to produce superior forms of culture which in turn allow the victors the spoils, among which are female subordination in the interest of maintaining home as hearth and as solid foundation for the nation.

Beyond the consequences attributable to their own inferior culture, failure on the part of African men to suppress their innate tendencies also means they are thought to be incapable of approximating the stereotypically Anglo-European culture pattern inherited from the colonial order. Given the otherwise presumed inferiority of their own culture, this "borrowed" culture is deemed their best hope of moving themselves and their families of procreation into the ranks of the middle and upper classes. And thus, so the stereotyping concludes, such households do not reproduce the available model of Anglo-European culture, the superior culture of the mother's racio-religious group, or even the better characteristics of the inferior Afro-Guyanese culture. Not surprisingly, local arguments framed around these stereotypical constructions generally end with alarmist prophecies about the dire consequences of a future national culture based on this continually degenerating "African-based" version of a Guyanese culture.

As I have argued elsewhere (Williams 1983, 1991), building on the work of Bartels (1977), Wagner (1977), and Rodney (1981), the particular patri-racial criteria which contemporary Guyanese produce or choose to emphasize as they construct these conceptions of cultural distinctiveness, masculinity, gender role responsibility, and the relation between cultural and biogenetic capabilities have their roots in the hierarchical ideological precepts around which dominant members of the Anglo-European colonial population initially constructed conceptions of cultural distinctiveness. It was to these notions of cultural distinctiveness that they imputed implications for the legitimacy of a particular socioeconomic and political arrangement of ethnic stratification. In the distribution of economic tasks and views of the legitimate sociopolitical order, these stereotypes (when viewed dialectically and diachronically) were both *cause* and *product*.

Moreover, as I have also noted in detail elsewhere (Williams 1991), members of the different racio-religious groupings initially utilized these stereotypes (the positive ones about themselves and the negative one's about other groups) in an effort to maintain any advantages associated with the socioeconomic and political arrangement that had been, in part, a motivating force behind the initial structuring of the stereotyping process. Beginning during the colonial era and intensifying their efforts in the postcolonial, postindependence eras, each group augmented, reinterpreted, and assimilated the elements of stereotypes of self and other to their integration of the competing hierarchical and egalitarian ideological precepts to produce a hierarchy of ethnic groups as givers or takers. They did so in efforts to conceptualize a redistribution of economic tasks and sociopolitical rights and obligations, and thereby to ultimately reformulate grounds adequate to lend political legitimacy to ethnically biased images of a new sociocultural order.

What, in the end, is deemed a positive stereotype of self and a negative one of others depends on the synchronic aims of interpretation. Hence the consequences for the racial dimension of masculinity as humanity floats with variation in interpretations and the logico-meaningful integrations of ideological precepts these produce. For contemporary African masculinity in Guyana, this means that African males are likely to consider the stereotypes grains of positive truths distorted by the innate tendencies of other racio-cultural groups as their members try to gain for these racio-cultural groups "properties" that are not theirs. These, according to African men and women, are the consequences of other groups' covetousness and their efforts to jealously besmirch the good name of the Afro-Guyanese group to which they know that these material benefits, higher group status rank, and greater control over the politico-economic structure, rightly belong (Williams 1991). They express such rationales for accepting the grains of truth in stereotypes while pointing to individuals who seem to fit the stereotype in all its negative particulars, and who therefore "give the race a bad name" and "hold back" its "progress."

In the views of Afro-Guyanese male informants, because African men in particular, and African people in general, experienced the full horrors of slavery they know that if human life is to be meaningful human interaction must be structured so as to balance a concern for sociability (enjoying one another's company and cooperation) against a concern with economic mobility (the quest to improve one's material condition). In short, they believe they know better than anyone that the demands of the egalitarian precepts must be emphasized first and foremost in the organization of life goals and daily interpersonal action. In their interpretations, they are more genuinely egalitarian than any of the other groups or, in terms they are more likely to use, they know better what it really means to be "wan famili." In sum, rather than being racially fixed, the intersection of these ideological precepts results in a set of "logical" interpretations that argue that race as history constructs nature and defines its relation to humanness (quantum and quality) as the quintessential measure of moral and political worth.

Less than human are the members of a group which lives only to work and amass material goods, as Africans, in slightly different stereotypical constructions, accuse Guyanese of East Indian, Portuguese, and Chinese descent of doing. To the least charitable of African informants, persons in such a group might as well be animals for all the value they place on their human dignity. To be a good human in these terms means that one must, in the process of making a living (becoming somebody), guard against becoming a slave to a job, money, or an employer. In the process of "making life" (living well with *mati*) one must guard against becoming a "duppy" (i.e., a spirit or shadow of the real self; a fool to be used by others), as one intent on meeting the demands others make but failing to demand from others that they reciprocate in a manner that respects (i.e., does not take 'vantage, or eye pass) one's human dignity. Hence, informants contend that if Africans are to remain in the ethnic competition for the highest rank in the sociocultural hierarchy, they must fashion around these conclusions a style of life consistent with them and recognizably distinct from the styles of life stereotypically attributed to or claimed by other groups. Within that style of life masculinity must not be equated with "becoming a slave" or to the frequently used term "living the life of a coolie," a reference to one who has adopted an "East Indian work ethic."

In the context of these positive and negative stereotypes of their masculinity and of the Afro-Guyanese culture, we may view African men's emphasis on being outside the house, being in the company of other men, and trying to give the appearance of having control over more than one woman as, in part, a symbolic expression of how they manage the intersecting demands of egalitarian and hierarchical ideological precepts, rather than, as Wilson (1973) has argued, a direct anti-colonial confrontation with respectability as symbolic core of the colonial order. In fact, as works on the cultural construction of gender and the "cult of True Womanhood" have demonstrated, male constructed forms of absence have been a demonstrated feature of colonialism and industrialization at different points in time throughout Anglophone societies (see, for example, Melosh 1993, Roper and Tosh 1991, Managan and Walvin 1987, Epstein 1981, Demos 1974, Welter 1966). The construction of femininity as respectability, taken as one version of the cult of true womanhood, which Wilson attributes to a female continuity/reproduction of the colonial order in Providencia in particular, and the English-speaking Caribbean in general, can reasonably be interpreted as a dialectical response to various reconstructions of masculinity within the changing economic bases of the overall cultural order of dominance and subordination. Hence, Wilson's male/female dichotomy, in a very limited sense, is accurate. It is also besides the point.

Put in terms Afro-Guyanese men and women use, African male conduct is intended to express how they can be men and African in a particular ethnically and class-stratified sociopolitical order. Their models of masculinity image how *African* men can be good *male-the-providers* without becoming the *whitemen* of the past or (and no less significantly) the *coolies* of today. Such models are constructions of how they can be good cooperative husbands/lovers living well with *mati*. Seeking the means to get out the barrels of "crab antics," they weave a fine rope of competing ideological postures which they hope will allow them moral and material freedom without having to engage in acts that make of them both de-racionated and de-humanized duppies. They seek to enculturate their "male nature" without loss of its humanity or undermining its racio-ethnic rank positioning.

Through the high visibility gained by frequenting public spaces informants, especially younger men (ages 18 to mid-30s), claim that it is made clear to anyone interested that they are not to be taken for coolies, always working, always in the house, under the feet of women and children, or as Chinese or Portuguese always grubbing for money, never stopping to enjoy life until often it is too late. In short they say, "When I wuk, I wuk," expressing their sentiment that, on the one hand, African men can accomplish more in a shorter time than others because, stereotypically speaking, they are stronger than other men and therefore do not have to spend as much time working to complete a task, and, on the other hand, that working all the time robs one of the benefits of labor (i.e., having the means to assist and share with others one's self and one's material goods).

Although these actions and the reinterpretation and augmentation of stereotypes that underpin them allow African men to fashion a pattern of behavior in the early years of their life that is oriented towards resolving the dilemmas of how to be African and male while living well with *mati* (i.e., being human), in the years after they are married and have children this solution works less well, not merely because they are drawn into a female circle of respectability but also because the egalitarianism, out of which they must construct their humanity, demands a cooperativeness that presses harder on them to forsake the streets, the company of drinking buddies, and the display of control over more than one woman. Men with daughters must alternate between appearing the dog and watching for the dog's first appearance in their daughters' lives. Other modes of conduct become necessary to demonstrate their ability to live well with people by respecting *mati's* daughters, cooperating with a wife, providing for the support and guidance of children, and, in general, representing a household in the local system of status evaluations, generalized reciprocity, and conflict mediation.

To fail in any of these regards is, as discussed above, to expose one's face and name to damage and potentially indelible stains. In addition, these egalitarian demands are reinforced by hierarchical demands that in order to become somebody, and to symbolically represent that accomplishment as a member of the middle-to-upper classes, the construction of masculinity must be fit into the constraints established by the stereotypical image of Anglo-European culture. Most specifically, it must fit this model's construction of morally worthwhile domesticity as the establishment of legally monogamous unions where the business of biological and social reproduction are conducted in neolocal, nuclear, male-dominated households. It must meet the demands of this feature of hierarchical ideology at the same time it manages those of the egalitarianism produced in resistance to it. However, as with women, men's most difficult problems come from the fact that *neither set of precepts speaks directly to one another* and, hence, cannot comment on relations of subordination among subordinates when the mode of subordination is *other than, but simultaneously part of, gender construction.* There is less a singular patriarchal ideology to which males can apply for legitimacy and authority than there is a unitary expectation that male agency will be employed to produce a mode of domination wherever it enters the pragmatic and symbolic order of human relation. Yet, and ironically so, domesticity is not about gender relations per se, but rather is about social reproduction. The social here is possible and meaningful only with reference to the pragmatics of ideological intersections manifest in the sociability of racio-ethnic competition. Hence, while gender dichotomies build on real and presumed biological diacritica associated with maleness and femaleness, these overlap with or are encapsulated by the physical diacritica of race/ethnic designations and their juxtaposition to historically constituted class qualities as demonstrated racial inequalities.

The Dilemmas of Domesticity: Race and Its Polarities in Gendered Constructions of Ethnic Humanness

How men are to be African while providing regular support for a wife and children when such activities ideologically are deemed "White," "Indian," or any ethnicity other than African stands in contrast to how women are to be human when the character of humanity is ideologically defined in opposition to their gender stereotype. Surely the "broken" families, female-headed households, varieties of concubinage, and "serial monogamy," so much a part of the Caribbean landscape drawn by anthropologists, reveal the consequences of a complex of economic and ideological factors. Yet it is through examinations of cases of long-term domesticity that have handled successfully some key features of economic marginalization that we might further clarify the role of female autonomy and male racial identity on gender stereotypes in the domesticity of nation-building. Attention to such cases of domesticated gender formations allow us to better identify those factors according to which succeeding and failing matters to those who succeed and to those who fail.

To briefly explore this possibility, I will close the discussion with a case of long-term, legalized domesticity. In this case we can glimpse the interwoven implications of the male and female dilemmas as they confront one another in the joint effort to construct domesticity. As we do so, we may recognize that the construction occurs in an ideological space of definite character and constraint. Masculinity and femininity, in the ideological space we have interrogated, are constructed of racio-ethnic and sociopolitical interpretations *interior* to the Guyanese ideological field but *exterior* to the space typically and stereotypically associated with mating and reproduction.[12] That is to say, these dimensions of the masculine and the feminine are exterior to, but become the context for, a logico-meaningful construction of economic production and biological reproduction. This arena is the space in which are realized the material *prerequisites* and the moral *perquisites* of childrearing (i.e., the benefits derived from domesticity constructed by a proper balance of attention to face, name, and "living well with the people dem"). As the following case will suggest, here the ideological field tells both African males and females you will make both love and money between a rock and a hard place.[13] At the time they were observed and interviewed, Mr. and Mrs. C, the subjects of our case, had been legally married for over thirty years.

Case in Point: Domesticity as a Matter of Gendered Deafness

Everyone knows, so the story goes, that Mr. C has no voice in his house. He has been silenced by his wife's deafness; deafness brought on by money sent from America and Canada by "her children." If one doubts this fact, those who tell this story point to an unfinished house across the path from Mr. C and Mrs. C's house. They will tell you the house belongs to Mr. C, and that it is a house he started several years ago on land that belongs to him. They will also tell you that Mr. C did so in order to have a place to which he can retreat when he disagrees with Mrs. C.

Across the path in this unfinished house he often sits, silently, as Mrs. C yells across her dissatisfaction with him on a timely vexation. In these public broadcasts she reminds him that she is a big woman, a woman with grown children, a woman who is living in a house built on *her* family land. And though it was Mr. C who put most of the funds into making the house what it is today, Mrs. C prefers to remind him that now it is her children who contribute the funds necessary to maintain it. Although all of *her* children are also *his* children, during these quarrels she refers to them as *her* children.

What bothers the men who talk about Mr. C's predicament is that he has no voice with his wife and children despite the fact that he, at least in their estimation, has been a good husband and father for more than thirty years. Although, in pity for him, they probably exaggerate his qualities as husband and father, they are convinced that no man could have done more to bring up his children, maintain a home, and look after a wife. They say that Mrs. C was always a woman concerned with her status. She was very selective in her associations and she always wanted the best for her children. But in her early years she was also a hard worker. With Mr. C away in the gold and diamond fields of Guyana's interior region, or busy with the farm and any other work he could find to earn a living, Mrs. C was a good wife, taking care of the children and the home. She was not one to neglect her responsibilities or to be frivolous with time and money. She, her mother, and the five children she eventually bore lived a quiet life, first in the small house that belonged to her mother and later in the same but continually expanded house made possible by the proceeds that Mr. C acquired through his labors in the gold and diamond fields.

Although viewed as a hard worker and a good husband and father, neither male nor female informants painted Mr. C as an angel in male skin. He was always a fellow who liked the company of other men; men who, on his return to the community from his porkknocking (gold prospecting) junkets, he sought out to entertain and by whom, as reciprocal drinking buddies, he expected to be entertained. And whereas he did not neglect his family, he was no "coolie"; he was generous with his funds, buying drinks for others and being sociable as is expected of an African man. He was never a grand playboy, neither was he a henpecked wimp. As one of his drinking buddies summed up the matter, he was "ordinary, an African man trying for 'e self and 'e family."

It is Mr. C's past pattern of reasonable conduct that all male informants, and more than a few female informants, say makes his current predicament so sad. He could have been like more "wuthless" men and would not today be in a much worse situation. Male informants, in particular, bemoan the fact that he often finds it necessary to sleep across the path in his unfinished house in order to have peace and quiet.

His troubles are not new. They are, informants say, the same troubles that were always there under the surface. His "voice" was never very "strong" in the house, but he was not truly silenced until his children were grown and began to intercede in quarrels between him and his wife. She, at the same time, argued with him in front of the children when they wanted to do something of which she approved and he did not. One of the things they argued about was their three girls' desire to "take a walk"—to go abroad and seek a livelihood in the United States, Canada, or England. Mrs. C not only supported them in this desire, while Mr. C was away in the gold fields she did everything she could to help them secure the appropriate papers and the funds necessary for their eventual departure. Despite Mr. C's disapproval and refusal to assist them, two of the girls eventually migrated (one to the U.S., the other to Canada). Their two sons sought a better livelihood in the bauxite mine at Linden (nee Mckenzie), leaving behind only the youngest daughter.

Even before the children left home, informants say they no longer showed much respect for Mr. C. They talked back to him and when he attempted to reprimand them Mrs. C interceded on their behalf. Mrs. C also interceded on behalf of her children in conflicts. She seldom admitted or accepted that they had wronged others. She and they engaged in transactions with friends and neighbors but they failed to honor their part in these transaction when it suited their purpose (e.g., asking a seamstress to sew a garment then refusing to pay the agreed upon fee when the item was completed). Living abroad now, the children's primary contact is with Mrs. C. Both Mr. and Mrs. C agree that it is to Mrs. C that they send funds to help out with living expenses, to maintain and expand the house, and to do other things that improve the family's material well-being and, in their eyes, if not those of all community members, the status of the family. Mr. C, who is still involved in porkknocking and who receives a small pension, contributes to the household budget but it is with the assistance of funds sent by their children that Mrs. C is able to hire the services of a young girl, a distant relative, to assist around the house, making her household the only one in this section of the community with hired domestic labor. Residents' knowledge of the outside source of income and gossip about her bragging, proud ways has gained her the reputation of being one who cannot be trusted to treat others fairly. Looking to her children for assistance, and feeling that her household is of higher status than those of her neighbors and less well-to-do relatives, informants complain that she has come to feel she no longer has to live well with the people.

Conclusion: Gendering Race to Nationalize Encultured Humanity

The concept of living well with the people and its egalitarian ideological underpinnings allow us to understand both Mr. C's predicament and his wife's conduct, which led up to it. Mrs. C considers Mr. C a good man. Mr. C considers Mrs. C a good woman. And of course, whereas it is they as *persons* who argue and disagree, during calm interludes each tends to chalk-up the difficulties they encounter to an acceptance that *men* and *women* are "by nature" at cross-purposes. By definition a point comes when in order to hear the needs of their gender each becomes deaf to wants of the other's personal concerns.

"Nature" is the culturally constructed constraints and advantages confronted by anyone interacting on an ideological field the dilemmas and contradictions, pulls and pushes of which are defined by the simultaneous relevance of egalitarian and hierarchical precepts. It is in terms of the interactional integration of these ideological precepts that informants' understandings and evaluations of Mr. C's predicament were generated. It is also in accordance with these terms that their understandings and evaluations did not differ fundamentally from their evaluations of the predicament in which those who have less, in terms of material goods and status, find themselves when they interact with persons who have more and who claim a higher status. Although "big people" recognize that they might fall at some future point and this recognition tempers their conduct in subtle and important ways, they consider one of the advantages of "becoming big" to be freedom from certain types of obligations. And "bigness" should, thereby, enhance one's ability to minimize others' control over one's decisions and actions (see Williams 1991). In the same terms, becoming a big woman in both senses of big (i.e., grown and materially well-off) should mean gaining one's autonomy, defined as a decrease in the control husbands/lovers have over one's decisions, actions, and the products of one's sexuality.

Thus, as humanness gendered in maleness and femaleness and culturally constructed as feminine and masculine natures, men and women confront, on the same ideological field, the same tasks: the construction of gender *in* domesticity. How they manage one partially shapes the space within which they construct the other. However, they engage in these productions and reproductions as different forms of subordination; forms of subordination that have different histories and, hence, different historical reactions to one another and to the present and its nation-building future. As such, their efforts to further subordinate one another (to act as subordinated subordinators), to equalize relation in forms of domesticity, or to confront the forms of gender represented by the men and women of other ethnic groups all take place within the constraints of a historically constituted process of subordination that conflates race, class, and culture to produce gender.

Contradictions and intersections in the integration of this field's precepts pose similar dangers to the good faces and names of men and women. Influenced by different aspects of the same ideological precepts, however, they do not undertake the tasks for the same reasons. That is to say, men do not participate in the production and rearing of children simply or primarily as a means to increase their control over women as wives/lovers or to demonstrate their racial identity. Instead, more accurately, they can be said to forsake a biologically given autonomy in favor of a culturally constructed humanity, but that culturally constructed humanity ultimately consists of racionated cultural stereotypes out of which they produce African masculine stereotypes. Women do not simply get married to have children or simply have children in order that they may develop more autonomous interactions with males as husband/lover (to ultimately regain their humanity). Yet, taken together, these issues constitute a significant concern for

women as they attempt to construct a gender identity consistent with their egali-
tarian-defined humanity. In learning to make life as a big 'oman they also learn to
manage the paradoxes of a femininity hierarchically defined as "sitting on one's
hands" and a egalitarian defined humanity that proclaims to all that "wan hand cain
wash; wan hand cain clap."

Men do not become involved with women merely to demonstrate the equality
or superiority of their ethnic group. Nonetheless, on an ideological field in which
stereotypes of masculine and non-masculine conduct is a feature of ethnic competition for hierarchical dominance or to avoid ethnic subordination to a particular
nationalist formation, how a man, whether as saga boy or family man, interacts
with women of their own and other ethnic groups is neither practically nor analytically separable for the symbolic representation of racio-ethnic group status. The
field of analysis for masculine gender identity is also the field of racio-ethnic competition. Whatever their financial wherewithal, in the arena of domesticity,
successful African men and women struggle to produce a humanized femininity
while they maintain a racialized masculinity. In a nutshell, women struggle to give
birth to children who will grow up to be their futures while men struggle to give
birth to cultures that will "advance" to become superior foundations for a nation-
state which, it is assumed, will ensure the future of a race as it competitively
positions its members in the nation-state. In the meantime the everyday pragmatics of biological reproduction and family sustenance are carried out between a
rock and a hard place.

Notes

1. On these points see, for example, H. Kirke (1898). Describing practices in a period
   some 60 years after emancipation, Kirke reports:

   > One reason why such a minority of the coloured people in British Guiana are
   > married is that they won't marry unless they can do so like white people, with
   > carriages, white satin, and wedding cake. Some of the more respectable people
   > form unions which last for years, and finally end in marriage, the children often
   > acting as bridesmaids to their mother. It is also absolutely necessary that proper
   > wedding garments should be worn. A city clergyman, after long and patient
   > entreaty, had prevailed upon a man and woman, both well up in years, who had
   > been "living in sin," to get married. The day was fixed and the bride arrived at
   > the church, where the bridegroom had preceded her. What was her horror and
   > indignation to see that he was dressed in a short jacket, or jumper, instead of a
   > long black frockcoat, which is de rigueur on such occasions. It was more than she
   > could stand, the insult was overpowering; so she bounced out of the church, and
   > went back to her house, saying she would be d[amde]d if she would marry any
   > man in a common jumper. (263)

   Kirke also argues that marriage and setting up a household together was not a
   taken-for-granted assumption (264–70). And, he bemoans the status of children of
   the poor who, he claims, were given up by their mothers and mulatto women,
   some of whom "sold" them to Portuguese men at the age of thirteen or fourteen

(46). He also claims that "one of the saddest features of the colony is the condition of the children of the poor" who he further claims "evinced a spirit of 'lawlessness' and impatience of control, a thirst for independence and license which bodes ill for their future and future of the colony. The boys are idle and dissolute, the girls dirty, foulmouthed, and dishonest. At an age so early as to be almost incredible, many of the former become thieves, and the latter prostitutes" (46).

Taken with a pound of colonial sugar, these types of comments, nonetheless, direct our attention to the complexities of a social order in which African men and women made the transition to male-good-provider, female-the-nurturer gender stereotypes.

2. Many of these features associated with representations of control, equality, or agency were common in English and Dutch wedding rituals of the period, thus one cannot automatically assume that they are symbolic representations specifically developed among the African freed population. Nonetheless, the attention they received in the ritual and the remarks upon them by observers suggest that the symbolism was actively engaged rather than passively adopted.

3. It is, I am arguing here as I have elsewhere (Williams 1983, 1991), the manner in which elements of these sets of precepts are integrated, within and across everyday activities, that constitute the social order within which individuals, male and female, move. By contrast, Wilson (1973) argues that there are two principles—reputation and respectability—that order social life in English-speaking Caribbean societies. Although he indicates that his description of these principles and the order they regulate is intended as a model that is, of course, not the same thing as social life itself, he contends that it is reasonable to suggest that "reputation is largely specific to men, while respectability is most particular to women and concerns men only at certain times of their lives, or only certain men in the society. This, in turn, raises the point that there is, at a certain level, a clear distinction to be drawn between the structure of social life for men and for women, a distinction that is reflected in day-to-day life and activity." (9) And that, "reputation has its roots in the external colonizing (or quasi-colonizing) society, though in any given instance its reality depends on the integral role of the colonizing society in the social system of the colony (or quasi-colony) and is *both* an authentic structural principle and a counterprinciple. (9) In the construction of gender, race, and class, what I am referring to as the precepts of egalitarianism and hierarchy have different implications for men and women but they are simultaneously relevant throughout the lives of both men and women. They become especially problematic, as I hope to show, in the construction of domesticity, not because one is a female principle and the other a male one, but rather because one orders conceptions of class cooperation and the other of ethnic/racial competition. Both are influenced by the nation-building process and its class- and race-conflated hierarchies that pits presumed ethno-racial cultural practices against a stereotyped construction of middle-class bourgeois respectability.

4. *Mati* essentially defines those presumed to share equal social status and poverty. "Ties between such persons, rooted in their shared equality of opportunity, resulted in expectations of amity, cooperation, and solidarity with *mati* as members of a close-knit social group within which minor material differences were considered to

result from luck rather than from any ascribed or achieved superiority" (Williams 1991: 94–95).

5. Geertz, (1973) following P. Sorokin, distinguishes logico-meaningful integration from causal-functional integration. In logico-meaningful integration one has a unity of style, whereas in causal-functional integration one has unity of parts such that each is "an element in a reverberating causal ring which 'keeps the system going'" (145).

6. Evidence for the following discussion of gender and domesticity is based on data initially collected in 1977 and 1979–1980 when sixty-three life history interviews focused on marriage, and male-female relations in households were conducted with couples. Thirty-eight of these couples were composed of persons who self-identified as African descent Guyanese. They ranged in age from early teens to mid-seventies. Length of time married before the interview ranged from three months to 34 years. Additional life history and observation data were collected on eight couples (selected as representative of the ethno-racial and religious composition of the community), and their families through visitations (at least three times per week, many weeks daily contacts of 1–2 hours were maintained), casual conversations, and semi-formal follow-up interviews to more directly questioned descriptions, comments causally given, or assumptions based on impressions from observation were conducted periodically. These forms of data were supplemented by hanging out in the community, talking with individuals during occasional trips to movies or restaurants in Georgetown with single females or with young women and their spouses. Over the two field periods I attended 28 weddings, ten of which were between individuals at least one of which self-identified as being of African descent. Couples were informally interviewed numerous times before and after the weddings. In the intervening years, for some of the couples, (especially those who later moved to the United States) contact was periodically maintained by telephone, letters, or personal contacts, providing a longitudinal sense of how they negotiated various aspects of their relationship through good times, struggles, a few separations and, two divorces. My focus here is on the Afro-Guyanese couples, however, and despite my references to Guyana in general my conclusions are drawn from Demerara and are deemed most appropriate to Afro-Guyanese life in that region of Guyana.

7. Here, we would be on solid intellectual ground to equate what I am referring to among Cockalorums as a pragmatic trigger to North American scholars' discussions of the role and selection of the male-the-good-provider. (See, for example, Bernard 1983 and Pierce and Williams, this volume.)

8. In this sense, to eye-pass *mati* means to show utter contempt or careless disregard for his or her self-ascribed status relative to the status he or she ascribes to the one who commits the offense (see Jayawardena 1963, Williams 1991).

9. Bush affair refers to clandestine meetings in out of the way places, sometimes, though not always, for illicit purposes. It also harks to the symbolism of geographical space labels, according to which the interior regions of Guyana and the spaces external to the village communities, relative to the urban areas, are defined as bush and are associated with a wildness and an absence of civility that is "catching" if one is too long exposed to it. Once "caught," such reversions to wildness may socially contaminate those around the infected party. The nature versus civilization-domi-

nated spaces is here historically grafted onto more general notions of the status geography of space.

10. In some senses, this is a fine point of morality that may as much serve to distinguish pragmatic consequences from ideological precepts as it does to distinguish the masculine from the feminine. From the standpoint of either set of ideological precepts, neither men nor women are immoral because they are promiscuous, but rather because of the pragmatic consequences of their behavior for the construction of egalitarian aspects of humanity and for hierarchical aspects of ambition. From the standpoint of racio-ethnic competition, these pragmatics form the structure within which successful efforts at economic accumulation launch individuals and, in the long-run, families (names) into the middle-class status and, thus, the vectors of the ideological field are intersected in these consequences.

11. See Williams 1991, chapters 5–7 for a detailed discussion of the stereotyping process in Guyanese culture history.

12. My use of interior and exterior is partially informed by S. Barnett's use of this distinction in his definition of an ideological field. Barnett states:

> [A]t the same time a person is interior to an ideology, he is exterior to other ideologies (sex, class, race, kin, etc.) in the same society (all such ideologies constituting an ideological field). These exterior ideologies are at least partially understandable (sharing global symbols common to the whole society) but do not provide a direct frame for action. Placement (interior vs. exterior) is therefore critical and moves praxis to the center of the analytical stage (1977: 276).

13. See note 6 for a description of the database. Here I am providing only one case and, therefore, only one cut into and across the life cycle. A fuller description must await a genuine ethnography of domesticity from a much richer database than I have available at this time.

References

Barnett, Steve. 1977. "Identity Choice and Caste Ideology in Contemporary South India." In *Symbolic Anthropology: A Reader in the Study of Symbols and Meanings,* edited by Janet Dolgin, David Keminitzer, and David Schneider. Pp. 270–91. Chicago: University of Chicago Press.

Bartel, Dennis. 1977. "Class Conflict and Racist Ideology in the Formulation of Modern Guyanese Society." *Western Canadian Journal of Anthropology* 4(1): 73–81.

Basow, Susan. 1986. *Gender Stereotypes: Traditions and Alternatives.* Monterey: Brooks/Cole.

Bernard, Jessie. 1983. "The Good-Provider Role: Its Rise and Fall." In *Face to Face: Fathers, Mothers, Masters, Monsters—Essays for a Nonsexist Future,* edited by Meg McGavran Murray. Pp. 145–67. Westport, CT & London, England: Greenwood Press.

Clatterbaugh, Kenneth. 1990. *Contemporary Perspectives on Masculinity: Men, Women, and Politics in Modern Society.* Boulder, San Francisco, Oxford: Westview Press.

Craib, Ian. 1987. "Masculinity and Male Dominance." *Sociological Review* 35(4): 721–43.

Demos, John. 1974. "The American Family in Past Time." *The American Scholar* 43: 422–46.

Di Stefano, Christine. 1991. "Who the Heck Are We: Theoretical Turns Against Gender." *Frontiers: A Journal of Women Studies* Vol. XII (2): 86–108.

Dunn, James. (n.d.). *Glints of Guyana.* Georgetown: Royal Agriculture and Commercial Society.

Epstein, Barbara Leslie. 1981. *The Politics of Domesticity: Women, Evangelism and Temperance in Nineteenth-Century America.* Middletown: Wesleyan University Press.

Geertz, Clifford. 1972. "Deep Play: Notes on the Balinese Cockfight," in *Myth, Symbol and Culture,* edited by Clifford Geertz. Pp. 1–38. New York: W. W. Norton.

————. 1973. *The Interpretation of Cultures: Selected Essay by Clifford Geertz.* New York: Basic Books, Inc., Publishers.

Kirke, H. 1898. *Twenty-five Years in British Guiana.* London: Sampsonhow, Marston & Co.

Managan, J. A. and James Walvin, eds. 1987. *Manliness and Morality: Middle-Class Masculinity in Britain and America, 1800–1940.* Manchester: Manchester University Press.

May, Larry and Robert Strikwerda, eds., with the assistance of Patrick D. Hopkins. 1992. *Rethinking Masculinity: Philosophical Explorations in Light of Feminism.* Lanham, MD: Littlefield Adams.

Melosh, Barbara, ed. 1993. *Gender and American History Since 1890.* London and New York: Routledge.

Rodney, Walter. 1981. *A History of the Guyanese Working People: 1881–1905.* Baltimore: Johns Hopkins University Press.

Roper, Michael and John Tosh, eds. 1991. *Manful Assertions: Masculinities Since 1800.* London and New York: Routledge.

Schomburgk, Richard. 1922 [1847]. *Travels in Guiana.* Leipzig: J. J. Weber Vol. 1 Georgetown: Daily Chronicle Ltd.

Smith, Raymond T. 1988. *Kinship and Class in the West Indies: A Genealogical Study of Jamaica and Guyana.* Cambridge: Cambridge University Press.

Wagner, Michael J. 1977. "Rum, Policy, and the Portuguese: Or, the Maintenance of Elite Supremacy in Post-Emancipation British Guyana." *Canadian Review of Sociology and Anthropology* 14(4): 406–16.

Welter, Barbara. 1966. "The Cult of True Womanhood: 1820–1860." *American Quarterly* XVIII (2) Pt. 1: 151–74.

Williams, Brackette F. 1983. *Cockalorums in Search of Cockaigne: Status Competition, Ritual and Social Interaction in a Rural Guyanese Community.* Ph.D. diss. Baltimore: Johns Hopkins University.

————. 1991. *Stains on My Name, War in My Veins: Guyana and the Politics of Cultural Struggle.* Durham and London: Duke University Press.

Wilson, Peter. 1973. *Crab Antics: The Social Anthropology of English-Speaking Negro Societies of the Caribbean.* New Haven: Yale University Press.

Part II

"Wombs" of Nationalist Respectability and the Problem of Patri-Racial Redemption

6

"Feminism, the Murderer of Mothers"

The Rise and Fall of Neo-nationalist Reconstruction of Gender in Hungary

Éva V. Huseby-Darvas

"The ideal situation would be if from now on all women could stay home as Hungarian mothers should, and if men could, once again, earn enough to support their family." This comment was made to me in the summer of 1991 on the outskirts of Budapest by a 43-year-old worker, a father of three. The statement summarizes public and political attitudes that called for the return to traditional gender roles during the first half of the 1990s in Hungary (Adamik 1993; Béres 1991; Gál 1994; Goven 1993; Verdery 1994; Tóth 1993). A categorical emphasis on a conservative stance toward women was among the many manifestations of radical change in Hungary following the end of four decades of a socialist regime.[1] In the transition there appeared a desperate struggle to recapture a time that perhaps never was, when men were strong and women were beautiful, or rather, a time when men were powerful and women "knew and kept in their place."

Indeed, in the entire former Soviet bloc, following the revolutions of 1989, the trend was, as Gábor Gyáni (1993: 893–913) notes, the "turning back to a past, a very often mythologized form of the past."[2] While discussing the more general forms of this trend along with the political use and abuse of a "return to tradition," Gyáni also comments that "turning away from the recent past as an abnormality or even a kind of aberration and the increasing antipathy to its domestic opponents further increases the importance given to the more distant and dim past. This latter past seems to provide more favorable prospects for idealization, for the creation of a historical self-image that is free of critical reflections" (1993: 893–913).

This essay examines historical images of women in general and motherhood in particular. The focus of the work is on viewing these images through a contemporary lens, more specifically how they fit in the neo-nationalist reconstruction of highly idealized gender roles between the Hungarian elections of 1990 and 1994. In that period a conservative, nationalist, and, as time passed, increasingly right-of-center government was in power. The new regime was accompanied by an ethos whose "Trinity of Leitmotifs"—(1) the folk-national; (2) the Christian course; and (3) the healthy fertility of our own, i.e., selective pronatalism— embraced the issue of motherhood, with a spotlight on the high rate of abortion and the dismally low national fertility rate. There were attacks directed at feminists, "murderers of mothers," and, relatedly, at women's rights to choose abortion. The abortion issue became the major political controversy—in a country with reasonably liberal abortion policies since 1956 (Adamik 1993; Gál 1994; Szalai 1991). Abortion was not outlawed, although, in 1991, a fledgling, but highly vocal pro-life group brought before the Alkotmánybíróság (the Hungarian Constitutional Court), a demand that abortion laws be proclaimed unconstitutional (Adamik 1993: 208).

> Fertility is a very private area of human life. The same goes for the nation. Its bedroom secrets are among the most sensitive issues it faces and they are hardly ever approached dispassionately. Ethnic composition, continued demographic domination of a region, forecasts for future trends are questions apt to rouse both passions and collective anxiety. (Ildikó Vásáry 1989: 431)

A special issue of the most popular Hungarian women's journal, the *Magyar Nôk Lapja* (1990: 2: 2–47) was devoted to "Expecting a Child," and included articles entitled, "Invocation for a Child," "The Blessed Peace of Birth," "Coveted Motherhood," and "From Women to Goddesses." Immediately after she declared that Hungarian women should have a choice to work or not, Zsuzsanna Benczur, leader of the Women's Democratic Forum, said:

> That is why we emphasize their role as mothers [sic]. We are not feminists. We stress traditional values for women and their role in the family. We uphold women's sentiments of goodness, tolerance and a willingness to respond to children and their husbands." (quoted in Erlich 1990: 29)

Women's Issues: A Neglected Focus and the "Mother-cult"

Scholarship during the period under discussion reflects a similar trend: When looking at a volume of projected future studies (Gáthy 1990), containing nearly

30 research proposals by leading Hungarian social scientists, I noticed it included none that focused on or dealt with or even specifically expressed an interest in the situation of women in the 1990s. There were, among other themes, research proposed on the very important issues of Hungary's elderly population, on social work, on concepts of justice, on ecological damage, on agrarian systems, on the housing system, and so forth, but none on women's quandaries in post-socialism. In the particular nationalistic political spirit that prevailed in Hungary between 1990 and 1994 there appeared to be little, if any, support for those who may have ventured to undertake such a study—considerably less support than there was in the late 1970s and early 1980s when, for example, H. Sas (1984) conducted her study. A handful of Western students of Hungarian society have focused on the plight of Hungarian women in the post-1989 era. Here Chris Corrin, Susan Gál, Joanna Goven, Lynne Haney, and my own work come immediately to mind. However, a few publications, primarily supported by the George Soros Foundation, did appear in Hungary; the bulk of these were published at the very end of, or since the 1990–1994 period that is the focus of the present work (for example, Acsády 1994; Adamik 1994; Bollobás 1993; Fodor 1994; Koncz 1994a and 1994b; Szalay 1991; Tóth 1993 and 1994; and Neményi 1994a, and 1994b, who compellingly asks: *"Miért nincs Magyarországon nômozgalom?* [Why aren't there women's movements in Hungary?]"). In fact, there are over 20 registered women's organizations in Hungary, but none—save the Feminist Network—really deal with the obviously troubling gender issues, and even the few women who were active in politics, claim that women's issues are not political issues. Horváth's (1992) fascinating study, though its compelling title includes "women's lot in a Budapest workers' district," actually focuses more on poverty, migration, family dilemmas, and the Romaness (or the Gypsy identity) of some of the 30 women interviewees than on particular gender-specific issues. Thus, whereas the situation of women per se was decidedly not an issue that commanded much attention in Hungarian scholarly circles, one study during this period argued that family and motherhood must, once again, retrieve their true status in the Hungarian system of social values.[3]

Since the writings of the young literati of the Hungarian Reform Period in the early nineteenth century, the crucial centrality of the mother, and the mother-son relationship has been both idealized and deemed "typically Hungarian." Authors often contend that "Hungarian [sons] love their mothers more than [do] the sons of other nations" (Szerb 1934: 402). Very rarely has this stance been critiqued. A notable exception was the well-known Hungarian essayist-humorist-philosopher, Frigyes Karinthy, who dared to take issue with this sanctimonious image of the mother. In a serious essay, he wrote:

> I have great difficulties with [our] mother-cult, applied in such a theatrical and sentimental fashion. Throughout my life I felt that it is indecent in conversation, even in poetry when the word "anyám" [my mother] is uttered with such

emphasis and in quotes. The manner in which the word is pronounced, with quivering voice, I find artificial and dishonest. (Karinthy 1983: 235)

The mother was, and is, hailed as the very core of national identity, the perpetuator of a culture that is somehow untouched by foreign influence and thus "incontrovertibly Hungarian." Intriguingly this highly idealized mother-image persists, carried almost to the point of mother-worship—notwithstanding the disparity between the ideal and the everyday life of the majority of Hungarian mothers.

Hungarian nationalism's ideological constructs long ago specified that womanhood ranked below manhood.[4] The relationship between women and men, however, was not imagined completely in terms of hierarchical subordination. Rather, there was a particular kind of asymmetry in which women were consigned to be the supplementary counterparts of men and given the "noble assignment" to help and care for men. As Fél and Hofer (1969: 113) show, these divisions were clearly permeating traditional Hungarian peasant culture too, but in a definite hierarchy. Men were considered the head of the family, women the heart.

The position of each member of the family is defined by his [sic] sex and age. Men consider themselves superior to women: "Woman is merely the helper of man, man is always the first. As we know, man is the masterpiece of creation. . . . We feel ourselves above the women." . . . "Woman is of less value than man; they cannot even be compared" . . . Even in begetting children the role of the male is considered the more important, [as one informant said] "this is but natural." (Fél and Hofer 1969: 113)

Consistent with this view of nature and gender, in the nationalist concept, women, as nurturers and assistants, were to remain in the background, decidedly in the shadows of men and, yet, rather miraculously, to emerge from there and provide help in cases of emergency. For example, Hungarian nationalism, trying to anchor the roots of the nation in the past, focused on selected women heroes, such as Dorottya Kanizsai, who were to bury the fallen heroes on the battlefield of Mohács where Medieval Hungary was defeated by the Ottomans in 1526. Takáts notes that "after our nation's tragedy at the battlefield of Mohács, Dorottya Kanizsai, who was "merely a weak woman but who had moral courage and respect and love for her nation," accomplished what no men and no powers could achieve because "her heart was intense with selflessness and humanity and homage for the heroes who have fallen for her beloved homeland" (1982: 46). Kanizsai's figure was reinvented in nineteenth-century paintings and romantic novels aiming to indoctrinate younger generations of Hungarian women; to ready them for sacrifice in the period of "national awakenings."[5]

Heroic Women, Motherhood, and Male Agency

Another enduring heroic image of women was that of the group of women of Eger who were fighting with their bare hands against the Ottoman warriors attacking the Bastion of that city. According to the story of the heroines of Eger, which was also intensively perpetuated in the age of emerging nationalism in the nineteenth century, these women bravely fought for the bastion when no men were left to fight. The women were the last ones to die for the freedom of the nation, following the death of their fathers, husbands, and sons. Here again the motive of sacrifice stands as a contributing factor in Hungarian women's respectability (Mosse 1985).

National character is often assumed to be prone to be irrational and hopeless just before the end of a struggle, when the doom of defeat cannot be avoided. The association between hopelessness and women's sacrifice underlined, on the one hand, the stereotype of female irrationality and linked, on the other hand, this allegedly female attribute with Hungarian national character. Various "self- and other-" definitions of Magyars throughout the past few centuries show certain recurrent characterizations. From the early 1700s we have the example of the *Völkertafle,* illustrated character maps with descriptions of the various European peoples, that were usually hung in inns, markets, and other public places on trade routes. These national character maps were created by and for Germans, and they functioned as a guide to German-speakers as to how to recognize a member of a particular nationality group, what to expect from them, and how to treat these strangers.

The characterization of Magyars was not particularly flattering: Magyars were described as faithless traitors, wolf-like in their cruelty and blood-thirstiness, whose favorite activity was being revolting revolutionaries. Moreover, Magyars were declared extremely limited intellectually, but very colorful dressers. They were described as lazy and sloppy in their religious worship. They had plenty of fruit and gold in their land; those they disliked they considered their masters, and they died by the sword (cited in Vörös 1987: 17). Some of these descriptions found their way into often cited and influential studies by twentieth-century Western historians and other scholars. For instance, during the inter-war period, C. A. Macartney (1934: 113) summed up the "peculiar war-like character of the Magyars" as "fiery warrior people, intensely proud, impetuous and always inclining toward extremes. . . . [E]ven today this psychological factor remains one of the first importance."

Not surprisingly, the self-stereotyping is considerably more flattering. As Hofer (1991: 159–60) muses when writing about the nineteenth-century Hungarian "construction of the 'folk cultural heritage,'" when the Hungarians worked out their modern national identity, they wanted to be most of all different from the Austrians. In these stereotypes the typical Magyar was depicted (for example, in one inter-war period publication, Révai's Lexikon 1936: Vol. 13: 186) as a person of "beautiful posture, calm, with a regal walk, strong, dexterous, with noble pride and courage, honest, open, warm hearted, with limitless hospitality, and burning love for the homeland. Granted, Magyars are often hot-headed and hot-blooded, and they love and hate in extremes, [though] never in a sneaky, sly, underhanded manner, but openly and with evident honor. Actually, a certain seriousness, sorrow, a deep national sadness are typical for real Magyars, but their emotions vacillate: *sirva vigad a Magyar* [Hungarians cry while having fun]."

Again, some of these descriptions can be found in recent surveys about self-stereotyping. Lendvay (1989) shows for example, that Hungarians mentioned most frequently the feature of traditional Magyar hospitality as typical: national pride and love of homeland, "hot-head" along with the "typical Hungarian volatile temperament," hard-working, but fun-loving and "big spenders." In contrast to earlier self-definitions, however, by the late 1980s the very positive self-descriptions became less self-assured, more uncertain. For instance, in contrast to an earlier survey in which 36 percent of the respondents said Hungarians should be ashamed of something (the focus of shame was past oriented: the Horthy regime during the inter-war period, the country's role during the Second World War, the Arrowcross Party—i.e., the Hungarian ultra-rightist national socialist party). But by the late 1980s, 61 percent of the adults found something that Hungarians should be ashamed of which focused on current national problems, such as the exorbitant amount of money borrowed from and owed to the West, alcoholism, high divorce rate, suicide, or the dire state of the national economy.

In the context of these self- and other-stereotypes, the role of women in Hungarian national imagery serves to save the face of Hungarian men while, simultaneously, at least to some degree, protecting the nation from the much-feared danger, extinction. As Hofer (1991: 158) comments, the

> feeling of being alone was richly elaborated in conceptions of history and was often paired with a vision of "national death"—other, younger nations would take the place of the Hungarians, the Hungarian nation would disappear. These negative visions of the future were patterned, in part on the Polish case, their defeated battles of liberation, the divisions of Poland.

Indeed, the Polish were seen in a very gloomy light as we can see in the nineteenth-century publication *Honderû*,

> [Hungarians] look upon the Poles as their beloved lost sibling whose fate is a foreboding sign: "in the neighboring [country] a nation was lost, upon whose memorial a single heartbreaking word is written: "'was.'" Poland's 22 million residents ceased to be a nation. Poland exists no longer! (quoted in Mátay 1994: 64)

Women can take to the stage in these times of crisis, and their task is to try to stop the avalanche of *balsors* (misfortune), which is the central cause of historical change in Hungarian's self-justifying cognitive system (Csepeli 1989). Most important is the fact that a Hungarian heroine not act alone. First, she should act only as a last resort, when everything is lost, when there are no more heroes in sight, and then only as a subordinate in association with men, who are heroic sons, husbands, fathers, and (in rare cases) lovers. Nonetheless, there are many opportunities for heroines to act because, in the Hungarian construction of history, the hero almost always dies as the result of his heroism long before the never-ending battle for the nation is finally won. In these terms, the Hungarian case well fits Rubin's notions about the functions of martyrdom:

> martyrdom justifies one's own hardships, constriction, and emulated self-sacrifice. Keeping martyrdom of the leader alive in the forefront of awareness is all-important. It has a unifying, binding effect and sustains the power and glory of the group leaders. Carried to the ultimate, in some cultures the king is killed, martyred, and thus each king accumulates the glory and respect of his predecessor. (1990: 90–91)

Motherhood was another aspect of womanhood carefully utilized in nationalist imagery in Hungary. In the nineteenth century a powerful creation myth was reinvented showing again that being a Hungarian woman had much to do with heroism but only in the context of service to the national community, conceived as an organic, ethnically endangered entity. Looking for the roots of the Hungarian nation, nineteenth-century romantic-nationalist authors selected the figure of Emese, declaring her the mother of all ethnic Hungarians.

There are various versions of this ancient creation myth. According to one, Emese—whose name means "little mother" in ancient Hungarian, from the words "eme" meaning mother, and the agglutinating "s[e]," meaning little—had sexual intercourse with the Turul Bird. She was impregnated by this totem bird of the Hungarians and gave birth to Álmos, who not only led the Hungarians to the Carpathian Basin but was also the father of Árpád who, as chieftain of the Hungarian tribes, settled with the Magyars in the Carpathian Basin in the late ninth century. Árpád's offspring established the Árpád House Dynasty, which ruled Hungary until its members died out in the fourteenth century. According to another version of the Emese legend, Emese was either asleep when impregnated by the Turul Bird, or she dreamt the Bird landed on her lap while she was already pregnant with Álmos whose name is constructed from the root-word, *álom* (meaning dream). In all versions of the creation myth, Emese's dream included a vision in which fountains sprang from her uterus, giving birth to the first of a heroic tribe that multiplied to rule far away lands (Róheim 1917; Sándor 1977: 688; Szerb 1934).

The Turul has remained part of the Hungarian scene. For example, the Liberty Bridge across the Danube River has four large statues of the Turul, and in front of the Royal Castle of Buda there is another Turul looking down at the inhabitants of the capital city who are not really aware that they can thank the sperm of this huge bird for their existence, for it was Turul who copulated with the brave Emese, the Ur-Mother of all Hungarians. And, on November 29, 1992 the Turul once again made news when, in the northwestern Hungarian city of Tata, a consecration ceremony of a monumental statue of a Turul Bird took place, attended by highly enthusiastic Hungarian skinheads and others.

The related creation myth reinforced the belief in the peculiar role of women in Hungarian national development. It did not emphasize female subordination to males but rather focused on female sacrifice and resourcefulness. Over this pre-Christian layer of Hungarian-motherhood imagery there were Christian representations of the Holy Virgin who had been declared (by Saint Stephen, or István, the first Hungarian king and establisher of the state and who was later anointed) the Defender of all Hungarians and of Hungary. Thus Hungary became *Regnum Marianum,* the kingdom and protectorate of the Virgin Mother. As Katalin Sinkó notes, Saint Stephen

> put his country at Mary's disposal; thus it is Mary's country and Mary is the protector of the Hungarians. The most frequent iconographic scene in baroque representations of Saint István is that of his dedicating the country to Mary. It was directed not only against the Ottomans but also against those among the Protestants who did not exhibit any special respect for Mary. (1994: 12)

Thus, reinvention and sanctification of motherhood in the nineteenth century had roots in a pre-Christian myth of ethnic-community creation as well as in Christian perceptions of sanctity. In Hungarian national ideology, the confluence of these two factors centralized and made crucial the mother image.[6]

In the Age of Reform, writers, contributing to popular journals such as *Életképek* and *Honderû,* added a new dimension to the image of the Hungarian woman. For them, as for others already discussed, she was a supplementary hero and a brave mother whose exceptional motherly powers were seen as a major force in national awakening but their attention to the awakening as a political socialization centered mainly on language (Hungarian: *anyanyelv,* mother tongue). Language became, and remained, an important criterion of Hungarianness within the Carpathian Basin and was frequently used to "objectively" measure ethnicity and national identity. For example, answers to the questions: "What is your mother tongue? What language do you speak at home?" were, in the period between 1867 and 1918, gauges of nationality in Hungary. Moreover, nineteenth-century literature stressed the role of women in what Takáts calls the "struggle for Hungarian [language]" (1982: 350), that was viewed as the shifting from German to Hungarian in the use and maintenance of everyday language. Takáts devotes a chapter, entitled "Our women in the Service of National Ideas," to a discussion of noble women having been instrumental during the first half of the nineteenth century in "saving the mother tongue" (1982: 340–53). In spite of serious danger, he writes, these women shifted to and maintained the use of Hungarian language and national garb. The perpetual danger was the Habsburg secret police who kept files on these "dangerously patriotic women" and accused them of inciting against German language use and Habsburg rule, in both the public and private domains.

In accordance with nationalist education (as well as in language maintenance, the mother images, and female heroism) women were to follow Emese in their primary role as mothers, if not in the strict sexual sense, then in a metaphorical one. They were to breed culturally Hungarian children, mainly sons, but also daughters who in time would fulfill their "natural destiny" by becoming proper Hungarian mothers. Other aspects of female emancipation were also systematically discouraged (Kovács 1994; Mátay 1995). With the exception of the young, urban intelligentsia—a very narrow, privileged stratum—traditional gender imagery was maintained in Hungarian society (Adamik 1993; H. Sas 1984; Denich 1990; Lampland 1990; Jávor 1990; Huseby-Darvas 1990; Goven 1992, 1993; Tóth 1993). This romanticized and mystified image, fostered in a patriarchal system, survived the repeated transformation of society from feudal to pre-capitalist, to capitalist, to state socialist, and finally to the current pre-democratic order.

After the Treaty of Trianon, images of the white and virginal, but mutilated and bleeding, body of the beloved motherland, surrounded by four black, severed pieces, were displayed in schools, offices, and public parks (Bárány 1969: 288; Deák 1965: 372). Thus, another very powerful representation of the mother, in the configuration of the motherland, joined its predecessors to express the Hungarian ethos during the years between the First and Second World Wars. It played a crucial and disproportionately major role in the social history of this century (Huseby-Darvas n.d., and 1995: 161–95). The losses from the unjust Treaty were, and remain, devastating in human, material, and psychological terms because 67 percent of the territory of the Hungarian state was annexed to its neighbors along with over 50 percent of its total population—one that included 33.5 percent of the ethnically Hungarian inhabitants. In all, nearly three and a half million people were affected (Király, Pastor, and Sanders 1982). This reality was condensed and reified, distorted and transposed into a sadomasochistic representation, buttressed by captions such as "the savage violation of the 1000-year-old sacred frontier," "the mutilated Carpathian boundary," and "the revered body of the motherland, torn asunder and ravaged by barbarians" (Király, Pastor, and Sanders 1982: 97). As the national symbol, this image was impressed upon the consciousness of millions for a quarter of a century during the interwar period, giving it a tenacious power both to divide and incite, and also to unite and direct.

It incited a particular kind of nationalism, and represented a division of the people of Hungary from their neighbors and from the West. Yet it simultaneously united Hungarians spatially separated, encouraging them along a path of national destruction toward World War Two (Király, Pastor, and Sanders 1982). Elements of this ethos continued to be used and manipulated in the entire region during the socialist period, even if much more tacitly than in the quarter century between the two wars, in a process Elemér Hankiss (1989) calls the "nationalization of socialism." It was partly because of the still burning issues that resulted from the Treaty of Trianon and the West's role in that Treaty that some political factions were able to easily link evil connotations to the very notion of democracy. In this respect, the post-socialist (and, as it turned out during the elections of 1994, also pre-socialist) period between 1990 and 1994, in some circles the notion of democracy became very similar to what it was during the inter-war period, when democracy likewise stood for anti-Hungarian, dishonest, and hypocritical (Kertész 1953).

Women's Role and the "Aborted" Nation

In the post-socialist period (1990–1994), several politicians and scholars invoked similar imagery and related it to the country's low-birth rate and high numbers of abortions. Employing tenets of the American Pro-Life Movement, in 1991, Gábor Jobbágyi brought a request before the Hungarian Constitutional Court to protect the unborn.[7] Jobbágyi (1991), who teaches constitutional law at Miskolc University, linked the Treaty-mutilation imagery to the request for protection when he described the 35 years after 1956 (the year when abortion was legalized) as "Our biological Trianon" and the "Hungarian Holocaust." He campaigned against what he called nonsensical socialist phrases, such as "women's free decision power" and "the fallacies of such notions as 'abortion being part of women's human rights'" (Jobbágyi 1991: 75). Maintaining that behind these phrases are "the murder of [some five million Hungarians who were never allowed to be born]," he also pointed to the "16 months that have gone by since the" new coalition government came to power, as time in which 130,000 more legal abortions were . . . performed." In a similar vein, a leading member of A Magyar Szellemi Védegylet [the Association for the Protection of the Hungarian Values], Béla Sebestyén contended that "we need very drastic measures to stop legal abortions and [thus] return to the normal state of affairs . . . like we had during the interwar period when the Hungarian folk experienced a most wholesome growth" (quoted in Magyar Nemzet, October 5, 1991: 5). Hence, despite evidence that before the legalization of abortion in 1956, 100,000 abortions were performed annually (David and McIntyre 1981: 270), one of the main arguments of the members of this group is that during the period when abortions were illegal, the birth rate was much higher and, by implication, the nation was much healthier.

On December 28, 1990, the Day of Holy Innocents, Hungarian "pro-life groups prayed for the almost five million children who could not be born in the last 35 years because their environment decided there was no room for them" (Béres 1991: 11). On that day, church bells were rang throughout the country for these "Hungarian victims of abortion" (Béres 1991: 11). Then, on the 35th anniversary of the Hungarian Revolution, October 23, 1991, Cardinal László Paskai, in Abasár (County Heves), inaugurated and consecrated the "embryo memorial," a monument dedicated "to those five million Hungarians who were never born." As the Hungarian News Agency reported, the memorial statue, created by sculptor Mihály Lakatos, depicts a glistening embryo, brilliantly radiant like the Sun, made sacrosanct by the iron crosses that surround it."[8]

The abortion debate is embedded in racial overtones, because "as the five million Hungarians who were never born" are mourned, concerns grow over the increasing numbers of Hungarian Roma (Gypsies) who are simultaneously viewed as too fertile. In the context of the relation between gender and nationalism, the Roma are generally characterized by such nationalist politicians and authors as unmanly, effeminate creatures who irresponsibly reproduce, thereby giving birth to a new generation of "their kind." Their high fertility rate, it is argued by those who express this concern, endangers the "valuable gene pool of real Hungarians." István Csurka, author, extreme right-wing politician, and demagogue, has several times mourned the "degradation" of the Hungarian population, complaining both about the high birth rate of the Roma and the high rate of emigration among "real" Hungarians. Such views deepen the cultural and social gap between the Hungarians and what the nationalists claim are the non-Hungarian parts of the population. According to this nationalist-racist discourse, fertility and motherhood are worthwhile attributes only among those who had been selected as valuable transmitters of Hungarian nationhood. Others, in spite of their generations-long Hungarian citizenship, should not be allowed to procreate, because, for the *nem mély magyars* (literally, for the not "deep Hungarians," or not "real Hungarians," to use the parlance of the nationalist politicians and authors), the virtues of motherhood and fertility become vices practiced against the nation.

Some other politicians, explicitly and specifically, blame the dismally low birth rate on feminism and feminists. For instance, one of the founding members and leading politicians of the Hungarian Democratic Forum, Gyula Fekete (at the time, a party associate of István Csurka) condemned feminism and declared that feminists had exchanged motherhood for the comforts of material wealth and the pleasures of *dolce vita*. In the same breath he declares feminists the "murderers of mothers" because, he argued, their "dissemination of feminist tenets are immediately accompanied by the [total] devaluation and abuse of motherhood" (Fekete 1989: 60).

Indignant about these accusations and about "women [being] implicitly . . . held responsible for *nemzethalál* [the death of the nation]," Enikô Bollobás, a feminist, responded to Fekete's charges.

Feminists are not murderers of mothers, they are not the ones who kill fetuses. [Rather, they are] deeply concerned for mothers unknowingly dragged into motherhood, for women whose only way of escaping poverty, prejudice, and shame is by abortion. They are deeply concerned for those women who, locked into the domestic sphere, suffer housewives' neurosis and do not find joy in mothering. . . . Feminists are deeply worried about women brutally battered by their husbands, and about those women who trade with their own bodies, as well as for those men who—if only by their glances—become their business partners. . . . The feminists are, furthermore, concerned about those families where men are absent, and for that economy, science, art, public life and movement where women are not represented. (1989: 52–53).

Such protests notwithstanding, feminists, it is popularly held in Hungary, hate men, yet they want to be like men and take up jobs better suited to men. They refuse to have children, do not consider motherhood important, resist marriage, cannot abide sexual relations with a man, and do not know or care to know how to cook or keep house "like a good woman should" (Haney 1989: 40–43). Feminists, according to the intolerant "man or woman on the street," as Adamik notes, are "women who hate men and children, are sexually voracious, don't wear bras, and above all are very unhappy and are lesbians" (1993: 207).

Considering the small number of feminists in Hungary and the ways in which feminism is treated in the popular, political, and scholarly spheres, it is indeed curious that there is this connection made between the country's low birth rate and what Fekete and others evidently detect as the dangerous onslaught of feminism upon the red-white-and-green (the national colors) Hungarian social fabric. Indeed, while the figures of how many women belong to the Hungarian Feminist Network (HFN) vary, I was told in 1992 that there are just under one hundred women who are the members of and openly identify with the Feminist Network (Adamik 1993: 211 reports that this group, which she helped found in 1990, consists of less than fifty women).[9] In Esély (Chance), a Journal of Society and Social-policy that is edited by Zsuzsa Ferge who is, deservedly, one of the most highly regarded social scientists in Hungary, the HFN published the Declaration of the Network, which gives a brief background of Hungarian women's de facto social situation versus their de jure equality between the 1949 Hungarian Constitution and the end of the socialist period. This is followed by the various goals of the Network, mainly that women, men, children should have equal chance for self-actualization. It is noteworthy that the Declaration has neither a designated author nor signatories.

Whereas the Feminist Network and its declaration would be readily identified elsewhere as a feminist undertaking,[10] there were and are women's organizations that would not be. For example, in 1988 Sarolta Zalatnay, a pop singer of a decidedly faded luster, founded what she elected to call the Hungarian Feminist Party, because, she said, it concerned her that not one of the seventy newly-formed political associations were really by and for women. Her platform included the legalization of

prostitution and bordellos, the creation of exercise classes, make-up and diet courses, and the founding of what she called "pornography houses," the profits from
which all the other "feminist" activities were to be financially supported.

Regardless of the Party's rather debatable platform, it was quite courageous of
Zalatnay to include the word "feminist" in the name of her ambitious, but short-
lived organization. Why? As a member of the Feminist Network, Zsuzsa Béres
succinctly put it, because in Hungary "the word feminism is slander" (1991: 1,
11). Even before the formation of Sarolta Zalatnay's Party in 1988, feminism was
a "word of ill repute" (Béres 1991: 1, 11). As Lynn Haney, who, at the time of her
research, was a graduate student from the University of California at San Diego,
commented,

> in all my interviews, I met only two women who claimed to identify with fem-
> inism. Both were academics and had spent a great deal of time studying and
> traveling in . . . Western Europe. One . . . was very explicit about her beliefs
> and regularly gave public lectures on the subject. . . . During her lectures both
> the women and men in the audience constantly harassed her, calling her names
> and [often] forced her to end her lectures prematurely. . . . She received
> threatening phone calls on a regular basis. On the street, people often bom-
> barded her with derogatory remarks and even, on occasion, physical assaults.
> Her "womanhood" and sexuality was constantly called into question even by
> people she did not know. [University students and professors told Haney] that
> "this woman was dangerous, stay away from her, she writes things that are
> very dangerous for us." (1989: 42–43)

Haney cites another woman who told her that all the harassment occurs
because

> I call myself a feminist. Because I read Simone de Beauvoir and am affected.
> Because I tell women to look at themselves, at what is happening in our
> world. . . . This alone makes me evil, and a disgrace to the women of
> Hungarian society. (Haney 1989: 43).

Based on Rév's (1987) notions of resistance, Haney interprets the view of feminism in Hungarian society:

> Hungarian women respond most negatively to feminism because they associate
> feminist rhetoric with the Hungarian [socialist] state and by resisting [feminism
> and feminist rhetoric], they indirectly resist the state and the demands the state
> places upon them. . . . Given the fact that the state has often pulled out its
> feminist rhetoric whenever it wanted to do something special, these ideas are
> very understandable. Feminist discourse then is associated with the Hungarian
> state, with an authority which is trying to get women in certain ways. (Haney
> 1989: 51–52)

In a similar manner, Simpson quotes Orsolya Váradi, whom she identifies as "a Hungarian feminist academic," in saying that

> the concept of women's rights was discredited partly because the women in Communist Party positions *"were filling a quota."* They had no real political power. And independent feminists are unknown. They're in a state of waiting for a man. There is a lack of self-respect—but that is matched by no respect for them. (1991: 21)

Reflecting the general attitude, one Hungarian colleague, a thirty-five-year-old woman, was clearly upset with me and the topic when she said:

> Just forget feminism! But even if anyone would try now to focus on women's plight in our society, that individual would not be taken seriously. Really, think of it! Concentrating on women's interest would be a luxury at the present time of economic hardship and general confusion. (Field journal, Summer 1993)

Róza Hódosán, one of the few women active in Hungarian politics between 1990 and 1994, recalled the futility of stressing women-related issues during the 1990 elections: as if these were insignificant, non-issues, about which nobody cared or paid attention. In interviews Hódosán hastens to add that, although very concerned about women's lot, she is not a feminist (cited in Erlich 1990: 29). Olga Tóth (1993: 213–23) asks Western-feminist colleagues for "No Envy, No Pity" in an angry, powerful and moving essay by that title. She argues—certainly not without foundation—that "Western feminists have distorted the situation of women in Eastern and Central Europe." In her conclusion she, however implicitly, rejects feminist tenets by stating:

> Not to be envied, not to be pitied, [p]eople adapt to the societies in which they live. Hungarian women's lives . . . are certainly more difficult than those of our Western counterparts. We live not only in a poorer country, but in one with a different social and historical background, and different cultural traditions. We would like to have a better, more peaceful life without losing what we have already achieved.

Masculine Fear and *Férfias Nôk* Contamination

Overall, the antifeminist attitude in Hungary stems from at least four motives. First, it is the legacy of state socialism.[11] While it is true that official socialist ideology was replete with rhetoric about women's emancipation, the underlying logic was far from being identifiable as feminist. Women's emancipation as the practice of female forced labor resulted in women realizing that they were being utilized as a substitute work force in socialist production. Through experience they also learned that even when women performed intellectual work, for example, as physicians, teachers, and judges, they were paid considerably less than their male counterparts, and generally excluded from top management positions. Moreover, as Goven succinctly puts it, there is

> [m]isogynistic and explicitly anti-feminist discourse resulting from the particular conditions of state socialism. . . . Women are portrayed not as victims of state sponsored "emancipation" that overburdened them but rather as powerful agents who have responded to state emancipation by becoming destructive to men and children. (1993: 225)

Second, with the transition to a market economy, unemployment hit the Hungarian work force with an intensity that had been unprecedented for nearly half a century. The first to be dismissed were women, next were Roma workers, regardless of their gender. This reinforced the conservative stance on professional motherhood, reinstating the power of the nationalist metaphysics of the nineteenth century while serving as an ideological remedy for the frustrating economic effects of the post-1989 transition.

Third, even under state socialism, working women never were represented as independent actors who were the equal of men. Instead, as previously noted, they were heroines who sacrificed, and who were expected to perform several roles simultaneously (Borbély 1983; Goven 1992, 1993; Lampland 1990). They were to be working women, building socialism; women working at home (doing all the chores including washing, ironing, sewing, cleaning, and shopping for the family), parents, and desirable sexual mates to their husbands. In mass culture, heroic aspects of this kind of womanhood was stressed, demonstrating the excellence of socialist women in all spheres: the public sphere and its work places, and the private sphere with its kitchens, nurseries, and bedrooms.

While men continued to believe in and to act out their dominating role in the family, they also realized that their working wives were gradually discovering the external world and becoming increasingly independent. Although, in many cases this process was viewed by the women themselves as cumbersome, it exacerbated a far-reaching consequential resentment among men who came to realize that the traditional grounds of their existence had been lost. Their response, a fourth motive for an antifeminist stance, was to resort to anti-feminism as an expression of their fears, uncertainties, and the sexual dangers of gender role changes.

In this atmosphere, the growing concern among men about homosexuality in Hungary must be noted: the prospect of sexual equality and the emergence of existentially independent women elicited fear among men because they felt that this process would lead to their own effeminization. They had failed to redefine their own roles and adjust themselves to changing realities and, hence, responded with anti-feminism and anti-gay sentiments. At the same time that there are officially recognized organizations for male homosexuals (and also for divorced men), there are no such formal associations for their female counterparts (Adamik 1993). Instead, public discussions continue regarding the "loss of femininity" among Hungarian women. There is fear of and resentment toward what is perceived as *férfias nôk* (mannish women) and *fius lányok* (boyish girls). And, in Hungary, as Goven suggests, there is "a discourse of antifeminism that blames women for social disorder" (1993: 226). For example, Dávid Bíró (1992), among others, blames women for male loss of confidence, alcohol problems, and the high rate and early occurrence of death among men, whereas sociologist Miklós Hernádi blames most social ills, in general, and men's problems, in particular, on the lack Hungarian women's lack of femininity and their aggressiveness (see Goven 1992 and 1993: 224–40).

It is little wonder that the small constituency (estimated between 50 and 100 members) of the Feminist Network are predominantly from the urban intelligentsia, but, as I was told, very "slowly other strata of society are also beginning to be represented" (Acsády and Bullain 1993: 124). The Network has no money, and it has difficulties in trying to publish a periodical. Thus far it has produced three issues of its periodical, *Nôszemély*. The first, September, 1991, was a run of 1,000 copies and was mimeographed; the second, June, 1992 was increased to 1,500 copies; and the third, April, 1993, ran 2,000 (Acsády and Bullain 1993: 126). With so few volumes published, very little is known about the readership; it is, however, likely that the publications are not widely read, being consumed instead by a select, mostly urban and university-educated, clientele.

It is no less revealing of the stereotype formed about feminists, that one of the many typical outbursts against the group was that "whether they call themselves feminists or not, they look exactly like housewives," as a Hungarian social scientist commented to me. Ironically, while it appears that both men and women are explicitly antifeminist, and buy into a romanticized vision of society and traditional gender roles, the abortion issue brought a backlash among women. It certainly looked as if it had the power to bring women from various factions together. In response to the "Petition for Embryo Protection" that was submitted to the Constitutional Court by a woman identifying herself as "Dr. Gábor Jobbágyi's wife," a committee of the Feminist Network delivered a counter petition containing some 7000 signatures in which they demanded the continuation of legalized abortion in the country. In addition, also in response to Mrs. Jobbágyi's petition, 46 women, leading social scientists among them, submitted a counter petition to the Constitutional Court, demanding the status quo until better birth control is available to Hungarian women.

A number of opinion polls support a conclusion that these signatories actually represent the majority of women, meaning that women in the general population reject pronatalism. According to one public-opinion survey (courtesy of Eszter Bornemisza), 85 percent of the sample wanted abortion laws left alone. Another poll, designed and conducted by Mária Vásárhelyi, showed that the majority of the Hungarian women respondents did not want radical interference with the abortion laws, but wanted them left as they were (Adamik 1993; Gál 1994; Kis 1992; Szalai 1991; Tóth 1993). Moreover, on this issue there was, and remains, a convergence between otherwise opposing and antagonistic women's groups such as that between the Feminist Network and the Association of Hungarian Women. This Association is the official successor of the old Communist Women's Council, and as such several years after the changeover of political regimes still uses a villa on Andrássy Street it was permitted to occupy during the socialist period. I was told that, except on the abortion issue, members of this Association reject contacts, but on this issue they urge solidarity and cooperation with members of the Network. According to Judit Torma, president of the Association of Hungarian Women, "abortion is not a pleasure, it is not something anyone yearns for," but "a woman must have the right to get the help she needs. Without the right to abortion, women are slaves" (cited in *Magyar Nemzet,* October 5, 1991: 7).

Conclusion

Although I subtitled this essay "The Rise and Fall of Neo-nationalist Reconstruction of Gender in Hungary," I do not believe the issues are settled or that the battle ended with the elections of 1994. Pronatalists, pro-life conservatives, Christians, and other nationalists did not gain political momentum (conservatism of any sort has been defeated in 1994 and, unlike in Poland, the abortion laws remained essentially unchanged in Hungary), nonetheless, the underlying controversies discussed here remain very active. With the number of poor increasing, a relatively high and increasing unemployment rate, intense competition within the work force, and reductions in welfare services that were typical of the pre-1989 state socialism, there are no guarantees that amid such social frustration and hopelessness a turn to false, but easily credited, ethno-nationalist dogma and, with it, a blaming of women for most of the nation's ills will not yet occur. Hungary, for example, has a low birth rate, the world's highest suicide and cancer-related death rate, one of the highest mortality rates for middle-aged men, a high rate of divorce—and the list could go on and on.

Feminism, I believe, still has a long time before it will be accepted in the general contemporary Hungarian political consciousness and its people's understanding of nation and society. Of course, it is questionable whether the blustering words about "feminism, murderer of mothers," expressed by Gyula Fekete and the others, really were about the goodness of fertility and motherhood, and the evils of feminism, or whether they were about something else. I believe, and have attempted to show, that one can make a case for the latter. Although there is no doubt that Hungary's birth rate was (and still is) falling, and that the nation's abortion rate was (and remains) alarmingly high,[12] the talk about motherhood and a woman's place served in the period between 1990 and 1994 as a metaphor for deeper ills in Hungary. The charges against feminism and the valorization of motherhood and nation, must be understood in the context of competing and often ambiguous views. On the one hand, there is the outward gaze, looking toward autonomy and reform, while anticipating the so-called "reentrance to the European community of nations." On the other hand, there is a considerable dwelling inward, looking back into a past (whether actual or presumed) that suits the moment, and invokes an ethos with its triple leitmotif of the folk-national, the Christian course, and the healthy fertility and growth of "our own Magyar folk" (i.e., selective pronatalism).

In these times of radical social transformation and severe identity crisis, the cries for pronatalism, and the yearnings for traditional gender roles are very likely responses to a rather desperate search for a new national identity that is viable and at the same time recognizable, legitimate, and decidedly not "tainted" by the recent socialist past. The Hungarian example shows us once again that neo-nationalist sentiment brings revival of an archaic scheme of beliefs that valorize women's fertility and equate reproductive success with the health and survival of the nation. Whereas clearly some feminists are also mothers, and feminists tenets are not the killers of mothers, all feminists, along with feminism as ideology, can be made to stand for an alien idea onto which fears for the nation's survival are projected. The verbal struggle pitting feminism against motherhood uses images of the female body to encapsulate a broader struggle over the body politic, over Hungary's future course, and over the ability of different courses to adequately position the nation (and its men) for power and security in a changing world order.

Notes

For helping with data collection, I am most appreciative for the assistance of my friends and colleagues Eszter Bornemisza, Tamás Hofer, Martha Lampland, Ádám Levendel, and Mária Székelyi. For carefully reading and critically commenting on earlier drafts of this manuscript and for stimulating conversations about nationalism and gender, I am particularly grateful to György Csepeli, as well as to Joe Gaughan, Martha Lampland, Fran Markowitz, and Antal Örkény. Special thanks are due to Gábor Halmai for help with the Hungarian Constitution Court's stance on the abortion issue, and to Eszter Bornemisza and Tamás Hofer for calling to my attention to the statements quoted in the text from the Association of Hungarian Women discussed in relation to their cooperation with the Feminist Network on the abortion issue.

1. I am following Verdery here, and elsewhere when I use "'socialist' to refer to the forms of socialism that we have seen on earth so far, especially in Eastern Europe and the [previous] Soviet Union, not to *possible* organizations we might want to call socialism" (1994: 225).

2. This trend is also demonstrated by most of the contributors in the volume edited by Funk and Mueller, (1993); see also Adamik 1991, 1993; Böröcz and Verdery 1994; Gál 1994; Goven 1993; Tóth 1993; Verdery 1994.

3. See referenced essays in *Férfiuralom, Café Bábel,* and other publications. Very few of these studies appear indigenously motivated, as a matter of fact most were supported by Western organizations, specifically by the Soros Foundation.

4. I am most indebted to György Csepeli for his suggestion with this particular section of the essay.

5. Obviously this is an immensely complex issue. It is discussed in meticulous detail in Lampland's (1994: 287–316) noteworthy study, subtitled "Gendered Images of the Nation in Nineteenth-Century Hungary."

6. "Mother worship" as Preston reminds us, "is neither a simple phenomenon nor one that appears with equal intensity, application, or significance in all cultures or even within cultures" (1983: xvi).

7. Although I have not been able to substantiate it, widely circulating rumor has it that these movements, including Dr. Jobbágyi's, are not only morally but also financially supported by international right-wing groups, and specifically by pro-life groups from the West.

8. Reported by the Hungarian News Agency (Magyar Távirati Iroda, MTI) on electronic mail network, entitled *Hírmondó,* October 26, 1991.

9. There are various versions of the Feminist Network's "creation story." According to one, in the late 1980s Mária Adamik and others of the Sociological Institute of the ELTE [Eötvös Lóránd University in Budapest] advertised a course, "Woman in Society." Flyers advertising the course were posted both outside and inside the walls of the University, and women from the street came to sit in on some of the lectures. Toward the end of the course there were more women from outside than there were students (10 students to approximately 30 to 40 outsiders). Adamik and a number of the participants became convinced that there was a need for an alternative women's group. They considered a number of possible names, but most had been discredited during the socialist era. After considerable dispute about what they should name their organization, they decided on the name Feminist Network. A number of women in the organization are still very uneasy about the "feminist" part of the name. Some of these women worry that it can lead to confusion both within and outside Hungary, while others realize that they will have limited potential to bring in new members because of the way the concept, feminism, is perceived in the country. Even before the Feminist Network was officially registered as a formal group, there was forewarning that soon in Hungary abortion will be declared illegal. The Feminist Network collected thousands of signatures (according to some informants 7000 in all) on a petition demanding that women should vote on the abortion issue. The petition was delivered to the Constitutional Court early November, 1991. The Network inherited a large hall free of rent so even though they had very little money for years they did have a place to meet once a week, on Tuesday evenings: No. 18 Forgács Street, in Ujpest. Judit Acsády (1993: 122–28), a graduate student at the Department of Sociology, ELTE University in Budapest, a

founding member of, and continuously active participant in, the Hungarian Feminist Network, gives only a slightly different version of how the Hungarian Feminist Network was organized in her account of the Network's periodical, *Nôszemély*. What seems to be more important is that to date, *Nôszemély* has been published only three times.

10. Though Acsády (1993) notes that the Network is conservative rather than radical.

11. I have not dealt here with yet another motive: antipolitics. See Goven's studies, in which she proposes that "the roots of antifeminism can be found not only in misguided and coercive state policies but also in the "antipolitics" for which the political opposition in much of Eastern Europe became famous" (1992; 1993: 224).

12. Based on World Health Organization statistics, and taking into consideration Hungary's demographic profile, the annual number of abortions should not exceed 22,000–25,000. In 1988 there were 87,100, in 1989, 91,000, in 1990, 90,400, and in 1991, 90,000 abortions (*Magyar Statisztikai Zsebkönyv* 1992: 17). A very high number of spontaneous miscarriages is, in part, a result of the high number of abortions. Moreover, as in the past, abortions are still used as birth control, because, although the number of sterilizations doubled in the same time period, it is still not widely known that after three children and reaching age 35 sterilization is a legal alternative. As noted in the introduction of this essay, the Hungarian Constitutional Court, in Decision 64 of 1991 (XII.17), wrought the following.

> On the basis of petitions seeking a review of the constitutionality of laws and regulations and the ending of unconstitutional omissions of legislation, the Constitutional Court, with concurring opinions from Antal, Herczegh, Kilényi, Lábady and Zlinszky, JJ., has made the following DECISION: The Constitutional Court holds that non-statutory determination of the rules regulating the termination of pregnancy is unconstitutional. Accordingly, the first sentence of s. 29(4) of Law II of 1972 on Health, according to which "termination of pregnancy is permitted only in circumstances prescribed by law and in the manner set forth by regulations " s. 87(2) of the aforementioned law, as well as MT Decree 76 of 1988 (11/3/88) on the termination of pregnancy, and SZEM Regulation 15 of 1988 (12/15/88) implemented for its execution, are therefore found to be unconstitutional and the Constitutional Court declares them to be null and void as of 31 December 1992.

Petitions calling for the determination of the unconstitutionality of the omission of legislation are dismissed."
(Constitutional text, courtesy of Gábor Halmai).

References

Acsády, Judit and Nilda Bullain. 1993. "A nôi alternatíva. A magyar feministák és a Nôszemély [Women's alternative [publications]. Hungarian feminists and the [publication of] Nôszemély]." *Mozgó Világ,* 12: 122–28.

Adamik, Mária. 1991. "Hungary: A Loss of Rights?" *Feminist Review* 39: 166–70.

————. 1993. "Feminism and Hungary." In *Gender Politics and Post-Communism: Reflections from Eastern Europe and the Former Soviet Union.* Edited by Nanette Funk and Magda Mueller. Pp. 207–12. New York and London: Routledge.

————. 1994. "A Nagy Fehér Üzemmód." In *Férfiuralom. Writings about Women, Men, Feminism,* edited by Miklós Hadas. Pp. 142–54. Budapest: Replika Kör.

Bárány, György. 1969. "Hungary: From Aristocratic to Proletarian Nationalism." In *Nationalism in Eastern Europe,* edited by Peter Sugar and Ivo Lederer. Pp. 259–309. Seattle: University of Washington.

Béres, Zsuzsa. 1991. "Women's Liberation: Words of Ill Repute." *Budapest Week* (March) 1 (2–1,11): 21–27.

Bíró, Dávid. 1992. "A Teremtés Koronái és a Nôk [The Crowns of Creation and Women]." *Valóság* 9: 23–29.

Bollobás, Enikô. 1989. "Feminista Tövisek Fekete Gyulának [Feminist Thorns for a Hungarian Sexist]." *Hitel* (June 21) II (13): 52–53.

————. 1993. "'Totalitarian Lib': The Legacy of Communism for Hungarian Women." In *Gender Politics and Post-Communism: Reflections from Eastern Europe and the Former Soviet Union,* edited by Nanette Funk and Magda Mueller. Pp. 201–206. New York and London: Routledge.

Borbély, Sándor, ed. 1983. *Asszonyaink Arca [The Faces of Our Women].* Budapest: Kossuth.

Böröcz, József and Katherine Verdery. 1994. "Introduction, Gender and Nation." *East European Politics and Societies* 8(2): 223–24.

Corrin, Chris. 1994. *Magyar Women. Hungarian Women's Lives, 1960s–1990s.* New York: St. Martin's Press.

Csepeli, György. 1988. "Negativ Identitás Magyarországon [Negative Identity in Hungary]." *Társadalom Kutatás* IV: 27–38.

————. 1989. *Structures and Contents of Hungarian National Identity. Results of Political Socialization and Cultivation.* Frankfurt, Bern, New York, Paris: Peter Lang.

David, Henry and R. J. McIntyre. 1981. *Reproductive Behavior: Central and Eastern European Experience. Transnational Family Research Institute.* New York: Springer.

Deák, István. 1965. "Hungary." In *The European Right,* edited by H. Rogger and E. Weber. Pp. 364–407. Berkeley: University of California.

Denich, Bette. 1990. "Paradoxes of Gender and Policy in Eastern Europe . . ." *East European Quarterly,* Special Issue on "Gender Contradictions/Gender Transformations: Cases from Eastern Europe," XXIII(4): 499–506.

Diószegi, Vilmos, ed. 1971. *Az ôsi Magyar Hitvilág. Válogatás a Magyar Mitológiával Foglalkozó XVIII. XIX. Századi Mûvekbôl* [Ancient Hungarian Belief System. Selections from Eighteenth- and Nineteenth-century Works]. Budapest: Gondolat.

Erlich, Reese. 1990. "Feminists and the Free Market: As Capitalism Takes Over, East German Women Fight to Keep Social Services and Abortion Rights—but in Hungary, it Seems, No One's a Feminist." *The San Francisco Bay Guardian* (June) 13: 29.

Fekete, Gyula. 1989. "Anyák Napi Köszöntô Tövisekkel (Mothers' Day Greeting with Thorns)." *Hitel* II(9): 60.

Fél, Edit and Tamás Hofer. 1969. *Proper Peasants: Traditional Life in a Hungarian Village.* New York and Budapest: Wenner Gren Foundation for Anthropological Research, Inc. and Corvina Press.

Fodor, Éva. 1993. "The Political Woman? Women in Politics in Hungary. Pp. 171–200 In: *Women in the Politics of Postcommunist Eastern Europe.* Edited by Marilyn Rueschemeyer. New York and London: M. E. Sharpe, Inc.

Foucault, Michel. 1980. *The History of Sexuality, Volume I.* New York: Random House

Gál, Susan. 1994. "Gender in Post-Socialist Transition: The Abortion Debate in Hungary." *East European Politics and Societies* 8(2): 256–86.

Goode, Stephen. 1978. *Cultural Pessimism and Hungarian Society.* Ph.D. Dissertation, Rutgers University, Microfilm and Xerox no. 7910388.

Gáthy, Vera, ed. 1990. *Magyar Jövô? [Hungarian Future? A Sociological Approach].* Budapest: Institute of Sociology, Hungarian Academy of Sciences.

Ginsburg, Faye. 1989. *Contested Lives: The Abortion Debate in an American Community.* Berkeley: University of California.

Girard, A. and L. Roussel. 1982. "Ideal Family Size, Fertility and Population Policy in Western Europe." *Population and Development Review* 2: 323–47.

Goldstein, Laurence, ed. 1990. "The Female Body, Part One," *Michigan Quarterly Review,* a Special Issue, XXIX(4).

Goven, Joanna. 1992. *The Anti-Politics of Anti-Feminism: Gender, State and Civil Society in Hungary, 1949–1992.* Ph.D. Dissertation, Berkeley: University of California.

———. 1993. "Gender Politics in Hungary: Autonomy and Antifeminism." In *Gender Politics and Post-Communism: Reflections from Eastern Europe and the Former Soviet Union,* edited by Nanette Funk and Magda Mueller. Pp. 224–40. New York and London: Routledge.

Gyáni, Gábor. 1993. "Political Uses of Tradition in Post-communist East-Central Europe." *Social Research, special issue: The East Faces the West; the West Faces East* (Winter) 60(4): 893–914.

Hadas, Miklós, ed. 1994. *Férfiuralom. Writings about Women, Men, Feminism.* Budapest: Replika Kör.

Haney, Lynne. 1989. *Privatization and Female Autonomy: The Hungarian Woman's Experience.* Manuscript.

Hankiss, Elemér. 1989. *Kelet Európai Alternatívák [East European Alternatives].* Budapest: Közgazdasági és Jogi Könyvkiadó.

Hatschikjan, Magarditsh. 1991. "Eastern Europe: Nationalist Pandemonium." *Aussenpolitik* 42(3): 211–20.

Horváth, Zsuzsa. 1993. "Magyar Valóság: Nôi Sorsok Budapest Egyik Munkáskerületében [Hungarian Reality: The Lot of Women in a Budapest Workers' District]." *Esély* 5: 39–72.

H. Sas, Judit. 1984. *Nôies Nôk és Férfias Férfiak. . . . [Feminine Women and Masculine Men: the Life, Genesis, and Socialization of Feminine and Masculine Stereotypes.* Budapest: Akadémiai Kiadó.

Huseby-Darvas, Éva V. n.d. "The Hungarian Ethos During the Interwar Period: A Bibliographical Essay." Manuscript.

————. 1987. "Elderly Women in a Hungarian Village: Childlessness, Generativity, and Social Control." *Journal of Cross-Cultural Gerontology* 2: 15–42.

————. 1990. "Migration and Gender: Perspectives from Rural Hungary." *East European Quarterly, Special Issue on "Gender Contradictions/Gender Transformations: Cases from Eastern Europe"* XXIII(4): 487–98.

————. 1995. "The Search for Hungarian National Identity." Pp. 161–96. In *Ethnic Identity: Creation, Conflict, and Accommodation.* Edited by Lola Romanucci-Ross and George DeVos. Walnut Creek, CA: Altamira Press.

Jávor, Kata. 1990. "The Socialization of Boys Versus the Socialization of Girls: Dissimilar Gender Roles in Two Hungarian Villages." *East European Quarterly, Special Issue on "Gender Contradictions/Gender Transformations: Cases from Eastern Europe"* XXIII(4): 409–18.

Jobbágyi, Gábor. 1991. "Magyar Abortusz Ipar? Elhajtott Fejjel (Hungarian Abortion Industry? . . .)." *HVG* (October)5: 74–76.

Kapitány, Gabriella. 1991. "Nôszerep és Munkavállalás: Fajlenntartás (Women's Role and Work: Keeping the Population Down.)" *HVG* (October) 5: 72–74.

Karinthy, Frigyes. 1983. "Anyám [My mother]." Pp. 231–37. In *Gurul a Pénz [The Money Rolls].* Budapest: Móra Könyvkiadó.

Kertész, Stephen. 1953. *Diplomacy in a Whirlpool.* Indiana: Notre Dame.

Király, Béla, Péter Pástor and Iván Sanders, eds. 1981. *War and Society in East Central Europe, Vol IV. Total War and Peacemaking: Essays on the Treaty of Trianon.* New York: Brooklyn College Press.

Kis, János. 1992. *Az Abortuszról: Érvek és Ellenérvek [On Abortion: Arguments and Counter-arguments].* Budapest: Cserépfalvi.

Koncz, Katalin. 1994a. "Comments re. Férfiuralom? Körkérdés a Nôkrôl [Men's Rule? Questions about women]." *Replika* 13, 14: 73–78.

————. 1994b. "Nôk a Rendszerváltás Folyamatában [Women in the Process of Regime-change]." In *Férfiuralom. Writings about Women, Men, Feminism,* edited by Miklós Hadas. Pp. 209–22. Budapest: Replika Kör.

Kovács, M. Mária. 1994a. "A Magyar Feminizmus Korszakfordulója [The aqua Fortis of Hungarian Feminism]. *Café Bábel* 11 (1 and 2): 179–83.

————. 1994b. "The Politics of Emancipation in Hungary." In *Women in History—Women's History: Central and Eastern European Perspectives,* edited by Andrea Petô and Mark Pittaway. Pp. 81–88. CEU History Department, Working Paper Series 1. Budapest: Central European University.

Lampland, Martha. 1990. "Unthinkable Subjects: Women and Labor in Socialist Hungary." *East European Quarterly, Special Issue on "Gender Contradictions/Gender Transformations: Cases from Eastern Europe"* XXIII(4): 389–98.

————. 1994a. "Family Portraits: Gendered Images of the Nation in Nineteenth-Century Hungary." *East European Politics and Societies* 8(2): 287–316.

————. 1994b. "Családi Portrék: Nemi Szerepekben Megfogalmazott Nemzetkoncepciók a Tizenkilencedik Századi Magyarországon [Family Portraits: National Conceptions Gender Roles Defined in Nineteenth-century Hungary." *Café Babel* 11(1 and 2): 119–30.

Lendvay, Judit. 1989. "Magyarországgal és a Magyarokkal Kapcsolatos Nemzeti Sztereotipiák (National Stereotypes related to Hungary and the Hungarians)." *Janus,* Péter Niedermüller, ed. (Published by Janus Pannonius University in Pécs, Hungary) VI. 1: 37–41.

Macartney, C. A. 1934. *National States and National Minorities.* Oxford: Oxford University Press.

Martin, Emily. 1987. *The Woman in the Body: a Cultural Analysis of Reproduction.* Boston: Beacon.

Mosse, George. 1985. *Nationalism and Sexuality: Respectability and Abnormal Sexuality in Modern Europe.* New York: Howard Fertig.

Mátay, Mónika. 1994. "Nemes Nemzetálom Avagy a Reformkori Nyilvánosság Jellegzetességei a Honderû Câmû Divatlap Tükrében [Noble Nation-Dream, or Aspects of Public Life During the Age of Reform as Reflected in the Honderû Journal]." *Jel-Kép* 2: 57–68.

N.A. 1990. "Feminista Hálózat—Alapító Nyilatkozat (Founding Declaration of the Feminist Network). *Esély (Chance)* 90(6): 98–100.

Neményi, Mária. 1994a. "Miért Nincs Magyarországon Nômozgalom? [Why Is There No Women's Organization in Hungary?]." In *Férfiuralom. Writings about Women, Men, Feminism,* edited by Miklós Hadas. Pp. 235–45. Budapest: Replika Kör.

————. 1994b. "A Kötelezô Heteroszexualitástól a Kötelezô Feminizmusig [From Mandatory Heterosexuality to Mandatory Feminism]." *Café Bábel* 11(1 and 2): 163–70.

Petô, Andrea and Mark Pittaway, eds. 1994. *Women in History—Women's History: Central and Eastern European Perspectives.* CEU History Department, Working Paper Series 1. Budapest: Central European University.

Preston, James J. ed. 1983. *Mother Worship: Theme and Variations.* Chapel Hill: University of North Carolina.

Rév, István. 1987. "The Advantages of Being Atomized: How Hungarian Peasants Coped with Collectivization." *Dissent* (Summer) 34: 335–50.

Révai Lexikon [*Révai's Encyclopedia*]. 1936. Volume 13: 186. Budapest: Révai Kiadó.

Róheim, Géza. 1984. (reprinted from the original 1917 publication). "A Kazár Nagyfejedelem és A Turulmonda [. . . and the Turul Myth]." *Ethnográfia.* XXVIII: 58–98, 146–158 In *A Bûvös Tükör: Válogatás Róheim Géza Tanulmányaibol [The Magic Mirror: Selections from the Works of Géza Róheim].* Budapest: Magvetô.

Rubin, Theodore. 1990. *Anti-Semitism: A Disease of the Mind.* New York: Continuum.

Sándor, István. 1977. "Emese." In *Magyar Néprajzi Lexikon I. A–E,* edited by Gyula Ortutay. Budapest: Akadémiai Kiadó.

Simpson, Peggy. 1991. "No Liberation for Women: Eastern Europe Turns Back the Clock." *The Progressive,* (February) 55: 20–24.

Sinkó, Katalin. 1989. "Árpád Versus Saint István: Competing Heroes and Competing Interests in the Figurative Representation of Hungarian History." *Ethnologia Euroapea* XIX: 67–83.

Szalai, Júlia. 1988. "Abortion in Hungary." *Feminist Review* 29: 98–100.

————. 1991. "Some Aspects of the Changing Situation of Women in Hungary." *Signs* 17(1): 152–70.

Szerb, Antal. 1934. *Magyar Irodalom-Történet*. Budapest: Magvető.

Takáts, Sándor. 1982. *Régi Magyar Nagyasszonyok [Hungarian Noble Women Of Yore]*. Budapest: Szépirodalmi.

Tóth, Olga. 1993. "No Envy, No Pity." *Gender Politics and Post-Communism: Reflections from Eastern Europe and the Former Soviet Union,* edited by Nanette Funk and Magda Mueller, Pp. 213–23. New York and London: Routledge.

Vásáry, Ildikó. 1989. "'The Sin of Transdanubia': The One-Child System in Rural Hungary." *Continuity and Change* 4(3): 429–68.

Verdery, Katherine. 1994. From Parent State to Family Patriarchs: Gender and Nation in Contemporary Eastern Europe." *East European Politics and Societies* 8(2): 225–55.

Vörös, Károly. 1987. "Az Európában Található Népek Rövid Leirása." *História* IX(1): 17

Wolchnik, Sharon. 1991. "Women in Eastern Europe." *World and I* 6: 557–67.

7

"And Your Prayers Shall Be Answered Through the Womb of a Woman"

Insurgent Masculine Redemption and the Nation of Islam

Paulette Pierce and Brackette F. Williams

> When you control a man's thinking you do not have to worry about his actions. You do not have to tell him to stand here or go yonder. He will find his "proper place" and will stay in it. You do not need to send him to the back door. He will go without being told. In fact, if there is no back door, he will cut one for his special benefit. His education makes it necessary. (C. G. Woodson [1933] 1977: xiii)

> The code of honour weighs on each agent with the weight of all the agents, and the disenchantment which leads to the progressive unveiling of repressed meanings and functions can only result from a collapse of the social conditions of the *cross-censorship* to which each agent submits with impatience but which he imposes on all other agents. (P. Bourdieu 1977: 196)

Subordinated agency, laboring under the heavy weight of its own and others' tarnished honor, all too often reproduces the miseducation that encourages us to love the blemish and forget the cause of its making. With backs bent and necks crooked to angles that give the visionary advantage to Cyclops and his muse of myopia, within racial identity struggles, gender struggles often seem to do much to cut a back door to domesticity as a form of political consciousness in accordance with which we are asked to both praise and reproduce that greatest of all tyrannies—the seduction and control of the mind.[1]

As women—seeking both to get out of and stay in the place defined by this form of agency, so cogently described by both Carter G. Woodson and Pierre Bourdieu, we ask how we might enter the house without a chauvinist helping hand through the double-revolving back doors of racial and economic tyranny. We ask this boldly but empathetically. Yet we ask it no more boldly and no less sympathetically than we ask how we might dwell there comfortably and constructively without our agency becoming a heavy weight on the shoulders of men as other forms of humanity rather than as subjects of the tyranny of a male and female nature believed manifest in history and projected back on biology.

Although here we will present our quandaries directly through an analysis of the Nation of Islam's views of gender, domesticity, and racial redemption, we do so as an indirect means to address a series of questions critical to an understanding of the interpenetration of race and gender in nation-states and the identity struggles they spawn. Our overriding concern is to reveal the workings of these logics as they are wittingly and unwittingly incorporated, or appropriated wholesale into social movements, by leaders of politically and, hence, culturally, and economically subordinated citizens of the nation-states as these leaders reconfigure gender stereotypes as nature's given in strategies intended to achieve the group's economic transformation and political emancipation.

Every class may have its Jezebels, Miss Anns, Aunt Jemimas, but these ladies travel with class identities that interpellate them as particular configurations of a race, class, and culture conflation (Pease and Pease 1990). Thus, we begin with a discussion of the economic forces that characterized the age of industrialization in the United States, examining this era and labor regime as a source of the historical transformations that makes some and not other conflations of race and class, and of class and gender appear "logical"[2] in contemporary construction of gender and domesticity in the United States in general and in the Nation of Islam's reconfiguration of these in particular.

In this overview we are concerned with the manner in which gender politics, embedded in religious and educational movements, interpreted economic changes to construct and position the manliness of male-the-provider against the femininity of female-the-nurturer. We attend to how this politic gave rise to the "cult of True Womanhood" (Welter 1966, 1976; Gay 1993: 288–367). In relation to the forces set in motion by these processes, we explore the contemporary demographics of gendered racial participation in the labor market and its links to the stereotypes and realities of the gendered identity of the lower-class structure of contemporary African-American communities (i.e., most often seen as a world of women in a world of trouble or as a masculine matriarchy and its effeminized men). We then turn to consider, on the one hand, the symbolic import of these engenderings for nationalist mythologics of racial redemption, the construction of manliness, and the cult of true womanhood to suggest what an analysis of these reveals about the rigidity and flexibility, and the continuities and discontinuities of the ideological field made necessary, if not always possible, by the precepts of Western nationalisms, as set forth by Williams in the introduction to this volume. We aim to link these issues to the practices that erase women's agency in the history of struggle, thereby, expanding on issues raised by Pierce (in this volume) in conjunction with "boudoir politics." By carefully scrutinizing the rhetoric and practices of the Nation of Islam, we aim to situate such gender troubles better during the same time in which we flesh out the everyday realities and pitfalls of the general metaphysics underlying nationalist mythologics that make of women's agency, agency out of place (mannish) even among a racialized form of subordinated masculine agency, itself deemed out place when actively contesting control of the nature of history and its history of nature in particular nation-states. In short, we interrogate the point of paradox where men become "mannish" by seeking to seize what Sunquist (1993), in the context of a literary analysis, has called the "signs of power."

The Symbolics of Working Man in the Cult of True Womanhood

Sexuality, sexual preference, gender constructions, and the implementation of domestic modes associated with such constructions are all products of the differential linkages among the concepts of race, class, and gender. In dialectical terms, these *products* are also the *producers* of the concepts insofar as what each means, when, where, and to whom depends on the manner in which all the others have been fashioned out of these linkages (Mouffe 1983). Thus, each concept has a separate history and an analytically distinct contemporary configuration, but a full disclosure of those histories and distinct configurations requires simultaneous attention to the dialectical construction of each. Change in constructions of identity that would de-essentialize any particular gender stereotype depends on the character of the dialectic between and among the concepts and their shifting relations in economic regimes.

For example, while slipping into a class-related, de-essentialization (i.e., pattern and duration of unemployment) of masculinity, and taking a psychoanalytic view, Craib nonetheless tells us:

> Men are unlikely to change spontaneously. The change might be stimulated by structural changes—*perhaps* for a few men **long-term unemployment** might have such an effect—or more likely by individual and collective challenges by women influenced by or part of the feminist movement. But psychoanalytic theory suggests that the first reaction of men to such a challenge is for the defence system to re-assert itself all the more strongly. My argument does suggest that the process of change will involve a degree of agony. But for many men, this will not be news. (1987: 741, bold emphasis added)

For our concerns, the implied feminization through labor-regime position is indeed a big "perhaps," addressing questions of how subordinated men react and what role the race/class conflation in that reaction serves to point up the confusion of gender role, stereotype, and identity often still rampant in gender-studies literature. As Clatterbaugh notes in his effort to distinguish these terms:

> Gender roles are social roles that belong to *identifiable* groups of men who exist in reasonably specific historical, ethnic, or religious situations. . . . [s]tereotype of masculinity is a general idea of what most people consider to be the masculine gender role. . . .
>
> The gender role and the stereotype are quite distinct. If we were interested in the masculine gender role, we would have to study an identifiable group of men. If we were interested in the stereotype of masculinity, we would have to survey people and ask them what they thought was typical of those men. The stereotype of what men are and the role that men actually play need not agree; in fact, there is considerable evidence to suggest that gender stereotypes are inaccurate. "Gender stereotypes . . . may not be based on statistically significant differences in behavior between the sexes but, at best, are exaggerations of a grain of truth" [quoting from Bascow 1986: 12].
>
> The gender ideal is a widespread notion as to what the gender role for men should be. . . . [S]tereotypes and ideals, too, are historically situated; they reflect the ideas of specific groups about what men (of specific groups) are and should be. (1990: 3–4)

The key question then becomes one of how to identify the historically constituted relations between "gender stereotypes" and "cultural stereotypes" in both their internal and external manifestations for racial/ethnic groups and the class-stratified individuals that make up such groups. How, in short, are simultaneous responses to gender stereotypes and aspects of broad intergroups cultural stereotypes manifested in the cultural construction of masculinity and femininity within and across racio-ethnic group boundaries? In this task, we recognize that the race-class-gender conflation constructs these concepts and their varied group-based stereotypes that are simultaneously dimensions of personal identity formation. Such constructions are relational, and their uses, as often as not, are strategic. Interpretations of them are both intrapersonal (in a psychodynamic sense) and intergroup (in a sociopolitical sense). In short, as Goux argues: "Philosophical terms themselves (matter, ideas, nature, man, means of production, etc.) cannot be seen as simple or transparent, as pure concepts. There is no such thing as a pure concept. These terms must be considered in all their analytical and historical depth" (1990: 213).

The dynamics of such conceptual histories are notable even when we attend to only one racially identified group of men and women. For example, Jessie Bernard's (1983) work on the rise and fall of the male-the-provider role model illustrates the multitude of factors and reactions to them that served to diminish the range of possibilities out of which colonial U.S. American "white" males constructed masculinity during their transformation to wage laborers in a capitalist mode of production. It is during this transformation that women's legal rights and economic opportunities were greatly diminished, thereby placing a greater responsibility for the subsistence, social mobility, and symbolic status of the family on the shoulders of men. Conceptions of masculinity shifted from male-the-interdependent householder to male-the-provider and head-of-household in broader wage-labor regimes. Bernard is careful to note, however, first that the transformation of conceptions of identity had both positive and negative benefits for men and women, second, that both men and women resisted the constraints implied, and third, as we would of course expect, for men and women there were always a diversity of ways of performing the roles dictated by the domestication of these new forms of masculinity and femininity.

Male responses were not shaped merely by efforts to provide for women and children without benefit of publicly validated female assistance. The fact that the new model correlated *quality* of economic performance with *degree* of masculinity also shaped their responses. In terms of benefits, to the successful—the good provider—went the spoils of power and status outside the household, and authority and control within the household. Bernard argues: "The benefits accruing to the successful performance of the Good-Provider role constitute[d] a measure of the costs involved in the events of failure. Since everything depended on his success, everything was at stake. The Good Provider was playing an all-or-nothing game" (1987: 153).

Confronted with a situation of deep play—play where the stakes are so high it is irrational to play the game—some men wisely rejected involvement.[3] Perceiving the game of domesticity as one of what Bernard calls "all restrictions and burdens," (Bernard 1983: 157) they remained bachelors despite manuals and other public tracts which extolled the virtue of family life and responsibility. Others, having taken on the task, found themselves humiliated and demasculinized by their effort to do the job well. Escaping the industrializing U.S. North, some of these men headed to its western frontier to seek their fortunes; they planned or hoped to eventually return home. Others took to the high seas with the same hopes and goals in mind. Some managed to return whereas others became, according to historian John Demos, tramps—"men who just gave up, who dropped out of the role entirely" (1974: 438). In many instances, these men became destitute wanderers, preferring not to work at all, seeking a handout from other men's housewives and hoping these women did not ask them to perform even minor chores in exchange. Demos (1974) notes that by the nineteenth century, in locations of increasing urbanization in the United States, those who became wholly demoralized and chronic alcoholics were among the bums that came to populate the skid rows of growing cities.

Still other men became hobos and Wobblies—members of the International Workers of the World—who ideologically as well as practically rejected the constraints on their humanity implied by the male-the-good-provider measure of masculine quantums.[4] More typically, men assumed the role of the Good-Provider, as they took minor and petty forms of psychological revenge against women by means of tight-fisted stinginess that forced wives and children to grovel for spare change in the forms of allowances and household budgets. Bernard (1983: 155) concludes: "Between the areas of conformity—at whatever level—to the Good-Provider role and the area of complete non-conformity has been the non-good provider, the marginal worker, made up usually of the undereducated, the under-trained, the underemployed, or part-time employed, as well as the underpaid, and of course the unemployed. These included men who want— sometimes desperately—to perform the Good-Provider role but who, for one reason or another, are unable to do so."

It is at this point that Bernard finds it useful to invoke class stratification as racial difference. Citing the work of Elliot Liebow (1966) with its focus on the failures of the men of Tally Corner to act the role of male-the-provider, when she argues, "The Black man is under legal and social constraint to provide for them [their families], to be a husband to his wife and father to his children. The chances are, however, that he is failing to provide for them, and failure in this primary function contaminates his performance as father in other respects as well" (155). Confronted with such failures, Bernard concludes that this means "In some states leaving the family entirely is the best substitute a man can supply. The community is left to take over" (1983: 155). Here, however, it is *communities,* that take over. The nation as "welfare state" dictates the practices that further exclude race/class conflated masculinities from the spoils of domestic authority and power while the racial/ethnic community is left to find balms for such masculine wounds as it also seeks means to bind and to curtail feminine independence. In the overall scheme of things, the highest masculine quantum was to be derived by economic success over and above any practical, and perhaps ideological, concerns with its implications for masculine humanity.

The Economy of Masculine Quantums and Dialectical Constructions of Femininity

Within nationalist ideologies, from the standpoint of their gender stereotypes, at least those derived from British-influenced cultural stereotypes, the good-provider construction of masculinity eventually implied a particular construction of femininity as female-the-housebound-housewife, seeker after the good-provider, and eventually mother-the-nurturer, protector-of-the-household, and, by metaphorical extension, protector-of-the-national-morality. As Barbara Welter comments:

> a true woman was a true woman, wherever she was found. If anyone, male or female, dared to tamper with the complex of virtues which made up True

> Womanhood, he was damned immediately as an enemy of God, of civilization and of the Republic. It was a fearful obligation, a solemn responsibility, which the nineteenth-century American woman had—to uphold the pillars of the temple with her frail white hand.
>
> The attributes of True Womanhood, by which a woman judged herself and was judged by her husband, her neighbors and society could be divided into four cardinal virtues, piety, purity, submissiveness, and domesticity. Put them all together and they spelled mother, daughter, sister, wife—woman. Without them, no matter whether there was fame, achievement or wealth, all was ashes. With them she was promised happiness and power. (1966: 151–52)

Welter further contends that [mainly White, Protestant] men as good-providers and overperformers salved their conscience with the knowledge that women, as housebound wives and mothers, remained hostages to moral and religious values the men of necessity left unattended as they chased the almighty dollar as the measure of their masculine quantums.

"White" women's responses to these cultural stereotypes of femininity and their implications for the construction of domesticity varied. Needless to say, facing legal constraints and economic limitations greater than those of men—even when we consider the issues involved only from the standpoint of "White" men and women—women's responses were both more limited and tended to be indirect: manipulating spaces and possibilities created by competition among men and the remaining forms (sexual and material, or practical if you prefer) of interdependence to mediate relations between self as human and self as culturally constituted femininity. Bernard provides telling examples of "White" women's reluctance to redefine their "selves" to assist unemployed or underemployed men whom they had married because these men had initially show promise of being good providers. The problems were especially acute during the Great Depression and in the aftermath of World War II as women's relations to the labor market changed. This suggests that we understand Craib's (1987) conclusion about the predominance of traits of "aggressiveness" in the lower classes and "rationality" in the middle classes as part of the very construction of those classes. The constructions were consequent to vacillations, not simply between "baby and bully" (Craib 1987: 733) but also between struggles for different criteria to measure and evaluate masculinity and femininity, which in turn were consequent to changes in the sociopolitical context of interpretation.

Bernard and others working in this vein in the United States suggest that historical analysis focused on changes in identity constructions of gender and domesticity must be situated in real historical and economic time and social structure. The work of such scholars as Barbara Epstein (1981) further indicates the need to include in historical analyses attention to uneven regional variation and the cultural demographics of racial and class populations under consideration. For example, during the nineteenth century, among "White" Protestant women of the industrializing northeast, Epstein locates the politics of domesticity in the intersection of evangelism and temperance. More importantly, the ideological context in accordance with which these women interpreted and understood this intersection was the prior extreme responses of men such as tramps, bums, hobos, and Wobblies, or just plain barflies. Men of these types were the extreme whereas in between were the passive resisters who evaded home by frequenting the local pub. When not chained to a job, they avoided dull accountability by constructing and valuing forms of absence. These absences not only left women isolated, homebound, and almost totally responsible for child care, but as forms of passive resistance they also made women dependents—sometimes humiliated and abused ones—of men whose separateness from the home often made of them virtual strangers.

Under such conditions, Epstein argues, women of the evangelical temperance movement constructed and valorized the sanctity of home, family, the critical function of the male-the-good-provider role, and upheld the essentialness of the female as naturally moral. In large measure for these women isolation and economic insecurity was met with Welter's "cult of True Womanhood." Hence, when we analyze race, class, and gender, we must seek to do so in a specific context, defined in its ideological, economic, and cultural aspects, in order to attend to the constraints implied by the concepts' shifting intersection. That is to say, domesticity (as a role formation linked to gender construction) is mediated by the simultaneously ongoing constructions of race, class, and culture as modes of middle-class respectability. This is especially so where popular, politicized definitions of culture view it as an interlocking set of ethnicities whose members and cultures competitively interact in the political and economic arenas of a nation-state. In such situations, superficial treatments of the politics of race and class in relation to constructions of sexuality most dangerously neglect the manner in which the continual interplay of these politics differentially limits the space within which males and females construct gender and domesticity as essential aspects of personal and group identities within and across the shifting barriers that are imposed by these same politics.[5]

Respectable Woman as the Measure of Racial Destiny and Masculine Accumulation

The stereotypes regarding Black manhood and womanhood engendered during slavery to rationalize a brutal profit-driven system have proven to be a tar baby that relentlessly clings to Black men and women; the more desperately they seek to clean up their images, the more tenaciously the negative stereotypes stick. Meanwhile White Americans deny any part in the tar baby's conception. According to the master narrative of United States' history, within the legal and economic constraints of the racialized slave system as it developed in the United States, there was no place for the Black man to play the provider role; also any attempt to play the protector role to defend either his woman or his children would almost certainly end disastrously, indeed, often in death. Thus, in this traditional view of slavery, the Black man was at best a "visitor" in a house run by the slave woman who could remain for as long as it suited her whim or the will of the master.

To little avail, revisionist historians have tried to correct this master narrative of American slavery which portrays the Black man as doubly castrated—primarily by the White man and secondarily by the Black woman. Despite factual errors, omissions and distorting truths, the images of the Black matriarch and the emasculated Black male contain too much symbolic power to be easily or permanently relinquished by the various and unequally matched contestants in the racial, gender, and class wars that have been and still are fought on the interpenetrating and continually shifting economic and cultural terrains in the United States as nation-state. That White men would be drawn to the image of the omnipotent, and in their view benevolent, slave master is predictable. Surprising, at least at first glance, is the enduring appeal of this master narrative to Black men, who, within this persuasive mytho-history of the American nation, are portrayed as eternally dependent children: little Black Sambos, Black studs plowing the master's literal and symbolic fields, or as castrated Uncle Toms. And, notwithstanding their leading role in the slave household, Black women are likewise reduced to a set of demeaning stereotypes. Clearly out of place, in terms of the dominant gender prescriptions defining appropriate forms of femininity in American culture and society, this mannish Black woman was the usurper of masculine agency—simultaneously as the demonic Black whore and the Black matriarch, representing forms of agency said to threaten destruction of the Black family, the race, and the future hopes of a once great Black civilization.

Ironically, in their efforts to rescue Black women, gallant defenders such as Alexander Crummell and W. E. B. Du Bois have more often than not reinforced disparaging images of Black womanhood, portraying them as the tragic victim of slavery who was stripped of all civilized features, especially feminine submissiveness, domesticity, refinement, and, most importantly, sexual modesty. Du Bois's pronouncement on the damnation of Black women still chills the soul: "I shall forgive the white South much in its final judgment day: I shall forgive its slavery, for slavery is a world-old habit; I shall forgive its fighting for a well-lost cause, and for remembering that struggle with tender tears; I shall forgive its so-called 'pride of race,' the passion of its hot blood, and even its dear, old laughable strutting and posing; but one thing I shall never forgive, neither in this world nor the world to come: its wanton and continued and persistent insulting of the black womanhood which it sought and seeks to prostitute to its lust" ([1920] 1969: 172).

Written early in Du Bois's long career, it would appear that all of the White man's crimes against the Black race were forgivable except his determination to make of the Black woman his race's whore. Du Bois, like all the major Black leaders of the nineteenth and early twentieth century, was steeped in the Victorian proposition that all of civilization depended upon the quality of a nation/race's womanhood. If she was fallen and unredeemed; indeed, all was ashes. From the horror of this sin, the Black woman could be reformed, thereby saving and redeeming the entire race. No one expressed this hope of national redemption through the domestication of women more eloquently than Rev. Alexander Crummell as he sought the prescription for "permanent and uplifting civilization" ([1891] 1992: 221).

> If you want the civilization of a people to reach the very best elements of their being, and then, having reached them, there to abide, as an indigenous principle, you must imbue the *womanhood* of that people with all its elements and qualities. Any movement which passes by the female sex is an ephemeral thing. Without them, no true nationality, patriotism, religion, cultivation, family life, or true social status is a possibility. ([1891] 1992: 221–22)

Crummell explained further that whereas the male could achieve extraordinary accomplishments, these were naught if the woman was not prepared to nurture his achievements and safely pass them to future generations as racial patrimony. The idea of the home as a refuge and of woman's sacred role as the first teacher of the children was also rhapsodized by a leading Black female educator when she stated: "Woman, Mother—your responsibility is one that might make angels tremble and fear to take hold!" (Cooper [1892] 1988: 22). Despite this effusive praise for Black womanhood, for most, the depravity of her real life circumstances was shaped by ongoing racism and centuries of slavery; the sublime destiny of Black womanhood could be attained only after she had been drastically reformed. Even the most elemental features of civilization had, in Crummell's estimation, to be taught in that she might do accurately all domestic work, such as sweeping floors, dusting rooms, scrubbing, bed making, and washing and ironing, sewing, mending, and knitting" (1992: 222). As part of Crummell's effort in 1883 to secure the future of the race through the proper training of its women, he called upon the more privileged Black woman who enjoyed the benefits of bourgeois domesticity, cultivation, and higher education, to put "aside all fastidiousness" and, as a "Sister of Mercy," "to enter the humble and, perchance, repulsive cabin of her black sister, and gaining her confidence, . . . lead her out of the crude, disordered, and miserable ways of her plantation life into neatness, cleanliness, thrift, and self-respect" ([1891] 1992: 220). And across gender, female leaders such as Anna Julia Cooper, in 1886, boldly suggested to a distinguished group of Black clergymen that, "'I am my Sister's Keeper!' should be the hearty response of every man and woman of the race" ([1892] 1988: 32). Cooper spoke to convince all that to continue to pour limited available resources into the education of Black men while slighting the educational advancement of the Black women would be a grave mistake from the perspective of Black women's needs but, more importantly, those of the entire race.

> [n]o man can represent the race. Whatever the attainments of the individual may be, unless his home has moved on *pari passu,* he can never be regarded as identical with or representative of the whole. . . . We must point to homes, average homes, homes of the rank and file of horny handed toiling men and women of the South (where the masses are) lighted and cheered by the good, the beautiful, and the true—then and not till then will the whole plateau be lifted into the light.
>
> Only the Black Woman can say "when and where I enter, in the quiet, undisputed dignity of my womanhood, without violence and without suing or special patronage, then and there the whole *Negro race enters with me."* (1988 [1892]: 30–31)

The small number of elite Black women living in the North and South tied their *individual* reputations to that of their less fortunate sisters. As Fannie Barrier Williams defiantly reminded her White female audience at the 1893 World Exposition in Chicago, "I regret the necessity of speaking of the moral character of our women," but "the morality of our home life has been commented on so disparagingly and meanly that we are placed in the unfortunate position of being defenders of our name" (quoted in Giddings 1984: 86). Josephine St. Pierre Ruffin agreed when she stated, "[T]oo long have we been silent under unjust and unholy charges" ([1895] 1973: 442). In 1895, she issued a call for the first National Conference of Colored Women. It quickly resulted in a powerful national movement that took as its aim the moral, educational, and domestic improvement of its female members. If properly trained in the new domestic and industrial sciences and Christian virtues, the middle-class leaders of the Black women's clubs firmly believed that as they climbed the socioeconomic ladder through hard work and respectability, they could likewise lift their less fortunate sisters.

When examining the consequences of the "Black holocaust" in slavery, most twentieth-century scholars, echoing nineteenth-century Black leaders, simply legitimated the worst stereotypes about Black manhood and womanhood (see, for example, Patterson 1993: 20). "It came to be the consensus of a vast body of scholarship that the taproot of racial inequality was the historically inherited sexual immorality of blacks, which was perpetuated in the demoralized Negro home. Central to this consensus was the notion that the decrepitude of the black family was the cause as well as the effect of Negro pathology, and in turn that the linchpin of this was the inadequacy of Negro women as women" (Morton 1991: 73). Although E. Franklin Frazier's major works on the Black family and community life were published in the 1930s and 1940s, as the most influential scholar in this tradition, the unintended and ill-fated consequences of his arguments still command the attention, and often the support of leading contemporary researchers. Daniel P. Moynihan and William J. Wilson, two of the more widely known and influential researchers, have launched extraordinary careers in the field of public policy building on the presumed political economy of a "backward" Black family morality.

The Political Economy of a "Backward" Morality

In sum, Frazier maintained that two types of Black families emerged out of slavery. One was a relatively well-organized patriarchal form which was able to adjust to the new status of freedom. The other was disorganized, demoralized, and matrifocal, and that near invariably produced cross-generational social disintegration and moral depravity. While noting the strength of the Black maternal bond, Frazier concluded that absent paternal authority and a mother's love was a potentially destructive force. Like Craib's contemporary psychoanalytic model, Frazier argues: "Of course, these elemental expressions of love and solitude for their offspring are often detrimental to the welfare of the children" ([1939] 1966: 112) because the unchecked attachment of children to their mothers kept both sons and daughters at home. Although Black women love their children (perhaps too much), in this view they are incapable, in the absence of paternal authority, of being good mothers; on occasion their over solicitousness even inadvertently kills their children.

Therefore, for Frazierians, the reform of the Black woman and the improvement of Black family life through creation of proper bourgeois domesticity was the *sine qua non* of racial redemption in U.S. society. Such required restoring the Black male to his "natural" position as household head. The positive experience of those Black families where the husbands played male-the-provider and reaped the rewards of domestic authority was, for Frazierians, convincing proof that Black inequality in American life was not due to inherent racial differences but rather to the legacy of slavery that had usurped the Black man's power and authority—even within his own family. Ironically, lost in this view of masculine Black racial redemption was the fact that the economy of slavery had made possible for other racialized families the potentials of the nuclear family form and its middle-class respectability against which the excluded Black woman was now judged.

The most controversial reiteration of this well-worn thesis came in 1965 when Daniel P. Moynihan, as a policy advisor for the U.S. Labor Department, authored *The Negro Family: The Case for National Action*. Notwithstanding the new Civil Rights laws and rising expectations, racial equality would remain, Moynihan warned, an elusive dream until Black men were economically empowered to become the good-provider. The frequent pattern of role reversal in Black families, he advised, must be prevented even if this meant taking "women's jobs" and redesigning them for Black men. Looking to the barnyard for inspiration, he concluded that "real men," like the "bantam rooster," must be allowed "to strut" (quoted in Giddings 1984: 326). Moynihan was understandably shocked by the outrage the *Report* sparked in the Black community because he correctly saw himself as merely confirming and updating Frazier's thesis. Yet, coming from the pen of a White man, Moynihan's conclusion drew blood: "Obviously not every instance of social pathology afflicting the Negro community can be traced to the weakness of family structure. . . . Nonetheless, at the center of the tangle of pathology is the weakness of the family" (quoted in Valentine 1968: 33). Clearly "out of place," standing at the center of Black family and community life, the Black woman's agency was, even for Moynihan's critics, believed to reinforce a pathological situation that was the initial product of the manner in which slavery had stripped the Black man of authority.

Economic realities were not so easily redesigned by such symbolic posturing. In 1965, 25 percent of Black households were headed by women, compared to approximately 66 percent today. William J. Wilson, while leading the call for a major overhaul in the United States' domestic policy, has argued that if we are to stem the disintegrating consequences for inner-city Black communities of recent structural changes in the United States' economy that have made it almost impossible for a major portion of the Black male population to become good providers and heads-of-household, federal policy must enable them to play such roles. Wilson claims, White liberals, intimidated by the vociferous attack on Moynihan from within the Black community, ignored the escalating crisis that made possible the formation of an "underclass" in the Black inner-city communities.

Within this emergent "underclass," men's inability to find employment leaves Black women unable to find good-provider husbands and unable to raise children alone. Backward moral reasoning again simplistically blamed the absence of paternal authority for rising poverty, crime, and homicide rates, and this class's isolation and alienation from mainstream society, leading Wilson to insist that the "tangle of pathology" labeling was absolutely appropriate and long overdue. Absent an honest national dialogue on the causes of underclass dysfunctional domestic life of poor Blacks, and lacking policy enabling Black men to assume their "proper place," Wilson warns, the cycle of illegitimate births, female-headed households, welfare dependency, and crime will continue to intensify. Wilson finds no need to advocate moral reform; instead, in a classic liberal, rather than, as often charged, a conservative stance, he calls for a serious federal commitment to full employment and income support for all American families. That Black families could be expected to benefit disproportionately from such a policy stems from their over concentration among the nation's poor. Unfortunately this is not simply a liberal or conservative limitation. Even the more radical "insurgent" critics of the existing race hierarchy in the United States unwittingly accept the underlying ideas about the character of race/nation, class, and sex differences that provides sources of criteria for its reproduction and maintenance.

Thus, whether we consider the writings of early political-religious nineteenth-century nationalist such as Alexander Crummell, or turn to twentieth-century academics, politicians, and scholar-activists, whether Black or White, experts are amazingly consistent in their call for the "restoration" of the Black man to create conditions adequate to an agency for the proper domestication of the Black woman. This common short-sighted rearticulation of oppressive ideology is, needless to say, particularly ironic and tragic when implemented in the name of national liberation. For this reason we turn our analysis to the pattern of "insurgent masculine redemption" found in the Nation of Islam in order to further disclose the dangers of such misbegotten appropriations of "the master's tools."

Taking Back His Own: An Insurgent Masculinity for Racial Redemption?

The Nation of Islam (NOI) has developed a highly successful strategy of national mobilization and organizational resurgence. The NOI's central racial myths, gender metaphors, and class mores, to which we now turn, bear stunning resemblance to the most cherished notions of race, manifest destiny, gender precepts, and the bourgeois ideals of (White) American nationalism, particularly during the Victorian period. Within the potent symbol system of the NOI, the capture, rape, and degradation of Black women constitute the central metaphors for the enslavement and for the continued exploitation of the Black race by the White man. Starting in the 1930s, through uniquely stylized and highly formulaic sermons and speeches, the NOI's ministers inculcated their listeners with the idea that Black people were destroyed through the Black woman and can only be redeemed by recapturing control of her thoughts, actions, and especially her sexuality.

In 1971 Minister Louis Farrakhan reiterated the core elements of NOI teaching: "Now the Honorable Elijah Muhammad says to us—'No man can think of reforming a people unless that man thinks in terms of re-building and reforming the woman of that people.' . . . We didn't fall down in this condition without a design. The white man knew exactly what he was doing; brother, he destroyed us through our woman" ([1971] 1992: 16). Although woman, in NOI's view, represents the race, this is obviously not good. Indeed, it is disturbingly similar to the biblical story of the Fall wherein the woman is portrayed as the weaker sex through which the devil is able to trick the first humans and cause the lost of paradise and immortality.

NOI mythology portrays the White man as the devil. Substantiating the biblical analogy, paradise lost becomes a key metaphor of Western civilization the entailment of which, in the Christian tradition, represent a sex-specific punishment imposed for opposing the Will of God. With paradise lost, man must live by the sweat of his brow; he must become a *producer,* and woman, submitting to the rule of man, through the pain of labor, brings forth future generations from her womb. Thus, until the coming of the Messiah (the second Adam), the only form of salvation mankind can know is that produced of masculine labor and represented in the collective immortality of cross-generational procreation and sustenance. Countless feminists have noted how this and other stories in the Book of Genesis have provided powerful mythical underpinnings for the subordination of women in Western societies over the past several millennia.

Parallels between Christian metaphysics and the NOI religious cosmology are quite evident. According to Elijah Muhammad, the man revered as "the Messenger of Allah" and founder of the NOI, Black man was the original man, made in the image of Allah/God and declared by Him, "vicegerent"/ruler of the universe. According to the Messenger, the White man, a devil created by a mad Black scientist, by prophesy was expected to rule for 6,000 years. The White man's reign was to end in 1914. Allah postponed the apocalypse in order to allow the Messenger sufficient time to resurrect the Black man in North America; to refashion his true identity as the original man and natural ruler of the universe. Time, declares NOI, is short and followers of the Messenger of Allah must spread the Word. "Allah gave [the Black] man," Minister Farrakhan tells rapt audiences today, "power and dominion over the foul of the air, the fish of the sea, and every creeping thing that crawls" (1994a: 21). God created woman, Farrakhan continues, to be man's "help mate": "He put woman there to help man to meet what Allah (God) had put on man to do. . . . The nature of you [woman] is to console a *productive man*. The nature of you is to speak to his mind that which consoles him in his effort to do Allah's (God's) Will" (Farrakhan 1994a: 21). Absorbing Christian dogma, the NOI takes male supremacy and "traditional" sex roles as a natural order. God has built the good/natural order into human's nature:

> NATURE makes a man desire to provide for a woman. NATURE puts within a man to secure a woman, and this is why men are the maintainers of a woman. All women by nature look to a man for maintenance. They LOOK to man for guidance. They look to a man for sustenance. They look to a man for provision, so naturally the man is out front. ([1971] 1992: 16)

More importantly, it is only through a *return to nature,* that is, by following the Will of Allah that the Black race will be able to defeat the devil and recapture paradise on earth. (There is no belief in resurrection or the hereafter in the NOI's theology.) There is no escaping nature or the Will of Allah, but evil and human weaknesses can interfere. In the fertile imagination of the Nation's myth makers, the White man constitutes a demonic interference with the divine order. In the aforecited 1971 speech, Farrakhan also explained:

> Now when a conqueror comes up against a nation and he conquers the men of that nation, he's conquered the vanguard or the wall that keeps the woman protected. So when the man is destroyed, the woman is the prize that the conquering army gains, is that right? Therefore, she's called in some slang filthy terms, "booty." . . . And since by nature women LOOK to strength; women

LEAN toward that which is strong and move away from that which is weak, the conqueror, by coming in, automatically has an attracting point with the women of that conquered people. And then the conqueror moves to put his seed into the woman that he conquers. . . . So through the woman he has destroyed a whole nation of people because every baby BORN to that woman is BORN in love with the conqueror; BORN to admire the conqueror; BORN to bow down to the conqueror. So until another conqueror comes to conquer that man that conquered the man that woman belongs to, that woman remains in the camp of the conqueror. ([1971] 1992: 16–17)

Hence, the key assumptions in this representation are: 1) that the race was destroyed through the woman; 2) that the dominant race perpetuates its power through control of *the womb* (the physical and cultural reproductive activity of women); 3) that women are property of the men of their racial identity; 4) that the Black woman, appropriated by the oppressor, is a collaborator who cannot be trusted, and; 5) that the Black race is doomed unless the Black man can reestablish, repossess, and control the Black woman by overpowering the White man.

Although this oft-told tale of Black enslavement and racial holocaust relies upon such familiar and degrading assumptions about the nature of woman, Black women no less than men nod their heads and shout approval when spokesmen for the NOI insist that "She [the Black woman] has been a free-for-all woman, for any man that wanted her." They declare: "he had her" and the Black man did nothing "to protect THIS Black Woman from the men of other nations coming in to use her as they will—is that right?" ([1971] 1992: 17). Black women who welcome such characterizations of Black womanhood are, no doubt, affirming the unaccustomed recognition of the extreme vulnerability and frequent violation they have suffered in White America over the past several centuries and expressing a deep yearning for protection, security, and respect. Unfortunately, the price of this recognition and of seeking protection within the NOI's discursive space are to be paid in coins of the implicit and explicit acceptance of her portrayal as a *whore* in need of tight *external control* of her sexuality. It is a double bind; she can remain free as the White man's whore or she can become the Black man's property, to be honored as the passive but *sacred womb/Mother* of the Nation. The destiny of the entire Black race, the NOI charges, depends upon her choice.

Without you sister, the nation is finished. With you properly taught, we have a beautiful nation and a great hope for a great future, but we don't need any ignorant, uninformed woman. An ignorant, uninformed woman is really an enemy to the nation. . . . You can bring forth greatness today if you will reform yourself sister. You can bring forth from yourself the type of people that the nation needs to deliver it from bondage if you reform yourself. But if you keep yourself as you are sisters, you will keep our nation in the same condition that the white man put us in. ([1971] 1992: 21 and 24)

The Womb: Reforming the Best Piece of Woman

Never has so much depended upon the womb of a woman, for it is indeed the womb in the woman and not the balance of woman surrounding it that must be protected. The obvious flattery in this particular appeal to Black women to help create a new Black Nation does little to conceal the increasingly thinly veiled threat to sisters who would resist the NOI's teachings. In addition, the frequent use of militaristic images in the NOI's rhetoric (army, vanguard, oppressor, conquest, booty, enemy camp) clearly indicates that compromise or even ambivalence is to be regarded as treason or betrayal.

Malcolm X, the most electric and effective spokesman for the NOI during its heyday in the early sixties, was known for his damnation of Black women who continued to follow the ways of the White man. When he charged that, "The trickiest [humans] in existence [are] the black woman and the white man," as explanation for the degradation of the Black man, his venom was as much focused on the Black woman as on the White man. Her collaboration with the White man was seen as institutionally structured into the functions of everyday life. Malcolm thus argues: "If you go to court with your wife, she will always win over you because the devil can use her to break down more of our black brothers. . . . It is this evil black woman in North America who does not want to do right and holds the [Black] man back from saving himself" (quoted in Cone 1991: 275). In his autobiography, Malcolm expressed surprise that he loved his wife Betty. Formerly, he did not consider "it possible . . . to love any woman" ([1965] 1966: 226). His past as pimp and whoremonger had provided him with "too much experience that women were only tricky, deceitful, untrustworthy flesh. I had seen too many men ruined, or at least tied down, or in some other way messed up by women. Women talked too much" ([1965] 1966: 226).

Moreover, while he credited Islam's "very strict laws and teachings about women," and "the teachings of the Honorable Elijah Muhammad" for helping him overcome his profound distrust of women, he also admitted that he, consistent with complaints from sisters in his Temple, "did tell the brothers to be very, very careful" ([1965] 1966: 226). As much as his general distrust might have been diminished by NOI teachings, his sense of the *conditions of trust* in relation to control and male agency was also honed by NOI teaching. Following a trip to the Middle East and Africa in 1959, Elijah Muhammad held up gender relations in these countries as a model for the Black man in North America to emulate: "Everywhere we went, the Black man recognized his woman. He had great respect for her. We dined in many of the "top (as you say in slang) homes." . . . [W]e never did see any of their family, only men" (reprint, *The Final Call,* July 20, 1994: 18). Like prize possessions, Elijah Muhammad taught, women were best kept out of sight and/or properly covered and strictly guarded.

Malcolm's deep fear of disorderly women and his corresponding need to maintain absolute control over female agency had traumatic consequences for his marriage. In a recent interview, Betty Shabazz described how she was forced to leave Malcolm on three separate occasions in conjunction with her desire to work outside the home. Malcolm uncompromisingly insisted that Betty not work outside of the household despite having a college degree in nursing and literally begging his permission to work. According to Betty he refused because, "He didn't want anybody to have any influence over [her] that would in any way compete with his" (1992: 109). In addition to traditional Islamic beliefs and the more idiosyncratic teachings of Elijah Muhammad, the man Malcolm revered not only as a the leader of the NOI but also as a surrogate father, it is likely that Malcolm's early tragic family history also contributed to his ferocious determination to keep Betty in the home. His natal family had been literally torn apart when his mother failed to hold the household together after his father's murder. She could not both provide for and adequately supervise the children, leaving the boys, especially Malcolm, to run wild until the state stepped in and took control, separating and placing the children in foster care settings and locking his mother away in a state mental institution where she would remain for more than twenty years.

In this quest to retake possession and control, as indicated earlier, no aspect of a woman was more precious, hence, in greater need of protection, than her womb. Using the metaphor of woman as a field (passive object) and man as a seed (generative principle), Elijah Muhammad warned his followers that "The woman is man's field to produce his nation. If he does not keep the enemy out of his field, he won't produce a good nation. . . . Until we learn to love and protect our woman, we will never be a fit and recognized people on the earth" (reprint, *The Final Call*, July 20, 1994: 18). In efforts to rebuild the nation through the woman, possession and control of her womb was paramount.

In this reckoning of procreation woman is raw material while man is generative principle and creator who gives identity/essence to unformed matter. Note, it is the male seed (masculine identity) planted in the female body that exclusively determines the likeness of the offspring, thereby, emulating the ancient and medieval myths of "sperm children" reproduction analyzed by Nancy Tuana (1993) and raises the problems of "resemblance" (Huet 1993). Woman is regarded as merely a convenient container; her seed is dismissed as either nonexistent or ineffectual, making Black woman's most significant contribution to the procreative process a clean vessel/womb into which the Black man can plant his seed without fear of pollution that might jeopardize the reproduction of *his image*. Such NOI reasoning predisposes its leaders to emphasize the duty of Black men to be "a wall of protection around the Black Woman," and "to keep the enemy out of his field." That a woman be pure and submissive is crucial to guarantee that she not interfere with the procreative process. The reward for such "happy" female submission to male rule, is the idealization of motherhood (Farrakhan [1971] 1992: 19–22).

Yet even this narrow space of achievement and honor for the woman shrinks in NOI patriarchal cultures, as a male god and/or men are represented as the real woman/womb whence life comes. In the Western world's march toward patriarchal dominance, Nancy Tuana notes that the female gods were progressively stripped of agency as male "substitution" rendered their creative powers nonexistent or ineffectual (Tuana 1993). For example, Zeus swallowed his wife (embodied the womb), and through his head subsequently gave birth to a fully formed Athena. In the Judeo-Christian tradition, by the power of his word, another male god is said to have created the universe and all living things. Also, within this same creation mythology, man is portrayed as giving birth to woman. Thus, through various cultural myths and religious beliefs, women are denied even the most obvious agency which they possess in biology, thereby deprived of an important source of cultural capital and its role in determining status and power across groups in a society.

In these terms, NOI also "borrowed" from the Western cultural tradition the mythologic for the concealment of female generativity/power, transforming it into a property of the male body. This erasure of even maternal female power and the associated forms of agency is evident in the NOI's birthing myths and metaphors. Despite the fact, the NOI unquestionably idealizes the Black woman as mother and its top male leadership symbolizes both the Father *and* the Mother of the new Black Nation, disguised female creative power in male bodies is put forth by even its highly respected female elder, Sister Tynetta Muhammad, a frequent writer in NOI publications and a former wife of Elijah Muhammad. NOI finds the imagery for this womb transfer in the Book of Revelation and in the teachings of Master W. Fard Muhammad, a shadowy figure who appeared in Detroit in the early 1930s, who NOI believe to have been Allah incarnate. Sister Muhammad puts forth the following to explain the counterfactual image of the birth of the Nation:

> The Honorable Elijah Muhammad has stated in a series of articles published in 1957 and 1958 on the true history of Jesus, that "We have made the son of Mary and his mother a sign," . . . what are they a sign of? . . . Who is the Originator of these teachings? Their origin is from the Founder of the Nation of Islam in North America, Master Wallace Fard Muhammad. He placed our entire Nation under sign upon His coming and finding of us and by His choosing of one from among us, the Hon. Elijah Muhammad, as His Apostle, to shine The Light of Truth upon us all.
>
> Thus, the Hon. Elijah Muhammad becomes the Messenger of Allah, stylized in scripture, as a woman giving birth to a child [Book of Revelations, ch. 12] as Mary gave birth to Jesus. And in this spiritual sense, we, as His chosen people, become the little Jesus that he is giving birth to. In this sacred union, Master W. Fard Muhammad becomes the Father who initiated the process of our birth.
>
> In another spiritual metaphor, Master W. Fard Muhammad also comes under the sign of the woman who gives birth to the baby Jesus, the Hon. Elijah Muhammad, who under the same sign (the Woman) is giving birth to a New Nation. This process of spiritual rebirth and enlightenment comes down in suc-

cession to Minister Louis Farrakhan, who again, under the sign of a woman, being heavy with child (the Nation of Islam) is about to be delivered as he travails in pain at the approaching moment of birth. (Tynetta Muhammad 1992: 10)

The fuzziness of the NOI's mythologic as with myth in general, is a useful source of flexibility and picturesque richness. The womb of the new Black Nation has been figuratively absorbed by the father figures, hence, the most powerful metaphorical images of national redemption are *all* male and it is man who bears the supreme pain of birthing the new Nation. Hence, the womb, the locus of racial reproductivity though literally in the woman is mytho-symbolically a male generative property and must be protected for that role. Minister Farrakhan comes directly to the point:

We all will die, sooner or later, right? Oh, yes. No man lives forever. So when you're dead where's future coming from? From her. So every time a man looks at a woman, he's looking at what? His future. Every time a man mistreats a woman, he's mistreating what? His future. Every time a man shows respect for a woman, he's showing respect for his future. Why? Because SHE brings forth from her loin or from her womb your image—your likeness—your fur- therance—your generation—this is how a man lives, he lives THROUGH a woman. Now if a man is dumb enough to allow his woman to be destroyed then that man also is destroyed, is that right? ([1971] 1992: 18–19)

Given these contentions it is not surprising that the NOI's religious and meta- physical assumptions maintain that the womb does *not* belong to the woman but instead to Allah, God who made the Black man His vicegerent with the authority to rule on earth.

Black woman, you are a sacred individual [because] . . . the secret of Allah (God) Himself is bound up in you. . . . When you respect Allah (God) you must respect woman, because the womb of the woman is the place of sacred- ness and it should be reverenced. When Allah (God) and woman co-operate, Jesus comes forth, Moses comes forth, Abraham comes forth, greatness comes forth. But when women are estranged from Allah (God), then the womb pro- duces a bitter fruit. The woman must be reconnected to Allah (God) so that the fruit of her womb will once again be the kings, the rulers, the masters of every discipline, whether it is male or female. (1994a:21, Atlanta speech, June 25, 1994)

Through procreation, G/god continues to reproduce the original creation. This is God's space and He supplies the creative principle for those who would labor in His workshop. And, in this "conception of conception" (Goux 1990), God as craftsman no longer needs the active participation of woman. His charac- ter is imprinted in man to be continually reissued through the womb as long as the proper form of woman provides passive cooperation. Inappropriate female agency around the womb can, NOI warns, distort the divine purpose and result in monstrous birth which if repeated over time will lead to a race of "maggots and flies" that will destroy all hope of national redemption.

> Man is what he eats. As a woman thinketh, so is she. If you're feeding your mind garbage, then you become a garbage pail. And as a garbage pail you can't produce anything but maggots and flies. . . . If we want to rise, then we've got to lift up our women and you've got to go to the pinnacle of knowledge, wisdom and understanding. (1994b: 21)

Here, as in Huseby-Darvas's Hungarian case (in this volume), abortion is therefore deemed a direct attempt to subvert the Will of God and to murder a race/nation. The dangers of such a subversion are both individual and incalculable because, according to Minister Farrakhan, Allah is pursuing His plan for human salvation through the womb of a woman. Thus without recognizing the enormity of her decision, a woman might foolishly abort the baby that would have grown up to discover the cure for AIDS or cancer. She might even abort the next Moses, Abraham, or Jesus. Surely, with so much at stake, the control of a woman's body cannot be left to her. Farrakhan uses the story of his own birth to underscore this teaching and in so doing more tightly link NOI's mytho-construction to the general pattern and the role of nativity stories in the legitimation logics of nationalist gender hierarchies.

Bad Wombs as Child-Consuming Earth Mothers Eating Up the Prophets

Nativity stories are frequently prominent parts of religious mythologies and very instructive regarding the nature of woman. By focusing on the Earth Mother, the Mother of God, or the first humans, nativity stories tell us how a particular people/religion see Woman, particularly her creative/procreative and/or destructive potential. Woman may be portrayed as active, powerful, creative, and nurturent (i.e., Earth Mother birthing a physical universe and/or humanity from her own body), as a contrary combination of good and evil; creative and nurturent but also violent and destructive, consuming the children she formerly gave birth to with pleasure or indifference. In short, as Tuana's work bears witness, these stories reveal a great deal about a religion's prescriptions and proscriptions regarding women in relation to power, often supplying answers to such questions as: should they have it and, what will happen if they do? Nativity stories which focus on the birth of a God/Savior also supply an image of ideal motherhood or the Madonna (the Holy Mother) by which all other mothers ought to be judged.

Consistent with these general features of nativity stories, Farrakhan's oft-repeated story of his own conception and birth is most telling. Although not yet a formal part of the NOI's theology, Farrakhan's rendition of his nativity places it within the framework of the Nation's redemption mythology that maintains, based on a unique interpretation of the Book of Revelations, that: "The slander and the flood is on its way. But yet under the Sign of adultery and illegitimacy, under the Sign of a Son of Mary and His Mother, God is bringing to birth a New Nation who will be the stars and the New Rulers of the Nations" (Tynetta Muhammad 1983: 18).

As Farrakhan tells his nativity story it reinscribes all of the NOI's major precepts concerning the nature of woman, the power of God, and the nature of true paternity. Farrakhan was an illegitimate child born to an unwed woman. Alone, frightened, poor, and desperate, she decided to abort her baby. After three unsuccessful attempts, in complete desperation, she turned to God in prayer. God, Farrakhan goes on to explain, heard her prayers and delivered her; not as she hoped for by aborting the seed but, instead, through the power of his Holy Spirit, molding the child into a boy (she had at the very least hoped for a girl) who would one day, after being further molded by the spiritual father on Earth, the Honorable Elijah Muhammad, become the Honorable Louis Farrakhan, the Savior of his people. As the story goes her attempts to exercise agency within the womb would have meant both the destruction of individual life and the loss of a savior for an entire race/Nation; but God knew better, and when she submitted to Him, His Spiritual agency in the womb permitted her to bring forth and nurture a God-Strengthened God/Child. Farrakhan tells this already compelling story with maximum effect, informing the women in his audiences that they too might be carrying the child in their womb who will grow up to provide answers to the most pressing problems facing the Black race today—if only they submit to God's reproductive Will.

The Nation does not need nor can it tolerate, "any ignorant, uninformed woman"; hence, rejecting abortion, the NOI is also greatly concerned about the quality of children Black women produce and how these children are reared. Sharing the degrading beliefs and prescriptions of nineteenth-century Black culturally conservative thinkers, NOI's opinions of contemporary Black women's intellectual capacities and mothering capabilities are equally negative. Again, the Black race is said to be dragged down by its ignorant, morally loose women who are incapable of maintaining healthy bodies and wholesome households without the morally, mentally, and spiritually superior guidance of the race's male members. The nineteenth-century Black club women invested in bringing Black women's respectability in line with the model of "True Womanhood," were, as noted above, ready to go into the disreputable and despicable hovels of their less fortunate sisters in order to "lift as we climb." In 1995 the NOI, still in pursuit of elusive bourgeois refinement and respectability, like the nineteenth-century Black women's club movement stooping to enter hovels, also argues, "If we want to rise, then we've got to lift up our women" (1994b: 21), by eliminating male absence, providing proper female education, and reinstating appropriate male control. Black women are not, Farrakhan explains, inherently bad. In fact, "[t]he Honorable Elijah Muhammad said to me that there is no such thing as a no good woman. He said that wherever you find a no good woman there's a no good man that made her that way" (1994 Atlanta speech). Yet, in the larger NOI frame, it is not merely *a* man but *the* Man, defined as the conquest of the Black man which left a historical *her;* "the prize of the conquering army" ([1971] 1992: 16), into which the conqueror "puts his seed. . . ." in the forms of "[an] education. . . . [such] that the woman now brings forth seeds that admire the conqueror." ([1971] 1992: 17)

> Allah (God) is not here to condemn you but to uplift you and offer you for-giveness. Now look at what our children are doing. . . . Never was there a time when so much murder and destruction was being carried out by children. . . . [T]hey're cold and heartless. But they are your fruit; they come from your womb. . . . Sisters, you do have the choice. . . . what you don't know is that you have prepared your children for The Messiah. They're wild, they almost appear to be crazy. They're fearless; they're strong; they're cold; they're not listening to their teachers, and sometimes they don't listen to you. . . . *A mind has to be put in you sisters,* so you can reconnect with your children. I am sixty-one years of age, but I can talk to your children and your children listen." (1994b: 20–21)

Therefore, with the restoration of racially appropriate *Black* male authority there is hope for proper female redemption as well. Speaking and thinking for and as G/god, it is Farrakhan's mind that is to be put into Black women. Minister Farrakhan is frequently referred to as the Messiah by NOI ministers who intro-duce him at the mass rallies the Nation began holding across the country January 1994, as part of its highly successful "Let Us Make Man Tour." (Elijah Muhammad is on occasion also referred to as the Messiah and from the perspective of the NOI it is a bit confusing just how many Messiahs the Black race has or needs.) If the Black woman will allow the Messiah's mind/seed to be planted in her mind, which Farrakhan refers to as her "second womb," she will once again bring forth greatness. The teachings of the Nation and the example of Minister Farrakhan will show her the way out of the camp of the conqueror and onto the path to personal salvation and racial collective liberation. But time is running out.

The crisis of the Black family and of gender relations, according to the current teachings of the NOI, has worsened in the post-civil-rights era as racial integra-tion and the women's liberation movement "spearheaded by white women to lift the oppressive boot of white men from their necks," has made "deeper rifts . . . in the relationship between Black men and women" (Editorial, *The Final Call,* July 20, 1994: 16). Affirmative Action has encouraged the White man, the NOI charges, to hire the White woman or the Black woman who counts as a "two-fer" in preference to the Black man. As a consequence, the NOI claims increasingly Black women are abandoning their domestic and maternal duties in order to enjoy "the 'secure' world offered by the white man" (Editorial, *The Final Call,* July 20,

1994: 16). In recent speeches, NOI ministers plead with the Black woman to stop putting "career first" rather than fulfilling Allah's "help mate" role.

Neglect of her sacred duties is the causal factor in the procreation of individual depravity and with it, a collective monstrosity. To Farrakhan, a mother who bottle-feeds her babies will raise children who will bond with a cow instead of their mother, producing the present cold and heartless young generation. Mothers who send their children to child-care centers are molding a generation that will not know the benefits of a loving family setting. We are, he warns, creating the conditions for our own destruction as a people, because the woman is no longer in her proper place to take care of her husband and children. Eva Muhammad, the most popular female minister in the Nation, dramatically informs women that microwave cooking is probably poisoning their families, encouraging a preference for the more time-consuming preparation of fresh nutritious meals as a sacred duty given to woman by Allah. Typical of the logic of evidence relied upon to support many of the Nation's most controversial teachings, she asks her audience to ponder the significance of the letters e-a-t as the center of the word "create."

Yet, notwithstanding the supposed naturalness of sex roles and gender relations, the NOI consistently relies on mandatory formal classes to teach males and females their proper places in the Nation and their respective roles in the domestic sphere. In his autobiography, Malcolm X describes the rigid procedures by which the Nation hopes to ensure production in its members of the appropriate quantums of ideal masculine and feminine traits. By detailing their focus on the domestic "responsibilities of a husband and father; what to expect of women; the rights of women which are not to be abrogated by the husband; the importance of the father-male image in the strong household; current events; why honesty, and chastity, are vital in a person, a home, a community, a nation, and a civilization; why one should bathe at least once each twenty-four hours; business principles; and things of that nature" ([1965] 1966: 227), Malcolm eagerly corrected the mistaken assumption that NOI's manhood classes focus on military training. The women, in separate classes, were instructed in the typical duties of wives and mothers, with additional attention to public comportment and how a proper Muslim woman should behave when traveling abroad. Respectability also claimed attention: "Fridays [were] devoted to Civilization Night, [with] classes held for brothers and sisters in the area of the domestic relations, emphasizing how both husbands and wives must understand and respect each other's true natures" ([1965] 1966: 227). Heaven will come to Earth as men and women act according to their supposedly divine/true natures. Although a woman will test a man's strength, unless she finds him lacking in strength and wisdom, she will eventually submit and be "*happy to be under his rule.*" With wise and just male rulers "The Black Woman should not belong to any women's liberation movement. That's for the white woman" ([1971] 1992: 22). We must assume here that despite the competition of having White women in the labor force and the negative consequences such might carry for Black women's chances of finding a "productive male," partially resulting from successful White women's liberation, for the Black race such an outcome would, in the long run, be balanced by the corruption of white gender relations and, hence, in NOI logic the presumed weakening of White racial reproduction.

Conclusion

Through an examination of the rhetoric and practices of the Nation of Islam, we have explored complications consequent to how those who are oppressed by the institutional and symbolic structures enabled by a particular system of ideological precepts make use of those same precepts in their efforts to forge strategies adequate to break the psychological chains that bind them to these institutional and symbolic structures. We contend that despite the emancipatory language of racial redemption, the symbolic strategies for the contestation of subordination, in the face of entrenched economic depravation, displaces tyranny onto women rather than confronting its reproduction. Agreeing with Peter Gay (1993: 299) that a charge of hypocrisy does not explain a social ideology, we have explored the Nation's positioning of male and female natures as a dependent discourse, demonstrating how it structures its protest against Black masculine subordination on the field and within the coordinates fixed by the metaphysics of nature, history, and race in the general configuration of Western nationalism (Mosse 1985; Goux 1990). Within those coordinates it is highly difficult, if not impossible to envision a role for domesticity that transforms the economic and social conditions of the race as *a* nation, encapsulated in *the* nation as a state. Locked into the logic that has been part of the production and maintenance of both class stratification and the conflation of race and class that specifically positions the enduring illegitimacy of blackness, we further contend, any racial redemption imagined as a transformation reproduces rather than voids the reproduction and strengthening of the very elements of the classificatory system that are most strongly linked to the legitimation of those categoric distinctions of race and gender on which the past inequalities in the social relations of economic production and biological reproduction have depended. The back door through which NOI's masculine redemption imagines entrance to the power grid is well and truly cut.

Delving into the gender ideology of this religion-based "Black" nationalism has allowed us to consider why possibilities of such appropriations and transformations are made more difficult or remote, or both when the oppressed are, by both classificatory fiat and material practices, ideologically deemed the polar opposite of the constructive forces of that social order (Copeland 1939; Roediger 1991). In essence, confronting the gender stereotypes employed by the Nation of Islam allowed us to ask, with respect to a specific imagining of the relation between cultural and gender stereotypes, whether members of groups that are symbolically and pragmatically defined as the "blackguards" of a nation-state can make themselves constructive forces for their own redemption without being transformed into "white knights" in "blackface" that merely assume their position as controller of the key stake—the classification codes in accordance with which both moral and material hierarchies are justified in conjunction with distributions of goods, services, and responsibilities—in the order of power relations (Bourdieu 1977; Touraine 1977).

We recognize that the ability of the categoric distinctions of the classification system to lend moral credence to an economic order, depends on the relationality of identity struggles and their politics (Weeks 1987; Williams 1991, 1993). That is to say, the gender constructions and prayed for patterns of domesticity among the NOI must be understood as features of a politic of identity that is dialectical in its construction of the multivocal interpellations out of which a variety of class-fractured subjectivities are created. As a result any and all hailing of the racial subject—the Black man and woman in White America—becomes an instantiation of an identity representative of a particular conflation of race and class. This conflation produces the everyday understandings of the symbolics of gender within a race and, though NOI gender ideology focuses on race as if races can contest one another's positionality solely through male dominance, such interpellations cannot invoke a class neutral subject. Therefore, they cannot avoid the stickiness of the tar baby that clings to the race's gendered reputation.

Above all we draw from this case the lesson that these constraints and the rhetorical maneuvers such as those NOI encourage are not dependent on whether Black women have been "good enough" mothers and respectable humans—even women. Subordinated Blackness as a form of masculinity is, and will remain a paradox insofar as masculinity is defined as a dominant agency attributable only to a particular—White—class formation. Even if there were no historical grounds on which to defame Black women such needs must be invented in order to authorize a rhetoric of masculine redemption which helps to explain how Black men can be both masculine and subordinate. Likewise, clearly such a discourse does not depend on the fact of Black male failure—master narrative notwithstanding—for while Black men have, under very difficult circumstances, struggled to protect and to assist their mothers, sisters, and wives, short of displacing the synecdoche of White masculinity in the national ideological formation they lack the *ideological ground* on which to claim the success deserved for their economic, social, and moral efforts. The problems they, and the women they would reclaim, face are embedded in the precepts of the nationalist imagination that serve to misrecognize the race/class conflation and its explanation of how race becomes overdetermined in its association with positions of power and economic privilege. It is a system that eats up the profits while producing subordinate prophets who feed on females.

Notes

1. As Anna Julia Cooper saw the matter of women's passivity in problem solving:
   Man's work is only impoverished by her remaining dumb. The world has had to limp along with the wobbling gait and one-sided hesitancy of a man with one eye.

> Suddenly the bandage is removed from the other eye and the whole body is filled with light. It sees a circle where before it saw a segment. The darkened eye restored, every member rejoices with it. (1988: 122–23)

2. By which we mean logical in Bourdieu's sense of a "poor" or "economical" logic wherein social sense and meaning develop within limits imposed by the politicoeconomic position of class fractures, encouraging its members to eschew the necessity of employing the full range of "logic's logic."

3. See Geertz 1971, "Deep Play: Notes on a Balinese Cockfight" (1–38).

4. Quantum, in the sense we mean it here, is more often used in discussion focused on labeling portions of different types of racial blood (especially among Native Americans) an individual contains as an indication of the strength of his or her other- or self-ascribed identity. In the context of male-the-good-provider, blood is transformed into money, as Jessie Bernard (1983: 150), quoting John Demos, tells us "There was a myth 'that endows a moneymaking man with sexiness and virility,' and is based on man's dominance, strength, and ability to provide for and care for 'his' woman."

5. For examples of studies of nationalism, economic change, and its relations to intra- and interclass reconfigurations of manliness and masculinity in Great Britain and the United States, see Managan and Walvin (eds.) 1987, and Roper and Tosh (eds.) 1991. Such issues remain relevant whether we consider internal or external models of psychosexual development. We must explore gender developments in relation to racio-ethnic based construction of dependence and independence. The measure of psyche growth—even the vacillations between "bully" and "baby" which psychoanalytic approaches (Craib 1987) suggest are consequent to them—must be considered within the ideological field (competing nexi of ethnoracial genderings) whence are generated the criteria for such measurements.

References

Bernard, Jessie. 1983. "The Good-Provider Role: Its Rise and Fall." In *Face to Face: Fathers, Mothers, Masters, Monsters—Essays for a Nonsexist Future,* edited by Meg McGavran Murray. Pp. 145–67. Westport, CT & London, England: Greenwood Press.

Bourdieu, Pierre. 1977. *Outline of a Theory of Practice.* Cambridge, London, New York, and Melbourne: Cambridge University Press.

————. 1987. *In Other Words: Essays Towards a Reflexive Sociology.* Stanford: Stanford University Press.

Chodorow, Nancy. 1978. *The Reproduction of Mothering: Psychoanalysis and the Sociology of Gender.* Berkeley: University of California Press.

Clatterbaugh, Kenneth. 1990. *Contemporary Perspectives on Masculinity: Men, Women, and Politics in Modern Society.* Boulder, San Francisco, Oxford: Westview Press.

Cone, James H. 1991. *Martin and Malcolm and America, A Dream or a Nightmare.* Maryknoll, New York: Orbis Books.

Cooper, Anna Julia. 1988 [1892]. "Womanhood a Vital Element in the Regeneration and

Progress of a Race. *A Voice From the South.* Pp. 9–47. New York: Oxford University Press.

Copeland, Lewis C. 1939. "The Negro as a Contrast Conception." In *Race Relations and the Race Problem: A Definition and an Analysis,* edited by Edgar Thompson. Pp. 152–79. Durham, NC: Duke University Press.

Craib, Ian. 1987. "Masculinity and Male Dominance." *Sociological Review* 35(4): 721–43.

Crummell, Alexander. 1992 [1891]. "The Black Woman of the South: Her Neglects and Her Needs" In *Destiny and Race: Selected Writings, 1840–1898 Alexander Crummell,* edited by Wilson Jeremiah Moses. Pp. 211–23. Amherst: University of Massachusetts Press.

Du Bois, W. E. B. 1969 [1920]. *Darkwater: Voices From Within the Veil.* New York: Schocken Books.

Editorial. 1994. "Developing a Proper Relationship." *The Final Call* 13(20): 16 (July 20).

Epstein, Barbara Leslie. 1981. *The Politics of Domesticity: Women, Evangelism and Temperance in Nineteenth-Century America.* Middletown: Wesleyan University Press.

Farrakhan, Louis. 1992 [1971]. *7 Speeches.* (no location provided) WKU and the Final Call Inc.

———. 1994a "The Black Woman Is Sacred," edited text of June 25, 1994 speech in Atlanta, GA., *The Final Call,* 13(20): 20–21 (July 20).

———. 1994b "The Black Woman Is Sacred, Part 2." edited text of June 25, 1994 speech in Atlanta, GA., *The Final Call* (August 3) 13(21): 20–21.

———. 1994c "Let Us Make Man!" Part 8, audio tape of speech in Baltimore, MD. June 27th.

Frazier, Franklin E. 1966 [1939]. *The Negro Family in the United States.* Chicago: The University of Chicago Press.

Gay, Peter. 1993. *The Cultivation of Hatred: The Bourgeois Experience, Victoria to Freud, Vol. III.* New York and London: W.W. Norton & Co.

Geertz, Clifford. 1972. "Deep Play: Notes on the Balinese Cockfight." In *Myth, Symbol and Culture,* edited by Clifford Geertz. Pp. 1–38. New York: W.W. Norton.

Giddings, Paula. 1984. *When and Where I Enter: The Impact of Black Women on Race and Sex in America.* Toronto: Bantam Books.

Goux, Jean-Joseph. 1990. *Symbolic Economies: After Marx and Freud,* translated by Jennifer Curtiss Gage. Ithaca, NY: Cornell University Press.

Huet, Marie Hélène. 1993. *Monstrous Imagination.* Cambridge, MA: Harvard University Press.

Liebow, Elliot. 1966. *Tally's Corner.* Boston: Little, Brown & Co.

Lorde, Audre. 1984. "The Master's Tools Will Never Dismantle the Master's House." In *Sister Outsider: Essays and Speeches.* Pp. 110–13. Freedom, CA: The Crossing Press.

Managan, J. A. and James Walvin, eds. 1987. *Manliness and Morality: Middle-Class Masculinity in Britain and America, 1800–1940.* Manchester: Manchester University Press.

May, Larry and Robert Strikwerda, eds., with the assistance of Patrick D. Hopkins. 1992. *Rethinking Masculinity: Philosophical Explorations in Light of Feminism.* Lanham, MD: Littlefield Adams.

Melosh, Barbara, ed. 1993. *Gender and American History Since 1890.* London and New York: Routledge.

Morton, Patricia. 1991. *Disfigured Images: The Historical Assault on Afro-American Women.* Westport, CT: Praeger.

Moses, Wilson Jeremiah. 1978. *The Golden Age of Black Nationalism 1850–1925.* New York: Oxford University Press.

Mosse, George L. 1985. *Nationalism and Sexuality: Respectability and Abnormal Sexuality in Modern Europe.* New York: Howard Fertig.

Mouffe, Chantal. 1983. "The Sex/Gender System and the Discursive Construction of Women's Subordination." In *Rethinking Ideology: A Marxist Debate,* edited by Sakari Hänninen and Leena Paldán. Pp. 139–43. New York and Bagnolet, France: International General/IMMRC, Argument-Sonderbana AS 84.

Moynihan, Daniel P. 1965. *The Negro Family: The Case for National Action.* Washington: Department of Labor.

Muhammad, Elijah. 1957. *The Supreme Wisdom, Solution to the So-Called Negroes Problem.* Newport News, VA: The National Newport News and Communicator.

———. 1994. "The Black Woman." *The Final Call* (July 20) 13(20): 18.

Muhammad, Eva. 1993. "Muslim Woman: Removing the Myths." Audio tape of May 7th speech at Mosque 45 in Houston, Texas.

———. 1993. "21st Century Female." Audio tape of June 12th speech at Mosque 80 in Plainfield, New Jersey.

Muhammad, Tynetta. 1983. *The Women in Islam Educational Series: Families of Muhammad; Study Into the Birth of a Nation; Articles Based on Muhammad's History and the Holy Quran.* Chicago: The Final Call, Inc.

———. 1992. "Mary and Her Son Jesus: A Sign of the Chosen People of God." *The Final Call* (November 30th) 12(2): 9–10.

Patterson, Orlando. 1993. "Backlash: The Crisis of Gender Relations Among African Americans." *Transition* 62: 4–26.

Pease, Jane H. and William H. Pease. 1990. *Ladies, Women, & Wenches: Choice and Constraint in Antebellum Charleston & Boston.* Chapel Hill: University of North Carolina Press.

Roediger, David. 1991. *The Wages of Whiteness: Race and the Making of the American Working Class.* London and New York: Verso.

Roper, Michael and John Tosh, eds. 1991. *Manful Assertions: Masculinities Since 1800.* London and New York: Routledge.

Ruffin, Josephine St. Pierre. 1973 [1895]. "The Beginnings of the National Club Movement." In *Black Women in White America: A Documentary History,* edited by Gerda Lerner. Pp. 440–43. New York: Vintage Books.

Shabazz, Betty. 1992. "Loving and Losing Malcolm." *Essence* (February) 22(10): 50, 110.

Touraine, Alan. 1977. *The Self-Production of Society.* Chicago: University of Chicago Press.

Tuana, Nancy. 1993. *The Less Noble Sex: Scientific, Religious, and Philosophical Conceptions of Woman's Nature.* Bloomington and Indianapolis: Indiana University Press.

Valentine, Charles. 1968. *Culture and Poverty, Critique and Counter-Proposals.* Chicago: The University of Chicago Press.

Weeks, Jeffery "Questions of Identity." In *The Cultural Construction of Sexuality,* edited by Pat Caplan. Pp. 31–51. London and New York: Tavistock Publications.

Welter, Barbara. 1966. "The Cult of True Womanhood: 1820–1860." *American Quarterly* XVIII (2) Pt. 1: 151–74.

————. 1976. *Dimity Convictions: The American Woman in the Nineteenth Century.* Athens: Ohio University Press.

Williams, Brackette F. 1991. *Stains on My Name, War in My Veins: Guyana and the Politics of Cultural Struggle.* Durham, NC: Duke University Press

————. 1993. "The Impact of the Precepts of Nationalism on the Concept of Culture: Making Grasshoppers of Naked Apes." *Cultural Critique* (Spring) 24: 143–191.

Wilson, William Julius. 1987. *The Truly Disadvantaged: The Inner City, the Underclass, and Public Policy.* Chicago: University of Chicago Press.

Woodson, Carter G. [1933] 1977. *The Mis-Education of the Negro.* New York: AMS Press.

X, Malcolm. 1966 [1965]. *The Autobiography of Malcolm X with the Assistance of Alex Haley.* New York: Grove Press, Inc.

8

Boudoir Politics and
the Birthing of the Nation

*Sex, Marriage, and Structural Deflection in the
National Black Independent Political Party*

Paulette Pierce

"The history of a nationalist movement is almost always," Cynthia Enloe reminds us, "a history filled with gendered debate" (1990: 59). If this is so, why are women usually overlooked by most theories of nationalism, written out of masculinized histories of nationalist struggle, and silenced in the actual movements? Why, given the fact that females are often among the most devoted supporters and sometimes ranked among the top leadership of nationalist movements, are their names generally unknown and few monuments or myths constructed to immortalize their numerous contributions to the birth of the nation? In sum, why and how are women's experiences with nationalism consistently erased in different cultures and at different times? The Black Power movement in the United States offers an excellent opportunity to examine gender dynamics in a nationalist-based movement that has experienced major changes related to the "women's question." In less than a decade, advocates of Black nationalism swung from an official policy demanding total female submission to male authority inside the family and in the movement to one mandating absolute male-female equality inside a revitalized Black Power movement. The purpose of this essay is to analyze, first, how this dramatic change of policy came about, second, why it ultimately

216

failed to create real equality and, third, and most troubling, why it even failed to significantly alter women's role in Black nationalism as manifested in the continued exploitation of their labor, sexuality, and needs for human intimacy.[1]

In November 1980 more than two thousand Black participants drawn from across the country eagerly crowded into a West Philadelphia high school to create a new party to realize the long-deferred dream of Black Power. There was an all-star line up composed of many of the legendary leaders of the Black nationalist movement dating back to the late sixties including those who had by the mid-seventies converted from one of the many variants of Black nationalism to one of the competing versions of marxism-leninism that made up the "new communist" as opposed to "old left" party formations.

It was quite an event. On one side, forming a loose nationalist block, were a major hero of the civil-rights movement, recently exonerated and released from prison, who seemed to embody the righteousness of the nationalist cause; the first head of the Congress of African People (CAP), the leading cultural nationalist organization of the early seventies, eager to resume leadership of a national movement; the man who wrestled control of the National Black Political Assembly (NBPA) from the new communists in 1975 attended by his remaining loyal troops; and several nationally known scholar-activists institutionally linked to the Black Studies movement. On the other side, the marxist opposition, composed of the national Black leadership of old- and new-Left parties as well as independent marxists, did not lack its share of "superstars." Veterans of earlier battles who had earned reputations for theoretical brilliance, unflinching courage, and/or the use of brute force during the internecine struggle between marxism and nationalism that aimed to determine the future direction of the Black movement in the mid-seventies, commanded both visible admiration and fear as they moved through the assembly issuing instructions to strategically placed cadre.

Much of the excitement at the founding convention stemmed from the unexpectedly large turnout on relatively short notice but also from the realization that a major power struggle between old enemies was about to commence. The nationalists had initiated "the Call" to organize a new independent Black party, but it was clear that the Black Left wanted control and was prepared to submerge internal differences in order to usurp leadership of the revitalized Black movement organization. To those who yearned to reunite the radical wing of the Black movement, it was unfortunately apparent that the old race-versus-class debate had been resurrected along with the scattered movement forces and many feared that it would abort the birth of the new party before mobilizing efforts could seriously get under way.

Womanist Stirrings in the Black Nationalist Movement

There were however encouraging signs that some things at least had changed since the Black movement last peaked during the early 1970s.[2] Black women historically have been the backbone of Black resistance and civil-rights struggles in the United States. Though rarely acknowledged in the written histories of these movements, women usually represented a major, if not, the majority share of the participants and often served in primary as well as secondary leadership roles.[3] Notwithstanding the exaggerated macho imagery of the Black nationalist movement, recent publications clearly establish that women were often vital contributors to many of its leading organizations including the Universal Negro Improvement Association, the Black Panther Party, and the Congress of African People. What has yet to be explained adequately is how—despite their crucial work and sacrifices—women's contributions to Black nationalism are so systematically ignored.[4]

After the male nationalist leadership dramatically issued the Call at the August meeting of NPBA in New Orleans, as usual, women did most of the actual work of organizing the founding meeting in Philadelphia. Many of the local women who took on the herculean task of convention organizing were long-term veterans of the Black movement and knew the ropes. This time however the women decided to do some things differently. Specifically, they agreed that this convention (unlike those in the past) would provide child care for the participants and seek equality for women in the leadership.[5] Recognition of the significance of child care no doubt stemmed from their own experience. Many of the convention organizers were single mothers working full-time jobs. Sensitized by contact with the women's movement, and/or the new visibility of "women's issues" in the mass media, they felt that it would not be fair to let women who desired to attend this historic meeting of Black movement forces scurry around to make their own provisions for child care. And, because they were the ones doing the actual work they neither anticipated nor encountered any opposition to this new dimension of convention organizing.

They were less certain about the fate of their decision to seek full equality in the leadership of the proposed party. As veterans of SNCC, the Black Panther Party, the Nation of Islam, CAP, and other militant Black organizations, they had first-hand knowledge of women's extensive role in the leadership of these organizations as well as the extreme manifestations of Black patriarchy and sexual exploitation in the radical Black movement. This time, however, they claimed they were prepared to fight. According to the stalwart leader of the local organizing committee: "We were used to having to work, having to do this and that. We were strong-willed women. We weren't going to take any foolishness." Apparently they were disarmed by what occurred. With tensions already at the flash point as nationalists and marxists braced for another showdown, the women's resolution calling for absolute gender equality inside the party at every level of leadership easily passed without significant discussion.[6] Naturally the women were both stunned and relieved.

The sense of relief was, they soon discovered, premature. In the eyes of the male leaders the decision to pass the new gender rule was an expedient maneuver.

Neither the old-guard Black nationalist nor the new-communist/old-left Black male leadership could risk alienating the women at such a crucial moment. Both hoped to maintain the loyalty of female participants already identified with their respective ideological positions and to win over the uncommitted as well as those who might be alienated if their opponents decided to resist the women's move to equalize male-female relations.

And so it came to be that the newly created National Black Independent Political Party (NBIPP) inscribed the principle of gender equality into the founding documents, organizing procedures, and eventually the constitution of the new party. Although the anti-patriarchal sentiment of the local group of women who promoted the resolution was undoubtedly strong, there is little evidence that the majority of participants at the Philadelphia meeting or those who subsequently joined the movement (women as well as men) were either very attuned to the issue of sexism in the Black community and movement or committed to its eradication. Moreover, no efforts were made to educate Black movement veterans or new recruits about the nature of sexism in general or, in particular, how male supremacy had previously affected the Black movement, nor the kinds of fundamental changes that would be necessary to make gender equality a reality instead of a pleasing but ultimately empty symbolic gesture.

The failure of the women on the organizing committee to follow up on the gender equity resolution is not, as it may initially appear, surprising or indicative of insincerity. They were not a separately organized group of women prior to joining the party-building effort nor did they have or subsequently develop an explicitly feminist agenda they hoped to pursue in the new party. In fact, it is fair to say that even the most women-centered advocate among them lacked a clear feminist/womanist consciousness at the time. It was without question their shared sense of *racial injustice* and deep commitment to self-determination for the oppressed Black nation which individually led them to join NBIPP; their *consciousness of themselves as women* and the problems related thereto although real did not motivate their decision to sacrifice their time, energy, and talents to this organization. Like most women in nationalist movements around the world, these women unequivocally put group unity and the welfare of the nation *before* their interests as women per se. The oppression and exploitation of racialized/colonialized subordinated peoples is frequently so intense that women within the dominated communities cannot reasonably hope to improve their situation separate from their men despite internal tensions and contradictions based on male supremacy.

The decision to submerge the women's question in the Black movement in the United States in the face of overwhelming external threat is quite old. For example, driven from the public stage in her role as dynamic abolitionist speaker in the 1830s, Maria Stewart continued to dedicate her life's work to the liberation of Black people, which she envisioned in terms best described as proto-nationalist; however, she subsequently did so in ways deemed appropriate to a woman. Her published speeches clearly demonstrate her awareness of and opposition to women's subordination but there is also no doubt that she put the women's question second when forced to choose (1987: 48). The same reluctant subordination of the women's question is seen in the political biographies of Francis Ellen Watkins Harper, the nineteenth-century abolitionist and women's-rights activist; Ida B. Wells-Barnett, the fiery anti-lynching publicist and all around crusader for justice; Mary Church Terrell, a major leader of the Black Women's Club Movement and numerous civil-rights struggles from the close of the nineteenth century through the period of World War II; and several other distinguished Black women leaders.[7] Reluctantly, they all accepted what Enloe, looking at global patterns within nationalist movements, characterized as the "not now, later," rule as the only practical way to proceed (1990: 62).

Nationalist Precepts of Gender and Sexuality

It's a man's world and nowhere is this clearer than in politics. Even when not on the political stage or visible in the public arena, sex and gender exert powerful direction over the actions and the interpretations of the plays. Indeed feminist theorists are in broad agreement that the show could not, in fact, go on without the first act of sex. In the beginning there was man and woman. From this fact of sexual difference men have spun many varied and competing tales of the "political" and given birth to many a nation. Carole Pateman and Mary Shanley describe this new feminist insight as follows:

> Notwithstanding all the differences between theorists from Plato to Habermas, the tradition of Western political thought rests on a conception of the "political" that is constructed through the exclusion of women and all that is represented by femininity and women's bodies. Sexual difference and sexuality are usually treated as marginal to or outside of the subject matter of political theory, but the different attributes, capacities and characteristics ascribed to men and women by political theorists are central to the way in which each has defined the "political." Manhood and politics go hand and hand, and everything that stands in contrast to and opposed to political life and the political virtues has been represented by women, their capacities and the tasks seen as natural to their sex, especially motherhood. (1991: 3)

Despite the obvious link between fundamental Western political concepts such as citizenship, political virtues, rationality, democracy, individual rights, self determination, the state and the idea of nation, few feminists have extended their analyses of power and politics to include the study of nationalism. The oversight is probably related to the fact that leading feminist theorists interested in politics, most notably Carole Pateman (1989), Susan Okin (1979), Carroll Smith-Rosenberg (1989), Joan Landes (1988), and Joan Scott (1988), have focused upon the political significance of sex and gender ideologies in determining power relations between upper-status and upper-class men and women in Western nations. In short, they have tried to explain the overdetermined nature of the "political" in social life as primarily dependent upon relations of domination and subordination between elite White men and women. Therefore, while correctly highlighting the hidden but crucial role of sex and gender systems in politics, White feminists living in imperial nation-states have generally failed to ask how deeply gendered political concepts operate when doubly distorted through the oppressive structures of racial and colonial subordination.

If White men have claimed superordination on the basis of their manly attributes and political virtues closely tied to masculinity, then how have they interpreted the masculinity of male members of subordinated groups and nations? And, following the twisting trail of gendered political thought, what attributes of femininity have imperial Western theorists ascribed to the female members of subnationalities? Once we recall that the broadest stage of politics is after all the world and not the bedroom, it is obvious why the hegemonic definition of manhood cannot in fact be a universal category: this would make all males equal, which would never do. And because men are defined in opposition to their women, all women of the world cannot be the same either. In sum, if assumptions about masculinity and femininity are the foundation of political discourse in the Western thought, then Third-World nationalisms which are umbilically connected to First-World Nationalisms will have to work with these gendered blocks to build their separate nations to house their competing/alternative forms of manhood and womanhood.

It is therefore necessary to extend feminist analysis of the "political" to embrace nationalist discourses of both hegemonic nations and dominated nations. There are, as Nira Yuval-Davis and Floya Anthias point out in the Introduction to *Woman-Nation-State,* broad similarities in the ways racial/national/ethnic collectivities and states or all rely upon women to achieve their objectives, i.e., reproduce members, socialize the next generation, mark group boundaries, and so forth. Nevertheless, they are careful to stress the multitude of serious differences that characterize nation- and state-building processes depending upon unique group histories, cultural heritage and the balance of current political forces both inside and outside the different nations/states. It is only against this shifting backdrop of racialized difference, colonial and anti-colonial struggle that we can begin to make sense of the gendered discourses of competing nationalisms improvised by actors united in movements they hope will give birth to free nations wherein they will become real men and true women as prescribed by their own nationalist precepts of gender and sexuality.

Nationalist precepts of gender and sexuality are essential to the identity and critical to the practice of nationalists. As implied above, it is often in terms of their shared ideas about what it means to be a man or woman that a group comes to see itself as constituting "a people" or "a nation." And, it is frequently out of a commitment to live in accordance with these precepts of manhood and womanhood that they claim the right to self-determination, and subsequently launch nationalist movements to achieve their unique vision of peoplehood, that is, of their being a particular type of man/human and [wo]man. Ironically, several researchers have found, it is women, not men, who are most central or critical to the related processes of nationalist identity formation, demarcation of group boundaries, ideological reproduction, and community-building. Because the idea of nation almost always involves some sense of shared blood/descent and common destiny, it is not surprising, as Carol Smith points out (in this volume), would-be nations or "imagined communities" put great stock in controlling the marital, as well as sexual, practices of its members. The question of the sexual purity and vulnerability of the nation's women is always a burning issue in the nationalist mind. Men are glorified as warriors but it is the women who must properly bear the future generations and safely pass on the cultural patrimony if the nation is to survive undefiled.

According to Cynthia Enloe (1989: 54), this kind of thinking confronts women with an uncomfortable paradox. The more importance attached to women's role as mothers of the nation, the more thoroughly the nationalist movement or state will seek to control their body/sexuality and appropriately define/restrict their activities in the public sphere. In other words, there is an inverse relationship between the symbolic significance of "Woman" as "sacred womb" to nationalist ideology and real women's actual freedom and participation in the nationalist project.[8]

The need to protect the nation's women does not stem only from a concern for sexual purity but also is strongly related to the belief that women are naturally more susceptible to cultural corruption (assimilation) and co-optation than are men. The colonizer (always assumed to be male in the patriarchal world view of nationalism) is much more able to penetrate the (weak) mind of a woman and transform her into a tool of his oppression. Thus, *both* the mind and the body of the colonized woman is portrayed as an easy target of racist-imperialist rape. It is therefore common practice within nationalist discourse to interpret the rape of women not so much as an outrage against womanhood as an assault on the manhood of the subordinated community. He/man is rendered the victim while she/woman is represented as merely the object/tool of this national disgrace, a tragedy in which the real actors (the colonized and the colonizer) are, of course, men.

The incredibly sexist logic of nationalist thinking was unfortunately all too evident in the speeches of Malcolm X throughout his years with the Nation of Islam and, as he tells us in his autobiography, also governed his handling of the intimate details of his private life. Based on his own experience on ghetto streets, the teachings of the Honorable Elijah Muhammed, the Holy Qur'an, and the Christian Bible, Malcolm X was absolutely convinced that all "women were only tricky, deceitful, untrustworthy flesh" (1965: 226). Apparently even the sisters in the Nation were not to be trusted. Following the Nation's strict rule of premarital chastity, Malcolm carefully kept his distance from even the pure obedient women of Islam and strongly urged the young warriors in the Fruit of Islam to do likewise

(1965: 226). James Cone observes that Malcolm X's "misogynic view" was so bla-
tantly insulting that sisters in the Nation frequently complained to Elijah
Muhammad whenever Malcolm taught one of the women's training classes (1991:
275). Black women visitors not feeling any special obligation to the Nation were
more likely to just walk out as Cone describes in the following scene:

> In 1956 at the Philadelphia Temple, Malcolm gave a series of addresses on
> black women, accusing them of being the "greatest tool of the devil." "How do
> you think this black man got in this state?" he asked his audience. "By our
> women tricking him and tempting him, and the devil taught her how to do
> this." "The trickiest in existence is the black woman and the white man." "If
> you go to court with your wife, she will always win over you because the devil
> can use her to break down more of our black brothers. . . . It is this evil black
> woman in North America who does not want to do right and holds the man
> back from saving himself." (1991: 275)

It would be reassuring if Malcolm X's views about women and their role in
subordination of the Black race/nation could be dismissed as the extreme opinion
of a religious fanatic on the fringe of Black-nationalist discourse in the United
States but this is not the case. Secular variants of Black nationalism during the
1960s likewise had scathing criticism for Black women who were presumed to
become the tools of White men if they were not appropriately controlled by
supermasculine Black male nationalists who swore to die for the nation if they
could find no space to be real men within America. None articulated this misogynic and suicidal dimension of Black nationalism better than Eldridge Cleaver in his
wildly popularly book, *Soul on Ice.* Cleaver unabashedly explained that women are
primarily a means of communications between men, ". . . I know that the white
man made the black woman the symbol of slavery and the white woman the symbol of freedom. Every time I embrace a black woman, I'm embracing slavery, and
when I put my arms around a white woman, well, I'm hugging freedom. The
white man forbade me to have the white woman on pain of death. . . . I will not
be free until the day I can have a white woman in my bed and a white man minds
his own business" (1968: 160–61). He went on to explain that as long as this
"war" between the White man and Black man went on the Black woman would be
the White man's "silent ally" even if she failed to realize it. "That's why, all down
through history, he has propped her up economically above you and me, to
strengthen her hand against us" (1968: 162). According to this nationalist logic,
the defeat of the Black nation would remain self evident as long as the White man
could "bind [the Black man's] rod," "fetter [his] bull balls" and "fuck" all the
women, Black as well as White while the Black man only had access to women of
his own kind (1968: 165). Such were the most influential musings of the fertile
imagination of Black nationalists during the sixties as they labored to birth a free
nation or die in the process.

Building a Nation of Neo-African Men and Women

The men and women who came together in the independent Black political movement in the early 1980s had for the most part been socialized into Black
movement culture of the late sixties. At that time Black nationalism displaced
civil-rights liberalism as the dominant movement ideology. The young Black mili-
tants who claimed leadership of the movement questioned everything: the old
assumptions about White liberal allies, violence versus nonviolence, separation
versus integration, human rights versus civil rights, and so forth. But somehow it
all seemed to be summed up in the debate about the character of Black manhood
and, the "burning question" of the role of Black women in the movement.
Writing in 1969 Toni Cade insisted that Black liberation and women's liberation
were inextricably linked but ominously warned,

> there is a dangerous trend observable in some quarters of the Movement to
> program Sapphire out of her "evil" ways into a cover-up, shut-up, lay-back-
> and-be-cool obedience role. . . . She is being encouraged—in the name of
> revolution no less—to cultivate "virtues" that if listed would sound like the
> personality traits of slaves.

Blind to the intrinsic dependence of nationalism upon gendered thinking, Cade
naively suggested: "Perhaps we need to let go of all notions of manhood and femininity and concentrate on Blackhood" (1970: 102–03).

Clearly, whereas Cade did not understand that Black manhood metonymized
the race, such was self-evident to Nathan Hare, the editor and publisher of the
Black Scholar, a journal that served at the time as one the major organs of the cultural-nationalist movement.

> The oppression of the black male essentially means the oppression of his
> kind—the black race. Historically, the white oppressor has pitted male against
> female and, in the analysis of Franz Fanon, forced and seduced the female to
> take on his values and through her emasculated and controlled the man.
>
> This is the day of the black male. . . . This is the era of liberation . . . the
> black man will be able to bring the woman along in our common struggle, so
> that we will not need a black women's liberation movement. . . .
>
> In our time, the struggle to restore the black male's position, black male
> consciousness, arose simultaneously with the general rise of black conscious-
> ness. Thus it had as its goal the re-unification of the family. The black man has
> an obligation, then, to halt this desertion of his woman, to head-off the sexual
> aggression of the white female and show the black female that she has to exhib-
> it the qualities he wants her to possess. (1971: 32–33)

It was an appealing offer in the eyes of many Black women, especially younger
Black women on White college campuses who for the first time (in the wake of
integration) found themselves in open competition with White women for the

attention of Black men. A good Black-nationalist man promised to treat a Black woman as his "queen," to love, to respect, to protect, to provide for her, and to grant her the supreme honor of becoming the mother of his beautiful Black babies (Males preferred, of course, as future warriors!).

All this in exchange for Black women's acceptance of their "natural roles." According to Maulana Kargena, the leading cultural-nationalist theorist of the period, "What makes a woman appealing is femininity and she can't be feminine without being submissive." A neo-African woman was suppose to inspire her man through public rituals of deference and submit to his supreme authority in the "house/nation" because "his knowledge of the world is broader, his awareness is greater, his understanding is fuller and his application of this information is wiser."[9] Ironically, it tended to be young, better educated Black women with some college experience who flocked to the new cultural-nationalist groups which promised to put women *back* into their traditional roles and proper place, for example, Karenga's U.S. organization on the West Coast and its East Coast and Midwest off-shoots collectively known as the Congress of African People.

Black-nationalist precepts of gender and sexuality simultaneously managed to naturalize a masculinist image of the "imagined community/nation" as a return to tradition/Mother Africa and idealize relations of domination inside the family/"house" as the restoration of the home as a place of refuge. A woman's place was in the home where she and the children would be protected. When the exigencies of the nationalist struggle required her to enter the public/political sphere it was understood that the natural order would not be upset: her duties would "complement," never challenge or overshadow, those of men.

Idealized images of home and family as refuge and protection did not prevent and, in fact, may have encouraged the exploitation of women in the private sphere. It was not uncommon for women to outnumber men in the Black-nationalist organizations of the sixties and seventies. In addition to the masculinist ideology, the sex-ratio imbalance furthered privileged men. Many took advantage of the situation to carry on intimate relationships with several women simultaneously, often openly. Indeed, polygamy was frequently advocated as both a legitimate and supposedly culturally authentic way to handle the surplus of women to men in the Black community. Thus demographics and nationalist definitions of acceptable gender behavior made it easy for men to reap the fruits of women's domestic labor (a well-kept house, clean laundry, good meals, and reliable child care for their off spring) while freely indulging their sexual appetites—all in the name of nation-building!

The mix of sex and politics is not, let me hasten to add, by any means peculiar to the Black movement. *Boudoir politics,* that is the manipulation of human needs for physical and/or emotional intimacy, has always played a major part in public life; yet it rarely has received the serious attention it deserves. Women as well as men play the game of boudoir politics. It is common knowledge that many women in high positions of power have gotten there by virtue of their familial and/or sexual ties to men in power.[10] Nonetheless, in the game of boudoir politics men have the clear advantage. On the one hand, men frequently use sex and/or the promise of intimacy to recruit women who will serve their interests in organizations or political parties. Love, sex, and intimacy as currency often buy enormous labor and loyalty. Hence, some men are able to significantly enhance their power position (as well as their ego) through strategic use of intimacy. Indeed, a man's ability to control and manipulate women is still in many quarters seen as evidence of the killer/hunter instinct that is often valued in a leader. On the other hand, women may rise to great heights of power using the bonds of intimacy but, in most cases, they remain dependent on their male benefactors, and, if they get too ambitious and transgress the acceptable limits of surrogate/dependent power, they are soon viciously attacked. Once the formerly powerful woman slips from grace, the assumptions that typically surround her tenure are made manifest: overnight she may be denounced as a "whore."[11]

Humiliating and degrading stereotypes of women in power pervade most human cultures and, according to Suzanne Dixon, have proven remarkably consistent over great periods of time. The stereotypes are, she argues, extremely effective means of limiting women's aspirations and undermining the achievements of those valiant and determined enough to pursue public power against the odds (1992). Whether true or false, women who acknowledge their desire for high position and power (that is, pursue it in their own right instead of as surrogates for men) are likely to be portrayed as hypersexual deviants, clearly out of control and dangerous to good public order.[12] Nice, normal, respectable girls/women simply don't act in ways associated with the acquisition and exercise of real power. Meanwhile, men who announce lofty ambitions and unabashedly pursue the pinnacle of power are revered as models of manhood young boys should look up to. Furthermore, where men are concerned rumors of hypersexuality often serve to enhance their image of strength and power. In light of these deeply rooted cultural patterns, it is not surprising that men are much more likely to deliberately and successfully use the sheets in their climb to power while women are more likely to risk reputation and position when they enter the boudoir and mix sex and politics.

There Is No Victory Without Struggle

Confronting this general and racially particular mysogenist dynamic, it looked as if Black women had won a great victory inside the Black-liberation movement when the resolution calling for equal sharing of all party leadership breezed through unopposed at the founding convention of the National Black Independent Political Party. Organizing literature used to recruit membership and mobilize mass support over the next several months in preparation for the first party congress held in August 1981 proudly cited the new Party's commitment to gender equality along with the more usual pledges to fight racism and class exploitation. In fact, women who joined the Party shortly after the founding convention recall that the fifty-fifty rule was already treated as if it was a standard-operating procedure in the Black movement. They never thought to inquire about its origin. And the principle of gender equality was carefully followed in the organizational and leadership structure laid out in the new Party's constitution.

At the national level the constitution called for: male and female co-chairs responsible for policy and administration; male and female national representatives to handle public relations; a presiding officer for the annual party congress and central committee (if the first was male then the latter had to be female and vice versa); and, male and female co-chairs of finance and fundraising. The central committee which was the highest decision-making body between party congresses was composed of these eight top officers, the male-female co-chairs of all standing committees, and two male-female representatives from each of the local chapters and from the state coordinating committees. The same formal structure of gender equality was reproduced at the local and state level. There was even a constitutional mandate to organize a women's commission to oversee the Party's work in this supposedly vital area.

It was not immediately apparent to women in the Party that the formal structure was anything but fair. Their gender was not suppose to matter; they were equal leaders with their paired associates to be treated and judged "just like men." Only with much painful experience did it begin to dawn on a few of the women in leadership that the structure of the organization itself, as well as the very idea of "the leader" was in fact thoroughly gendered. Most never did get it. Removing the veil of formal equality/universalism that conceals so much of the relations of gender, race, and class domination in modern society is no easy task.

The Gendered Subtext of Formal Organization

Feminist theorists have only recently began to seriously think about the subtleties involved. In *The Bonds of Love,* Jessica Benjamin analyzes rationality as a discourse of domination par excellence:

> It is difficult to grasp the fact that the center of male domination lies not in direct expressions of personal violence (rampant though they are) but in the societal rationality which may or may not be defended by men. Male domination, as Weber said of rationalization, works through the hegemony of impersonal organization: of formal rules that refer to the hypothetical interaction of autonomous individuals. . . .
>
> The presence of women has no effect on its rules and processes. The public institutions and relations of production display an apparent genderlessness, so impersonal do they seem. Yet it is precisely this objective character, with its indifference to personal need, that is recognized as the hallmark of masculine

power. It is precisely the pervasive depersonalization, the banishment of nur-
turance to the private sphere, that reveal the logic of male dominance, of
female denigration and exclusion. (1989: 216 and 187)

The family (where personal needs supposedly are met) is of course the women's
sphere where there's no pretense of equality. Thus, as Benjamin astutely argues,
the very possibility of an impersonal order governed by rationality and formal
equality presupposes the existence of a domestic sphere based on tradition and
"natural" inequalities.

Joan Acker's critique of the gendered subtext of modern organization pursues a
similar line of reasoning. Modern bureaucracies are, Acker reminds us, instruments of control and anything that gets in the way of goal-oriented activities is
formally ruled out. It is not surprising, Acker observes, that foremost among the
disruptive influences, bureaucracies have historically attempted to exclude or at
least suppress is sexuality. Fleshing out Benjamin's more abstract analysis, Acker
sadly concludes,

> the abstract worker is actually a man, and it is the man's body, its sexuality,
> minimal responsibility in procreation, and conventional control of emotions
> that pervades work and organizational processes. Women's bodies—female
> sexuality, their ability to procreate and their pregnancy, breast-feeding, and
> child care, menstruation, and mythic "emotionality"—are suspect, stigma-
> tized, and used as grounds for control and exclusion. (1990: 152)

Under the circumstances, to merely include women in the existing structures of
modern society without directly challenging the male-biased set of assumptions
which underlay the supposedly impersonal rules, roles, and practices of modern
social organization is a sad hoax.

This is however the standard response by hegemonic classes to demands, from
marginalized groups, for greater inclusion in modern systems of control and
resource distribution. I refer to this popular deception as *structural deflection*.
Structural deflection is characterized by an adroit substitution of a formal equality
for a true equality that would require fundamentally changing the way things are
done, or even changing the goals of the organization or both. In the case of the
NBIPP, the adoption of the fifty-fifty rule preserved male privilege in two important ways. First, because the separation of public and private life, based on an
implicitly male model of the activist and/or leader, was not questioned, the new
policy simply earned women the right to prove themselves *as men* in a male-
defined space. If they succeeded in their new leadership roles they would do so by
adopting the same attitudes and behaviors associated with respected male leaders.
If, however, they failed it would reinforce the belief that women just don't have
"the right stuff" to be leaders. Either way, the patriarchal ideals which have historically characterized Black nationalism and the more recent macho style of
leadership would be further valorized. Second, the Party's sex-paired leadership

structure limited electoral contests to members of the same sex thus protecting males from the status deflation implicit in direct competition with members of an inferior group/sex.

Despite how little was actually given, the new policy nonetheless enhanced the reputation of Black male nationalists who were praised for what one participant characterized as their "eager embrace" of women as equals. Alas, only in retrospect, as painful wounds slowly healed, have women begun to figure out why, notwithstanding what looked like a level playing field, so few of them made it past first base. In order to illustrate gender dynamics within the tension-ridden and contradictory structures of egalitarianism and patriarchal nationalism as thus far broadly defined, we will now turn to the experiences of three Black women who shared NBIPP's top leadership with the Black men who, from the very beginning, were regarded as the dominant or superior half of the supposedly equal partnership.

Women in NBIPP's Top Leadership

Two of the three top female leaders were new to the Black movement at the national level. Before joining the NBIPP their activism was restricted to Black student politics on individual campuses and piecemeal community organizing. The younger of the two neophytes, who I will call Beverly, had concentrated on her professional education and recently graduated law school. Women in the Party's national leadership saw her as tough, bright, and very ambitious. Aside from one strong female ally in her local chapter, Beverly was not close to other women in the Party. Most women agreed that she acted just like the men: "She never fit in with the other sisters very well. . . . She went after leadership. . . . [She] knew how to compete with the males" (K. F. 1990, Washington, D.C.). This mannish behavior which alienated most women did not win her great favor among the men in the organization. In fact male members of the local chapter in North Carolina, which was at the time her home, berated her character and performance with the usual stereotypic imagery invoked to discipline or dismiss women who have the temerity to openly seek power. They claimed that she was selfish, manipulative, ignorant of politics, and simply wanted to use the Party to make a name for herself and establish a national network. They seemed to take special pleasure in the fact that she not only failed to distinguish herself at the national level but frequently suffered public embarrassment.

Beverly lacked the leadership skills and experience needed to function equally with her male counterpart. The difference in their treatment as NBIPP's national representatives was, she confesses, obvious and frequently humiliating. She described herself as an adequate public speaker, who was more adept at writing. Unfortunately for her, orality is far more esteemed in the Black community and its movement culture than is the written word. Supporters tend to demand "great speakers," by which they generally mean someone who has mastered the art of public speaking that most closely approximates the style associated with Black preaching—a calling that until recently was almost exclusively reserved for Black men. Local chapters would invite the male national representative to attend special organizing and/or publicity events and would protest when instead she was sent. When she went public, ignominy was always a distinct possibility. Despite the wounds, which have only partially healed, Beverly nonetheless credits the Party with having offered her extraordinary learning opportunities. Moreover, she does not question whether or not the Party's masculinist definition of leadership was in fact best suited to the stated goals of grassroots empowerment and the eventual liberation of the Black community.

In contrast, her male counterpart was already an experienced movement leader and dynamic orator when he joined the party. In fact, he was a charismatic preacher with a national reputation established during the earlier civil-rights phase of the Black movement. And, notwithstanding the clerical collar and a beautiful wife, he was also known to be quite a lady's man who regularly used women to satisfy his political as well as personal agenda.[13] Given the obvious discrepancies in their ability to exercise leadership, how, I inquired, did they handle the situation? According to Beverly, they "never, never" discussed it!

The situation was even more frustrating for the woman I will call Eva who had additional responsibilities to juggle as a single mother with two children to support. She was also working on her doctorate. Not surprisingly, the Ph.D. was put on hold as she slowly sank beneath an increasing burden of movement work that was shifted to her shoulders by her male national co-chair. He frequently taught at different colleges and universities while also slowly pursuing his doctorate, and he too had children. Nonetheless, the similarities were more apparent than real. Eva was frequently torn between her desire to be a "good mother," which implied putting one's children first, and the desire to be a "good leader," which meant putting the nation first. The tension between her public and private life was most acute in terms of time. She recalls that it was both painful to take time away from her children in order to attend frequent party meetings and often a nightmare to arrange for child care, especially when these meetings lasted a weekend or longer.[14] He, on the other hand, had a wife who helped to financially support the household and, because she was not active in the Party, child care was not a problem for him. Moreover, her typical absence from party affairs freed him, if he so desired, to play the game of boudoir politics with little risk of disrupting his domestic life.

Although inexperienced at this level of movement activism, Eva was initially confident about her leadership abilities. In the past, people had always affirmed her work and talents. This was not to be the case in the NBIPP. She just didn't fit the dominant (implicitly male) model of a "real leader." Eva is a beautiful, petite woman with refined mannerisms. Possessing what, in the pre-Black Power days, was called "good hair" and a "high yalla" complexion, she more closely resembled the popular image of the tragic mulatta than the radical Black nationalist leader. Nor did Eva *act* like the stereotypical militant Black leader. She was soft spoken to an extreme, neither enjoyed public speaking nor the limelight, and preferred neither to oppose nor to embarrass anyone publicly. Her public silence became a topic of gossip inside the party. Many, according to Eva, saw her quietness as evidence of low intelligence and proof of her inability to be a real leader. She was dismissed as "the men's flunky."

Other women in the leadership eventually confronted her on this point. While sympathetic to Eva's desire to transform the macho style of party leadership, they wanted her to publicly challenge the male co-chair. She refused the confrontational approach and continued to discuss behind closed doors their differences over styles of leadership, policy, and the division of labor. As she explained it to me, "He was not the type of person who could handle being criticized; definitely not public criticism." She believed her only hope of getting through to him was to approach him discreetly and to continue to accept a disproportionate share of the tedious and unglamorous work required of the co-chairs.

This pattern of female public deference is common among subordinated racial/national groups. The obvious shortcomings and often abusive behavior of subordinated men are usually excused by their women and attributed to the systematic attack upon their manhood by the dominant group. With their public deference women of the subordinated community hope to assuage the status wounds of their fathers, husbands and sons, or, at least, avoid the charge that they are the ones responsible for emasculating the race/nation.[15] The release of the infamous Moynihan Report that resurrected the myth of the Black matriarch who castrates Black men at the same time as the Black movement swung towards nationalism further exaggerated the existing pattern of female public deference in the Black community.[16] Eva's pains to avoid hurting the male co-chair's fragile (albeit inflated) male ego was characteristic of most women in the Party's leadership.

Eva's male co-chair not only fit the image of the radical Black-nationalist leader but had actually been one of the nationally recognized leaders of the movement since the sixties. His movement credentials (by which informal status in the Party was allocated) were impeccable. He was, after all, the man who had managed to out maneuver the new communists when they had tried to seize control of the radical Black movement from the nationalists back in the mid-seventies. Experienced and well-versed, he could be fierce in debate and, unlike Eva, he relished the spotlight.

Paradigmatic Privilege and the Preservation of Patriarchy

Even if Eva had chosen to publicly confront the male co-chair it is very unlikely that she would have been successful. In order to be heard, let alone respected, in the Party, a person had to be able to frame his or her remarks in terms of the reigning paradigm of the radical Black movement. The paradigm defined both what are considered to be legitimate topics of discussion and how they are to be presented. Hence inside the Black movement the paradigm controlled both the substance and style of all discussions. From the sixties to date, Black ghetto culture, specifically the "masculine mystique" associated with it, pan-Africanism, and marxist-leninist theory have been the most obvious influences on this paradigm.[17]

In the public space claimed by Black radicalism style counts for almost everything. Fighting words, an attitude of toughness, the appearance of the street warrior can create and sustain a reputation of powerful/effective leadership as readily as can deeds. Malcolm X, more than any other recent Black leader, both fit and helped to define this ideal of Black leadership as supermasculinity. He was, Ossie Davis eulogized, our manhood, "our shining Black Prince." Malcolm X was tall, handsome, obviously intelligent, and charming, but just beneath the gracious manners and alluring smile was a palpable rage, raw energy, and the hunger hunter waiting to strike. The electricity produced by these opposing poles of his personality was positively seductive.

Sophisticated news reporters, experienced civil-rights leaders, college professors, and Oxford debaters—all were sitting ducks when Malcolm X took aim. His words were weapons, which he masterfully used to trap, wound, or destroy his enemies. In his arsenal of words, humor and sarcasm could be just as deadly as a barrage of facts. The Black community delighted in the way the Brother could, as folks on street described it, "Tell it like it is!" Friends and critics alike were forced to recognize Minister Malcolm's extraordinary communication skills. In fact, some media experts credit him with inventing the thirty second sound-bite before we had the term. Through brilliant and calculated use of the mass media, Malcolm X created an image of leadership that effectively challenged the authority of Dr. Martin Luther King, Jr., and quite unintentionally that of his mentor, the Honorable Elijah Muhammad.

Few paid close attention to Malcolm X's critique of his own leadership as a Minister and National Representative of the Nation of Islam after he was forced to leave: he admitted that he had actually *done very little* other than talk for the entire period he was with Elijah Muhummad's separatist movement. His inactivity was not however of his own will; Elijah Muhammad strictly forbid Black Muslims from becoming involved in the intensifying Black struggle for civil rights. In a candid interview with Gordon Parks, Malcolm X shared a devastating portrait of the NOI and his own role as a leader, "I did many things as a Muslim that I'm sorry for now. I was a zombie then—like all Muslims—I was hypnotized, pointed in a certain direction and told to march. Well, I guess a man's entitled to make a fool of himself if he's ready to pay the cost. It cost me 12 years" (1965: 29). Unable to take action, Malcolm confessed that the militant reputation of the Muslims was without real substance, "Not involved in anything but just standing on the sidelines condemning everything" (1989: 174). Finally free of the suffocating restraints of a brutally repressive authoritarian organization, Malcolm promised to lead the most militant Blacks in a new organization which would not only talk tough but take meaningful action (1989: 142–43). He was assassinated before he could keep this promise.

Memory is a tricky thing. Groups no less than individuals often remember most clearly what best suits their present needs. In the wake of Malcolm's and King's assassinations, militant Blacks needed a clear-cut hero to sustain their commitment to struggle so they ignored the self-confessed limitation of Malcolm X as a model of radicalism and turned him into their "shining Prince," the image of the super-macho Black leader that reigns to date. To be like Malcolm would-be leaders had to prove their loyalty to the Black masses (most easily achieved by adopting ghetto behavior), demonstrate an appreciation of the African heritage of Blacks (most readily signaled by African garb and/or name change), and accomplish a verbal "put down" of any contenders to leadership. The eruption of marxism-leninism in the Black movement in the mid-seventies augmented the masculine mystique and neo-Africanism by adding a new "scientific" aura to the image of the radical Black leader. Now intelligence and strength would also be measured in terms of one's fluency in the new revolutionary jargon.

Taken together, it is not surprising that struggles for leadership in the radical Black movement tend to be exciting spectacles wherein incredible verbal combat usually suffices in place of actual blood-letting. In the NBIPP, the contest was supposedly open to men and women alike. In fact, the radical Black paradigm favored men. Of course, not all men were able to compete. Nonetheless, men were more likely than women to be comfortable with the aggressive and threatening style that characterized party debates and to be more familiar with marxist theory. Competition was highly intellectual but the threat of violence also hung in the air.[18]

According to several respondents, the floor was dominated by the handful of men who had mastered marxist-leninist theory, pan-Africanist theory or both, and who knew the histories of Black nationalism and of the Left in the United States. They "insisted" that any contributions to the debate had to be presented in one or more of these frameworks or else, as one woman recalled, "you'd be cut to ribbons." Regarding one of the most "ideologically advanced" men in the Party, another woman recalled: "He was very rigid. If you couldn't speak in that [marxist] construct, he would really eat you up. You would have to speak in it" (K. F. 1990, Washington, D. C.). Or shut up. One of the male leaders, himself adept at debate, admitted that participation in these events took training. "You need[ed] to up your pain tolerance, emotional tolerance, and concentration level" (T. M. 1989, Philadelphia). Women increasingly came to see the debates as "dick fights," "sick," and as a "male construct." At one point a top female leader even suggested that what they needed was a "process observer" whose intervention could serve to reduce intimidation and allow for open discussion. Most women merely sulked and complained that "the men disenfranchised or dismissed [them]." Others maintain that they wanted no part of the leadership discussions anyway. In general, the women in the party (along with the majority of men) were silenced by the exercise of the paradigmatic privilege which was essential to the preservation of patriarchy in the Party.

Unfortunately, it was in the arena of public debate that a would-be leader had to win respect and a following within the Party. By refusing to participate in such contests, Eva eliminated herself from consideration as a "serious" political leader. She was admired for her personal morality and for her willingness to endlessly work behind the scenes, but, alas, this was not the leadership criteria the Party used. Eva consciously strove to change the masculinist bias of the leadership model. She readily admits that she failed. Her most telling failure is revealed by the following incident during which Eva did the unthinkable for a leader of nationalist organization, she cried.

For several days, with little or no sleep Eva had been working to get everything ready for a major national meeting of the Party. Without time for preparation she was asked to hold a press conference. When Party members insisted that she must hold a press conference, she refused and ultimately broke down in tears. Like wildfire, word of her unprecedented behavior spread through the Party. Responses included shock, outrage, disgust, and pity, but little real compassion, and no approval. Leaders are supposed to be strong and tough to act like real men! Sure, they can express emotions like joy, anger, and even, properly controlled, pain and disappointment but *never* weakness which is what tears are thought to symbolize. When she tried to explain to those who would listen that they should *not* want a leader who would not cry in public, she fully felt how different her own evolving understanding of the requisites of leadership was from that of the Party majority. Not surprisingly, they thought that she was crazy or just making excuses for herself.

Boudoir Politics and Womanist Consciousness

The new road along which Eva sought to walk was especially lonely because, with few exceptions, not even the women in the Party tried to understand her position and beliefs. Of course this merely suggests that like most men most women have internalized patriarchal standards.[19] Fortunately there was another woman in the top leadership who did empathize with Eva and shared her struggle to reimagine the Black movement from a womanist perspective.[20]

Zelda (a pseudonym) was in fact the woman who headed the local committee that organized the Philadelphia meeting and put forth the demand for fifty percent of the party leadership. Her determination to change women's position in the Black movement grew out of years of first-hand experience. She was a leader in SNCC when that organization tore itself apart in the debate over Black nationalism. She and her activist husband sided with the nationalists and later joined the Nation of Islam when it became clear that SNCC would continue to unravel. He was assigned important work but the Black Muslims expected her to step into the shadows and display proper respect for the brothers who would lead the movement. Unhappy with this explicitly patriarchal definition of her role she and her husband left the Nation and joined a Black nationalist group advocating armed struggle. She laughed as she recalled how close to prison or death this flirtation with the coercive forces of the state brought her. Her husband actually was incarcerated for a number of years, leaving her with a baby girl to raise on her own. After his release from prison they split up.

By 1980 when she was asked to help build a new Black nationalist party, Zelda said she was prepared to resist the old patriarchal practices. It was more than a matter of improving the status of women. She was increasingly convinced that the Black movement would never succeed until it gave serious attention to the special needs of Black women—particularly poor Black women who are struggling to raise the next generation, usually without the help of Black men. These women, Zelda explained, are in dire financial shape but, just as importantly, lonely and desperately in need of sexual and emotional intimacy. Any movement that hopes to empower them as opposed to just mobilize them for the purpose of exploitation will have to, Zelda argues, deal directly with these issues.

It is difficult to imagine a more fundamental challenge to politics as usual which is premised on the presumed split between the public and the private spheres. Zelda's insistence that the need for love and sexual intimacy are political issues flies in the face of traditional political thought which maintains that such personal/sexual issues ideally should be kept out of the public arena. Nationalist movements consistently challenge their subordinated status in the dominant political order, claim the right to separate from it, or both, but to date they have not questioned the separation of public and private life which is the cornerstone of the modern political order. But it is precisely this vitiating split which must be healed if subordinated nationalists are ever to get beyond the destructive patterns of nation-building borrowed from the West and blended with their own ancient phallic traditions of male honor, female purity, and territorial possession/domination. If the *whole human being* does not become the focus of political attention even so-called successful nationalist movements will, recent feminist scholarship warns, simply create new patriarchal states which reproduce most of the old abuses from which the people sought liberation.[21]

The provision of child care at the founding meeting was the first evidence of Zelda's growing commitment to womanist transformation of the Black nationalist movement. The resolution calling for gender equality was the second major sign. In both instances she was able to win the necessary support of other women. However neither of these innovations met with significant opposition from the men which meant that women did not have to struggle with the men and thereby put their relationships on the line. In other words, the women in the Party backed Zelda when they had much to gain and little to lose. Tragically, when the risks increased, Zelda found herself alone.

Like many other women in the Party leadership, Zelda was sexually involved with one of the men in the Party. When the relationship became abusive she tried to bring the matter before the Party. Like the female co-chair had contended, Zelda argued that *personal* morality should be a significant criterion of party leadership. Hence, the Party should be concerned about the behavior of her consort who was one of its leaders. Her case was not an isolated one. Although many women felt that they were being exploited in intimate relationships they kept silent.[22] "A lot of the sisters who were in leadership positions was very tied to the male figures. . . . And I don't think most of them will tell you because they know how bad it got" (K. F. 1990, Washington, D. C.). She was partially right; most would not talk about their own situation but they did acknowledge that boudoir politics was a serious problem in the Party. When asked about the problem, the female national representative grimly remarked, "Intimate relationships were very, very destructive" (B. A. 1990, Washington, D. C.). She declined to elaborate. Other women in leadership suggested that boudoir politics was a major obstacle to the development of the Women's Commission as well as individual female bonding.

The consensus was that the men used the women and the women let it happen:

> Without them they [male leaders] would have never made it. They [women] were the workforce. . . . They [the men] can always attract the naive sisters. It was a pattern. . . . The women were dogged. (K. F. 1990, Washington, D. C.)

Yet women did not resist because they were often desperate for companionship. Zelda explained the problem as follows:

> How can you carry on when you have no one who loves you? . . . I think that often the men hit on the women at these meetings. Women let that happen or participated with that happening because that's the only time they are getting stroked. The problem of being perceived as an Amazon, being ostracized and hated. . . . On the one hand, you pat the sister on the back who's strong, but look who [the men in the Party] marry [sic]. (Zelda 1989, Philadelphia)

Unlike the women leaders, many of the men in leadership had wives that looked as if they had stepped out of *Good Housekeeping*. Zelda continued:

> We were sick of having sexual exploitation. We were sick and tired of all the men being married in the Party and the women being single. . . . We are sick and tired of raising the kids. (Zelda 1989, Philadelphia)

The women in the Party were hurt and angry but clearly compromised by their own sense of desperation. The competition for men inside the party was intense and, according to one woman, the brothers knew this: "They played this card." The women regularly got together around kitchen tables and complained about sexist exploitation inside the party, but brave words of defiance hatched there dissolved in public settings—even when it meant abandoning Zelda, who was described by almost everyone as a person who had nurtured anyone in need of kindness and support. Zelda asked the Party to take up her complaint of abuse in an intimate relationship with a Party leader but she was rebuked and told this was obviously a private matter. Forced to choose between their men and Zelda, the women chose loyalty to their lovers and to men in general over womanist solidarity and an open confrontation with sexism.[23] Zelda left the Party after being hospitalized for a spastic colon and suffering deep emotional wounds. To make matters worst, her three years of selfless devotion to the Party seriously damaged her relationship with her daughter who today claims she will never join the movement and neglect her children as she charges her mother did to her.

Conclusion

Women should not be forced to choose between their commitment to nationalism and the full development of themselves as human beings. But as things stand, these are precisely the choices patriarchal nationalism provides them. The precepts of nationalism require women to choose race/nation over sex at the same time that it defines the nation in terms of manhood. In order to be "good nationalists" women must submit. Their bodies are not their own but the womb of the nation to be planted and protected by their men alone. Their principle responsibility is to the home where they will dutifully raise the children (the nation's future) and where they will provide a comforting refuge for the nation's warriors. Should the exigencies of the nationalist struggle demand their participation in the public arena, on the battlefield or both, women must nonetheless never overshadow the men of the nation.

It has proven extremely difficult to change the sexist assumptions of nationalism even in the context of a growing international women's movement. Part of the problem, no doubt, is that much of the masculinist bias undergirding nationalism is unconscious. Nationalist precepts of gender and sexuality are understood to represent the "natural" order and, no less importantly, are equated with "cultural authenticity." In both cases resistance can be easily dismissed as dangerous, treacherous, or both.

Ironically, one of the best defenses of patriarchal nationalism may be an acceptance of the principle of women's equality. The case of the NBIPP is sobering evidence of the huge gap that often remains between the promise of equality by dominant groups and the realization of the principle in reality. Gender equality in the party resulted in *structural deflection,* which merely adjusted the form of male domination without altering its substance. Women were then free to prove themselves as men but nothing was done to challenge the masculinist definition of leadership nor the sexism of the Black radical paradigm. Given the masculine mystique of nationalist leadership and the exercise of *paradigmatic privilege,* which silenced all but a few exemplary models of Black manhood, women never stood an equal chance—notwithstanding the formal rule of equality.

Just as damaging to the cause of women's equality was NBIPP's acceptance of the fiction of the separation of the public and private spheres. Feminists have agreed that this split is the key to women's continued subordination in both presumedly separate spheres. Crucial human needs, i.e., sexual intimacy, procreation, and nurture have along with women, been relegated to the devalued domestic sphere. It is here that humans satisfy their personal needs and receive the recognition they crave as whole human beings. According to the dominant ideology none of this, often messy, stuff is supposed to enter the public/political sphere where the important business of society is said to take place. By upholding this social fiction the party allowed *boudoir politics* (the manipulation of the needs for emotional and sexual intimacy) to remain a major strategy in the internal struggle among men for power and advantage.

A few brave women did resist the patriarchal character of the new nationalist party, but these hidden and primarily unchallenged masculinist assumptions meant that their desire to bring forth a new kind of party failed. Part of the fault for the aborted birth must rest with the women of the Party. Even when they did recognize implicitly sexist attitudes and practices that made a mockery of the principle of gender equality, they kept silent rather than risk being without a man—the ultimate sanction in a patriarchal society.

This silence is literally and figuratively killing us. Nationalism becomes, Cynthia Enloe has warned us, more masculinized every time women keep quiet. What the world needs is a womanist/feminist vision of nationalism which would heal the split perpetuated by patriarchal nationalism. In the tradition of the Black club women who stepped to the forefront of the Black movement in the late 19th century, womanists must reimagine nationalism for the benefit of the *entire* nation.[24] Extending the vision of our foremothers, *a womanist nationalism* must both challenge phallic images of victorious nationalism which promote dangerous, even suicidal enactments of masculinity, as well as continued oppression and sexual abuse of women, and insist that private matters, the human need for love, emotional and sexual intimacy, are rightfully a part of our political interests and of the nationalist agenda.

Notes

1. Data for this study was gathered between 1987 and 1990 when I conducted interviews with the principal leaders and core activists in the National Black Political Assembly and its successor the National Black Independent Political Party. The organizations considered themselves the legitimate heirs to the Black Power Movement of the sixties. This research has been supported by a Ford Foundation

Minority Post-Doctoral Fellowship, the Research Foundation of the City University of New York and a Grant-in-Aid from the American Council of Learned Societies.

2. Although it is widely assumed that the Black movement rapidly declined after the death of Dr. Martin Luther King, Jr. in 1968, this is inaccurate. The Black Power movement continued to gain momentum as many nationalists turned their attention to the electoral arena in the wake of the Voting Rights victory. Nationalists played a leading role in electing the first Black mayors in several major cities including Newark, Cleveland, and Gary; and, in 1972, help bring roughly 10,000 participants to the National Black Political Convention in Gary, Indiana to determine a unified Black strategy and agenda for the upcoming presidential election.

3. Several recent works focus on women's crucial behind the scenes work in the creation and maintenance of Black movement organizations. See Giddings 1984; Robinson 1987; Crawford, Rouse, and Woods 1990; Clark 1990.

4. Black women's leadership role in Black nationalist organizations is even less well-known than their rarely appreciated contributions to civil-rights struggles. Nonetheless, women were among the primary leaders of such male-identified organizations as the Universal Negro Improvement Association, the Black Panther Party, and the Congress of African Peoples. See Adler 1992; Brown 1992; Baraka 1984; Woodard 1991.

5. The Black Power movement held a series of national conventions starting with a planning conference in 1966. The first major convention took place in 1967 in Newark, N.J. as the fires from the rebellion literally still smoldered. In 1970 the yearly convention process culminated in the formation of a new organization, the Congress of African Peoples, which in turn spearheaded the convention process which lead to creation of the National Black Political Assembly in 1972. The NBPA then assumed leadership of the convention process and organized major conventions in 1974, 1975, and 1976 by which time the organization was virtually destroyed by factional fighting. A remnant managed to pull together the NBPA's final convention in 1980 where the Call to organize a new Black party was issued.

6. In 1975 "the women's question" emerged as a pivotal issue in the struggle for control of the NBPA between Black radicals who remained loyal to nationalist ideology and the followers of Amiri Baraka in CAP who suddenly converted to marxist-leninism-maoism. CAP like other cultural-nationalist organizations had up to this point in its history been extremely patriarchal but now critiqued its former position and sought to use the women's question to hammer away at its opposition which continued to espouse a cultural-nationalist position.

7. Paula Giddings describes how on a number of different occasions Harper, Wells-Barnett, and Terrell were forced to publicly separate themselves from White feminists who, notwithstanding often impressive reform work, betrayed racism or at least gross racial insensitivity (1984: 66–68, 87–94, 179–81).

8. The Nation of Islam is a prime example of this nationalist exaltation of the womb accompanied by the strict control and subordination of real women in the movement. See Pierce and Williams, in this volume.

9. These quotations are taken from the official documents of the founding convention of the Congress of African People which was held in 1970 in Atlanta, Georgia. See,

Imamu Amiri Baraka (ed.), *African Congress: A Documentary of the First Modern Pan-African Congress* (1972: 177, 179).

10. Throughout history women have had to rely upon sexual and familial ties to men to gain access to political power and high positions. As far back as ancient Egypt we find that the few women who shared in governmental power were, according to V. G. Callender, related by blood or marriage to the principal male leaders as mothers, mother-in-laws, daughters, and wives. Nebet, vizier of Upper Egypt, who is thought to be the first female prime minister in recorded history, was the mother-in-law of the then reigning king, Pepy I. Vizier Amenirdi, the next women in Egyptian history to hold such high authority, was daughter to the king (1992: 15–16). Callender also underscores the point that both ancient and contemporary historians of Egypt have tended to erase or minimize women's leadership roles. Even when evidence suggests that Egyptian Queens played substantial political roles they are dismissed in historical writings simply as wives (Callender 1992: 19). Some of the most obvious recent examples of women who have exercised great political influence or power by virtue of their ties to men are Eva Peron in Argentina, Corozon Aquino in the Philippines, Madame Mao Zedong in the People's Republic of China, Eleanor Roosevelt and Hillary Rodham Clinton in the U.S., and Intisar al-Wazir, widow of Khalil al-Wazir, Arafat's revered military commander and strategist, in the Palestinian National Authority, which will govern the Gaza Strip and West Bank town of Jericho until elections. When during the presidential campaign, the present first Lady of the United States was forced to bake cookies in order to diminish her image of power and autonomy and conform to traditional American precepts of domesticity, we were once again reminded that even powerful women walk a thin line of respectability.

11. Ross Terrill offers an engrossing account of the rise and fall of Madame Mao Zedong who was publicly denounced as a whore following the Chairman's death in *White Bone Demon: A Biography of Madame Mao Zedong.*

12. Todd Gitlin himself a prominent SDS leader during the mid-sixties, observed that "the befuddlements of sex" seriously compromised the self-image and confidence of women who worried that their private activity was undermining their public roles as movement leaders. Men similarly were confused about whether they most valued women as competent and trusted comrades or sexy and submissive bedmates (1987: 368). It was also obvious to women newly conscious of their oppressed status in society and the movement that some SDS male leader used their sexual virility to enhance their organizational prowess. "Some leaders," Gitlin agreed, "in effect recruited women in bed—what Marge Piercy in a classic polemic called 'fucking a staff into existence.' Women might be attracted by a show of sensitivity or an aura of bravery, but in any case there were staffs that were, in effect, serial harems" (1987: 371).

13. Beverly's private life also intersected with the party but it was not a source of leverage as she struggled to legitimate her position of leadership. She apparently maintained a monogamous relationship with a man in the party.

14. Child care was not provided at Central Committee and Administrative and Policy Committee meetings, which often required participants to travel to distance cities primarily at their own expense.

15. Elaine Brown (1992) offers numerous examples of the rule of public deference.

16. The wide publicity given to the Moynihan Report had an extremely damaging impact on women in the Black movement. On the one hand, Black activists denied the truth of Moynihan's characterization of the Black family as pathological; but, on the other hand, Black men used it to force Black women into a posture of submission. Cade sadly noted that, "Unfortunately quite a few of the ladies have been so browbeaten in the past with the Black Matriarch stick that they tend to run, leap, fly to the pots and pans, the back rows, the shadows, eager to justify themselves in terms of ass, breasts, collard greens just to prove that they are not the evil, ugly, domineering monsters of tradition" (1970: 163).

17. Sara Evans notes a similar development of "macho street youth style" in the White Left movement during the sixties (1980: 149–51).

18. On rare occasions violence did break out at party meetings but no one was ever seriously hurt, physically that is.

19. In fact, Eva admits that her own critique of what she called "the male construct" developed gradually only after she assumed leadership and was still rather vague five years after she had left the party. Even at this late date she still saw her duties as a single-mother as "a separate issue" from her role as a party leader.

20. I use Alice Walker's term "womanist" because of its close association with women of color. While similar to feminist in its concern for women's empowerment, it differs from traditional feminism in its explicit identification with the needs and interest of the whole community instead of an oppositional view which pits women against men. This primary concern with all of the members of the Black race clearly characterized the political vision of these women—even when they were deeply disturbed by the destructive impact of sexism on the party. Most importantly, I believe these nationalist women would object to the term feminist as a bourgeois White-identified label.

21. Noting how little things have changed in the wake of successful Third-World nationalist movements Enloe concludes: "But a nationalist movement informed by masculinist pride and holding a patriarchal vision of the new nation-state is likely to produce just one more actor in the international arena. A dozen new patriarchal nation-states may make the international bargaining table a bit more crowded, but it won't change the international game being played at that table" (1990: 64). Reflecting on the situation in the Middle East, Accad warns: "Outside powers may continue to play with and on Lebanon, trying to impose their views and interests. . . . In this respect, nationalism (although often mixed with sexism) may appear to be the more urgent need. But I would argue that if nationalism remains at a sexist stage, and does not move beyond ownership and possession as final goals, the cycle of hell will repeat itself and the violence will start all over again" (1991: 246).

22. Accad draws attention to the widespread phenomenon of "autocensorship" among women of subordinated nationalities who for various reasons keep silent about the abuse and injustice they suffered within their own communities. However noble the motivation, the practice is, Accad contends, "killing creativity and freedom" of at least half of the nation (1991: 240).

23. Ironically, Eva and Zelda, who were more womanist in their thinking than other female leaders, both claimed that they did not have time to devote to the development of the Women's Commission because of the overwhelming amount of work associated with their leadership roles in the Party. It was question of priorities and in the pinch they chose race over sex as have the vast majority of Black women involved in the Black movement historically.

24. In her speech at the First National Conference of Colored Women held in 1895, Josephine St. Pierre Ruffin, one of the leading organizers in the Black Women's Club Movement, clearly set forth the unique purpose and vision of the new organization:

> Our woman's movement is woman's movement in that is led and directed by women for the good of women and men, for the benefit of all humanity, which is more than any one branch or section of it. We want, we ask the active interest of our men, and, too, we are not drawing the color line; we are women, American women, as intensely interested in all that pertains to us as such as [sic] all other American women; we are not alienating or withdrawing, we are only coming to the front, willing to join any others in the same work and cordially inviting and welcoming any others to join us. (Lerner 1973: 317)

References

Acker, Joan. 1990. "Hierarchies, Jobs, Bodies: A Theory of Gendered Organizations." *Gender and Society,* 4(2): 139–58.

Adler, Karen S. 1992. "Always Leading Our Men in Service and Sacrifice": Amy Jacques Garvey, Feminist Black Nationalist. *Gender and Society,* 6(3): 346–75.

Accad, Evelyne. 1991. "Sexuality and Sexual Politics: Conflicts and Contradictions for Contemporary Women in the Middle East." In *Third World Women and the Politics of Feminism,* edited by Mohanty, Chandra, Ann Russo, and Lourdes Torres. Pp. 237–50. Bloomington: Indiana University Press.

Baraka, Amiri. 1984. *The Autobiography of LeRoi Jones / Amiri Baraka.* New York: Freundlich Books.

Baraka, Imamu Amiri, ed. 1972. *African Congress: A Documentary of the First Modern Pan-African Congress.* New York: Morrow.

Benjamin, Jessica. 1988. *The Bonds of Love: Psychoanalysis, Feminism, and the Problem of Domination.* New York: Pantheon Books.

Brown, Elaine. 1992. *A Taste of Power: A Black Woman's Story.* New York: Pantheon Books.

Cade, Toni. ed. 1970. *The Black Woman, An Anthology.* New York: Signet Books.

Callender, V.G. 1992. " Female Officials in Ancient Egypt and Egyptian Historians." In *Stereotypes of Women in Power: Historical Pespectives and Revisonist Views,* edited by Barbara Garlick, Suzanne Dixon, and Pauline Allen. Pp. 592–99. New York: Greenwood Press.

Clark, Septima. 1990. *Ready From Within, A First Person Narrative,* edited and with Introduction by Cynthia Stokes Brown, Trenton: African World Press, Inc.

Cleaver, Elridge. 1968. *Soul on Ice*. New York: Ramparts Books.

Cone, James. 1991. *Martin and Malcolm and America: A Dream or a Nightmare*. Maryknoll, New York: Orbis Books.

Crawford, Vicki L., Jacqueline Anne Rouse, and Barbara Woods, eds. 1990. *Women in the Civil Rights Movement: Trailblazers and Torchbearers, 1941–1965*. New York: Carlson Publishing.

Dixon, Suzanne. 1992. "Conclusion—The Enduring Theme: Domineering Dowagers and Scheming Cucubines." In *Stereotypes of Women in Power: Historical Perspectives and Revisionist Views*, edited by Barbara Garlick, Suzanne Dixon, and Pauline Allen. Pp. 209–25. New York: Greenwood Press.

Enloe, Cynthia. 1990 [1989]. *Bananas, Beaches and Bases: Making Feminist Sense of International Politics*. Berkeley: University of California Press.

Evans, Sara. 1980 [1979]. *Personal Politics: The Roots of Women's Liberation in the Civil Rights Movement and the New Left*. New York: Vintage Books.

Giddings, Paula. 1984. *When And Where I Enter: The Impact of Black Women on Race and Sex in America*. New York: Bantam Books.

Gitlin, Todd. 1987. *The Sixties: Years of Hope, Days of Rage*. New York: Bantam Books.

Hare, Nathan. 1971. "Will the Real Black Man Please Stand Up?" *Black Scholar* 2:10: 32–35.

Landes, Joan. 1988. *Women and the Public Sphere, In the Age of the French Revolution*. Ithaca, NY: Cornell University Press.

Mohanty, Chandra, Ann Russo and Lourdes Torres. 1991. *Third World Women and the Politics of Feminism*. Bloomington: Indiana University Press.

Okin, Susan Moller. 1979. *Women in Western Political Thought*. Princeton, NJ: Princeton University Press.

Pateman, Carole. 1989. *The Disorder of Women, Democracy, Feminism and Political Theory*. Stanford: Stanford University Press.

Parks, Gordan. 1965. "'I Was a Zombie Then—Like All Muslims, I Was Hypnotized,'" *Life* March, pp. 28–30.

Robinson, Jo Ann. 1987. *The Montgomery Bus Boycott and the Women Who Started It: The Memoir of Jo Ann Gibson Robinson*, edited and with a Forward by David J. Garrow. Knoxville: University of Tennessee Press.

Ruffin, Josephine St. Pierre. 1973 [1895]. "The Beginnings of the National Club Movement." In *Black Women in White America, A Documentary History*, edited by Gerda Lerner. Pp. 440–43. New York: Vintage Books.

Shanley, Mary Lyndon and Carole Pateman, eds. 1991. *Feminist Interpretations and Political Theory*. University Park, PA: Pennsylvania State University Press.

Scott, Joan. 1988. *Gender and the Politics of History*. New York: Columbia University Press.

Smith-Rosenberg, Carroll. 1985. *Disorderly Conduct: Visions of Gender in Victorian America*. New York: Oxford University Press.

———. 1989. "The Body Politic." In *Coming to Terms*, edited by Elizabeth Weed. Pp. 101–21. New York: Routledge.

Stewart, Maria W. 1987. *Maria W. Stewart: America's First Black Woman Political Writer, Essays and Speeches,* edited with an Introduction by Marilyn Richardson. Bloomington: Indiana University Press.

Terrill, Ross. 1984. *White Bone Demon: A Biography of Madame Mao Zedong.* New York: W. Morrow & Co.

Woodard, K. Komozi. 1991. *The Making of the New Ark: Imanu Amiri Baraka (LeRoi Jones), the Newark Congress of African People, and the Modern Black Convention Movement. A History of the Black Revolt and the New Nationalism, 1966–1976.* Ph.D. dissertation: University of Pennsylvania.

X, Malcolm. 1989. *Malcolm X, The Last Speeches,* edited by Bruce Perry. New York: Pathfinder.

X, Malcolm with Alex Haley. 1966 [1965]. *The Autobiography of Malcolm X.* New York: Grove Press.

Yuval-Davis, Nira and Floya Anthias, eds. 1989. *Woman-Nation-State.* London: Macmillan.

9

"Business Story is Better Than Love"

Gender, Economic Development, and Nationalist Ideology in Tanzania

Deborah S. Rubin

On Maktaba Street in downtown Dar es Salaam, a block from the main post office, a small kiosk was perched on a sidewalk corner in July 1991. Its wares included consumer items such as stationery, rubber sandals, candies, bars of soap, and tape cassettes of prerecorded African and Caribbean music. This particular kiosk stood out due to its corner location and its solidly constructed box stall, exhibiting an air of permanence that contrasted with the rickety tables and packing crates used by neighboring sellers, or the ground displays of even more itinerant hawkers of fried snacks. But the decoration of the stall made it unique: above vividly colored landscapes of Mt. Kilimanjaro and Indian Ocean beaches, a painted header proclaimed in English, "Business Story is Better than Love."

This phrase encompasses multiple meanings about the trajectory of Tanzania's strategies for economic development from its independence in 1961 until 1991. On a first reading, the statement seems simply to voice approval of the program of economic liberalization begun in the 1980s. The slogan supports government policies that acquiesced to pressures pushing for a capitalist "business story" to replace the "love" represented by former President Julius Nyerere's *ujamaa* program to establish a socialist nation.

In Tanzanian Swahili the word *ujamaa* labels a specific form of political and social organization glossed by the label of "African Socialism." Julius Nyerere, the president of Tanzania (until 1964, Tanganyika) from 1962 until his retirement in 1985, constructed the *ujamaa* philosophy and authored many of its policies. He envisioned *ujamaa* as the application of principles drawn from supposedly traditional African familial organization—love, cooperation and shared property, and hard work—as an organizing framework extended to the whole society. He wrote:

> The first of these basic assumptions, or principles of life, I have sometimes described as "love," but that word is so often used to imply a deep personal affection that it can give a false impression. A better word is perhaps "respect," for it was—and is—really a recognition of mutual involvement in one another. . . . Each member of the family recognized the place and the rights of the other members, and although the rights varied according to sex, age, and even ability and character, there was a minimum below which no one could exist without disgrace to the whole family. (Nyerere 1967, reprinted in Clark 1970: 48)

Discourses of development carry nationalist messages (Woost 1993). From this perspective, "business story" and "love" each declares a position in a vocal and wide-ranging debate[1] over the defining content of Tanzanians' vision of themselves as a nation. The dominant (if also contested) position, or national ideology,[2] for much of the twenty-five years after independence defined Tanzania's uniqueness among African nations as a product of striving towards Nyerere's stated goals of socialism, multiracialism, and egalitarianism. To be a Tanzanian implied some level of acceptance (if not always the practice) of the principles of President Nyerere's conceptualization of "African socialism" in Tanzania's national economic, social, and political affairs. A marked shift towards capitalism, towards "business story," as occurred in the mid-1980s, therefore involved not only another transformation of Tanzania's economic and political infrastructure, but also a change in both the official and popular views of what constituted Tanzanian identity.

Development practice and ideology also carry assumptions about gender relations. "Business" and "love" are both gendered activities. Cultural constructions of gender in Tanzania, as elsewhere, influence both with whom and how business is transacted and loving relationships are formed. The two activities establish connections between actors that can be simultaneously egalitarian and hierarchical, cooperative and competitive. In theory, *ujamaa* policies envision national development as extending the principles of kin-based production, building on established gender relations, whereas capitalism envisions economic actors as individual workers, detached from familial ties, and responding directly to the needs of the workplace. In practice, both are equally, if differently, gendered systems.

This essay takes the kiosk's slogan as the starting point for an exploration of the interconnections between the discourse of economic development, national ideology, and gender relations in Tanzania. Tanzania's economic-development policies contain both ideas about the nation and about appropriate gender relations among its citizens. As development objectives have shifted from those of *ujamaa* to those of structural adjustment, there has been an accompanying shift in ideas about gender. Although the kiosk's slogan asserts that, economically, the new policies are an improvement over the old, this assessment is not equally true for all Tanzanians. In particular, the gendered aspects of the new economic policies have made life difficult for many women. While Tanzanian women were perhaps not fully liberated by "love," they now find themselves newly restrained without the coin to buy their independence in the new economy.

Linking Gender, Development, and National Ideologies

Anthropologists have only recently begun to analyze the discourses[3] of development (e.g., Escobar 1988, Woost 1993) bringing a new dimension to earlier studies of development malpractice,[4] the cultural sensitivity of project design, and peasant resistance. Woost, looking at development ideology in Sri Lanka, writes: "Development . . . appears today to be much more than merely the introduction of new technologies and funds into agrarian economies. It is a complex array of material resources and cultural activities that provides an ideal context for the dissemination of nationalist ideologies" (1993: 504). An important element of Woost's approach is the assertion that peasants and other targets of development are cognizant of the discourse and often attempt to use it to achieve their own ends, if not always successfully. The development discourse

> is not just a coherent system of ideas constructed by elites and imposed on the populace from above. To the contrary, it represents an articulation of diverse ideological elements, both old and new, yielding a new ideological configuration of society. In this articulation, changes in the representation of society and identity are made to resonate with the past in crucial ways. As Brow has pointed out (1988: 312, 322), the fact that the dominant discourses mobilize themes already existing in local culture only increases the likelihood that people will recognize themselves in the forms of address contained in those discourses. (1993: 505)

Development discourse often links nationalism with particular notions of progress. It emphasizes a linear progression towards one vision of "modernity" in which industry replaces agriculture, urban replaces rural, rationality replaces affect, and business replaces love. As a national ideology, the development discourse asserts claims about "what is and is not a good society, what its customs and practices should be, or how it should even view itself" (Dominguez 1990: 132). To piggyback "progress" to cultural symbols and practices with enduring cultural values is, however, a complicated and nonlinear project. National ideologies have multiple components, with complementary as well as contradictory meanings. Progress and modernity are lent credence when justified in cultural symbols of stability.

Nationalist messages of development are accompanied by both explicit and implicit assumptions about gender. Gender is understood here primarily as a system of cultural categories that is often, though not exclusively dichotomous or heterosexual[5] (Yanagisako and Collier 1990; Rubin 1994). Culturally specific gender ideologies are those historically shaped beliefs and understandings that define gender categories. The ideologies offer culturally appropriate guidelines shaping how individual men and women engage in social action. Cultural systems vary as to how intractably they link the content of gender categories to the structure of categorization itself. That is, it may be possible to change ideas about what men and women do without disturbing the idea that there are, for example, only two gender categories. Enduring categories permit changing content. Since peoples' understanding of gender often seems inextricably linked to cultural rules about labor, it is understandable how ideologies of development, nationalism, and gender become entwined. Important for the argument presented here is an examination of how historically forged social and cultural processes have connected gender and economic activity to support nationalist goals. Paulette Pierce notes elsewhere in this volume: "Nationalist precepts of gender and sexuality are essential to the identity and critical to the practice of nationalists. . . . [I]t is often in terms of their shared ideas about what it means to be a man or woman that a group comes to see itself as constituting 'a people' or 'a nation.'"

Recognizing the gendered constitution of familiar concepts such as "peasant," "nationalism," or "development" involves analyzing the assumptions about gender relations that form the very basis of these systems. All societies build their institutions onto assumptions about difference of various sorts and then "naturalize" them—justifying cultural and historical constructions on the basis of a supposedly natural and supposedly obvious set of differences: age, biology, intelligence, skin color, or sexual orientation. Analyses of these processes of naturalization provide a new appreciation for how specific cultural assumptions have been embedded in dominant theoretical frameworks (e.g., Haraway on museum displays (1989: 26–39), Okin on justice (1989: 8–9), and Enloe on militarism (1989: 96)).

Analysis has demonstrated that these core cultural assumptions are not neutral. Systems of power and dominance create and maintain cultural codes—about gendered behavior and gender categories, about the legitimacy of state institutions over "tribal" ones, or about the benefits one economic system over another.

To apply this framework to the Tanzanian case requires, first, a brief summary of the history of Tanzania nationalism from which to garner the central tenets of *ujamaa* principles and its gendered and nationalist themes. Against this background I will examine village production in Kwakombo village in northeast Tanzania during the early 1980s, followed by a second look at Kwakombo village in 1991 that is framed within a discussion of the characteristics and impacts of the structural adjustment program initiated in the mid-1980s. The threads of development discourse, gender, and nationalist ideology are then rewoven, finally, to trace out the differing models of nation and gender described by the development discourse of the two periods.

Building the Independent Nation

Studies of early nationalist sentiments in the region now known as Tanzania assert that the character of the movement was unusual for Africa in its early appearance and peaceful development (Feierman 1990; Geiger 1987; Iliffe 1979; Lonsdale 1972). Pan-territorial movement of traders during the nineteenth century, and multi-ethnic resistance to early German rule had, by the time of formal German administration in 1898, already created a sense of a "Swahili society" that extended inland from the coast, and was "based on towns and trading centres, the vehicle of a literary culture predominantly but not necessarily Muslim, linked by a common language and non-tribal in its social and political focus" (Lonsdale 1972: 25).

Akidas, or local government officials, were appointed by the Germans from among existing chiefs or chosen from Swahili speakers from Zanzibar and mainland coastal communities to collect taxes and try cases (Iliffe 1979; Lonsdale 1972). The Germans preferred to use Muslim traders because of their knowledge of Swahili, and their familiarity with the region through trading.

The British, who replaced the Germans as overseers in 1914, established an administrative system relying even more strongly on indigenous leaders, but also "continued the German practice of transferring African employees of the administration through the territory," reinforcing a sense of nation united under foreign rule (Lonsdale 1972: 27). In the northeast the British replaced most of the *akidas* with local leaders, a move that helped "to slow the process of economic and ideological integration across political or linguistic boundaries" (Feierman 1990: 122). Local leaders under the formal Native Administration system were required to carry out colonial administrative directives. Anti-colonial sentiment emerged gradually and was channeled through other pan-territorial movements such as occupational unions rather than through, what Lonsdale calls, "the politics of local focus," that is, ethnically based leadership (1972: 25).

It is too simple, however, to see a Swahili-based national identity emerging and replacing ethnic identities at that time without contestation, or to assume that ethnic mobilizations played no part in the nationalist efforts. A richly detailed study of the history of the Kilindi chiefdom and the Usambaras in northeast Tanzania, shows that localized cultural and political forms—particularly language—also influenced the style and content of colonial administration. Colonial objectives were transmitted to local populations through the cultural imagery of their appointed leaders, using methods and metaphors often unintended, uncontrolled by, and unknown to the colonists (Feierman 1990: 120–21).

The struggle for nationhood in Tanzania also had explicitly gendered aspects. Though more research is needed, apparently both women and men actively and directly participated in the movement, becoming members of the Tanganyika African National Union (TANU). Women recruited new members through cultural organizations such as dance groups (Geiger 1987) and spoke out against colonial economic and political policies (Feierman 1990; Mbilinyi 1990). Even women who were not activists in nationalist politics played critical supportive roles through their work in the fields, in homes, and in a variety of small-scale entrepreneurial activities, maintaining households so that their fathers, husbands, sons, and brothers could take part in leadership and organizing roles in the nationalist movement. The specific forms of their support were variably shaped by local cultural definitions of gender roles, by class, and by religion. Comparing the involvement of Christians and Muslims in TANU, Geiger notes that "both gender and religion shaped the women's direct experience of colonial oppression and, therefore, their positive response to nationalist objectives as expressed through TANU [the Tanganyika African National Union]" (1987: 18).

Nationalist sentiments collided with the concerns of the colonial administration about the process of transforming "tribesmen" into peasants and workers. Both colonial administrators and early researchers alike envisioned this process as inherently unstable. The creation of a peasantry or a stable urban workforce, with its concomitant increase in contact with bearers of "modern" ideas, was fraught with concerns for the maintenance of community in the face of enormous economic and social change. The use of the term "detribalization" indicated to many academics, development specialists, and local political leaders, the risk of loss of an important source of values and customs, as expressed by the International Institute of African Languages and Culture:

> The fundamental problem arising from the interpenetration of African life by the ideas and economic forces of European civilization is that of the cohesion of African society. African society is being subjected to a severe strain, and there is danger lest the powerful forces that are entering the continent may bring about its complete disintegration, the results of which must be calamitous for the individuals who compose it and at the same time render impossible an orderly evolution of the community. (1932, quoted in Kuper 1975: 132)

Under colonialism settlements near Korogwe in northeastern Tanzania were shaped by the plantation economy established by the Germans. Sisal estates provided wage employment for men, many of whom were drawn from labor-exporting regions to the south and west and differed ethnically from the local population. Estates were situated within a region of geographical and ecological diversity that was home to peasant farmers from several local ethnic groups. This estate-centered production system relied on a gendered division of labor. The plantation laborers were mostly men who, as contracted laborers, left their wives and families in their home areas for periods of several months or longer to live on the estates; their wives remained on the farms cultivating fields and managing household affairs. Local men and women from the area, of Shambaa, Zigua, and Bondei ethnic backgrounds, produced food—maize, beans, bananas, and fish—to feed migrant workers on local plantations and to raise cash to support of their own families (Iliffe 1979).

Among the Zigua, one of the more populous local ethnic groups on the plains outside Korogwe in the 1950s and 1960s, a gendered division of labor organized household production and consumption. Men were expected to fish and raise cattle, as well as to clear and burn agricultural land and to cultivate. Women also farmed and provisioned the household with water, firewood, and cooked food while bearing primary responsibilities for the care of children. Dichotomous characterization of these activities as "domestic" vs. "public" or "reproductive" vs. "productive" obscures their local character because the work involved both men and women in a variety of tasks that jointly helped to maintain the household.

Notwithstanding some overlapping practice by men and women of both agricultural and household tasks, symbolically, gendered labor patterns were central to Zigua conceptions of masculinity and femininity. The digging stick or hoe was considered to be the model of manliness, and a boy was urged to work hard and never turn down agricultural work, on the grounds that "there can be no life without farming" (Muya 1974: 7). A woman was closely identified with the cooking. Rituals carried out soon after birth involved demonstrating the various tasks for which they would be responsible as adults: infant girls were shown how to pound maize and millet into meal to be cooked into the staple dish of stiff porridge; infant boys were shown how to clear land for planting and to care for cattle. Various tasks were thus seen as entering into definitions of Zigua personhood in distinctly gendered ways.

All activities centered around an extended family. "Home" in both Swahili (*nyumba*) and Kizigua (*kaya*) stands equally for a physical structure, and for those who live in a house. *Nyumba* in Swahili is related to the word "*umba*"—to give form to—usually used only to describe God's creation, of the forming of man and woman. This notion of creation in the physical sense is carried over in the word "*unyumba*," which refers to the relation of husband and wife, a union from which children are supposed to be created. The Swahili phrase, "*nyumbani kwetu*" or "our household" is used to refer to all those who live together and share meals. Except for visitors, those who regularly eat together also share a responsibility to contribute to what goes into the pot. This relationship between consumption and production is reflected in the Swahili proverb, "A guest is a guest for three days; on the fourth day, give the person a hoe."[6]

This image of interdependent production and consumption processes was held together not by ties of equality, however, but by explicit and well-understood principles of age and sex differentiation. Adults and children, and men and women were taught tasks appropriate to their stage in life and their sex. Instruction was contained in everyday practice as well as more formal rituals marking life stages such as those described at birth and *mwali*, the ritual separation for girls at puberty. It is difficult to demarcate precisely difference from inequality or partnership from complementarity. Life histories of Zigua women in Kwakombo village reveal restrictions on women's opportunities that challenge assertions of non-hierarchical gender complementarity in pre-colonial or colonial African village life. Regional similarities in the contours of gendered labor were prevalent, though each ethnic group followed different cultural proscriptions for defining gendered persons (Feierman 1990).

Early Post-Independence Development

Tanzania (then called Tanganyika) achieved independence from Great Britain in 1961. Until 1967, the Tanzanian government followed a development plan devised with the assistance of British advisers that depended on large infusions of foreign capital to promote rapid industrialization and to expand agricultural production through mechanization and other capital intensive inputs. Low prices in sisal and other major export crops and low levels of foreign aid, however, made it impossible to achieve these goals (Mighot-Adholla 1979: 166). During this period of restricted resources, as in the colonial period preceding it, peasant agriculture was in practice largely neglected by the government.

Earlier concerns about the potential social instability of "detribalization" took a different slant in the immediate post-independence years from 1961–1967 as efforts were made to enter the "modern world." Now "peasants" were not moving forward quickly enough. "Peasant" agriculture was backward, not sufficiently oriented towards the market, and needed an infusion of expert technical advice and infrastructure to put it on the right track. The First Five-Year Plan for the United Republic of Tanganyika, for example, states that the "greater part of Tanganyikan peasant agriculture continues to be characterized by primitive methods of production and inadequate equipment. . . . Attitudes will evolve through social emulation, co-operation, and the expansion of community development activities" (1964: 19 quoted in Coulson 1982: 161).

The issue for the newly independent government became how to most effectively transform peasant society to best achieve "modern" nationhood. For the first few years of independence, a variety of techniques and institutional structures were put in place, among them, cooperatives, community development programs, and agricultural extension services. None, however, seemed able to achieve significant improvement in rural conditions. Instead, while production levels increased, they did so by virtue of expanded capitalist practices, contributing to growing inequalities in the rural sector (Coulson 1982: 166–67).

Ujamaa: A Nationalist, Gendered Discourse on Development

In 1967, a major policy proclamation known as the Arusha Declaration initiated a massive period of social, political, and economic transformations, and marked the formal start of Tanzania's socialist experiment. The turn to socialism was, according to then President Julius Nyerere, a response to an increasing pattern of economic inequalities in Tanzania. Regional imbalances, rural-urban inequalities in standards of living, and growing economic disparities among rural producers were all intensifying in the years following independence. Nyerere argued that colonial policies had introduced exploitative, capitalist relations that were inappropriate and detrimental in the Tanzanian context: "it is wrong for some people to live in luxury while others are destitute" (Nyerere 1977: 2). To halt these growing inequalities, the Arusha Declaration nationalized industries, banks, and other services to stop capital flight. It identified a program to reduce the country's dependence on foreign financial sources as the motor of development by increasing agricultural production and promoting village-based self-help programs. The aims of the new nation were succinctly expressed in the national motto, *Uhuru na Umoja,* Freedom and Unity, and the slogan of the Arusha Declaration, *Ujamaa na Kujitegemea,* Socialism and Self-reliance. Freedom, initially from colonial rule and later, as in self-reliance, from the dictates of the international economic system, has been an open and much valued part of Tanzanian national identity.[7] Unity has been consciously and successfully promoted through the adoption of Swahili as a national language and the initiation of universal primary education programs.

The Arusha Declaration and related policies had three themes: increased production, egalitarianism, and self-reliance. The cornerstone was national cooperation to increase production, particularly agricultural production. The obligation to work was a vital part of the *ujamaa* philosophy, as in the phrase "Uhuru ni kazi" (Freedom is work) and in Nyerere's exhortations to citizens that "[E]very one of us has an equal duty to do the work entrusted to him—whatever that work may be—as if he too had taken a solemn oath to devote himself, without thought for his own advantage, to building our Republic of Tanganyika." (Nyerere, quote reprinted in Meienberg 1966: 147).

The process of achieving "socialism in the villages" included several organizational changes such as decentralizing the national administration by placing government officials, often from different regions, into the new villages to monitor their activities, and creating parastatal organizations to control crop marketing and to distribute consumer goods.

Most important however, was the policy of villagization, or the gathering together of scattered rural residences into nucleated villages. As Nyerere said,

> [W]e shall achieve the goals . . . if the basis of Tanzanian life consists of rural economic and social communities where people live together and work together for the good of all, so that all of the different communities work together in cooperation for the common good of the nation. . . . [T]his . . . organization of society is different because its dominant characteristic would be cooperation, not competition, and its criteria for individual success would be good service, not the accumulation of private property. (Nyerere 1968: 348)

As part of the process of building rural socialism, each Tanzanian village was required to set aside a piece of land for cooperative farming and to use the proceeds from the sale of its harvest for achieving village goals. In both the villagization program and the emphasis on cooperative farms, Nyerere was drawing on a long history of cooperative farming in Tanzania (Rubin 1985). But the effort to build and maintain cooperatively owned and jointly cultivated plots was historically never a practical success. Plots farmed under the umbrella of the household have always formed the backbone of peasant agriculture.

Nyerere's writing reveals the state's relationship to the villages in *ujamaa* policy. To Nyerere, the *ujamaa* village program was the concrete expression of African socialism, grounded in the principles of what he perceived of as a "traditional African" way of life. It is based upon three assumptions of "traditional" living, in which members of a community were thought to have respect and concern for each other, to share basic goods and property with one another, and to have an equal obligation to work. In Nyerere's view, these positive values, which he maintained had been generally present among Tanzania's many ethnic groups, were marred by two severe inadequacies: an acceptance of human inequality and of great poverty (Nyerere 1968: 338–39). Contemporary *ujamaa,* on the other hand, was formulated to include only the positive values of this "traditional" society and to overcome its inadequacies.

If meant to be an accurate snapshot of Tanzanian rural life, this vision of Tanzanian society is seriously misleading. It ignores the diversity of ethnic traditions in the country, and the different principles of organization manifested by them. Tanzania includes pastoralists and foragers, neither of which fit the model of rural cultivators that form the basis of Nyerere's socialist society. Stratification existed both within and between various ethnic groups as described in the *nyarubanja* system of the northwest (see O'Neill 1990). Nyerere's formulation further glosses over the gender and age-based systems of inequality that served to limit access to resources to older, male heads of households. On the question of inequalities, Nyerere states, "Inequalities existed, but they were tempered by comparable family or social responsibilities, and they could never become gross and offensive to the social equality which was at the basis of the communal life" (Nyerere 1968: 338).

It is, however, inappropriate to dismiss Nyerere's writings as naive representations of traditional life. Though not a snapshot, his speeches describe a commissioned portrait of Tanzanian social organization: it does not look exactly like the image you think you project, but everyone finds something recognizable in it. The generalizations of rural life are part and parcel of what Benedict Anderson (1983) terms the nation as "imagined community" and what Williams labels an ideology of "traditionalism" in reference to British Guiana:

> Traditionalism, as an effort to return to either presumed precolonial traditions
> or to authenticate creolized or syncretized elements of the heterogeneity cre-

ated during the colonial era, is taken here to be one among many strategies used to link the aforementioned roles of nationalism to the two dimensions of the process of cultural authentication. (1990: 128, fn. 1)

"Traditionalism" provides a useful way to think about Nyerere's articulation of principles drawn from "African" traditions as laying the foundation for the "modern" Tanzanian society. By identifying local cultural values of cooperation, hard work, caring, and social equity in such general terms, and attaching them to Nyerere's vision of the forward movement of the nation into modernity, each ethnic group was free to read into the President's statements the specific formulation of these values specified by their own cultural codes.

The ideology of traditionalism helps to explain the attractiveness of the *ujamaa* policies to the Tanzanian population. Working sometimes in concert with it and sometimes against it, however, was the ideology of "developmentalism," defined by Shivji (1985) as a focus on economic development as separate from politics. By articulating the position that economic development was an independent process, the Tanzanian state could suppress mass political organizations without acknowledging that such actions contradicted other elements of the national ideology, such as widespread political participation (1985: 1–2).

The relationship between government and its citizens embedded in Nyerere's model of African socialism can be used to support the idea that economic development is in some ways separable from political action. First, government is paternalistic; as quoted above the use of the family idiom extends to the government the role of father in the extended family. Second, government is the initiator and the developer, although not the source of the finances. In discussing the role of the government, Nyerere says, "[p]romises of great government help will only lead to disaster. . . . it must not be expected everywhere. . . . the Government will not be able to give much help to any one [village] that is established" (1968: 358). Finally, there is the sense in Nyerere's model that the government and the people are all on the same side, and that they share the same goals. The conflicts of society which Nyerere identifies are not between social groups or social classes, but between the individual and the larger society. These assumptions make possible the formulation of rural development policies founded on increasing government intervention into all aspects of social life, yet which at the same time not only ignore the asymmetrical power structure supporting the state and subordinating the peasantry, and the unequal relationships of men and women to agricultural production, but also the intricate alliance between the state's economic and political infrastructure.

The nationalist attributes of *ujamaa* have been laid out: the unifying principles of the national language of Swahili and in the ideologies of traditionalism and developmentalism. Perhaps less obvious are the components of the national ideology which connect economic activity and gender. Here the elaboration of *ujamaa* or Tanzanian socialism as a distinctive form of social organization based on the supposedly "traditional" "African" extended family and its associated values is relevant. The paternalistic model encoded unequal gender relations even as it proclaimed greater recognition of women's contributions to the economy and offered new opportunities for education and political leadership. The Tanzanian government, for all its use of traditions of complementarity, still utilized an attitude toward women that borrowed, supported, or paralleled Western and local paternalisms towards women and maintained specific and circumscribed ideas about women's correct roles in society, ideas which emphasized domesticity and dependence, and encouraged autonomy, if at all, only through gradual training and education (see Geiger 1987). This paralleled a more general shift from political activism to political consumerism, "where the perceived need to expand centralized control and establish development priorities frequently obliterated local dynamism, popular initiative, and grassroots leadership" (Geiger 1987: 25).

Ujamaa as Everyday Practice

In Kwakombo village, implementation of *ujamaa* policies meant that in 1974, previously dispersed families were resettled, at first voluntarily and later forcibly, to an area along the main road. Land was reallocated to village households according to a complex and not terribly systematic set of criteria including length of residence in the area, existing landholdings and their location relative to the new settlements, number of people in a household, and strength of political influence. Policies specified that *households* were to be the unit of allocation, but were vague as to the understanding of what members of households were entitled to allocations. Thus, influential men in the village were able to obtain independent allocations for both themselves and their multiple wives, while others, less well placed, obtained only single allocations for entire families. Often no allocations were made either to women without male partners or to single mothers (Rubin 1985).

Agricultural work under *ujamaa* policies took two forms: private farming on plots allocated to households, and cooperative farming on village plots. Farming on individual plots continued in much the same way as in the pre-Arusha period, in culturally prescribed patterns. The scheduling of work, the choice of crops and crop combinations, the preference of one crop over another—all of these are choices made with consideration not only of prices and availability, but also against the history of what it meant to be Zigua or Ngoni, or a Zigua man or Ngoni woman. As described for the earlier period, in the 1980s the division of labor in agricultural production continued to reproduce gender categories. Certain tasks were appropriate for men but not for women, for the young but not for the old, for Zigua but not for Ngoni. As a result, increasing agricultural production as a whole or changing the balance of crops farmed, was not a simple matter of reallocating something called "labor." Men often balanced their agricultural labor with care of livestock and earning cash. Women balanced their agricultural tasks with the scheduling and energy demands of cooking, collecting firewood, child care, and cleaning, as well as *kibarua* or daily labor for cash or bartered for food.

Labor for maize and cassava was contributed by both men and women, although they cultivated these crops at different points in the agricultural cycle. Rice and vegetables were grown by women; sweet potato fields and tree crops were tended by men. These gross categorizations of male and female work are belied by variations on this pattern that emerge when ethnicity and class position interpenetrate these gender dichotomies. Women in some wealthier households or with extended kin networks had access to cash resources that purchased farm labor even when hired labor was ideologically suspect and in some cases legally prohibited by *ujamaa* policies.

Cooperative farming on village fields was to be carried out equally by all men and women in the village, with harvests designated for use by the village community as a whole. Cash from crops sales were to offset village expenses for building and furnishing public structures, and for financing a grain milling machine or a village store. The crops themselves might provide a communal store of grain for distribution to the needy or to supplement poor harvests. The benefits of these fields were not well-defined and villagers often perceived this unpaid labor as an extra tax.

Although adult men and women were nearly equal segments of the population in Kwakombo, women were in the early 1980s less frequent and less active participants in communal work (Rubin 1985: 278–79). Some women found cooperative work particularly problematic because participation was expected without any attention as to how women's other work was to be accomplished, such as care of young children, meal preparation, and household chores. It was not always possible or feasible to find other family members, usually younger girls, to take over these chores and free up their mothers for cooperative work. Women responded by bringing children with them to the village fields, making active farming work difficult; by arriving late or leaving early and using the travel time to collect firewood, wild greens for cooking, or water; or by participating irregularly or not at all. Women were expected to do the same agricultural work on the cooperative farm as on their own fields, thus technical skill was not the issue. Rather, women were using the social construction of their "real" "women's work," their home responsibilities, to avoid participating in cooperative farming.

At the same time, however, other women used the promise of more egalitarian relations envisaged by Nyerere to argue the reverse. They used their "duty" to participate in cooperative and village work as a way out of unpaid, unrecognized family labor. Initial reports of women's eagerness to volunteer for *ujamaa* activities are perhaps best understood in this light (Fortmann 1982, Mbilinyi 1990), with their enthusiasm fading only after several years of hard work without obvious benefit. These women were "resisting their position as unpaid labor" by moving into village projects and government-sanctioned activities (Mbilinyi 1990: 91).

The period from 1967 to 1986 corresponded to the policies beginning with the Arusha Declaration and ending with the initiation of Tanzanian-International Monetary Fund agreements on structural adjustment programs. It represents a time of increasingly greater demands on labor among the peasantry. Cooperative farming was seen as an additional expenditure of time and effort over private farming, over the same period that returns to agriculture, as measured by crop prices, were declining (Ellis 1982). Inflation was growing, consumer goods were scarce or expensive and available only on the unofficial markets, and regulated crop prices were low. Peasants responded by diverting crops to unofficial markets and shifting inputs from regulated crops into unregulated ones, such as from coffee or maize to tomatoes (Mbilinyi 1990: 90–91; Rubin 1985). Production strategies in Kwakombo, as in other regions, were shifting from the sale of staple crops for cash established during the colonial period to the sale of vegetables and, unofficially, of daily labor (*kibarua*) during these years.

The economic crisis experienced by the state during this period was characterized by declining volumes and/or prices of agricultural exports, while prices for oil and imported goods were rising and debt levels were increasing. Peasants experienced these conditions in the form of scarce and expensive consumer goods, and higher taxes—in the form of low producer prices and extra labor demands. As wage labor—both casual and salaried, and both regulated by the government and primarily male—became less able to provide for daily subsistence, women's labor became increasingly important. Women's efforts to cultivate for home consumption and to earn cash through informal and small-scale entrepreneurial activities helped to fill the gap between men's wages and the cash requirements for everyday existence. In many ways, development projects for women have contributed to this intensification, as many involve supplying "appropriate technologies" such as wells and hand pumps, grain mills, and solar cookers as ways to free up women's time for more "productive" tasks, such as time spent producing food or cash-earning crops. As mentioned above, this greater need for women's cash contributions, unpaid labor or both was met with contradictory responses by women themselves, with some embracing new government definitions of appropriate women's work as a means of resisting increasing family demands and others resisting perceived taxation or proletarianization by embracing familial definitions of women's work.

I have argued elsewhere (Rubin 1985) that Goran Hyden's (1980) representation of Tanzanian peasant society as an "economy of affection" severely distorts the international, national, and community interconnections that shaped the historical conditions of peasant production in Tanzania's Tanga Region. More recently, Hyden has elaborated the idea of affection on which his model depends:

> if these units of production and these economies are so weakly linked together, structurally and functionally, what is it that holds them together? I suggest that what really holds them together is *affection*. Affection here is a word that

describes what is essentially the networks of support, communication, and interaction that exists among not only kinship units but also communities and other groups that might be described as held together on the bases of mutual sharing of positive sentiments for each other. . . . In Africa, I'm suggesting that because markets and state are so weak and have not really penetrated societies, affection is not just a marginal or peripheral phenomenon, but sits there in the middle and is actually the core that holds societies together. (Hyden and Peters 1991: 305)

Where Hyden saw peasants as minimally incorporated into the world economy and having "the unique prerogative of choosing to withdraw" (1980: 32), it is also possible to see that peasants' circumvention of a political and economic system not to their immediate gain was *not,* as Hyden saw it, a sign of their autonomy and isolation but instead reflected precisely the extent to which peasants productive and exchange relationships were shaped by extra-local forces (Rubin 1985: 292).

Pauline Peters has pointed out that Hyden's formulation not only "misrepresents the conditions under which most African rural dwellers live and work" but also ignores the gendered character of peasant production: "Hyden is unable to attend to this crucial aspect of African rural systems because the economy of affection excludes social differences of all kinds, including those based on gender" (Hyden and Peters 1991: 316, 317). Peters argues that the collective, cooperative ideology underlying the economy of affection glosses over the inequalities which are part of the internal organization of production work among the peasantry (1991: 318), precisely the point which emerged in the village study of production processes in Kwakombo from the individual household, to the village, and to the state.

Ujamaa policies of cooperation thus articulated contradictory statements about women's rights to equality within a set of hierarchically gendered production and political systems. Tanzanian women, as good citizens, were being praised for their important and necessary participation in building the national economy,[8] but they were actually restrained from making significant progress by the double burdens of domestic and field work. Some rural women actively recognized and fought against this contradiction by withholding labor: either by resisting calls to participate in cooperative farming, or by more fully engaging in official activities and refusing domestic work. These responses support the position, as outlined earlier, that not only does the development discourse carry nationalist and gendered precepts to the peasants, but they in turn also use the formulations to obtain their own ends.

Overall, the principles of *ujamaa* were problematical as a blueprint for increased smallholder production at the village level, and failed to institutionalize successful forms of cooperative production. What is important, however, is that they did articulate a national ideology that legitimated rural women's contributions to village and national economic and political life. During the *ujamaa* period, expectations were set for achieving education for both girls and boys, women were elected to village councils, and many women gained positions as village managers. Women's contributions to agricultural production were increasingly recognized, as were the constraints facing women—lack of inputs and transport, simple and inefficient tools, and insecure tenancy, among others. Though efforts to address these problems were only partially possible as the economic crisis deepened, the vocabulary of *ujamaa* and its emphasis on cooperation illuminated how women's work needed support to make them equal contributors to the state-building process.

By the mid-1980s, little was left of the *ujamaa* policies except the rhetoric of equality and cooperation. The market-based economic reforms of the late 1980s and early 1990s have also shifted the characterization of women's work in the state's development ideology.

Gendered Consequences of Structural Adjustment

In 1986, after years of disagreement and several unsuccessful efforts at national reform, Tanzania accepted conditions laid down by the International Monetary Fund for initiating economic "liberalization." These included currency devaluation, debt reductions, limits on new borrowing, and a variety of "free" market policies such as raising interest rates, prohibiting protectionism, and encouraging private investment and entrepreneurship (Stein 1990: 1). The results have been mixed. Beneficiaries have primarily been the large scale agriculturalists and industrialists, as well as urbanites of all sorts. The freeing up of import restrictions and foreign currency exchange regulations has meant that imported goods of all types have become available in shops (Cooksey 1989) and urban construction is booming. David Booth notes that "[R]eal GDP growth rates seem to have averaged around 3.6 percent per annum over the five years 1984–89" (1991: 6). The reforms, generally praised by well-off urban dwellers, have uneven consequences for rural residents and the urban poor. Prices for farm inputs and rural services increased dramatically without a corresponding increase in availability, but producer price increases have not kept pace (Meena 1991: 170–75). Government and private investments in social services, such as health, infrastructure, and education, have declined, and the availability of such services has deteriorated, while costs have increased (Rugumisa 1990: 10–11). In the early 1990s, the government announced a "cost-sharing" program for university students in which students will be expected to contribute to the financing of their educations, a cost previously borne by the government. School fees and development taxes are other similar examples.

For the majority of urban dwellers, life in Tanzania in the 1990s means "chasing after shillings" (Rugumisa 1990), in which multiple avenues of salaried and casual wage employment, self-employment, garden plots, and backyard livestock all contribute their share to daily upkeep. Men and women benefit differently, however, from urban employment. It seems easier for young men than for young women to find wage work and, whether employed or not, to call on the labor of female kin—sisters and sisters-in-law, aunts and grandmothers—in fashioning an urban home. Pregnancy, the burdens of child care, and the expectations that women will be responsible for organizing household work all place significantly different demands on young employed women. As a result, instability in urban employment often has greater consequences for women than for men.

In many rural areas, opportunities for earning cash incomes are less plentiful than in towns; costs for consumer goods are higher because of added transport fees; the availability of imported goods and domestic manufactured products is lower; and small-scale agriculture is not significantly more profitable than in the 1980s. The structural-adjustment policies aim to increase production of export crops, the great bulk of which are produced by larger-scale farmers or the transnational agribusiness companies. Observations in Kwakombo village confirmed other published reports that peasant agriculture is becoming marginalized in the structural-adjustment process (Maganya 1990: 112). Approximately 80 percent of the nation's population continues to rely on small scale agriculture, therefore production problems in the peasant sector negatively affect the nation's food supplies.

Kwakombo village is in an area in which staple food crops, such as maize, rather than export crops, such as tea or coffee, have been the mainstay of peasant agricultural production. During the 1980s and into the 1990s, producers have tried to grow staple crops for their own use, selling some surplus, and to experiment with cultivating some vegetables and fruits for sale. Problems of transport, however, have made reliance on domestic marketing for cash returns uncertain, especially with highly perishable crops. In July 1991 huge heaps of rotting oranges waiting for transport sat by the side of the trunk road in the "northeast development corridor," evidence of both the productivity of orange tree orchards planted in the late 1980s and of the underdeveloped-infrastructure problem.

Village demographics both reflect and contribute to the problematic conditions of small-scale agricultural production in the 1990s. Many of those remaining in Kwakombo are in their forties and older as well as numerous children under eighteen. Many younger women in the village are single—never married, divorced, or widowed. Many of them left at some point during the 1980s for jobs as bar girls and domestic servants in town, citing no other alternative for earning money and a dislike of the hard work and low returns of farming. They returned to the village as a result of pregnancy, illness, or unworkable relationships established in town. Young men, in their twenties and thirties, have traveled to larger urban centers to find work sometimes leaving behind new wives and small children. These demographics point out the unequal consequences for men and women trying to find work in urban areas. The village population today is therefore not the best equipped to invest in newer agricultural techniques and equipment. They continue to farm their small plots, earn small, irregular cash incomes, and send food supplies to their relatives in urban centers in return for remittances of cash and consumer goods.

The structural-adjustment policies are partly responsible for redefining and newly appropriating women's work. As Meena (1991: 171) reports, women become the "'shock-absorbers' of socio-economic crises" following in the wake of these policies. Economic liberalization during the late 1980s and early 1990s has promoted individualism and political democratization, while downplaying the emerging issues of gender equity and declining social welfare. Studies of structural adjustment and its consequences (Cooksey 1990; Mbilinyi 1990; Meena 1991; Tripp 1990) reveal that many of the political, legal, and economic gains offered to all women under *ujamaa* policies diminished unevenly. Women differ in their abilities to take advantage of the opportunities offered by "business story" in relation to their position in class, ethnic, and regional frameworks. Poor and rural women seem to be hardest hit by economic restructuring (Mbilinyi 1990; Meena 1991).

One study of urban women's income-generating strategies in Tanzania in the late 1980s argues that women must now pursue multiple avenues to earn cash because it is no longer possible to survive on the single salary of a male employee. Urban women, however, in choosing their earning strategies, stay largely within "projects that were considered within the sphere of female work, e.g., making pastries, frying fish, braiding hair" (Tripp 1990: 167). While providing needed cash and, in consequence, some small degree of autonomy, these activities, fitting as they did within existing gender definitions, were not threatening to male authority within the household (Tripp 1990: 168). The continuation of women in historically demarcated "women's work" reflects the difficulty that women have in obtaining vocational training and salaried employment. At the same time, the economic difficulties which face most Tanzanian households today, both rural and urban, are creating new patterns of gender relations and changing urban definitions of their gender roles. Historically urban women were limited, culturally and legislatively, to relatively fewer economic opportunities, especially when married. Tripp argues that in contemporary Dar es Salaam, many men are accepting the increasing involvement of their wives and daughters in the urban informal and formal economy, and that women see such work as empowering because of their ability to contribute directly to the household's fund of cash to pay school fees, development levies, and to cope with inflation.

The informal, small-scale entrepreneurial activities identified above, as well as the intensification of agricultural labor both act to buffer urban wage earners from the full impact of the removal of subsidies (such as the end of price controls) and devaluation. As peasant production becomes less profitable, entrepreneurial activities are taking center stage. On all fronts, the Tanzanian government is encouraging investment from foreign and local sources, and suggesting ways to improve operations.

Women are the target of special attention in many of these efforts in capitalist economic development. The vocabulary of their involvement, however, emphasizes their contributions of labor rather than their intellect, or it emphasizes their "natural responsibilities to family" rather than their managerial or leadership capacities. This is a different vocabulary from that of earlier decades of *ujamaa*. The new terminology reflects a tension between, on one side, the ideology that empowerment of women is crucial to national development, and on the other, an ideology of female domestication. It is indicative of a tension which is starkly reflected on the pages of Tanzania's major newspaper, the *Daily News*. On one side, Anna Makinda, the Minister for Community Development, Women Affairs, and Children, said, "Women's development underlies the development of the whole society" and that "women are working longer hours than anybody else for the benefit of the whole society" (*Daily News*, 1 August 1991: 1). Also in August 1991, during a speech opening a meeting of the Tanzania Women's Organization (UWT), the Party Secretary General reportedly noted that "the Party and the government had charted out a strategy that would facilitate easier acquisition of capital for women, including funds, land, and technical know-how," and that "more credit, appropriate technology, and responsive agricultural extension services could improve women's productivity" (*Daily News*, 2 August 1991: 1).

Despite these rhetorical assertions of progress and improvement, other articles attest to another side of the picture, the continued insistence by banks on the use of land as collateral for loans, a provision which is discriminatory to women who often have no access to land (*Daily News*, 13 July 1991: 6). A front page editorial, entitled "Let's Support Women" highlights the "crucial role of women, and particularly the role of the rural women to the country's economy, given the fact that 86.7 percent of them are based in rural areas and are the main workforce in this area" at the same time it notes that the "inheritance law and other customary laws which are oppressive to women." It goes on to argue: "There is a need also for the society to change [its] attitude, so that equality is truly reflected in all sphere of social endeavors. . . . enhancing women's status will go a long way in consolidating the care for children; for a society whose gender [sic] live in harmony will focus more positively on the child" (*Daily News*, 1 August 1991: 1).

What is so intriguing in the editorial is that after documenting the need for women's equality, the article ends by closely associating women and children's welfare. These discussions are not being phrased in terms of either gender equality or gender complementarity as in any way associated with "traditional" Tanzanian cultural practices. Rather, the discussions assume the existence of "women" as an identifiable and isolable category of economic worker, a category that has on the one hand been unfairly treated but which is nonetheless still seen as having primary responsibility for the welfare of society's children.

Similarly, another front page photo of a mother nursing her child is subtitled: "It's feeding time . . . mother and her children are inseparable as picture above shows" (*Daily News*, 6 July 1991: 1). Women are not frequently depicted in the news photos of the paper, and privileging the maternal, breast-feeding woman— in the center of the front page—sends a strong message that women's importance to the nation lies first in her reproductive capacity, outweighing the importance of women's participation in other sectors of economic life.

The policies of adjustment contain a new discourse of development. The nationalist and gendered messages it carries are at variance with those of the *ujamaa* years. The image of the new Tanzanian citizen highlights efficiency, competitiveness, individualism, and capabilities in the marketplace rather than cooperation in the field and in the home. Men and women should be equally suited to taking on these new economic roles. A return to the kiosk, so firmly positioned on the Dar es Salaam sidewalk, where this journey started, however, suggests otherwise.

Business Is Better . . . For Whom?

At the kiosk, we find that its owner, a *man* in perhaps his early thirties, set up his shop in the late 1980s with the help of kin, and that he operates the kiosk while living with relatives in town. The itinerant hawkers displaying their wares on the surrounding sidewalks are *women* selling *mandazi* (a sweet fried cake) and other cooked foods, prepared each morning at home with ingredients purchased with the cash from sales of the previous day. The new practice of "business" creates opportunities for many, but the ability to act on them presumes gendered networks of labor and financial support within which men and women are differently, and often unequally, situated. The kiosk owner, assisted in part by his female relatives, both financially and domestically, was able to obtain sufficient capital to start his business. If the trade is good, with the right contacts, he could expand—maybe selling beers and cassettes of European and U.S. music. The women surrounding him are conducting businesses that grow out of their of domestic experience; which, as Tripp pointed out, does not threaten male autonomy in the household—business that does not threaten love. Hence, the "business story" slogan invites recognition of a shift not only of *how* Tanzanians are now doing *business,* but also of how Tanzanians are *Tanzanian* when doing business. And more, it invites us to look at how men and women in Tanzania do business differently.

In Nyerere's early visions of Tanzanian nationhood, "business" and "love" were in theory conflated, since the essence of *ujamaa* or "familyhood" was to imagine the nation as the African extended family writ large, with cooperative economic practices a natural extension of kin ties. In this projection, complementary gender relations were seen as a vital part of the ideology and practice of socialist political economy. As state policies over the last decade have reshaped the Tanzanian economy and reformulated the content of Tanzania's national ideology, they have created and been challenged by gendered constructions of work. In adopting capitalism, however, the national ideology has detached economic practice from a distinctive Tanzanian identity as well as from an ideology of necessary gender equity. Economic actors are in theory genderless even as the goal of gender equity persists. Thus the assumptions about the relationships between economic development and ideologies of gender and nationhood are differently constituted in the last ten years of economic liberalization and structural adjustment policies than they were previously. This detachment of "business" from "love" sets the stage for finding "business" to be the better deal, at least for some—those in positions to appropriate resources and the labor of others.

Economic development, gender relations, and the creation of Tanzanian national identity are positioned around the shifts in the practice and definition of women's work. By twists and turns a colonial state model of paternalistic assistance and integration into a world capitalist system was replaced by a socialist state model of carefully articulated hierarchy under a gloss of cooperative effort, equality, and self-reliance. Most recently the state has sanctioned a glorification of entrepreneurship and the rewards of consumerism. The discourse of *ujamaa* proclaimed an ideology of sexual equality; its implementation built upon patterns of male achievement and female support. The new discourse of economic liberalization, in contrast, promotes an ideology of individualism and democratization, whereas practice continues to produce gender inequities and promises increasing class stratification. At this juncture it is difficult to measure either the practical or the ideological impact of these changes on Tanzanian society, but clearly the nation that Nyerere imagined—egalitarian, cooperative, and united—remains elusive.

Notes

Research in Tanzania was conducted with the permission of UTAFITI, the Tanzanian National Research Council. It was supported by a Fulbright-Hays Research Grant from 1980–83 and by the Eberhardt Faculty Summer Research Grant from the University of the Pacific, Stockton, California in the summer of 1991. Additional brief visits to Dar es Salaam and to Kwakombo village were made in 1986 and 1988. Earlier versions of this paper were presented at a University of the Pacific School of International Studies Faculty Seminar in March 1992 and at the American Anthropological Association meetings in San Francisco in December 1992. I would like to acknowledge the comments of the participants at those sessions, and well as the helpful criticisms and suggestions made by Deb Amory, Evie Blackwood, Debbie Caro, Rafik Hirji, Longina Jakubowska, Helán Page, Louisa Schein, Brackette Williams, and Harvey Williams. This version of the paper could not have been completed without the help of Karen McNickle, Diane Paull, Daisy Plovnick, and Sandy Richardson.

1. A review of the vast literature on Tanzania's development policies since independence is not possible here. A collection that provides a good presentation of the various debates written by both Tanzanian and foreign scholars of Tanzania is Norman O'Neill and Kemal Mustafa's 1990 *Capitalism, Socialism, and the Development Crisis in Tanzania.*

2. I draw here on Richard G. Fox's use of the term:

    Nationalist ideologies "refer to the production of conceptions of peoplehood . . . we emphasize the relationship between a nationalist ideology as a set of cultural meanings and a national culture. That relationship is contingent and processual: the creation of nationalist ideologies anticipates a larger project, the forming or reforming of a national culture. A national culture starts out as a nationalist ideology, that is a consciousness or perception of what the nation is or should be, which then may gain public meaning and be put into action. Usually there are several coexisting and even contradictory perceptions, which constitute competitive nationalist ideologies." (1990: 3 and 4)

3. John Sorenson's (1993) use of discourse links texts to the conditions which produce them:

Discourse refers to dispersed groups of statements, which form coherent unities, and involves a common object, style of reference, conceptual unity, persistent themes, ordered systems, connected transformations, and regularities.
. . . to avoid the flaws of the deconstructionist approach . . . I have supplemented the idea of discourse with an analysis that is more firmly grounded in concrete historical conditions and examines the roles of interests of those who produce these discourses, such as nationalist intellectuals, mass media, and representatives of the state. (10–11)

4. This marvelous phrase to describe development projects with unintended negative consequences was used by Sarah Hoagland in a seminar at the Institute for Development Studies in Nairobi, Kenya in the mid-1980s.

5. One difficulty in doing gender analysis lies in confronting the belief that we already know what the gender categories we are dealing with are: "men" and "women." Using dichotomous, sexually based categories to talk about gender is problematic, heterosexist, and ignores how cultures variously categorize the diverse "raw facts" of biology (see Fausto-Sterling 1993). Given the existence of three or more gender categories in other cultures, it becomes important to problematize the content and definition of "gender" as well as other analytical categories, following Yanagisako and Collier (1990) and others. For this paper, however, I will use "gender relations" and "gender" to refer to the categories of "wanaume" (men) and "wanawake" (women) in Swahili. There is no single Swahili word which translates as "gender."

6. Access to land was regulated through patrilineal ties among the Zigua, and, in colonial times, was passed down primarily from father to son (although they have been variously listed as matrilineal in some works, see Beidelman 1967). Women gained usufruct rights of access to land primarily through their husbands; on his death they held it in trust for their sons.

7. The assertion here is that Tanzanians for the most part agreed that self-reliance was "a good thing," not that it was actually practiced as it was laid out in Nyerere's policy paper, "Socialism and Self Reliance" (in Coulson 1982).

8. A 1966 Tanzanian civics textbook (Meienberg 1966: 144) quotes D.N.M. Bryceson, Member of Parliament: "I want to put it to all of you, particularly to girls, that agriculture has the most important task in planning the country's economy. I want to see more of you study to go to universities to learn about agricultural science."

References

Anderson, Benjamin. 1983. *Imagined Communities*. London: Verso.

Beidelman, T.O. 1967. *The Matrilineal Peoples of Eastern Tanzania*. London: International African Institute.

Booth, David. 1991. "Structural Adjustment in Socio-Political Context: Some Findings from Iringa Region." *Tadreg Research Report III*. Dar es Salaam: Tadreg.

Brow, James. 1988. "In Pursuit of Hegemony: Representations of Authority and Justice in a Sri Lankan Village." *American Ethnologist* 15: 311–27.

Clark, Leon E. (ed.). 1970. *Through African Eyes: Cultures in Change, Volume VI: Nation-Building: Tanzania and the World*. New York: Praeger.

Cliffe, Lionel. 1972. "Nationalism and the Reaction to Enforced Agricultural Change in Tanganyika During the Colonial Period." In *Socialism in Tanzania, Vol. 1: Politics*, edited by Lionel Cliffe and John S. Saul. Pp.17–24. Nairobi, Kenya: East African Publishing House.

Cooksey, Brian. 1989. "Incentive Goods in Rural Tanzania, 1986–1989: A Summary of Research Findings." Unpublished paper.

———. 1990. "Girl's Educational Opportunities and Performance in Tanzania," *TADREG Research Report No. 2*. Dar es Salaam: Tadreg.

Coulson, Andrew. 1982. *Tanzania: A Political Economy*. Oxford: Clarendon Press.

Daily News, Editorial: "Let's Support Women." 1 August 1991, 1.

Dominguez, Virginia. 1990. "The Politics of Heritage in Contemporary Israel." In *Nationalist Ideologies and the Production of National Cultures*, edited by Richard G. Fox. Pp. 130–47. Washington, D.C.: American Anthropological Association.

Ellis, Frank. 1982. "Agricultural Price Policy in Tanzania." *World Development* 10(4): 263–83.

Enloe, Cynthia. 1989. *Beaches, Bases, and Banana Republics: Making Feminist Sense of International Politics*. Berkeley: University of California Press.

Escobar, Arturo. 1988. "Power and Visibility: Development and the Invention and Management of the Third World." *Cultural Anthropology* 3(4): 428–43.

Fausto-Sterling, Anne. 1993. "The Five Sexes." *The Sciences* 33: 20–25.

Feierman, Steven. 1990. *Peasant Intellectuals: Anthropology and History in Tanzania*. Madison: University of Wisconsin Press.

Fortmann, Louise. 1982. "Women's Work in a Communal Setting: The Tanzanian Policy of Ujamaa." In *Women and Work in Africa*, edited by Edna Bay 1. Pp. 130–47. Boulder, CO: Westview Press.

Fox, Richard G. 1990. "Introduction" in *Nationalist Ideologies and the Production of National Cultures*, edited by Richard G. Fox. Pp. 1–14. Washington, D. C.: American Anthropological Association.

Geiger, Susan. 1987. "Women in Nationalist Struggle: TANU Activists in Dar es Salaam." *International Journal of African Historical Studies* 20(1): 1–26.

Haraway, Donna. 1989. *Primate Visions*. New York: Routledge.

Hyden, Goran. 1980. *Beyond Ujamaa in Tanzania: Underdevelopment and an Uncaptured Peasantry*. Berkeley: University of California Press.

Hyden, Goran and Pauline E. Peters. 1991. "Debate on the Economy of Affection: Is it a Useful Tool for Gender Analysis?" In *Structural Adjustment and African Women Farmers*, edited by Christina Gladwin. Pp. 303–37. Gainesville, Florida: University of Florida Press.

Iliffe, John. 1979. *A Modern History of Tanganyika.* Cambridge: Cambridge University Press.

Kuper, Adam. 1975. *Anthropologists and Anthropology: The British School, 1922–72.* Great Britain: Penguin Books, Ltd.

Lofchie, Michael. 1989. *The Policy Factor: Agricultural Performance in Kenya and Tanzania.* Boulder: Lynne Rienner.

Lonsdale, John. 1972. "Some Origins of Nationalism in Tanzania." In *Socialism in Tanzania, Vol. 1: Politics,* edited by Lionel Cliffe and John S. Saul. Pp. 25–28. Nairobi, Kenya: East African Publishing House.

Maganya, E. N. 1990. "The Structural Adjustment Programmes and the Agricultural Sector: The Case of Tanzania." *Taamuli: A Political Science Forum* 1(1&2): 103–15.

Mbilinyi, Marjorie. 1990. "Structural Adjustment and Agribusiness in Tanzania: Struggles over the Labour of Women Peasants and Farm Workers." *Taamuli: A Political Science Forum* 1(1&2): 76–102.

Meena, Ruth. 1991. "The Impact of Structural Adjustment Programs on Rural Women in Tanzania." In *Structural Adjustment and African Women Farmers,* edited by Christina H. Gladwin. Pp. 169–90. Gainesville: University of Florida Press.

Meienberg, Hildebrand. 1966. *Tanzanian Citizen: A Civics Textbook.* Nairobi: Oxford University Press.

Mighot-Adholla, Shem. 1979. "Rural Development Policy and Equality" in *Politics and Public Policy in Kenya and Tanzania,* edited by Joel Barkan with John J. Okumu. Pp. 154–70. New York: Praeger.

Muya, Mwalumwambo. 1974. "Grandparent-Grandchild Utani Relationships in Zigula Society" in *Utani Relationships* edited by Steven Lucas. University of Dar es Salaam: Dar es Salaam, Tanzania. Unpublished manuscript.

Nyerere, Julius. 1968. *Freedom and Socialism: Uhuru na Ujamaa.* Dar es Salaam: Oxford University Press.

———. 1973. *Freedom and Development: Uhuru na Maendeleo, 1968–1973.* Dar es Salaam: Oxford University Press.

———. 1974. *Freedom and Unity.* Dar es Salaam: Oxford University Press.

———. 1977. "The Arusha Declaration: Ten Years After." Dar es Salaam: Government Printer.

———. 1979. "On Rural Development." IFDA Dossier 11: 1–15.

Okin, Susan Moller. 1989. *Justice, Gender, and the Family.* New York: Basic Books.

O'Neill, Norman. 1990. "Politics and Development Strategies in Tanzania" in *Capitalism, Socialism and the Development Crisis in Tanzania,* edited by Norman O'Neill and Kemal Mustafa. Pp. 1–21. Brookfield, VT: Avebury (Gower Publishing Company).

O'Neill, Norman and Kemal Mustafa (eds.). 1990. *Capitalism, Socialism and the Development Crisis in Tanzania.* Brookfield, VT: Avebury (Gower Publishing Company).

Pierce, Paulette. "Boudoir Politics . . ." (this volume).

Rubin, Deborah. 1985. *People of Good Heart: Rural Response to Economic Crisis in Northeast Tanzania*. Ph.D. Dissertation, The Johns Hopkins University. Ann Arbor: University Microfilms.

———. 1994, "Review of Henrietta Moore's Feminism and Anthropology." *American Ethnologist* 21(4): 902–903.

Rugumisa, Salvatore. 1990. "A Review of the Tanzanian Economic Recovery Programme (1986–89)." Dar es Salaam: Tadreg Research Report I.

Shivji, Issa. 1985. "The Transformation of the State and the Working People." In *The State and the Working People in Tanzania,* edited by Isaa Shivji. Pp. 1–15. London: Codesria.

———. 1990. "The Politics of Liberalization in Tanzania: Notes on the Crisis of Ideological Hegemony." *Taamuli: A Political Science Forum* 1 (1&2): 138–52.

Sorenson, John. 1993. *Imagining Ethiopia: Struggles for History and Identity in the Horn of Africa*. New Brunswick, NJ: Rutgers University Press.

Stein, Howard. 1990. "The Economics of the State and the IMF in Tanzania." *Taamuli: A Political Science Forum* 1 (1/2): 1–25.

Tanganyika, Republic of. 1964. *The Tanganyika Five-Year Plan for Social Development, July 1964–June 1969 (the First Five-Year Plan)*. Dar es Salaam: Government Printing.

Tripp, Mari Ali. 1990. *The Urban Informal Economy and the State in Tanzania*. Ph.D. Dissertation, Northwestern University. Ann Arbor, MI: University Microfilms.

Williams, Brackette F. 1990. "Nationalism, Traditionalism, and the Problem of Cultural Inauthenticity." In *Nationalist Ideologies and the Production of National Cultures,* edited by Richard G. Fox. Pp. 112–29. Washington, D.C.: American Anthropological Association.

Woost, Michael D. 1993. "Nationalizing the Local Past in Sri Lanka: Histories of Nation and Development in a Sinhalese Village." *American Ethnologist* 20 (3): 502–521.

Yanagisako, Sylvia and Jane Collier. 1990. "The Mode of Reproduction in Anthropology." In *Theoretical Perspectives on Sexual Difference,* edited by Deborah Rhode. Pp. 131–41. New Haven: Yale University Press.

Notes on Contributors

Richard G. Fox is professor of anthropology at Washington University in St. Louis and editor of *Current Anthropology*. His publications related to nationalist movements include *Lions of the Punjab: Culture in the Making* (1985), *Gandhian Utopia: Experiments with Culture* (1989) and the edited volume *Nationalist Ideologies and the Production of National Culture* (1989). He has been a Guggenheim fellow and a fellow at the Institute for Advanced Study, Princeton.

Éva V. Huseby-Darvas was born and raised in Budapest, Hungary. After the Hungarian revolution of 1956, she fled her homeland and arrived in the United States as one of 34,000 other refugees from Hungary. Stemming from her experiences as refugee woman, Huseby-Darvas researches the relationship between women's identity and social change, and the ramifications of migration, nationalism and ethnicity on individuals and communities. She has conducted research in rural and urban Hungary, and North America.

Louisa Schein is an assistant professor in the Department of Anthropology at Rutgers University, New Brunswick. She is the author of "The Consumption of Color and the Politics of White Skin in Post-Mao China," which appeared in *Social Text,* and is currently working on a book on cultural politics in contemporary China. Her ongoing research includes a project on the forging of transnationality between Hmong in the U.S. and Miao in China.

Carol A. Smith, professor of anthropology at University of California, Davis, has written many articles and edited three influential books in which she was primary author. But she has never written a book, nor has she written on gender before. But having reconstructed herself recently, in California, she is undertaking a major field project on race, class, and gender ideologies in four countries of Central America, where the state project of *mestizaje* is currently unravelling.

Paulette Pierce, associate professor, Department of Black Studies, the Ohio State University, is a sociologist, specializing in Black political movements and gender relations in the Black community. She has conducted research in both the United States and the former British colony, The People's Co-Operative Republic of Guyana. She is author of *Noncapitalist Development: The Struggle to Nationalize the Guyanese Sugar Industry,* and numerous journal articles analyzing independent Black politics and Jesse Jackson's Rainbow Coalition.

Deborah S. Rubin is a cultural anthropologist specializing in gender and development issues in East Africa. Now an associate professor of Anthropology and International Studies at the University of the Pacific in Stockton, she has also taught at Stanford University. Before entering academics she acquired ten years of applied experience in international development on a Rockefeller Foundation postdoctoral fellowship in agriculture and rural development and as a consultant for the World Bank, the International Food Policy Research Institute, and the German aid agency, GTZ. She has carried out fieldwork in Tanzania and Kenya.

Jacqui True is a Ph.D. student in the Department of Politics and a Researcher in the Centre for International and Strategic Studies at York University, Toronto, Canada. She is a New Zealand citizen with degrees in Political Science and International Relations from New Zealand, Australian and American universities and has studied in Poland and the Czech Republic. With an academic background and publications in feminist and international relations theory, her current dissertation research is focused on gender transformations in post-communist East Central Europe. De-naturalizing one's own nationalism and identity-formation, she believes, is vital preparation for studying *other* cultures and for rethinking international relations.

Brackette F. Williams has conducted anthropological fieldwork in Guyana, Alabama, and New York City. She received her Ph.D. in cultural anthropology from The Johns Hopkins University in 1983. Her related publications include *Stains on My Name War in My Veins: Guyana and the Politics of Cultural Struggle,* "A Class Act: Anthropology and the Race to Nation Across Ethnic Terrain," "Nationalism, Traditionalism, and the Problem of Cultural Inauthenticity," and "The Impact of the Precepts of Nationalism on the Concept of Culture: Making Grasshoppers of Naked Apes."

Index

abolitionist movement, women in, 219–20
abortion:
  Hungarian nationalist opposition to,
    162, 170–78
  in Nation of Islam thought, 205–206, 207
Acker, Joan, 228
Adamik, Mária, 172
Affirmative Action, 208–209
African-Americans, gendered nationalism
    among, 29–30, 186–238
Africanness within Guyanese conceptions
    of masculinity, 144–49
"African Socialism," 246
Afro-Guyanese, the, 29, 130, 132–54
Age of Reason, the, 18
agency, gendered views of, 17
agriculture:
  in nationalist development, 252–53,
    255–56
  as gendered activity, 256–60, 261–62
AIDS, 206
"Ain't Nobody's Business If I Do," 140
Alkotmánybíróság (Hungarian
    Constitutional Court), 162, 170, 176
Allah, 200, 205–206, 209
"All Blacks" rugby team, 111
All-India Women's Congress, 39
Alloula, Malek, 84
American Civil War, 111

Anderson, Benedict, 254
Anglo-Maori wars, 111
Anglo-Saxons, the, 28–29, 110–11, 122
Anthias, Floya, 221
Aotearoa/New Zealand, 103, 108, 122
"April 8th Festival" (Beijing), 88
Árpád House Dynasty, 167
Arrowcross Party, 166
Arusha Declaration (Tanzania), 252–53,
    258
Asian games 1990, 95
Association of Hungarian Women, 177
Athena, birth of, 204
athletics as war, 16, 21
Aunt Jemima stereotype, 187

Bankinchandra (Indian nationalist), 54–55
Bartel, Dennis, 146
Basu, Aparna, 39
Benczur, Zsuzsanna, 162
Benjamin, Jessica, 227–28
Béres, Zsuzsa, 173
Bernard, Jesse, 189–90, 191, 192
Besant, Annie, 41
Bhaba, Homi, 118, 121
Bible, Christian, 222
Bíró, Dávid, 176
Black nationalist movement, gendered
    activities within, 199–210, 216–38

Black Panther party, 218
Black Power movement, 216–17
Black Sambo stereotype, 194
Black Scholar, 224
Black Studies movement, 217
Black Women's Club Movement, 220
blood:
 and class position, 52–54
 in colonial society, 56–59
 female, 14–15
Bollobás, Enikô, 171
Bonds of Love, The (Benjamin), 227–28
Booth, David, 260
Bornemisza, Eszter, 176
Bossen, Laurel, 61–62
boudoir politics, 225–26, 234–37
Bourdieu, Pierre, 187
British Empire, the, 28–29, 103–106,
 108–16, 119
British House of Commons, 119
Bronfen, Elisabeth, 24–25

Cade, Toni, 224
Centipede Queen, the, 131
Central Nationalities Institute (Beijing), 88
Certeau, Michel de, 39
Chatterjee, Partha, 38, 39, 40, 48, 54–55,
 97, 108
Chaudharani, Sarladevi, 45
Chiang Kaishek, 81
childrearing:
 and autonomy for women, 140–41,
  150–52
 benefits of, 150
 as element of hierarchical evaluation of
  the self, 138–39
China, gendered nationalisms in, 79–97
Christian views of creation, 12–13
citizenship, 3, 259, 264
Civil Rights laws (U.S.), 197
Clarke, Edward, 15, 16
"classless society, the," 111–13
Clatterbaugh, Kenneth, 189
Cleaver, Eldridge, 223
"Cockalorum" (research site in Guyana),
 129, 133–54
colonial "symbolics of blood," 56–59

Communist Women's Council (Hungary),
 177
community as component of nationalism, 2
Condliffe, J. B., 108–109
Cone, James, 223
Congress of African People (CAP), 217,
 218, 225
Cook, Captain James, 108, 110
Cooper, Anna Julia, 195–96
cooperative farming vs. traditional gender
 roles, 256–60
Corrin, Chris, 163
costume and national identity, 92–93
Craib, Ian, 188–89, 192, 197
creoles of Guatemala, 57, 59–60
Crummell, Alexander, 194–95, 198
Csurka, István, 171
Cultural Revolution, the, 93
Custom Survey Society, 81

Daily News (Tanzania), 263
dance as production of identity, 88–89
Davis, Ossie, 232
Declaration of the Network (Hungarian
 Feminist Network), 172
Demos, John, 190
descent, ideologies of, 50, 52–54
development, economic, as gendered
 activity, 245–65
Dharsana salt works, 46
Dictionary of Australian Colloquialisms
 (Wilkes), 115
Dixon, Suzanne, 226
DNA, 3
domesticity:
 and African-American nationalism,
  196–99
 and economic development, 246–47,
  251–52, 259–61, 263–64
 and feminism in modern nationalism,
  162–78
 and gendered space, 116–17
 within race, 149–54
 in aftermath of slavery, 129–33, 197
dominant gaze, women's response to,
 87–88
drinking and national identity, 95–96

dual marriage system, 131–32
Du Bois, W. E. B., 194–95

Earth Mother, woman as, 206–10
Eger, heroines of, 165
Életképek, 168
elites, post-colonial, 59–60
Emese (mythic mother of Hungary), 167–68, 169
English as We Speak it in Ireland (Joyce), 116
Enloe, Cynthia, 216, 220, 222, 238
Epstein, Barbara, 192–93
Esély (Chance), 172
essentialist images of women in Gandhian nationalism, 37–48
ethnic cleansing, 2
ethnicity vs. class position, 50–71
exogamy, 90
export vs. food crops, effect on gender roles, 261–62

"face" in Guyanese gender construction, 133–41
Farrakhan, Minister Louis, 199–201, 205–209
Feathersone, Dr. Isaac, 110
Fekete, Gyula, 171, 177
Fél, Edit, 164
feminine other, the, 82–83
femininity:
    as construction of racialized nature, 19–25
    "face" in the construction of, 133–41
feminism:
    in Black nationalist movement, 217–38
    lack of study of nationalism in, 220–21
    vs. traditional, gendered nationalism, 161–78
Feminist Network (Hungary), 163, 172, 176, 177
Ferge, Zsuzsa, 172
First Five-Year Plan for the United Republic of Tanganyika, 252
Forbes, Geraldine, 39
Foucault, Michel, 27, 52
Fox, Richard G., 27
Frazier, E. Franklin, 196–98

freedwomen, domesticity of, 130–33
"Fretful Sleepers" (Pearson), 113
frontier myth, 114
Fruit of Islam, 222–23

Gál, Susan, 163
Gandhi, 27, 37–48, 54–55
Gandhian Constructive Programme, 44
Gay, Peter, 210
Geiger, Susan, 250
Gender, Culture and Power (James / Saville-Smith), 115
gendered subtext of formal organization, 227–29
Genesis, Book of, 11, 200
"Godzone" as New Zealand nickname, 28–29, 103, 112
Good Provider role, the, 190–91
Goody, Jack, 52, 55
Goux, Jean-Joseph, 9, 189
Goven, Joanna, 163
Gramsci, Antonio, 47–48, 118
"Great Chain of Being," 111
Great Depression, the, 192
"Great New Zealand Clobbering Machine," 113
Grimmond, Joseph, 105
Guatemala, gendered nationalism in, 27–28, 50–71
Guatemala's Civil Code, 61–62
Gu Hongming, 80–81
Guizhou Culture Bureau, 86
Guizhou province, development in, 86–88, 94–95
Guomindang, the, 81
Guyana, 29, 129–54
Gyáni, Gábor, 161–62

Half-Gallon, Quarter-Acre, Pavlova Paradise, The (Mitchell), 115
Hall, G. Stanley, 16
Han vs. non-Han Chinese, 80-97
Haney, Lynne, 163, 173
Hankiss, Elemér, 170
Hare, Nathan, 224
Hayes, Carlton, 2
Hernádi, Miklós, 176

heroic women, 165–70
historicity and nation-building, 104–107
Hoberman, John M., 11, 20–21
Hobson, William, 108
Hódosán, Róza, 174
Hofer, Tamás, 64, 165–66
Holbrooke, M. L., 17
Holiday, Billie, 140–41
Holmes, Oliver Wendell, 16
Holy Virgin as protector of Hungary, 168
Honderû, 166, 168
Horme, Pottier L', 109–10
Horthy regime (Hungary), 166
Horváth, Zsuzsa, 163
hospitality and national identity, 93–94
Huet, Marie Hélène, 11, 17–19, 21
humanity, construction of women's vs.
    male ideal, 133–41, 149–50, 152–54
Hungarian Constitution of 1949, 172
Hungarian Democratic Forum, 171
Hungarian Feminist Party, 172–73
Hungarian News Agency, 171
Hungarian Reform Period, 163
Hungarian Revolution, 171
Hungarian Women's Forum, 162
Hungary, gender and nationalism in, 29,
    161–78
Hunn Report of 1961 (New Zealand), 120
Huseby-Darvas, Éva, 29, 161–85, 206
Hyden, Gordon, 258–59

ideological production, sites of, 3–4
India, gendered nationalism in, 27, 37–48
Indian National Congress, 47
insider, racialized, 8–9
International Institute of African Languages
    and Culture, 250
International Monetary Fund, 258, 260
International Workers of the World,
    190–91, 193
István, (King of Hungary), 168

James, Bev, 115, 117
Jobbágyi, Gábor, 170
Joyce, P. W., 116
Judeo-Christian Godhead, 107
Jurchen people, the, 80

Kanizsai, Dorottya, 164
Kapferer, Bruce, 113
Karenga, Maulana, 225
Karinthy, Frigyes, 163–64
Katrak, Ketu, 38, 39
Kaur, Amrit, 44
Kilindi people, the, 249
King, Dr. Martin Luther, Jr., 232, 233
Koonz, Claudia, 69–70

Ladino people of Guatemala, 27–28,
    50–51, 57, 58, 59–71
Lakatos, Mihály, 171
Landes, Joan, 220
Lazaro, Maria, 64–65
leadership as gendered activity, 231–34
Lendvay, Judit, 166
Lerner, Gerda, 52–53
Less Noble Sex, The: Scientific, Religious, and
    Philosophical Conceptions of Woman's
    Nature (Tuana), 11
"Let's Support Women" (Daily News,
    Tanzania), 263
"Let Us Make Man Tour" (Nation of
    Islam), 208
Liebow, Elliot, 191
Liu Shaoqi, 87
Livermore, A. A., 16
Lloyd, Henry Demarest, 112
local leaders, role in spread of national
    idea under colonialism, 249–50

Macartney, C. A., 165
McCreery, David, 58
Madonna, the, 206–207
Magyar Nôk Lapja, 162
Magyars, the, 165–66, 167–68
Magyar Szellemi Védegylet, A (Association for
    the Protection of Hungarian Values),
    170
Makinda, Anna, 263
Malaparte, Curzio, 22–23
"man alone, the," as national hero, 117
Manchu conquest of China, 80
Mani, Lata, 97
mannish woman, the, 19, 176–77
Mansfield, Katherine, 104

Maori, the, 28, 103–23
Mao Zedong, 87
marriage:
  dual system of, 131–32
  and modernity, 90
  and race/class position, 60–63, 134–39,
    150–54
  rules of, 50, 56–59, 90
  following slavery, 130–33
Marsden, Samuel, 110
Martinez-Alier, Verena, 27
Martínez Pelaez, Severo, 57–58
Marxism-Leninism, 67–68, 70, 217,
  233
masculinity:
  and fear of feminism, 174–78
  as construction of racialized nature,
    20–25, 141–49
  and unemployment, 188–91
Maya people, the, 27–28, 50–52, 59, 60,
  63–69, 70, 71
May Fourth movement (China), 80
Meena, Ruth, 262
Meigs, Charles, 14–15
Messiah, the, 199, 208
mestizaje, the, 58
Miao people, the, 28, 79, 82–86, 87–96
Miao Studies Association, 94, 96
Minault, Gail, 39
Ming dynasty, 80
Miss Ann stereotype, 187
Mitchell, Austin, 107, 115
modern vs. anti-modern race/class/gen-
  der ideologies, 69–71
Mohács, battle of, 164
Molyneux, Maxine, 70
Morgan, William, 115
Mosse, George L., 4–10, 11, 12, 13,
  19–21
Mother Africa, 225
motherhood as gendered construction of
  nationalism, 161–78
Moynihan, Daniel P., 196–98
Muhammad, Honorable Elijah, 200,
  202–205, 207–208, 222, 232
Muhammad, Eva, 209
Muhammad, Sister Tynetta, 204–205

Muhammad, Master W. Fard, 204
Müller, Max, 41
Muslims, African-American, 29, 186,
  199–211, 218, 222–23, 232–33,
  234–35

Naidu, Sarojini, 39, 46
Nandy, Ashis, 42
National Black Independent Political Party,
  29–30, 216–17, 226–38
National Black Political Assembly (NBPA),
  217, 218
National Conference of Colored Women,
  196
national hegemony in international con-
  texts, 118–21
National Heritage, The (Guogu), 80–81
Nationalism and Sexuality: Respectability and
  Abnormal Sexuality in Modern Europe
  (Mosse), 4–6
Nation of Islam, gendered nationalism
  within, 29, 186, 199–211, 218,
  222–23, 232–33, 234–35
Native Administration system,
  Tanganyika, 249
nature:
  as constructed by nationalism, 9–19
  gendered view of, 14
  associated with minority women, 83–84
Nazi Germany, 21, 54, 69–70
Negro Family, The: The Case for National
  Action (Moynihan), 197–98
Nehru, 54–55
neolocality in marriage, 131–32
New Culture movement (China), 80
Newman, Gerald, 114
New Zealand, gendered nationalism in,
  28–29, 103–23
New Zealand Company, the, 109
New Zealand in the Making (Condliffe),
  108–109
Ngoni people, the, 256–57
Noble, Margaret, 41
"No Envy, No Pity" (Tóth), 174
Nôszemély, 176
Nyerere, Julius, 30, 245–46, 253–57,
  264, 265

Okin, Susan, 220–21
Omvedt, Gail, 39
Opium wars, 80
Orange, Claudia, 123
Orientalism: 40–41
    internalized, 83, 86–87, 96
origin myths, 2–3, 11–13, 165–70,
    203–205
Ortmayr, Norbert, 58
Ottoman Empire, 164–65
*Over Her Dead Body: Death, Femininity, and
    the Aesthetic* (Bronfen), 24–25
"own kind," production of, 14
Oxford English Dictionary, 115–16
Oxford Illustrated History, 103

Pakeha New Zealanders, 103–23
pan-Africanism, 232, 233
Paracelsus, 13, 17
paradigmatic male privilege, 231–34, 238
Park, Roberta J., 11, 15–16
Parks, Gordon, 232
Paskai, Cardinal László, 171
Pateman, Carole, 220–21
Pearson, Bill, 113
People's Co-operative Republic of
    Guyana, 129–54
People's Republic of China, 28, 79–97
Peters, Pauline, 259
"Petition for Embryo Protection" ("Dr.
    Gábor Jobbágyi's wife"), 176
Phillips, Jock, 114
Pierce, Paulette, 29–30, 186–244, 248
Poliakov, Leon, 109
Polish, the, as seen by Hungarians, 166–67
polygyny, 52
Poovey, Mary, 11, 17, 18
Potter, Jonathan, 112
public/private dichotomy, 30, 37,
    116–17, 259–60
public speaking as gendered activity,
    229–30
purdah, 38, 48

Qing dynasty, 80
Quit India Movement, 47
Qur'an, Holy, 222

race:
    vs. class and gender, 50–71
    domesticity within, 149–54
    and female biology, 17
    and construction of femininity,
        191–97
    and discourse of fertility, 171–72
    gendered conceptions of, 6, 141–54,
        191–97
    and nationalism, 6–25, 103–104,
        108–11
"racial" destiny, 2
racism as "scavenger ideology," 7–8
Ramakrishna, Paramahansa, 42
Ray, Bharati, 39
"resemblance," problem of, 203
respectability, 4–10, 114
Rév, István, 173
revolutionary societies, gender relations
    in, 66–69, 70
RNA, 3
Rodney, Walter, 131, 146
Roma (Gypsies), the, 171, 175
Rubin, Deborah, 30, 245–69
Rubin, Theodore, 167
Ruffin, Josephine St. Pierre, 196

Said, Edward, 83, 96
St. Jean Baptiste, the, 109
Salt March of 1930, women in, 45–46
Sangari, KumKum, 39
Sargeson, Frank, 117
Sas, Judit H., 163
Saville-Smith, Kay, 115, 117
Schein, Louisa, 28, 79–102
Schlesin, Sonya, 43
Scott, James, 40
Scott, Joan, 220–21
Sebestyén, Béla, 170
Seddon, "King Dick," 107
"serial monogamy," 150
settler culture, 105–106, 108–109,
    119
sexuality:
    and class position, 60–63, 134–39
    as attributed to minority culture, 81,
        84–86

as component of nationalism, 4–10,
    52–54
within nationalist movements, 43,
    46–47, 217, 220–23, 234–37
and race, 7–9, 53, 141–49
Shabazz, Betty, 202–203
Shambaa people, the, 250–51
Shameem, Shaista, 121
Shanley, Mary, 220–21
"sheila" as term for woman, 115–17
Shidong Dragon Boat Race, 93
Shivji, Issa, 255
Siegfried, Andre, 105
Sikhs, the, 40–41
Sinclair, Keith, 103, 109, 112
Sinkó, Katalin, 168
Sita (goddess), 39
Skin, The (Malaparte), 22–23
Skinner, G. William, 82
slavery:
    domesticity following, 129–33, 197
    gender roles following, 194–99
    gender roles under, 132–33, 194
Smith, Carol A., 27–28, 50–78
Smith, R. T., 131–32
Smith, W. Tyler, 17
Smith-Rosenberg, Carroll, 220–21
SNCC, 218, 234
social Darwinism, 110
"socialism in the villages," 253–60
Soros Foundation, 163
Soul on Ice (Cleaver), 223
South Asian diaspora, 44
Spencer (physiologist), 14
"sperm children," 13, 203
Stacey, Judith, 70
Steiner, Olive, 43
Stephen, Saint, 168
Stewart, Mary, 219–20
Stolcke, Verena, 27, 53–54, 56–57, 58,
    59, 70
structural-adjustment economic policies,
    262
structural deflection of gender equality,
    237, 238
supersexuality, 7–8
swadeshi program, the, 43

Swahili language, 249, 251,
    255–56

Takáts, Sándor, 164, 168–69
Tanganyika African National Union
    (TANU), 250
Tanzania, gendered nationalism in, 30,
    245–65
Tanzania Women's Organization, 263
Tasman (discoverer), 108
Terrell, Mary Church, 220
Thompson, E. P., 40
Tigress of Tiger Bay, 131
Tolstoy Farm, 43
Torma, Judit, 177
Tóth, Olga, 174
Touraine, Alan, 104–105, 106
Treaty of Trianon, 169–70
Treaty of Waitangi, 104, 108, 121,
    122–23
Tripp, Mari Ali, 262, 264
Trollope, Anthony, 110
True, Jacqui, 28–29, 103–28
"True Womanhood," cult of, 187, 193,
    207
Tuana, Nancy, 11–15, 203–204, 206
Turul Bird, the, 167–68

Ujamaa socialism, 30, 245–46, 253–57,
    259–60, 262, 263, 264
Uncle Tom stereotype, 194
unemployment, effect on gender roles,
    188–91
Universal Negro Improvement
    Association, 218
Untouchables, the, 45
Usambara people, the, 249
U.S. Labor Department, 197

Vaid, Sudesh, 39
Váradi, Orsolya, 174
Vásárhelyi, Mária, 176–77
Versailles Peace Conference, 80
Victoria, Queen, 104, 108
Vivekananda, Swami, 42
Vogel, Prime Minister (New Zealand), 112
Von Tempensky, Count, 110

Wagner, Michael J., 146
Wakefield, Edward Gibbon, 109
Watkins-Harper, Francis Ellen, 220
Weatherall, Margaret, 112
Weimar republic, 69–70
Weininger, Otto, 20–21
Wells-Barnett, Ida B., 220
Welter, Barbara, 191–92, 193
Westminster statute of independence
    (New Zealand), 119
Williams, Brackette F., 1–30, 94,
    129–58, 186–215, 254–55
Williams, Fannie Barrier, 196
Williams, Mark, 121
Williams, Raymond, 89
Wilson, Peter, 148
Wolf, Margery, 70
Woman-Nation-State (Yuval-Davis/Anthias),
    221
woman's nature, versions of, 12–15
womb, the:
    in Black nationalist thought, 237
    in early modern thought, 17–19

in modern Hungarian nationalism, 29,
    161–78
in imagery of the Nation of Islam, 29,
    199–210
in Roman thought, 13, 17
Women's Commission, NBIPP, 236
Women's Democratic Forum (Hungary),
    162
Woodson, Carter G., 187
Woost, Michael D., 247

X, Malcolm, 202–203, 209–10, 222–23,
    232–33

Young India, 41, 46
Yuval-Davis, Nira, 221

Zalatnay, Sarolta, 172–73
Zeus, swallowing of wife by, 204
Zhou Enlai, 87
Zhu De, 87
Zigua people, the, 250–51, 256–57